1

Pietro Belluschi

Publication of this book has been supported
by a grant from the Graham Foundation for
Advanced Studies in the Fine Arts.

This book was set in Helvetica Neue by DEKR
Corporation and was printed and bound in the
United States of America.

Library of Congress Cataloging-in-Publication
Data

Clausen, Meredith L.
  Pietro Belluschi : modern American architect /
Meredith L. Clausen.
     p.   cm.
Includes bibliographical references and index.
ISBN 0-262-03220-1
1. Belluschi, Pietro, 1899–   —Criticism
  and interpretation. 2. Architecture,
  Modern—20th century—United States.
  I. Belluschi, Pietro, 1899–   . II. Title.
NA737.B43C58   1994
720′.92—dc20   94-20789
                              CIP

Pietro Belluschi

Modern American Architect

Meredith L. Clausen

The MIT Press

Cambridge, Massachusetts

London, England

Contents

Pietro Belluschi

Preface

In the past several decades, as modernism with its moral imperatives and revolutionary fervor collapsed, no consistent set of architectural values emerged in its stead. Recent developments have been chaotic, marked by constant changes and abruptly shifting taste. Driving the process has been the quest for novelty, a preference for "cutting edge" projects that carved new directions in architecture, and a view of architecture as personal artistic expression. What seems to have been lost is a sense of lasting quality and the collective response on which it is based, a sense of what ultimately counts in architectural form.

It was precisely that Pietro Belluschi sought. Though intertwined with the history of modernism, his career was based not on intellectual premises but on an intuition about what constituted enduring values. Having grown up steeped in the architecture of Rome, amid traditional buildings with layers of accrued history, he was accustomed to think in terms of familiar types rather than newly created forms. Modernism, with its disruptive, antihistorical stance, its demand for new forms in response to new circumstances, hadn't hit Rome when he left. Arriving in the United States in 1923, and determined to succeed at all costs, he initially embraced the prevailing Beaux-Arts practice of copying literally historical forms, but quickly rejected it in favor of what struck him as a more reasoned modern approach. Throughout his long career, from the Portland Art Museum of 1931 to his churches of the late 1980s, Belluschi consistently sought not the unique or different, by definition ephemeral in appeal, but the more permanent values inherent in time-honored, accepted forms.

Over the first half of his career, until his move to the East Coast and change in *modus operandi* in 1951, he produced a series of buildings that have found a place in the modernist canon, among them the Portland Art Museum, the simple, regional houses and churches of the 1940s, and the Equitable Building in Portland. The aluminum-clad Equitable, completed in 1948, was the first major corporate office tower to be built after the Second World War and the first of a long line of sleek, flush-surfaced glass and metal buildings. Recognized the world over, it established Belluschi as one of the preeminent modern architects in this country. In its wake, he was appointed by President Truman to the National Commission of Fine Arts in 1950, became Dean of Architecture and Urban Planning at MIT in 1951, then was elected a Fellow of the American Academy of Arts and Sciences in 1952. Commissions for buildings of all kinds, from houses and churches to shopping centers and corporate towers, poured in.

The Pan Am Building, on which Belluschi collaborated with Walter Gropius less than a decade later, marked a turning point, not only in both men's professional careers but in the history of modern architecture. Finished in 1963, three years before Robert Venturi published his seminal *Complexity and Contradiction in Architecture*, the Pan Am Building, a hotly contested, tall and massive structure built in the heart of one of the most congested areas of New York, perhaps more than any other single thing turned the tide of public sentiment, triggering the widespread reaction against modernism that rocked the later sixties. Belluschi had until then been one of the most highly regarded men in the architectural profession, an unquestioned authority on architectural taste, much sought-after advisor and juror, and leading spokesman for the modernist tradition. Shattering the myth of the architect as cultural hero, the Pan Am Building marked his, Gropius's, and modernism's fall from grace, the selling out of its lofty social goals for the sake of personal gain.

After retiring from the MIT deanship in 1965, Belluschi continued to practice independently in association with local architectural firms. In this capacity he turned out, at least in name, an astonishingly large body of work, equally astonishing in its wide range of building types—churches, synagogues, tall office buildings, university buildings and master plans, concert halls, community centers, retail complexes, and large commercial developments. His work of this era aroused as much notoriety as that of the earlier era, but now critical rather than celebratory in tone. Seen as inhuman in scale and insensitive to the needs of the city and its citizens, his buildings, or those perceived as his, were by and large viewed as profit-oriented and at odds with the public good. Throughout the 1960s and 1970s, as progressive architects began exploring other issues, Belluschi aligned himself with big business, alienating the leaders of the profession and distancing himself from newer theoretical directions.

Nonetheless, he maintained a position of considerable power. Belluschi was unquestionably one of the most influential figures in the architectural profession at the time. As a key advisor to government officials, university presidents, and other major corporate clients, and as a regular juror on some of the most important competitions of the time, among them those for Boston City Hall, the Franklin D. Roosevelt Memorial, and the Vietnam War Memorial, Belluschi's voice carried weight. He played a pivotal role in securing some of the top commissions of the time for architects such as I. M. Pei, whom he favored, and seemingly blocking the careers of those, such as Robert Venturi, whom he did not; as such, he had a substantial impact on the course of architecture in the 1950s and 1960s.

As architectural values changed and former superstars were transformed into social scoundrels, Belluschi's own fundamental views remained the same. Though seen as a leading spokesman for modernism, he had never been comfortable with the modernist emphasis on originality, and he continued to use existing forms, sometimes those of his contemporaries, sometimes those of the past, never simply copying but always refining and adapting them to changed circumstances of time and place. At times hubris got the better of him and he tried his hand at the messianic role, with buildings such as St. Mary's Cathedral in San Francisco in the mid-1960s. Its shortcomings and his others' like it were as apparent to him as they were to others.

Unlike Philip Johnson, his archrival and nemesis since the 1950s when cracks in the modernist block first began to appear, Belluschi refused to change his views. The two men, two courtly, urbane gentlemen born seven years apart, with their old world manners and elegant ways, sparred continuously through the years. Johnson proclaimed architecture an art, Belluschi maintained that pragmatics came first. They finally squared off in 1979 in a well-publicized duel over Michael Graves's Public Services Building in Portland, Belluschi's hometown, with nothing less than the future direction of architecture at stake. As postmodernism spread in the 1980s, promoted by Johnson through his gaggle of younger architects, Belluschi delivered a series of hard-hitting speeches to the profession in defense of more solid values than those Johnson espoused.

In writing on Belluschi, my aim—difficult at times because I too, coming of age in the 1960s, have attitudes and ideals often at odds with his—was not to judge but to understand, and to consider him and his work in the context of a vastly complicated, constantly changing time. A great many people, cited individually in my acknowledgments, contributed graciously to this end. I would like to thank in particular Robert Frasca, who in the course of long hours of discussion saw what I was trying to do and helped keep my thinking in perspective. He enhanced my understanding immeasurably. Robert Brannen recognized the immensity of the project and the difficulties involved; I thank him, Jill Weber, and Jung/Brannen for their generous support. I'm grateful too to my colleague and eminent historian David Pinkney, who died before the work was completed, for his consistent support when things got rough, and to William Jordy, Robert Harris, and Walter Creese for their sympathetic reading of the text. Their suggestions were invaluable, and greatly improved the final result. Marjorie Belluschi was a constant help, indispensable in providing letters, photographs, and other archival material in Belluschi's possession. I want to thank Matthew Abbate for his careful, thoughtful editing of the text. And finally Roger Conover of the MIT Press heard my initial frustrations and sensed the significance of what I was doing. I'm grateful for his confidence, and hope it has proved warranted.

Pietro Belluschi

Pietro Belluschi

1   Italian Origins

Preceding page: Belluschi in uniform,
1918.

Topological map of Italy (Rand McNally).

Ancona, view of seafront (postcard).

*Belluschi in front of Via Pizzecolli 30,
Ancona, 1974.*

*Belluschi in front of Via Pizzecolli 30,
Ancona, 1974.*

Pietro Belluschi was born 18 August 1899 in Ancona, a major port on the Adriatic, where his family lived in an apartment near the seafront on the hilly slope of Via del Comune (now Via Pizzecolli). He was the anxiously awaited second child, only son and male heir of a devoutly Catholic, aspiring middle-class family of Lombard and Genoese extraction.[1]

As Guido Belluschi, Pietro's father, recorded in his memoirs, the men of the family—he, his younger brother Piero, his father and grandfather—had all worked in the Italian railways.[2] At the time of Pietro's birth, Guido was employed by the Adriatica, a privately owned railroad company headquartered in Ancona, as a minor official in the office of land assessment and acquisition. In 1905, when the railroad system was nationalized, he was transferred into construction, and the family moved to Rome.

There were four in the immediate family: Belluschi's parents, a sister four years his elder, and Pietro. Beyond them, however, was a wide net of extended family on both sides. Guido's brother had married Guido's wife's sister, and the two families remained close. Besides this uncle and aunt there was another aunt and a grandmother on his mother's side, all of whom at some point shared living quarters.

It was a proud family, aware of its accomplishments and with a strong sense of its role in history. An assiduous collector of family memorabilia, including what was thought to be the Belluschi coat of arms, Pietro's father traced its genealogy back to the time of the Holy Roman Emperor Otto I, to the region near Lake Como in Lombardy, and to a possible connection with the Roman city of Bellusco, or Belusco.[3] As Pietro himself later pointed out, northern Italians by nature were different from southern Italians, known more for their industriousness and entrepreneurial skills than for sensuality.[4] Pietro's grandfather, born in Milan in 1831, was by his own admission not much of a student, but he excelled in draftsmanship, attending the highly acclaimed Brera School of Fine Arts as a youth, where he produced precise, finely executed drawings, many of which were still in the family's possession in the 1930s. His sons, Guido (born in 1862) and Piero, on the other hand, proved themselves strong students with a genuine interest in learning. Guido showed a gift for poetry and languages but for practical reasons pursued a course in technical studies, concentrating in mathematics and the general sciences. Though engineering appealed to him, in deference to his father's expectations he gave it up and continued the family tradition of working for the railroad.

Belluschi coat of arms.

Belluschi, age one.

A highly disciplined man with a strong sense of order and precision, and, by his own account, a preference for simplicity in all matters of life, he was passive in manner, conciliatory rather than confrontational.[5] Outwardly serene, and leading, in Pietro's eyes, an uneventful and colorless life consumed by hard work and aspiring to nothing more lofty than improving his family's material circumstances, inside he cultivated a rich life of the mind, quietly pursuing his interests in poetry, the classics, and music. Rejected by his wife physically and emotionally after Pietro's birth, he doted on his son, to whom he often turned for companionship. The two took long walks during which Guido, given to rapturous poetic and philosophic musings in the nineteenth-century romantic manner, passed on to Pietro his love of language and literature.[6] The first of several crucial mentors, Guido remained an important figure in Pietro's life, someone he loved deeply and respected but in time rebelled against, fiercely rejecting his comfortable religious convictions and bourgeois tastes. Much like him in manner, the younger Belluschi vowed to be different in essence.

Pietro was less close to his mother. Born Camilla Dogliani of a well-to-do Genoese family, blond, blue-eyed, and, according to Guido, endowed with a certain physical grace, she too had excelled as a student, distinguishing herself with a quick mind and high grades in school.[7] Belluschi described her as a domineering, self-centered woman whom he feared more than loved. Both parents indulged him, however, hovering over him when he was sick and staging splendid parties on his birthdays, celebrated with gifts and garlands of fruits and flowers.[8]

As Belluschi reconstructed it decades later, he felt stifled by his parents' solicitousness and the confinement of their comfortable middle-class existence, and sensed at an early age an urge to assert his individuality. In an oft-repeated anecdote, he recalled outings with his family at the age of three or four in which he insisted on walking by himself on the opposite side of the street.[9] This determination to go his own way, to distinguish himself from others, led, as he put it, to a firm resolve to shape his own life and create his own destiny. Not immediately obvious under Belluschi's soft-spoken, modest veneer, this self-assertion was a character trait that had great bearing on the course of his career.

Margherita, his older sister, was an operatic singer, a mezzo-soprano of some skill, and there was talk of a musical career. Instead she married an engineer and settled down to a comfortable bourgeois life.[10] Intelligent, sensitive, warm, she was evidently as conventional as Pietro was determined to be different.

Gifted artistically as well as intellectually, the Belluschi family shared too a heightened concern over matters of health seemingly out of proportion with the family's tendency

Belluschi family, Rome, June 1908.

toward longevity. Pietro's mother felt weak after Pietro's birth and acquired a live-in maid, or personal companion, who cared for her throughout her life until just before she died; he was nursed by a peasant woman who lived in a village outside Ancona. Pietro's father, debilitated, according to his own account, by long hours of desk work, chronically suffered from a host of ailments and in 1928 underwent surgery for ulcers, an operation Pietro himself was to have several decades later. In his memoirs, Belluschi recorded all the skinned knees, sore throats, and bouts with pleurisy, pneumonia, yellow fever, and smallpox that peppered his past. This solicitousness in his childhood led to chronic worry in later life, with frequent complaints about his health, aging, and imminent death from the 1950s on.

His maternal grandmother, who lived with the family while Pietro was growing up, exerted a rather different influence. Pietro, who prided himself on his "innate sense of beauty," was very aware of his own good looks. He found repulsive her awkward gait, simple manners, and plain appearance. She had been raised in comfortable circumstances, then lost what had been a sizable dowry at the hands of her husband, a dashingly handsome free spirit (for whom Pietro admitted a certain sympathy) who died shortly after Pietro was born,[11] leaving his wife dependent on her daughter. Money acquired what Belluschi described as a "transcendent importance" in his grandmother's thinking, a trait passed on to his mother and to a large extent, he admitted, to himself as well. The grandmother was a devout Catholic, whose unquestioned religious convictions he viewed with contempt as a youth. Bored by mass and the droning of priests, unconvinced by the dogma, he rejected the formal teachings of the Church and was repelled by its external trappings, which he recognized, or so he told it years later, as nothing more than a seductive appeal to the senses of the uneducated.[12]

His grandmother's presence in the household had its positive side, however. Several years after the family moved to Rome her brother died, leaving her a substantial inheritance. This sudden wealth after years of abject poverty she saw as an act of God, which only deepened her religious fanaticism; but it also enabled the family to upgrade their standard of living. With their share of the estate, Pietro's father and uncle bought land on Via dei Villini near the Porta Pia, on what was then still largely orchard on the outskirts of Rome, and built a large apartment house, two apartments of which their families used, with servants' quarters for their three maids under the roof, while the other four units were rented. Belluschi recalled the excavation for the building uncovering bones and artifacts from a network of early Christian catacombs, and the weight of the past he sensed as human teeth centuries old dissolved into powder in his hands.[13]

Belluschi apartment building, Via dei Villini, Rome, circa 1910.

Pietro's maiden aunt on his mother's side also lived with them for a time. It was she, evidently, who was mainly instrumental in cultivating his interest in the visual arts. A painter of some skill who had attended the School of Fine Arts in Bologna, as an adult she continued collecting art works and painting. Belluschi described her work years later as competent but unadventuresome, leaning more toward the romantic landscapes of Corot than modernist works of Cézanne. He nonetheless recalled being aware of the work of the futurists while spending summers as a teenager with his family in Pistoia.[14]

Pietro did not attend school until 1905, after the family moved to Rome. Accustomed to center stage at home, he disliked the classroom setting. Bored by classes and impatient to get out, according to his later account, he rarely concentrated and insulated himself from others. Despite a quick mind, he proved, like his paternal grandfather, to be an indifferent student. His father had put great stock in his son's academic success; faced with his father's pressure to work harder, Pietro appealed to his mother and invariably obtained her sympathy. Highly perceptive and keenly aware of his effect on others, he became adroit at manipulating their emotions to get what he wanted. Much to his father's dismay, he failed the fourth grade and had to repeat it.

During his childhood, the Belluschi family spent summers on a distant relative's farm in the countryside near Piacenza. In his memoirs, Belluschi described it as a "paradise on earth,"[15] with its farm animals, bountiful crops, rich sights, and earthy smells. The memory, no doubt embellished over the years, represented a lifelong ideal: to be owner of a substantial estate with fertile soil, ample local peasant labor, and an unlimited supply of fresh meat, fruit, and vegetables. It was to him the perfect life, ordered, serene, free from want and the concerns of others, in harmony with the natural rhythms of the land. This ideal was to form the basis of his concept of the house as a private retreat, and led to his move to a farm in the suburban countryside outside Portland in 1944, and still later in 1973 to the Burkes House, secluded in the hills above Portland. Here he retired, overlooking the city but wholly removed from its noise and turmoil.

Schooled in the family history of swings of fortune and financial loss, and well aware of the fate of the owner of the idyllic estate of his childhood, who was talked into selling his farm during the war and died destitute in a *pensione* on the Riviera, Belluschi tempered his romantic visions with sober fact.[16] The insights gained from such experiences impelled him always to size up the fiscal implications of a given situation, potential pitfalls as well as promise. It was an inclination that proved useful later not only in his role as an architect and design critic but also in his dealings with clients and developers.

As he approached adolescence, the family took to spending summers in a rented villa near Pistoia in Tuscany. As Belluschi recounted it, not without flourish, it was here, rather than in his ordered, well-mannered, cerebral home life, that his love of the physical pleasures of life was developed: listening to the sounds of cicadas, soaking up the warm earthy smells of the damp soil, harvesting walnuts and chestnuts, trying out his first bicycle, and playing with the farmers' children in the open fields. It rounded out what seems to have been a carefree youth, free from material want and, aside from occasional childhood illness, largely without trial.

In 1910, the family moved to Bologna, where they lived for several years in a large apartment on the top floor overlooking the city. As a young adolescent with a growing awareness of his own identity, Pietro felt here the first pangs of rebellion against his family's conventional life. It was also a time when his intellectual horizons were expanding. He was fascinated by new advances in modern technology. Descending from a

Pietro with mother, sister, and aunt,
Bologna, 1911.

family whose livelihood had long been from the railroad, he was entranced by new modes of transportation, especially motorized vehicles; it led to a fascination with airplanes at a time when air flight was still experimental, as well as a lifelong love of cars. He recalled often fantasizing, as he launched toy planes from the terrace of their top-floor apartment, about flying off to escape the mundane existence of his too stolid, earth-bound family.[17] This childhood urge to flee situations he found boring or insufferable he was to feel repeatedly throughout life, suggesting a tendency not unlike his father's to withdraw from rather than confront situations he was unable to control.

The love of cars, trains, and planes also led to a passion for travel. Determined to surpass his father, who had never ventured outside Italy, at age 15 Pietro vowed to explore as much of the world as he could. This meant long hikes through the Italian countryside alone or with friends, and frequent train trips, which, because of his father's position in the national railway, he could take for free, always first-class. This zest for travel would lead to his decision to leave Italy in 1923 for the United States. It also led to a life as a consulting architect actively seeking out opportunities that would take him throughout the world.

In the late fall of 1912 Pietro moved back to Rome to live with his uncle and aunt, who were childless. His uncle, a supervisor for the railroad company in the department of construction, was a small, fiercely ambitious man, evidently far more enterprising than the more retiring Guido. Warm-hearted and generous, at least with his family, he lavished particular affection on Pietro, whom he regarded as a son. Pietro learned much from him not only about the building trades but also about the entrepreneurial skills required to run a successful business. A year or so later Pietro's father was transferred back to Rome and the two families were reunited, living together in the apartment house they had built on Via dei Villini. In 1922 Guido retired from the railroad, and with his pension he and Piero started a private venture in speculative housing. Sensing an excellent opportunity to profit in the overheated inflationary postwar era, Piero too left the railroad in order to build apartment buildings full time. With Guido administering the business and Piero in charge of construction, the enterprise flourished. This highly lucrative family business Pietro seemed destined to take over in due time.

In Rome he attended the Ginnasio Liceo Torquato Tasso, then the school of applied engineering at S. Pietro in Vincoli.[18] He began studying the classics, but finished, as had his father, with a more practical diploma in the technical sciences. Despite his keen mind his interests were not in academia, and the only subject he truly enjoyed was drafting, which came easily to him and provided an outlet for his artistic inclinations.[19]

It was at this time that he learned the principles as well as the classical forms of architecture. Drawing fluted Ionic columns, complicated Corinthian capitals, detailed moldings of Renaissance cornices over and over, he mastered lessons he never forgot.[20] This exercise also developed the discriminating eye—the sense of scale, proportion, rhythm, detailing—for which he later became known.

From an early age he had also possessed a remarkable visual memory. Moving from Ancona at the age of six, he remembered it well three-quarters of a century later: the neighborhood churches, the apartment he lived in, the layout of city streets. Growing up in the architecturally rich settings of Ancona, Bologna, and Rome, and traveling by foot or rail around the Italian penisula and beyond, to Sicily, Nice, Vienna—places steeped in history and endowed with renowned architecture—he was able to recall years later, when asked by staff members of his Portland office, the exact proportions of their buildings with astonishing accuracy. This ability to visualize cities and places, even those he had only seen through drawings or photographs, provided him a repository of ideas and potential design solutions rare among the American architects he was to encounter later.

Belluschi's engineering studies were interrupted by the war. Though he himself was unmoved by feelings of patriotism, military service was a longstanding family tradition in which it took great pride; then too, his older cousin had set a standard by becoming

Belluschi and family, Rome, 1916.

an officer in the Royal Grenadiers, one of the first to go to the front. As Pietro still had no idea what he wanted to do and sensed that he was likely to be drafted anyway, in March of 1917 he volunteered, hoping this might grant him some control over where and when he would go. After completing an accelerated officer training course, in September he was promoted to aspirant officer and assigned to the Third Regiment of Mountain Artillery in Bergamo. On the front for most of the rest of the war, he was stationed first at Pocol in the Dolomite mountains, serving in observation, then, after the retreat of Caporetto, in a special assault unit near Monte Grappa, where he was charged with reconnaissance. He participated in the battle of the Piave in June of 1918 that marked the turning point in the war, as well as the final battle of Vittorio Veneto in October.[21]

The experience was unforgettable. As he recounted it in his memoirs (the vividness of his prose no doubt heightened by his reading of Hemingway's *Farewell to Arms*), one night out alone on the trail, he panicked at an unexpected burst of gunfire. Eventually he overcame his terror, but it was a harrowing experience that brought home tangibly what courage meant, and what it took to conquer fear by sheer power of will. Tested a second time as he was delivering ammunition to the front and surrounded on all sides by the whistling of shells, he felt not fear but the exhilaration of battle. He describes it as a moment of self-discovery, and recalls the experience as a test of psychological as well as physical stamina.[22] Early in 1920, after three and a half years of service, Belluschi was discharged as a first lieutenant, decorated with two war crosses and a recommendation for a bronze medal.[23]

After the war, now 21 and still unsure what direction he would pursue, he attended the University of Rome, where, according to his father's account, he had matriculated after completing his studies at the polytechnic school. He took advantage of a special proviso issued by the Public Education Ministry easing requirements for returning veterans, and was able to receive credit for course work by exam in lieu of classes. Two years later, in December 1922, he was granted a "laurea di Ingegneria," the equivalent of an American bachelor's degree in civil engineering.[24] He was elated to be out of school, but the thinness of his formal training was later to haunt him, leaving an insecurity about his academic background that plagued him throughout life.[25]

The university did not have a school of architecture, which was only established in 1922, the year he graduated. Had it had, it seems unlikely that he would have enrolled in it, since before coming to Portland and securing a job in the office of A. E. Doyle, his own claims later to the contrary, there is no sign that he thought of becoming an architect.[26] Considered one of the fine arts, architecture was formal, abstract, and academic. His interests were more practical. As an engineering student he took courses in the sciences, mainly math and physics. He signed up for one course in architectural history from the then young architectural historian Gustavo Giovannoni, who was later to publish in sixteenth- and seventeenth-century Italian architecture. Remaining his only formal exposure to the discipline of architectural history, the course, according to him, consisted of little more than the succession of historical styles, and made no impression.[27]

After receiving his degree in 1922, the year Mussolini came to power and his father and uncle started their business in speculative housing, Belluschi secured through a friend a job as a housing inspector. Though no doubt it was useful for the family to have him in such a position, Pietro found the job dull and unlucrative. Then an opportunity arose to go abroad. The daughter of a well-known Italian general, Irene di Robilant, had just been given the task of finding a war veteran eligible for an exchange fellowship sponsored by the newly established Italian-American Society for a year of study in the United States. Time was running out and a candidate had not yet been found. Belluschi's English was weak, but with his good looks and charming manner he made a good impression, and through the Countess di Robilant he received a scholarship for a year of study at Cornell University. Though he hardly relished the thought of more schooling, he had been reading Rimbaud, the French symbolist poet, and inspired by his vivid accounts of foreign travel, Belluschi saw this as a chance to escape his mundane existence in Rome.[28]

According to his memoirs, he worried about his lack of English, but in fact spent more time concentrating on what clothes to take. Uncertain about what he should wear, he equipped himself with eleven new suits, including both black and white tie tuxedos.[29] Seen off by his family, he boarded the luxury transatlantic liner *Conte Rosso* in Genoa and arrived in New York eleven days later.

Pietro Belluschi

Belluschi remembered vividly the fear and excitement he felt on the morning of 27 September 1923 when the *Conte Rosso* slipped into harbor and the skyscrapers of New York loomed into view. He was met by the Countess di Robilant, who showed him his room in a hotel near Fifth Avenue and 14th Street. The quarters were considerably meaner than he had anticipated, and after wandering aimlessly around the city by himself, he left a few days later for Cornell.[1]

The situation there he found little more congenial. Compounding the anxiety about his English, the thought of taking a mandatory qualifying exam in engineering terrified him. He passed it, according to him, mostly by cribbing from other students, but not with a high enough score to get into graduate school; he was accepted only as a senior.[2] The year at Cornell passed quickly, and though he joined an Italian fraternity and made several friends, by his own account he was lonely and felt isolated by the language barrier. Painfully aware of his lack of preparation and panicked at the thought of returning home a failure, he threw himself into studying, taking courses in economics and thermo-dynamics in addition to required courses. The curriculum included one architecture course, a studio taught by the dean of the College of Architecture, Francke H. Bosworth. Subscribing to the then-conventional Beaux-Arts method with its emphasis on formal values, Bosworth gave students a problem and asked them to respond with a set of quick pencil or ink *esquisses.* He also taught them rendering with color and wash.[3] Belluschi was familiar with the classical buildings that served as models for student designs, and was already experienced in drawing and sketching; hence he found the

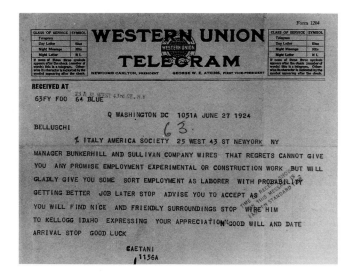

Telegram, Caetani to Belluschi, June
1924.

course easy. In retrospect, he said that he learned little from it, though one surmises he absorbed more than he realized or admitted.

It was expected that he would return to Italy at the completion of the school year. But as June graduation neared, he cast around for some means of prolonging his stay. Because of a childhood friend whose family lived in Japan, he thought of going there, but was persuaded by the Countess di Robilant not to unless he had assurance of work, and to think instead of remaining in the United States with whatever job he could find until something better turned up.[4] He was given a letter from the president of Cornell that testified to his "exceptionally good scholastic record and in addition his personal qualities," which had "won him a high regard in the Cornell community"; thus equipped, Belluschi applied to a number of engineering and construction companies in New York, indicating a particular interest in concrete construction. None of the companies to which he applied had anything to offer.[5] As time grew short, Belluschi appealed for help from the Italian ambassador to the United States, Don Gelasio Caetani, to whom he had been given a letter of introduction before leaving Rome and whose acquaintance he had made on the *Conte Rosso*. Caetani, a descendant of an old Roman family, had studied engineering at Columbia University and then gained firsthand experience working for the Bunker Hill and Sullivan Mining Company in Kellogg, Idaho; through him, Belluschi was able to secure him a job there in electrical engineering.[6]

Introduced as the member of a "distinguished Italian family" and a "protégé" of the ambassador, he was received well and taken by the head of the company on Sunday drives to experience the Idaho hinterland. He soon supplemented these with long hikes through the wilderness to explore the rugged beauty, vast spaces, and desolate cliffs of the Pacific Northwest, very different from the tamer landscape of northern Italy.

The job itself, however, in which Belluschi worked in a wide range of capacities from electrician's helper to drawing up the plans of a small hydroelectric plant, proved to be hard work. Moreover, the working conditions were less than genteel. Winters in Kellogg were even colder than in Ithaca, and the frustration of being stuck in a job with no clear opportunity for advancement took its toll; he began having the ulcer problems that were to plague him for the next thirty years. He endured it for nine months, then resolved to move on. Obtaining letters of introduction from the manager of the company, who had contacts with several architectural firms on the West Coast, in April Belluschi boarded a train west with the hope of finding an engineering position in Seattle, Portland, or San Francisco.[7]

After stopping first in Spokane, he continued to Portland, which was then in the midst of the biggest building boom in its half-century history. He had a letter of introduction to A. E. Doyle of A. E. Doyle and Associate, which was then known as one of the largest and most successful architectural offices in the Pacific Northwest. The affluence, urbanity, and sheer beauty of the city after the rough-hewn mining town of Kellogg impressed him. Then too, the presence of an established upper class offered a level of cultural sophistication commensurate with his own tastes and ambitions. These factors plus the flourishing business climate boded well. He went no further.

Portland and A. E. Doyle

Portland was by the 1920s a small jewel among cities in the West. Founded in 1843 on the west bank of the Willamette River just above its juncture with the Columbia, it had garnered a major share of the local commerce that depended on river and sea transportation; by the 1860s it was the hub of the steamboat trade, and a decade or two later of Henry Villard's railroad empire. Its prosperity marked it as the major metropolis in the region,[8] and, stretching out below steeply rising hills to the west, with the river winding its way through and the majestic snow-capped Mt. Hood looming in the east, it was a city of astonishing natural beauty. It also had a cultural heritage that was unique on the West Coast. Founded by a small but powerful elite of affluent, well-educated families from New England, it offered civic amenities—an art museum, public library, theaters, even two private colleges—compactly located and comparable to many on the East Coast. Much of this cultural sophistication was reflected in the architecture, which on the whole was of a quality unequaled in the West.

The tradition of fine architecture had been early established by Whidden and Lewis, whose roots were in the eminent New York firm of McKim, Mead and White. In the late 1880s William Whidden was sent out to Portland to supervise the construction of a new grand hotel for the railroad magnate Henry Villard. When Villard suddenly lost his fortune and abandoned the hotel project, Whidden was retained by local supporters to complete the building. Sensing a need in Portland for his skills, Whidden stayed, soon joined by Ion Lewis, a fellow former student at MIT. For the next several decades their McKim, Mead and White–derived architecture dominated Portland, establishing a precedent for highly sophisticated, well-designed, mostly classical buildings, characterized by the perfectly scaled, balanced proportions and fine detailing for which McKim, Mead and White were known.

Albert E. Doyle fell heir to this tradition. A Californian by birth, son of a successful building contractor who moved to Portland with his family in the early 1880s, Doyle was apprenticed at the age of fourteen in the Whidden and Lewis office. As part of his training he was sent to work in the New York office of Henry Bacon, who was later to design the Lincoln Memorial in Washington, and to attend Columbia University. A scholarship in the spring of 1906 enabled Doyle to attend the American School of Archaeology in Athens and to take the Grand Tour, mandatory in any ambitious American architect's education, through Europe and Great Britain. He returned to Portland in 1907 with sketchbook filled and opened his own office. Shortly thereafter, he and several other architects founded the Portland Architectural Club to propagate Beaux-Arts ideals in the local community.[9]

Although young and inexperienced, Doyle had talent. Tall and handsome, with a patrician bearing and the cultural polish of an eastern training but warm and congenial in manner, he rose quickly in the profession, gaining the reputation of a highly successful designer of some of the most important public, institutional, and commercial buildings of the time. It was, for example, to the Doyle firm, then under the name of Doyle, Patterson and Beach, that trustees of newly founded Reed College turned in 1911 for a master plan of the campus as well as design of the buildings. By the early 1920s, as Portland's economy expanded, Doyle was operating with a sizable staff of some of the city's best designers.

Portland, with Mt. Hood (photo: Walter Boychuk, courtesy Oregon Historical Society).

By the time Belluschi arrived April 1925, however, Doyle was already suffering from the Bright's disease that was to kill him within three years, and the office, following the departure of several key designers, was languishing. Because the vogue for classical architecture, particularly that of the Italian Renaissance, continued to grow nationally, largely due to the influence of McKim, Mead and White, Doyle was keenly interested in Belluschi's Italian background. Thinking he might use him as a draftsman, he took him on. Doyle's own background had leaned more toward the chaste, restrained forms of Greece and ancient Rome, and to broaden it he was about to leave for another trip abroad, this time specifically to Italy. He had also just recently sent his chief designer, Charles Greene, there to absorb what he could of Italian precedents, mostly of the sixteenth century. Aware now of the value of his Italian background, especially in culturally self-conscious Portland, Belluschi made the most of it. Sharp as his ear was to nuances of language, he made little effort to disguise his accent, continuing to speak in the disarmingly soft, hesitant, half-broken English he was to use throughout his career.

He began doing small-scale detailing under Greene's supervision, but moved quickly into larger jobs involving greater design responsibility. This appears to have been as much a

A. E. Doyle & Associate, Portland Central Library, 1913 (Oregon Historical Society).

A. E. Doyle & Associate, U.S. National Bank, Portland, 1916 (Oregon Historical Society).

matter of expediency as native skill. Almost immediately after Belluschi joined the firm, Doyle left on his trip abroad for two years, leaving the office in the hands of Charles Greene, who in turn turned to Belluschi for assistance. While privately contemptuous of Greene's attempts to imitate traditional Italian forms, Belluschi learned from him. He quickly realized that there was more to design than good draftsmanship, and envied Greene's natural talent which he felt he lacked.

Of the firm's projects from this period, the 10-story Pacific Building was particularly important. It was under design when Belluschi arrived and was the first project he worked on. Unlike the firm's other commercial office buildings, such as the Public Services Building, which were cast in a conservative academic classicism, the Pacific Building bore evidence of a more progressive source stemming from the Chicago School.[10] The steel-framed structure with non-load-bearing brick walls had straightforward exteriors of a plain, overall Chicago grid. Rather than a traditional rhythmic arched and pedimented composition, the windows were uniform, unframed, and flush, or nearly so, with the plane of the wall. Inspired by Chicago School prototypes but with a crispness

Belluschi rendering, Public Services
Building, Portland, 1926.

A. E. Doyle & Associate, Pacific Building, Portland, 1925–1926 (photo: author).

and elegance for which the Doyle firm, with its McKim, Mead and White background, was known, the Pacific Building marked a notable departure from the prevailing Portland norm. The Doyle office itself moved into a spacious loft on the tenth floor soon after it was completed. More importantly for Belluschi, the Pacific Building, with its clean, flat wall plane and deliberate expression of the structural grid, served as a point of departure for one of the most widely acclaimed buildings of his later career, the Equitable Building of 1948.[11]

The Terminal Sales Building was another of the half-dozen or so projects on the boards at the time. Designed in 1926 and built in 1927, it was progressive in a very different way from the Pacific Building. Reflecting newer stylistic trends sweeping the country, with its simplified form and flattened, stylized ornamentation it suggested a contemporary Euro-

A. E. Doyle & Associate, Terminal Sales Building, Portland, 1926–1927 (Oregon Historical Society).

pean influence, that of the Viennese Secessionists as seen through the 1925 Paris Exposition des Arts Décoratifs. Though Belluschi himself was not involved in its design, he remembers the interest it expressed in the Viennese architects Josef Hoffmann and Otto Wagner, and he was to draw on this idiom himself several years later.

A project in which Belluschi appears to have had the most design responsibility at the time was an addition to the Cloud Cap Inn, a resort hotel on the eastern slopes of Mt. Hood.[12] The original building, designed by Whidden after his arrival in Portland in the late 1880s, was a rambling one-story log structure, roughly U-shaped in plan, elementally rustic in character, with steeply pitched shingled roofs and massive stone chimneys. In 1927 the Doyle office was asked to do an addition. Modeled closely on the Multnomah Falls Lodge, a similar structure the firm had done several years earlier, the Cloud Cap Inn addition was another indication of the wide range of building types and stylistic idioms the firm was accustomed to producing. The addition was never built, evidently as a result of the weakening economy.

Belluschi's drawings for the project, however, are revealing. On the one hand, they attest to his adeptness at picking up and using whatever stylistic idiom seemed appropriate. On the other, his precisely drawn, formal, straight-edge elevation and loose, freehand perspective sketch of the proposed building, nestled into its natural setting halfway up the mountain, attest to his interest in drawing as an appreciable art form in its own right. Belluschi had by this time become involved in activities at the Portland Art Museum and was taking life drawing, composition, and painting classes from the painter Harry Wentz, a close friend of Doyle's who was later to become one of Belluschi's most important mentors. The Cloud Cap Inn perspective, with its careful composition and landscaped setting in particular, suggests Wentz's influence and Belluschi's growing involvement in the visual arts.

A department store in Boise, Idaho, of 1927, was, according to him, his first design on his own. Italianate in character, it suggests the influence of Charles Greene, who may in fact have provided the basic concept.[13] Perhaps because of this building in Boise, but more likely because of his convincing manner as well as his eagerness to travel and familiarity with that part of the country, Belluschi was asked to assume an advisory role hitherto filled by Doyle. Like Doyle, Belluschi proved to be charming and personable, a good listener and conscientious in his work. Despite his youth and inexperience, it was he who increasingly was sent out to negotiate with clients. The First National Bank of Idaho, a longstanding client of Doyle's, had asked the Doyle office to oversee the design of one of its branch banks in Boise. Belluschi was sent to review the design and advise

Cloud Cap Inn addition, Belluschi elevation (Oregon Historical Society).

Cloud Cap Inn addition, Belluschi perspective.

the client. It was his first experience in an advisory capacity, requiring the astuteness, tact, and diplomacy for which he later became well known.

In 1927 Greene precipitously left the firm, and in January 1928 Doyle died, leaving the office without clear leadership. A deathbed partnership was set up with William H. Crowell, a genteel, older man from New England and the only registered architect in the office, David Jack, the office's business manager, and Sidney Lister, supervisor of construction. Crowell, who had had several years of architectural training at MIT, managed the drafting room and supervised working drawings; Jack was the principal liaison with the community and scouted out new jobs. Belluschi was left, by default as it were, in charge of design. In 1928 they were joined by William Kemery, a young and highly regarded engineer. In all there were roughly a dozen people in the office, which continued to operate under the name of A. E. Doyle & Associates. Among their half-dozen or so current projects begun while Doyle was still alive were a theater, a sports stadium, several large commercial buildings, and a $450,000 Italian Renaissance mansion.[14]

It was a pivotal moment. Facing the decision of whether to bail out from what appeared to be a sinking enterprise and seek employment elsewhere or to remain, Belluschi sized up his opportunity within the firm. A chance to design a mansion for the locally prominent Corbett family helped him decide. Knowing he would get farther as an architect, a far more prestigious area of endeavor, especially in his parents' eyes, than in engineering

Boise Department Store, 1927, newspaper clipping.

*Drafting room, A. E. Doyle office,
Pacific Building, 1926; Pietro Belluschi
seated at rear right (Oregon Historical
Society).*

or construction, Belluschi spent several months studying for the state licensing exams, and in July 1928 passed them with the highest score of those who took them that year.[15]

Despite a high rent, the office continued to occupy the spacious quarters on the tenth floor of the prestigious Pacific Building in Portland's downtown. The receptionist's desk was in an entrance lobby, off which was a small office for business affairs. Beyond this was the reference library, with wood-lined walls bearing a large collection of architectural books, many of them old and rare, photographs, and current magazines. It was here, around a long, rectangular, elegantly carved table, that meetings with clients took place. Opposite the library was a spacious drafting room lit by a series of large monitor windows on the north and opening onto a landscaped rooftop garden to the south.[16] It was a tastefully designed and efficiently organized space, destined to appeal to well-to-do, sophisticated clients. As the economy began to slump in the later 1920s and fewer jobs came in, the office stepped up its efforts to broaden its clientele. Work meanwhile continued on branch buildings for the Pacific Telephone and Telegraph Company, an administration building for Linfield College, and a mansion for Hamilton F. Corbett.

This last was a job Belluschi himself brought in. Through his activities at the Portland Art Museum, Belluschi had met Harriet Corbett, the attractive young wife of Hamilton Cor-

Library, A. E. Doyle office, Pacific Building, 1926 (Oregon Historical Society).

*Corbett Residence, Portland, 1928–
1929 (Oregon Historical Society).*

bett, son of an Oregon state senator and descendant of one of Portland's wealthiest and most influential families. Enamored of the good-looking young Italian, she persuaded her husband to retain him as their architect despite his inexperience. Belluschi was of course delighted, largely because it gave him a chance to do some designing on his own. And it was a good job: a prominent client, with a substantial budget, on a large, secluded, wooded site in an exclusive neighborhood in the Portland hills.

To meet Mrs. Corbett's request for a French provincial house, Belluschi turned to plates in the Doyle library. His design was conventional by contemporary standards, and competent enough (though the roofline, Belluschi later thought, was too steep for French provincial), but greatly simplified in the final version as the economy waned. To keep costs down, he used recycled brick, which gave the building a rich, warm texture, and eliminated as much as he could expensive moldings and other architectural decoration.[17] Built at a cost of $125,000, a fraction of the original budget, the mansion still stands, in use as a Catholic convent.

Belluschi's Design Philosophy

In May 1929 Belluschi was suddenly called back to Italy to be with his father, who, it was believed, was dying. By the time he arrived in Rome his father had largely recovered, but Belluschi remained for a while, taking the opportunity to look around, now with fresh eyes, at what architecturally was going on in Europe. His correspondence with Dave Jack in the Doyle office suggests he was aware of the new developments, but not much impressed except for those in Germany. "As architecture [in Italy] nothing new that is good," he wrote to Jack in his still fragmented English. "Mussolini has standardized architecture (with laws) in a bad taste, baroque France is just as bad. I am hoping better for Germany through which I will return."[18] A second letter from New York several weeks later confirmed his expectation. "As far as modern architecture is concerned," there was little of interest except in Germany, which was "astonishingly advanced and is producing a really vital architecture." He met up with an architect who showed him around Berlin, then went to Paris before returning to the States in early July, four months before the economic crash of October 1929. His letters made no mention of what buildings he saw, and in interviews later he was unable to recall anything specific, except for Erich Mendelsohn's newly completed theater complex in Berlin. His letters to the Doyle office actually reflect a greater interest in, or at least conscientious study of, recent building in America. Instructed by Jack to return to Portland via New York, New Haven, Chicago, and Detroit, Belluschi was asked to study new developments in elevator installation, theater design, college libraries (specifically the new Yale University Library, which their client for the Reed College Library especially admired), art museums, storefronts (particularly the use of the new, glassy material, Vitrolite), bank interiors, and hotel lobbies. Sending him letters of introduction and money for the trip, Jack expressed the hope that he would return full of ideas for the year ahead.[19]

Remodeling the lobby of the more sumptuous and exclusive Benson Hotel was one of several projects Belluschi returned to. Like the Public Services Building lobby, one of the first jobs Belluschi worked on after joining the Doyle firm, it was relatively small, but the budget was ample, and he obviously enjoyed working with costly materials—rich marble wainscoting, patterned tiling, and new modern light fixtures—and drawing on some of the recent artistic developments he had been exposed to abroad. The job also enabled him to travel to New York, San Francisco, and Los Angeles, staying in the finest hotels at the client's expense.

The library for Reed College, a private college on some 86 acres southeast of Portland, was another project he faced on his return. Doyle had basically established the design

Public Services Building, lobby, 1926
(Oregon Historical Society).

Doyle, Patterson & Beach, Reed College, campus plan, 1912 (Oregon Historical Society).

as part of his campus master plan of 1912, and a preliminary drawing had been prepared, evidently by Charles Greene, in 1927. It was left to Belluschi to develop it, now with a far more limited budget. It was an important job, testing his ability to continue the high standards Doyle had set for the campus with substantially fewer means.

Tudor Gothic in character following the Doyle precedent, Belluschi's design was considerably reduced in both plan and elevation: a simple rectangular form, symmetrical in disposition, a central tower containing a great arched entrance, steeply pitched, battlemented roofs, mullioned arched windows and doorways, and vaulted ceilings. Of brick with limestone trim, it was built in 1930 for $128,700, more than Belluschi had aimed at but still substantially less than originally budgeted. Remarkably efficient in plan, it served as a model for a series of small college libraries Belluschi was to do in the 1930s.[20]

More challenging was the office tower project he was to do the same year. In June 1929, a group headed by Robert H. Strong of Strong and MacNaughton Trust Company had announced plans for a 27-story skyscraper, with an impressive 350-foot rectangular tower capped by a spire, set back on a broad, block-filling, two-story base, the whole to be spectacularly lit by immense floodlights marking the heart of Portland's financial district. Had the project gone ahead, it would have been the biggest and most expensive building in the city. Architects were A. E. Doyle & Associates. It was evidently with this job in mind that Jack had asked Belluschi to study elevator installations, lobbies, and other features of similar high-rise structures in New York and Chicago on his return home from Europe.

The project hinged, however, on obtaining a lease for the strategic site located in the downtown. When negotiations fell through, the clients regrouped in November 1929 under the name of the Commonwealth Trust & Title Company, among them the most high-powered businessmen in the city. With a new site and new board of directors, including Ralph H. Cake of the Equitable Savings & Loan Association, the project was revived the following year.

Ralph Cake was no ordinary client. A young, ambitious lawyer, he was also an aggressive entrepreneur with new ideas and the drive to carry them out. As part of the planning process, he and the other members of the Commonwealth board of directors had assembled an advisory team of leading experts in tall office building planning and management from across the country, under the direction of the National Association of Building Owners and Managers. Cake was charmed by Belluschi's youthful, earnest personality and remained unconcerned about his lack of experience, backed as he was by a firm with a long record of accomplishment. He welcomed Belluschi's receptiveness

Reed College Library, Portland, 1929–1930 (Oregon Historical Society).

Reed College Library, plan (courtesy Joachim Grube, Yost/Grube/Hall).

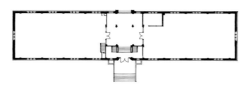

A. E. Doyle & Associate, proposed 27-story building, Portland, 1929.

to new ideas and eagerness to try them. Belluschi was also by now becoming known in the community in his own right through his work on Reed College, whose president was Bostonite banker (and former architect, trained at MIT) E. B. MacNaughton, of the Strong and MacNaughton Trust.[21] MacNaughton was also on the board of directors of the Portland Art Museum, as were many other members of the Commonwealth Trust consortium.[22]

In June 1930 Belluschi accompanied Strong, president of the Commonwealth Trust, on a trip east to study current developments in skyscraper design in New York, Philadelphia, and Chicago. Though no evidence confirms it, it seems likely they knew of Rockefeller Center and the Philadelphia Saving Fund Society Building, both in planning stages at the time, especially in light of Belluschi's particular interest in the work of Raymond Hood.

A revised proposal on a new, more restricted site on the corner of 6th and Stark, calling for a rectangular 27-story tower rising above a two-story base with staggered setbacks above the thirteenth story, at a projected cost of $2 million, was published in the local newspapers that spring. In the architect's statement prepared for the press, Belluschi, with his halting syntax and somewhat prolix prose but also the lofty rhetoric that was to become a trademark, declared the aim was to make the new Commonwealth/Equitable Tower one of the notable buildings in the country. It was to incorporate the most advanced mechanical equipment available, including high-speed, automatically operated elevators, to have a lobby of the most exquisite marble, bronze, and black opalescent granite, and to offer 150,000 square feet of high-quality rentable office space, with none wasted "for the sake of a so-called logical treatment which has proved to be a rather deceiving theory."

> Lately we have persisted in wasting good rentable space and money in order to express verticality. . . . But such expression of verticality applied to a steel structure which has both horizontal and vertical members isn't any more necessary or logical than the modern German horizontal treatment. They are just expressions of individuals and important as such. Naturally, it is always possible to create a theory on anything that happens, and man doesn't seem satisfied until he has labeled every expression of its individuality into definite formulas behind which he stands ready to attack and criticise. The truth is that science having given us new materials, we found ourselves free to follow new ways of creating and composing masses, although up to the present time we didn't know very well how to go about it. We may have dropped architectural classical orders, but we haven't necessarily become more logical in our buildings as we have been so fond of proclaiming. However,

Proposed Commonwealth/Equitable Building, 1930, as published in Oregonian.

through the centuries there has been a certain quality about architecture which seems to have always withstood all offense of time and fashion, and that quality is simplicity. Simplicity with mass is, or ought to be, the real expression of an age where waste is not tolerated.

The architects were convinced, Belluschi concluded, that this quality of simplicity is what "keeps a building ever modern through good and bad times." A functional, efficient plan was their primary concern, for which a team of experts from around the country had been assembled for advice. "Nothing will be left undone to make the building one of the most beautiful and successful in the northwest."[23]

It was a revealing statement, not only of Belluschi's ambitions but also of his familiarity with contemporary theories of modernism. How much of it was Belluschi personally rather than the views of the Doyle office is hard to ascertain. Still short of his thirtieth birthday, however, and in the United States but a little over five years, with virtually no architectural training and licensed only the year before, Belluschi was green by anyone's standards. The statement appears to have been prepared by him, and suggests basic convictions about architecture that he was to hold throughout his career: the primacy of the plan, the importance of efficiency, indifference to theory, contempt for fashion, and, above all, simplicity. It was evidently at this point that his personal design philosophy, based on the classical values he grew up with but informed by current modernist theory, began to take shape.

The Commonwealth Tower remained a project only, a victim of the deteriorating economy and a lack of consensus among the clients over a final solution. It proved a valuable experience for Belluschi, however, not only cementing his connections with some of the wealthiest and most influential clients in Portland but also exposing him to some of the most progressive thinking on skyscraper design and planning in the country. It also provided insight into the advantages of bringing in experienced consultants, whatever the short-term costs.

Instead of a new tower, a pair of existing two-story buildings on the site were remodeled to meet the clients' immediate needs. One of the buildings, intended for the Equitable Savings & Loan Association, was given new interiors and an up-to-date face of flush Indiana limestone with a polished black granite base, suggesting the influence of the PSFS Building by Howe and Lescaze in Philadelphia, at a cost of $40,000. The adjacent building to the south, providing headquarters for the Commonwealth Trust & Title Company, was given a late twenties styling, with the stripped, simplified classicism characteristic of the Art Deco, for $50,000. Both buildings were completed in 1932.[24]

*A. E. Doyle & Associate, Common-
wealth and Equitable buildings (remodel), Portland, 1932 (Belluschi
Collection, Syracuse).*

In the Doyle office, Belluschi's specific role varied from project to project. Typically, his function was to oversee design, working with the client to ascertain exactly what was needed, then conveying the essence of the program to whomever in the office seemed best suited to carry it out. In instances such as the Corbett House and Reed College Library, where the design responsibility was clearly his, his approach was to turn for a model to whatever visual sources seemed appropriate—books, photographs, the architectural magazines. His models were sometimes contemporary, sometimes drawn from the past; in either case, his approach was the same. He first analyzed the problem from all angles, then devised an efficient, economical plan for which a suitable three-dimensional form was to be found. Highly analytical, based on problem solving, and aimed at finding the best structural and functional rather than a formally innovative solution, his design approach basically remained the same from this point on.[25]

But times were changing, and so too architectural values. Of this, Portland, despite its isolation from the main headquarters of the architectural establishment in the East, was very much aware.

Portland's Architectural Community

In observing Doyle, Belluschi had seen the importance of maintaining close ties with the profession. Though basically reclusive by nature and not interested in joining clubs, he made a deliberate point to become involved with the local architecture community. In its brief existence, the Portland Architectural Club had aimed at raising the local community's level of sophistication and standards of taste. Though focused primarily on the Beaux-Arts, it had encouraged an awareness, through exhibitions and other activities, of other architectural traditions as well, such as the arts and crafts movement and the work of West Coast architects Bernard Maybeck and the Greene brothers. By the late 1920s, however, local attitudes toward the Beaux-Arts were changing and modernism was in the air.

William Gray Purcell, a leading proponent of the Chicago School who had moved from the Midwest to Portland in 1922, had much to do with this. An outspoken critic of the Beaux-Arts, Purcell argued forcefully on behalf of indigenous American traditions, urging architects and others in the art community to read Thoreau, Emerson's essays on art and beauty, Sullivan's *Autobiography,* and Lewis Mumford's *Sticks and Stones.* He also favored the works of British critics, such as Ruskin's *Seven Lamps of Architecture* and Fry's *Vision and Design,* for a fundamental understanding of art.[26] His lectures did much to undermine confidence in academic classicism, especially among younger Portland architects, and to introduce them to a new way of thinking.

Articles on Sullivan and other American modernists, then beginning to appear in the national press, lent credence to Purcell's theories. Fiske Kimball, in a major article in the *Architectural Record* of 1925, discussed the philosophy of the Chicago School and of Louis Sullivan in particular, whom he heralded as the first to give artistic expression to the steel frame skyscraper and to deal with it logically and openly. It was this vein of thinking that evidently lay behind the design of the Pacific Building on which Belluschi had cut his architectural teeth.[27]

Belluschi came to know Purcell, who was President of the Society of Oregon Artists, through his activities at the Portland Art Museum, and methodically purchased each of the books Purcell recommended. A well-thumbed, underlined copy of Emerson's *Essays,* still in Belluschi's library, suggests that this was especially meaningful. He was also familiar with Purcell's article on Sullivan tracing the development of modernism in America, which discussed Sullivan's midwestern banks in particular. It seems likely that the Sullivan banks, with clean, crisp brick forms, delicate terra-cotta ornamentation, their sense of French refinement and restrained elegance—an architectural language very different from McKim, Mead and White's Italianate academic classicism—formed a part of Belluschi's thinking at this time.

More influential than Purcell in introducing Belluschi to this train of thought was W. R. B. Willcox. Joining the faculty at the University of Oregon in 1922, Willcox, with the backing of the dean, Ellis Lawrence, had wrested the architecture school away from its Beaux-Arts orientation and ushered in newer methods of architectural education, turning it into probably the most progressive architecture school in the country in terms of pedagogy. Like Purcell, Willcox was a Sullivan disciple. With low-key Socratic discussions, which Belluschi found far more compelling than Purcell's imposing lectures, Willcox introduced students at the university to the theory of organic architecture and, according to Belluschi, to a reasoned approach to design rather than reliance on historical precedents. Belluschi was on the committee in charge of exhibiting the architectural work of University of Oregon students and faculty at the Portland Art Museum and kept abreast of campus activities. Thus it was that he became drawn into the debate between "modernism" and "tradition" in the late 1920s.[28] Two articles on modernism that Willcox published in the *Oregonian* in June and July of 1929, accompanied by a Sullivan-inspired skyscraper proposal, were particularly germane. It was these, more likely than not, that were behind Belluschi's thinking in his remarks on the Commonwealth Tower. Having worked in Chicago before coming to Portland, Willcox also knew Frank Lloyd Wright and was instrumental in bringing Wright to the University of Oregon campus in 1931 to deliver one of a series of lectures he was giving throughout the country.[29] Wright was by this time well known in the Portland community, especially after the publication of his essays in the *Architectural Record* of 1928 and 1929. Drawing on Sullivan's vision of an organic architecture, Wright's work, especially at Taliesin where the built forms were so thoroughly integrated with the natural landscape, found particular resonance in Portland. It proved to be a major source of inspiration to architects in the Pacific Northwest.

Harry Wentz and the Portland Art Community

Close ties between architects and the artistic community in Portland were longstanding. The Portland Architectural Club had held joint exhibitions with the Portland Art Association since its inception in 1907, and architects such as Doyle were typically members of both organizations. Doyle's connection with the Portland Art Museum was particularly close. Anna Crocker, curator of the museum, was a Doyle client; so too was Harry Wentz, who taught painting at the museum school and was one of Doyle's closest friends. Born in 1877 in The Dalles on the Columbia River, Wentz had studied art first in New York, then in Europe. He returned to Portland in the early 1900s, joined the faculty of the Portland Art School, and remained there teaching watercolors, life drawing, and composition until he retired in 1941.[30] An inspiring teacher and a man of rare personal integrity, Wentz played a major role in shaping the artistic values and philosophy of a whole generation of young artists and architects in the Portland community. His influence on Belluschi was particularly profound.

Wentz was deliberately ecumenical in his artistic judgment, open to what he deemed inherent quality or a fresh vision regardless of style. His approach was intuitive, a result of looking at and experiencing art rather than of formal schooling. Growing up amid Oregon's natural beauty and returning to it after studying abroad, Wentz was particularly sensitive to the aesthetic properties of the natural landscape. His watercolors and oils were typically of the mountains, seacoast, Columbia Gorge, farms, and small towns of Oregon.

Composition was his great strength. Informed by Cézanne, whose work he had pinned up in his studio, Wentz was interested in the unity of formal elements, in structurally integrating buildings and landscapes—the flat planes, pitched roofs, vertical chimney shafts of the one with the rocky outcrops, sloped mountains, and tall, upright trees of the other. Asian art, which comprised a substantial portion of the Portland Art Museum collection, was another major interest. Wentz's high horizon lines, mountainous rocks, structuring of planes in depth with a foreground, middle ground, and far distance, his brushstrokes, his subdued palette with its subtle gradations of tone, all bear evidence of Oriental painting. He himself had an extensive collection of Japanese prints that he later donated to the museum. Wentz's method of teaching, like Willcox's, was informal, one-to-one. He himself was a quiet, self-effacing man of simple Spartan tastes, frugal in his living habits; antipathic to Victorian clutter and the bourgeois accumulation of material goods, his life like his painting was pared to the essential. Spurning visual complexity and elaborate details, his outdoor sketches recorded, as he put it, "the spirit of a motif as I feel it and conceive it."[31]

Belluschi admired Wentz greatly, recognizing in him many of his father's virtues without his strictures. Wentz taught him not only how to look but how to understand what he saw, how the parts of a work of art were organized, what made a composition hold together, how scale and proportion were vital to the whole.[32] Wentz looked at architecture with an artist's eye, saw how architectural forms could be organized, balanced harmoniously, how they could fit in and become an integral part of the setting.[33] He showed how light coming in at an angle and focused on a single object affected the quality of the space as a whole, how the hard smooth surfaces of stone might be played off against the warm rough grain of unfinished wood: the purely artistic potentials of architectural elements and materials rarely acquired in architectural schools or on-the-job training. Harry Wentz more than any other spurred Belluschi's love of art.[34] From him Belluschi learned not only essential artistic values—the meaning of a work as well as its structure and use, the discernment of genuine quality as opposed to ephemeral style—but also how to teach, how to spot talent, encourage it, critique it constructively to bring out the best of what others could offer, insights that proved invaluable to him later in his own role as teacher and mentor.

Belluschi met Wentz shortly after joining the Doyle office. He began attended Wentz's evening lectures at the Portland Art Museum, then took several classes from him in life drawing and composition. With the Model T Ford he bought as soon as he could afford it (which he soon traded for a Buick, then in 1931 for a Hudson), Belluschi began touring the Oregon wilderness, sometimes alone, more often with Wentz and friends in the Doyle office. They often took long hikes together, as Belluschi had with his father, sketching and painting the Oregon countryside.

At times they were joined by John Yeon, also an architect and, like Wentz, a native of Oregon, who was to play a formative role in the development of Belluschi's regional thought and work. Eleven years younger than Belluschi, Yeon came from a well-to-do, culturally sophisticated family. His father was a French-Canadian who had made his

Harry Wentz, Neahkanie Cottage, *water-color (Oregon Historical Society).*

Belluschi, Pine Tree, *watercolor.*

Belluschi, Neahkanie Cottage, *water-color, 1929.*

Belluschi and a friend touring.

Belluschi on Mt. Hood, 1927.

money in timber, his mother a painter, and he grew up surrounded by art. He had also spent much of youth with his father, a conservationist, combing the backwoods, and developed a strong attachment to the wilderness. After a short stint at Stanford University, then Columbia University, he traveled abroad with his mother following the death of his father and returned with a passion for architecture. Bored by formal training, he sought instead an apprenticeship with a respected architect. It was in the Doyle office that he met Belluschi. Sharing an interest in the fine arts as well as progressive developments in modern architecture, the two became good friends. On his trip to Europe in 1930, Yeon, a great admirer of the Scandinavian modernists, saw Gunnar Asplund's Stockholm Exhibition, and he followed closely the work of International Style architects, especially Erich Mendelsohn, an interest he shared with, or more likely passed on to, Belluschi.[35]

Wentz owned a small vacation cottage that Doyle had built for him at Neahkanie, a small, isolated resort community on the Oregon coast populated largely by artists and intellectuals from the Portland area. Doyle had done several seaside cottages in the vicinity, all basically derived from the common bungalow type in use at the time.[36] The Wentz Cottage was different. Designed in 1916 with Wentz's close collaboration, it was conceived as an artist's studio, with a bank of large windows to the north framing a view of the receding coastline and gaunt, windswept cypresses in the foreground. The interior consisted of a lofty two-story space that served as a living, dining, and studio area, with kitchen and small bedroom off to one side. A master bedroom and bath were in the loft on the second floor. Everything was left natural: walls were of a warm, textured, unpainted wood, with framework exposed; beams and rafters of the roof were similarly open, creating a linear articulation that formed an inherent part of the overall composition. Opposite the bank of windows was a massive stone fireplace, its random, unhewn boulders rising the full height of the wall.

Simple, straightforward, economical, with clapboard exteriors of unpainted spruce blending into the landscape, the Wentz Cottage was conceived as an inherent part of its rugged coastal setting. Unassuming on the exterior, its artistic sophistication was reserved for the interior, where the basic architectural elements were handled simply but exquisitely, with everything hand-worked by local craftsmen. A soft raking light from the northern window gave a pearly luster, like the inside of seashell, to the smooth spruce walls. To Yeon, who with Wentz and Belluschi spent weekends and vacations there, it was one of the most beautiful structures he had ever seen, the first to strike him as true architecture.[37]

In designing the cottage, Doyle clearly drew on arts and crafts principles and most likely was directly inspired by the work of Bernard Maybeck, whose drawings had been featured in a Portland Architectural Club exhibition the year it was begun. The profile of the balustrade, both interior and exterior, is distinctly Maybeckian. It was a motif of special significance to Belluschi, who was to quote it some 70 years later in the Robert Packard House, Portland, a private testimonial to Wentz and his architectural values.

The Wentz Cottage bore signs too of a Japanese sensibility, possibly inspired by the California architects Maybeck or Greene and Greene, but very different in nature and more likely bearing the influence of Wentz's interest in Japanese art. The deliberately framed views, both of the receding coastline to the north, and out across the Pacific Ocean to the west through a lone cypress, bear the mark of Japanese compositional principles.

Modest as it was, the Wentz Cottage had a profound impact on Yeon and Belluschi and the regional tradition that was emerge in the Pacific Northwest. It represented the potential of a domestic architecture that responded to nature simply, directly, and unpretentiously. More than any other kind of building, it seemed to fit.[38]

A. E. Doyle, Wentz Cottage, Neahkanie,
view from northeast (photo: author).

Wentz Cottage, interior.

Wentz Cottage, exterior, balcony looking west (photo: author).

Wentz Cottage, view from window to west (photo: author).

Pietro Belluschi

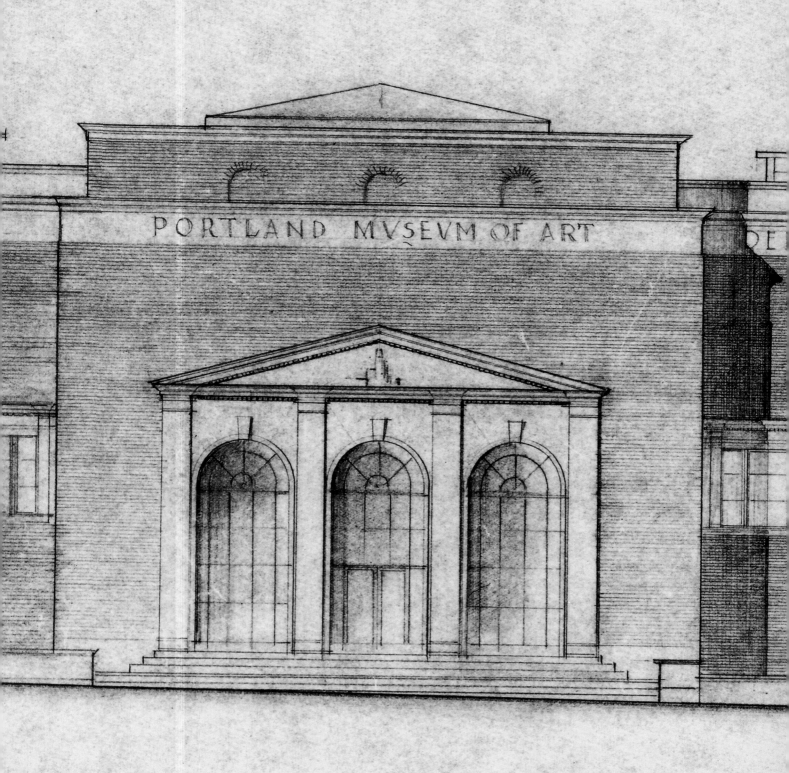

Pietro Belluschi

Preceding page: Portland Art Museum,
preliminary drawing, April–May 1931,
detail (Oregon Historical Society).

The impact in Portland of the stock market crash of October 1929 was direct and devastating. Jobs had begun falling off in the Doyle office as early as 1925, as the economy slowed in the latter part of the decade. By the spring of 1929, the Corbett House was nearing completion, the Reed College Library and Benson Hotel lobby were under way, a storefront for the large wholesale florist Tommy Luke was begun, and there was the $2 million Commonwealth/Equitable project, which was soon abandoned.

Doyle's traditional clients, the bankers, brokers, and businessmen of Portland, were especially hard hit. Membership in Portland's exclusive private clubs, which Belluschi himself eventually joined, dropped sharply, and civic affairs, supported largely by the city's well-to-do, were severely curtailed.[1] The worst was yet to come, with work in the office hitting an all-time low in 1933 and 1934. The office nearly folded for want of jobs, the staff shrinking to five. Kemery, the engineer, sought work elsewhere; Ken Richardson, who had joined the office in 1927 as an office boy and was to return in 1944 as Belluschi's chief designer, had a family to support and left; Frank Allen, fresh out of Benson Technical Manual Arts school and hired as a draftsman, saw months go by with no more than $5 in salary; even Lillian, their all-purpose office secretary, had to find supplemental work elsewhere.[2] Belluschi himself returned to Italy.

Portland Art Museum, 1931–1932

Private donations to civic institutions dropped sharply as family fortunes dwindled. Nonetheless, support for the Portland Art Museum as well as the Portland Symphony remained strong, a clear sign of the value placed on the cultural life of the city.

The museum had been founded in 1892 on lofty ideals. Departing from the traditional concept of the museum as a self-contained repository of art, the Portland Art Museum saw itself as an active force in the community, a progressive educational institution dedicated to cultivating the arts broadly through special exhibitions, lectures, gallery tours, and an art school, with close ties to the public school system. Hendrietta Failing, its first curator, was a social crusader who set the tone. Anna B. Crocker, her successor, shared her sense of artistic mission; committed to the goal of bringing the fine arts to the general public, Crocker emphasized the direct, personal experience of art over formal academic theory. By the time Belluschi enrolled in the art school in the late 1920s, the curriculum included drawing, painting, life class, composition, costume design, handicrafts, and children's classes, as well as courses in the history of art.[3] The focus was on cultivating the eye and powers of discrimination through practical experience, on understanding meaning rather than mastering technique. Belluschi, introduced to the school through Doyle, was deeply affected by the philosophy of the school and especially by Miss Crocker, whose sense of mission he found compelling.[4]

Doyle had been an active member of the Portland Art Association since 1907, when he opened his office and founded the Architectural Club, not only through joint exhibitions but also as lecturer, lender, and chairman of numerous committees. As the need for more gallery space became apparent in the early 1920s, he was appointed head of a special building committee. In 1926, he became president of the Association.

As talk grew serious of a new museum building, Doyle drew up a program, a long, thoughtful, detailed analysis of the museum association's needs. It included several pages of notes from both Anna Crocker, the current curator, and Hendrietta Failing, the museum's founder. The focus of the report was purely practical: what they should look for in a site, the plan, its convenience and efficiency, the "comfort," security, lighting, flooring, square footages of gallery spaces and storage areas, even color. Repeated references to other museums, such as Boston's, the Cardiff Museum in Wales, and the new Detroit Museum of Art, indicate the careful research their work was based on, and that they were very much aware of changing attitudes toward contemporary museum design.[5] Their questions focused on the special problems of the small art museum, and specifically what role the museum and art school should play in the city of Portland. Accessibility was a principal concern of Crocker's. Conspicuously absent from the report was any mention of the building's style. Crocker specified only that the appearance of the building should speak of its function, that the materials be good, its proportions and details fine, and that the "luxury," as she put it, be in the space, its lighting and "comfort." Failing was concerned about the galleries, which she wanted varied in size and shape to avoid user fatigue and monotony; their beauty should reside in their proportions, with architectural ornament minimized so as to enhance rather than compete with the art. Doyle too, from whom one might have expected some statement on style, given his McKim, Mead and White background, made no mention of it, commenting instead on modern tendencies in architecture.

Doyle's statement was a response to articles he had recently read on the relationship of architecture to culture, or what he called, using the terminology of the times, "civilization," a theme Belluschi was to pick up in his lectures a decade later. Doyle regretted the view of Leonard Cox, who denounced the contemporary trend in skyscrapers as unworthy of the times, finding far more important the comments of the New York architect Harvey Corbett, who rather than lamenting the situation sought practical solutions. "Architects are not over-modest men," Doyle admitted, "but they do not believe they are capable of changing the drift of civilization. They build for people and have always built what people want, using their imagination, and suggesting, if they are worthy of their calling, something better than their client imagined. But if the civilization in which they work wants skyscrapers and banks, architects cannot make that civilization build Cathedrals and Museums."[6]

Doyle's pronouncement differed fundamentally from the far more heroic, revolutionary stance of his contemporaries abroad. The European modernists proclaimed the architect as a social reformer; Doyle saw the architect more humbly as a professional whose first obligation was to the client. Embraced by Belluschi, this view was to raise the hackles of doctrinaire modernists in the 1950s and 1960s. Its deference to client demands also set him squarely at odds with Philip Johnson in a battle the two of them were to fight over basic architectural principles throughout the course of their long, in many ways parallel careers.

Doyle's death and the downturn in the economy put plans for a new art museum on hold. In 1930, however, the museum traded its old 1905 red brick Georgian building in the heart of the business district for a site just beyond the downtown. The Association also received a donation of $100,000 earmarked for a new building. An existing school building on the new site was to be remodeled, its wooden superstructure razed, leaving a concrete basement that was to be altered to house the museum and staff until new facilities were built.[7]

With Doyle no longer there, it seemed clear that the job would go to Jamieson Parker, an older, conservative architect and longstanding member of the museum's board. He was also a member of the building committee and had been commissioned to remodel the old school building for temporary use.[8] The job went instead to the young, untested Belluschi, the doing, apparently, of Anna Crocker, backed by C. F. Adams, chairman of the building committee. As president of the First National Bank and member of the Commonwealth Trust consortium sponsoring the Commonwealth Tower project, Adams knew Belluschi and was charmed by his earnest confidence and eagerness to please. Reassured by the reputation and experience of the Doyle office, he went along with Crocker's recommendation.

In February 1931, an agreement was drawn up with what were recognized to be very generous terms. The Doyle office offered to build the new unit for the museum at no more than cost to them, including overhead, and guaranteeing that their fee would not exceed 6 percent of the cost of the building. The museum in turn would pay a maximum of $100,000 for the new unit, including architect's fees; this was also to pay for a preliminary plan of the entire new building, of which this unit would be the first part.[9]

Although Crocker and Belluschi had discussed the project earlier, it was only now, with the site determined and the commission in hand, that he started work on the design. One of the first actions he took was to update Doyle's research in current museum design, compiling a list of recent articles from the architectural magazines.[10] Shortly after, he sent Crocker a typed, five-page memo of their preliminary thoughts. He began with the plan, which he described as "more or less the inevitable solution" of the problem, with two levels of galleries disposed symmetrically around a spacious lobby. Second in importance was lighting. Skylights, they found, were inappropriate because they cast light in the middle of the floor rather than on the walls where it was most needed, produced glare, and were hard to keep clean, hence expensive to maintain; side lights were also unsuitable, as they, too, created glare as well as casting reflections off the surface of paintings; moreover they consumed valuable wall space. Their conclusion was that monitor windows, casting a soft diffused light onto the opposite wall, with the use of Venetian shades where necessary to control direct sun, were most appropriate. They considered artificial lighting but found it not well studied and not good as the major source of illumination because of its monotonous evenness; it also was purported to have deleterious psychologic effects on visitors. As to the form of the building, Belluschi concluded that it "should be designed from the inside out, and that no good interior practical feature be sacrificed for a faked external appearance."

> Architecture should be a living thing and that to apply the externals of a past age when requirements were of an entirely different nature is a fundamental mistake. Contemporary architecture has been abused when new forms have been applied solely for the purpose of making something different and not with the idea of letting the interior function be the guiding element of design. Functionalism recreates the standards of beauty and if considered a sort of fourth dimension of architecture must work with the other three to produce something that is alive; that standard mask called "style," whether that be Georgian, Italian or English is just a bad formula and only our lack of imagination has tolerated its application on buildings where a new set of ideas had to be given a new form.

> The museum as we understand it today is a new institution with modern requirements, and a definitely alive function. Let us not try to maim and twist the body to fit the suit but let us build a new suit consistent with the body.[11]

Belluschi included a list of specific questions he hoped Crocker would address: Is a 16-foot 6-inch net ceiling height sufficient for the first floor, will a 15-foot net ceiling height on the second story accommodate future large paintings, what was her opinion

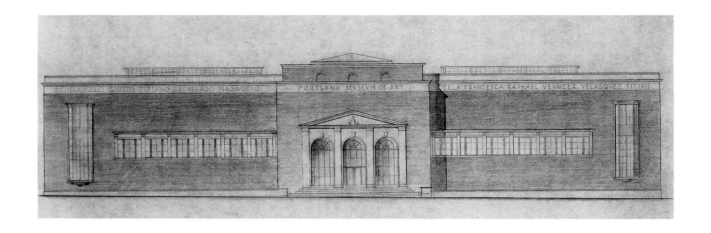

on artificial lighting, on removable partitions placed perpendicular to window walls, etc.[12]
Actively seeking her advice in light of her years of museum experience, Belluschi for his
part kept her well informed of their decisions as they progressed. She was thus a vital
component of the design process.

Wanting a second opinion, or perhaps seeking reassurance from a more experienced
source, Crocker sent Belluschi's memo to L. Earle Rowe, the director of the new Rhode
Island School of Design museum, who responded by commending them on their
straightforward, functional approach. Clearly intrigued by their problems, he addressed
Belluschi's points one by one. The two men continued to exchange ideas on Belluschi's
proposals, especially the pros and cons of skylights versus clerestory windows in view
of Portland's particular climatic conditions and the orientation of the building. It was
Rowe, for example, who called to Belluschi's attention a recent article on glare in
museum galleries that recommended the use of monitors, and he generously passed on
his experience with loading platforms and storage spaces, making several suggestions
that Belluschi incorporated in the revised plan.[13]

It wasn't until well into April that Belluschi began work on the elevation. He himself drew
up a number of different schemes, and had a model built that would allow them to try
on various facades.[14] The plan and overall massing remained constant; what varied was
the design of the parapet, moldings, fenestration (arched or rectangular, individual or
continuous, with or without muntins), central bay, and main portals, providing a range of
options from the most simple and modern to the traditional. Adams, the driving force of
the building committee and by then head of the board of trustees, had been greatly
impressed by the new Fogg and Rhode Island School of Design museums, then considered among the finest in the country. He wanted a Georgian building. The challenge for
Belluschi thus was reconciling what he had found to be the simplest, most practical and
economical solution to the problem with the client's demand for a traditional building,
and with what Anna Crocker had made clear she wanted: a welcoming, accessible,
unpretentious, functional-looking building.

Faced with resistance to his modernist leanings, Belluschi appealed to Frank Lloyd
Wright, whose name was in the news because of his recent University of Oregon lecture.
Belluschi described the problem of the small museum that was also to function as an
educational facility, basically a new building type without formal precedent. The budget
was limited, between $100,000 and $150,000, which he considered in this case a plus
as it precluded the use of marble, colonnades, statues, "and other monumental mausoleum accessories." His own preference was for a purely functional solution, but because
of the nature of the job he had to accommodate a symmetrical plan, and more impor-

tantly his client's demand for Georgian. "There is really no argument against a person's taste," he told Wright. "The worst part was that they were so nice about it and so unmovable. I am writing this to you because that is what we young architects are pounding our heads against. It seems almost impossible to be spiritually alive in the right sense. In this country we are inevitably kicked between fashion and dead tradition." Would, Belluschi asked, a letter from him to the client help?[15]

Wright responded immediately. The client was "making a serious mistake" in insisting on a Georgian exterior. He commended Belluschi on his "sensible modern exterior" and took the liberty of suggesting a few changes. The plan was simple and sensible, the exterior "would mark an advance in culture for Portland. Can't Doyle and Crowell stand up for Architecture?"[16]

Bolstered by Wright's response, Belluschi refined the design, making only minor adjustments, mostly to the central bay. The proportions of the central bay were changed, broadened, its side flanges reduced to make the whole lighter, less monumental in effect; the one entrance portal was changed to three and the stairs broadened, providing greater ease of access and creating a less imposing, more welcoming effect. The number of horizontal windows in the main galleries to either side was adjusted accordingly, and

Portland Art Museum, tentative elevation of April 1931, with Frank Lloyd Wright's suggestions of July 1931.

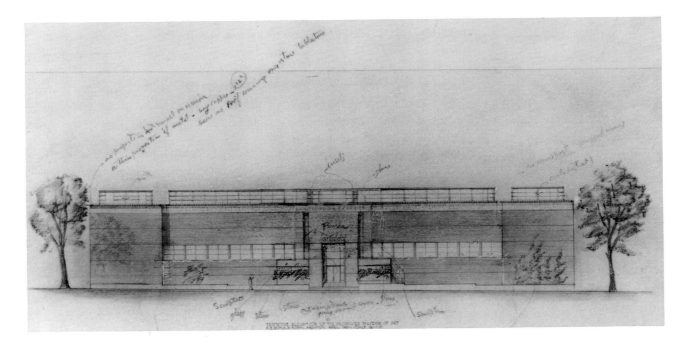

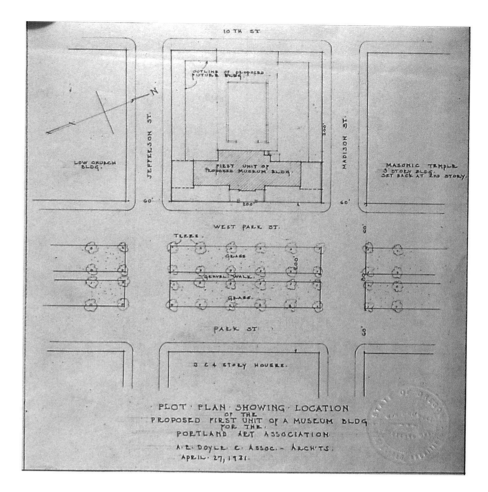

the wall above the main portal left plain, following Wright's suggestion, with the name of the museum inscribed in the recess below. By December 1931 the final design was ready. It was approved, construction begun immediately, and the building completed by the following fall. It opened to the public November 1932.

The site consisted of a 200-by-200-foot city block facing a long narrow park several blocks from the downtown. It was thus an easy walk for office workers on lunch breaks and after working hours. The sense of accessibility was deliberately enhanced by siting the building close to the street and keeping it low, with a minimum of stairs, rather than elevating it on a lofty podium. The entrance was broadly glazed to allow pedestrians to see in. Although the site was confined on three sides by streets and on the fourth by the old school building, Belluschi left a narrow zone around the periphery for the landscaping Hendrietta Failing wanted to create the appropriate mood.

The building consisted of a simple two-story rectangular block, with galleries disposed on either side of a main gallery space or sculpture court. Additional wings were to be

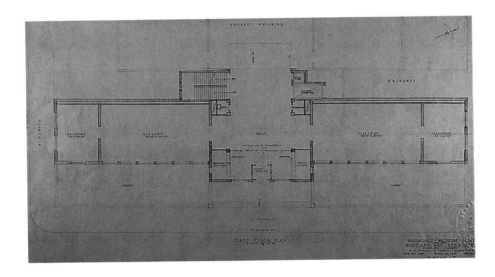

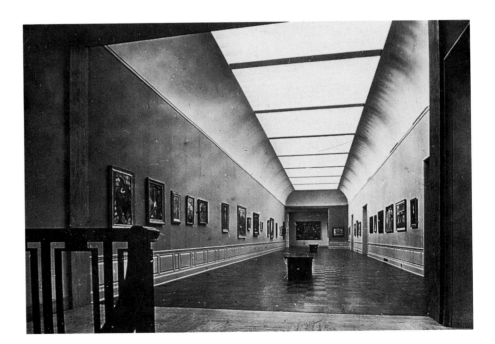

*Portland Art Museum, plan, 14 May
1931 (Oregon Historical Society).*

Portland Art Museum, interior.

added when resources were available. The main entrance hall into which one immediately stepped was large and spacious, filled with as much natural light as possible to give incoming visitors a sense of openness, in deliberate contrast to the confinement and oppressive gloom of the traditional monumental museum. Galleries were varied in size and proportion to provide flexibility in staging exhibitions and to avoid visitor monotony, and were lit primarily by natural lighting. Avoiding ornamentation, Belluschi aimed at keeping everything simple, with visual interest generated by purely architectural solutions such as long, dramatic perspectives. Galleries on the lower floor, destined for exhibitions of sculpture and small objects in glass cases, were lit by a continuous zone of 6-foot-high sidelights just below the lofty ceiling, freeing wall space below. The upper stories, intended for paintings, were lit by continuous monitor windows on all sides, with a 5-foot cove immediately below to shade the eyes of onlookers from direct glare.

The structure was of reinforced concrete, with exteriors of warm copper-red brick and creamy white Roman travertine trim. Bricks, obtained from the local Willamina Clay Company, were varied in color just enough to create a subtle texture without become garish. The mortar, tinted to match, was thicker than customary and only slightly tooled, again aiming for a distinctive but unobtrusive pattern. Belluschi used a Flemish bond he admired in the work of a local architect, sending bricklayers down the block to study his building. The warm color and distinctive grain of the travertine (less expensive than marble) were another part of the overall effect. This sensitivity to the harmony of color values and textures and attentiveness to detail enabled Belluschi to keep the architecture masses simple without the building becoming merely dull. Trim was minimal, a simple cornice, rolled molding around portals and windows, possibly Italian but more likely Scandinavian in derivation. The steel grillwork was French, apparently drawn from one of several books on the decorative arts that Belluschi acquired while in Paris on his trip abroad in 1929.

In his summary of the proposal for the new museum, Belluschi commented on the external form almost as an afterthought:

> As to the exterior appearance of the building, having come to the conclusion that windows of a certain peculiar shape placed at a certain location were the most efficient from the lighting point of view, it was not tried to disguise, cut or change them in any way in order to conform to any rule of style, but they were given their proper place and made a part of that subtle relationship of masses and materials which constitutes, or rather ought to constitute, the basis of real architecture, if it is to be alive and not be just popular or fashionable architecture. For these reasons classical proportions had to be abandoned, and for economic reasons colonnades

and other expensive architectural exercises had to be abandoned. The very best and most enduring materials were used and here the architects have tried to find a simple solution to a very peculiar problem, and tried to make it as consistent with the interior as possible, eliminating the more transitory qualities of style in the hope that by expressing the vital function of the structure in terms of the enduring they had fulfilled their most important duty.[17]

Belluschi's modernist stance was clear: function, not form, governed design. Starting with a list of the museum's needs, he worked out what he saw as the most logical plan, and only then proposed an elevation. His whole approach, as Anna Crocker noted, was fundamentally different from the old way: "Architecture to you," as she put it, "is not a matter of rigid styles."[18] Behind her thinking was an article on the *Atlantic Monthly* of January 1931, later quoted in the Art Museum *Bulletin.* Architecture, it maintained, could be defined as great only insofar as it satisfied the demands for which it was built; the standard by which it must be judged was "the degree of success with which it fulfills, with the best workmanship and most suitable and economical materials, the demands of the client, whether he be a pharoah, medieval priest, Renaissance potentate, or a modern industrial concern." This was modernist theory, beyond "style." It formed the core of Belluschi's thinking.[19]

Modern in theory, the new museum also looked modern. Although Belluschi had studiously avoided thinking in terms of style, with its crisp clean forms, flush surfaces, long low lines, and restrained ornamentation the Portland Art Museum was not unlike the work of the Italian or Scandinavian modernists, or even Mies, an analogy noted by H. R. Hitchcock a decade later.[20] These qualities readily appealed to photographers, as Belluschi must have intended. Harry Wentz had done much to hone his eye, but so had the photographic exhibitions regularly staged by the Portland Art Museum. In 1929, Belluschi was one of the jurors of an architectural photography exhibition cosponsored by the University of Oregon School of Architecture and Allied Arts. One dramatically angled photograph of the museum entrance, capturing the subtle texture of the brickwork as well as the bold simplicity of the architectural forms, caught the eye of A. Lawrence Kocher, editor of the *Architectural Record,* who wrote Belluschi in the spring of 1933 asking permission to publish the building. Kocher added, in an aside indicative of the heightening competitiveness among the architectural magazines, that he wanted to be certain "to obtain the job before it slips away to some other publication."[21] The following July, the *Record* published the Art Museum, bringing Belluschi national recognition.

By this time, however, Belluschi himself was not around. With the office out of work, he had returned to Italy in October 1932, just before the new museum opened. Throughout his nearly one-year absence, however, he kept track of the office's activities, writing long letters conveying his boredom at home and eagerness to come back. At the first sign of an economic recovery, he returned to the States, hitching a ride and sharing expenses with a vacationing couple from Portland. He arrived back in August of 1933.[22]

Essays and Speeches

Activity in the office remained slow. In part to justify his existence there, in part to satisfy his own passion for travel to new places, Belluschi talked the museum directors into sending him to Madrid in 1934 for a 10-day international conference on museums sponsored by the League of Nations. As it turned out, Belluschi, whose trip was paid for by C. F. Adams, was the only American delegate able to attend, as most institutions were unable to afford it. The focus of the conference was on the planning, construction, and equipment of the new museum. Belluschi presented a long, informative paper based on a document Crocker had drawn up, describing what went into the Portland Art Museum design. The paper was published under Belluschi's name in *Mouseion* the following year.[23]

After his return from Madrid, as things were still slow in the office, Belluschi became increasingly involved in the world of the fine arts. He was an active member of a group

Third International Conference of Museography, Madrid, newspaper clipping dated 28 December 1934.

of young artists and painters that showed at the Creative Art Gallery. He was also asked to delivered a series of lectures sponsored by the museum, his subjects varying widely among contemporary painting, architecture in Spain, the role of the museum in today's society, and modern architecture.

His talks on the last presented, in effect, his architectural credo. Long, diffuse, difficult to summarize, they revolved around three points: the anachronism of historical styles, hence their inappropriateness in modern society; the superficiality of recent attempts at novelty, and the emptiness of the work of the "ultra-moderns"; and finally, what he considered fundamental to true or "living" architecture. "Truly modern architecture reflects the will to create forms which are alive, appropriate, in tune with the life which is nourishing our thoughts and reactions; modern architecture reflects the determination to stand on our [own two] feet, to feel and think for ourselves." Echoing in the beauty of our cities and buildings is "a consistency of purpose obtained not just by intelligent planning, but by a spiritual rapport with life around us."[24]

Architecture today, he maintained, was in a state of confusion. Outdated styles were being rejected in favor of a more modern approach, which was good. The problem was, architects were turning to the work of a few moderns, more often than not from Germany, who were offering a new style just as superficial, and often just as inappropriate as the old. Architects today were losing a sense of what was eternal and universal in architectural form.

Finding it difficult to talk of "beauty," which was hard to define, he spoke instead of the admiration he felt on his recent trip through southern France, Italy, and Spain for the old cities and medieval towns, and their fit with the land. Unlike recent American towns with their imported styles, banal, always the same, Belluschi argued for an architecture that "springs from the very depths of the civilization that produces it," an architecture generated by contemporary spiritual values as well as material ones. More important than talent, or even creativity, for an architect is to learn "the essence of his own surroundings and the soul of his own people."

Distinguishing between the subjective and objective experience of architecture, the latter, he maintained, belonged to the critic, the intellectual, and professional, and dealt with the history of architecture, its philosophical content, its relationship to new engineering and materials. The subjective was harder to define, as it was personal and emotional and belonged to everybody, or to anybody who sees or uses the building. Both, he felt, were relevant in design.

The mission of the architect was not only creation but coordination. His task was to seek a balance between functional or practical requirements and "the proper knowledge of his civilization," which included what Belluschi called spiritual as well as scientific discoveries. The architect versed in contemporary cultural values "must become interpreter and prophet of his own people." This was a theme he was to return to time and again, even decades later in one of the last major essays of his career.[25]

Belluschi took issue with Le Corbusier, whom he referred to as "the French critic," and his conviction that the only American architecture worthy of the name were the grain elevators and factories. Grain elevators and factories were the result of material and utilitarian aims only, Belluschi said; that Le Corbusier and others found them beautiful was merely happenstance. Whereas true architecture includes a spiritual experience, presupposes a conscious spiritual or aesthetic effort, "a recreation through the guides and the restraints of functions." This was important, he maintained, because architects of the "ultra-modern" school denied this spiritual, creative aspect, and made extreme simplification an end in itself, "rather than as it was intended to be, a clarification from the fogs of a sentimental past."

"The architect must be an artist in the deeper sense of the word, an artist capable of forgetting the superficial manifestations for the lasting and the universal, an artist capable of deeply feeling his own mission, and above all his duty of being himself a part of a whole, that is, of having consideration for the harmony of surrounding things." It was this spirit of harmony, he said, that was responsible for the perennial beauty of medieval towns.

Today we look back to the centuries following the Renaissance with dispair "at the slow falling of this noble art of construction into the prostitution of fashionable prettiness, at the slow substitution of sweet modeling for the strong relation of forms, at the introduction of stucco in place of marble, stone, or brick—the beginning of an architecture made by sculptors yet lacking plastic quality, an architecture of sophistication instead of strength, of exterior and transitory meaning instead of universal significance."

While in Rome not long ago, he said, he admired again the old Roman walls, the relationship of their projecting masses, beautiful materials, and the fine color of the brick. An opportunity there has been lost; today the talk is of nothing but "the new style," the "novecento," which is "nothing but a new fashionable mask for an old face, and they fall more deeply into error, only with less craftsmanship and less delicacy. They have rigged up an exterior dress and compiled a new set of formulas and gone about applying them with compromise and uncertainty—they have missed the message of the new materials of construction, of the metals which have changed the engineering from one of compression to one of tension, which means strength, lightness, and plasticity, . . . [and] persist in showing heaviness where there should be lightness, covering the beauty of steel with enormous and useless masonry columns, again robbing people of sunshine, violating space into small cubic rooms, which were monotonous and oppressive." Belluschi decried the "enormous beehives full of ugly rooms inside, all patched up with styles outside." When have their authors tried to make the interior the main creative motive, this fourth dimension which is, after all, the raison d'être of construction?

Here in America, however, already there were critics and intellectuals "busy crystallizing these modern architectural expressions into ready-made formulas." Referring to the Hitchcock and Johnson catalogue for the 1932 MoMA "International Style" show, he described their book as "explaining in detail what to do when a person wants to design a structure in the 'international style.'" He saw this as an intellectual groping for externals, missing the deeper spirit of architecture. He found more interesting the interpretation of modernism in the Scandinavian countries. There, he said, they seemed to be addressing issues with more directness and sympathy.

There are no easy formulas in modern architecture, he said, just as there weren't in art. While it was easy to criticize, it was more important, and far more difficult, to search within oneself for answers. He urged learning introspection before the rules of Vignola and the sequence of styles, urged an understanding of one's people and culture, of materials and how to use them, an understanding of architecture as something that had its own life, in the present, growing naturally from the soil on which it sat, and an understanding of the reasons for which it was built. The sense of freedom felt today must be tempered with discipline, "a sacred allegiance to honesty, sobriety and restraint, a regard for the city surrounding and a sense of one's work in relation to the whole, . . . rather than [as] a discontented, envious, individualist person only bent to increase his personal prestige."[26]

Belluschi's lectures were delivered but two or three years after the Hitchcock and Johnson show at MoMA, and coincided roughly with an essay by Marcel Breuer in which he too focused on the principles, not the form, of modern architecture.[27] Their platforms differed, with Breuer's more universal and abstract, Belluschi's more particular and specific. Drawing on Sullivan and Wright, but also on Crocker and Wentz and on his own sense of the legacy of tradition, Belluschi called for a modern architecture that grew out of the *genius loci,* stemming from and geared to its people and the conditions that gave it rise.

This was the core of his philosophy. It served as the point of departure for innumerable future lectures, speeches, and essays addressed to students, congregations, legislative bodies, professional colleagues, corporate clients, learned societies, and the public at large.

Oregon State Capitol Competition

In a lecture delivered at the Portland Art Museum in November 1935, Belluschi had questioned the wisdom of building "a monumental building of oversized domes supported by an overgrowth of columns beneath," appropriate to ancient Greece or Rome but not to Oregon. "Why have a Greek or Roman building in Oregon in 1935? Would it not be far more appropriate to use simple undying forms, forms overflowing with logic, and to relate them in subtle and meaningful harmony to each other and to compose them into unity with commonsense, to design them so that each and every part could not be taken away or changed without destroying the whole composition, to see that the details are sensible and simple but refined and appropriate, and to use materials which are enduring, colorful, and in harmony with their surroundings?"

The issue was hardly academic. Earlier that spring, the old state capitol building in Salem had gone up in flames. A special session of the state legislature was held immediately to appropriate funds for a new building, with the architect to be selected by a national competition. With local architects hungry for work, the subject of a national competition drew hot debate. Some felt a national competition was the surest means of their getting the best architect for the job; others felt Easterners would have an advantage, as they had more funds for and were more sophisticated in preparing presentation drawings. Belluschi staunchly opposed it, at least ostensibly for a different reason. As he told fellow members of the Oregon chapter of the AIA, "The Oregon country is entirely different from the rest of the nation. It should be interpreted by men who live here."[28]

The Doyle office desperately needed work. Other than a few small jobs, mostly remodels and some Public Works Administration work, there was nothing. The Oregon State Capitol was the first major public building for the state since the 1926 Public Services Building. For Belluschi, it meant the chance to prove himself with an important large-scale job. The challenges were considerable, as the Doyle office had been reduced to a skeleton crew; moreover, it had never entered a competition before, and lacked experienced in the process.

OREGON STATE CAPITOL COMPETITION

OREGON STATE CAPITOL COMPETITION

A. E. Doyle & Associate, Oregon State Capitol Competition, 1935, front elevation of the traditional solution (Belluschi Collection, Syracuse).

A. E. Doyle & Associate, Oregon State Capitol Competition, 1935, front elevation of the modern solution (Belluschi Collection, Syracuse).

The competition, open to any architect or architectural firm with the proper credentials, called for "an outstanding solution" that would be "looked upon now and hereafter with an ever awakening interest by people of Oregon." The names of the jurors, of whom two were out-of-state architects, two were members of the competition committee, and one was a layman, were to be concealed until after the winner was announced. The site was in downtown Salem, the budget set at $2,200,000, including architects' fees.

Entries poured in from all over the country, 123 in all, mostly from the East Coast, 28 from New York City alone. Most were in the simplified, stylized classicism rooted in the work of Raymond Hood. Many entrants were longstanding architects of great repute in the profession, among them William Lescaze, Cram & Ferguson, Cass Gilbert, and Paul Cret.[29]

In Belluschi's eyes, the principal problem was style. The program had specified that competitors were "free to choose among traditional, functional, or modern style, or any combination thereof." Unsympathetic to this way of thinking about the architectural problem, and used to dealing directly with his clients and picking up cues from them about what they wanted, he tried to second-guess the formal preferences of the jury. To cover all bases, the Doyle office submitted three entries, ranging from modern to traditional. The traditional was a domed, pedimented, monumental classical structure, albeit somewhat stripped in the interest of economy. The modern was without a dome, but with a tall, highly stylized centralized tower instead. The third was stylistically in between.

They lost the competition to out-of-staters, the New York architects Francis Keally and Trowbridge & Livington, whose design Belluschi, in retrospect (and not without bitterness), saw as not significantly different from one of their own.[30]

The incident was nonetheless telling. In yielding to the pressure for a stylistic approach, Belluschi knowingly compromised the antistylistic modernist principles, especially those rejecting the use of anachronistic historical forms, that he had only recently espoused in his museum lectures. But when it came to principles versus practice, expediency won. Belluschi was determined to succeed, in his own words, "at all costs," which to him meant getting the job. The State Capitol competition was not the first time he was faced with the contradiction, and it was hardly to be the last. And although he was subsequently to serve on many a jury himself, it was also the first and last time he was to enter a competition.

Pietro Belluschi

*Keally and Trowbridge & Livington,
Oregon State Capitol, exterior (Oregon
Historical Society).*

Other Public Buildings of the 1930s

Aside from a small remodeling job for General Electric and a PWA project for the town of McMinnville, the only other job of note Belluschi was involved in at this point was an apartment house for his brother-in-law and sister, who had prospered in the family business, in Quercianella on the Italian Riviera.[31] It brought no money to the Doyle firm, however. The total income for the office in 1935 was $13,756.[32]

Among several other jobs that sustained the Doyle office during the bleak years of the Depression was a series of small libraries for schools and local municipalities. The Corvallis Public Library, an 89,800-square-foot building, was typical. It was based on the Tudor Gothic Reed College Library and bore traces of an Elizabethan influence, but it also showed the modern influence of the Portland Art Museum, which Belluschi worked on at the same time. The building consisted of a simple low rectangular form with a shallow, projecting central bay defined by a gable and broadly glazed, welcoming entrance. The structure was of reinforced concrete, with brick veneer, limestone trim, and a simple pitched shingled roof. Like the museum, its distinction lay in the warm yet dignified character, simple crisp geometric form, planar surfaces, minimum ornamentation, and subtly textured brickwork. It was completed in 1931 at a cost of $25,700, including the architects' fees.[33]

Its quality was not lost on others. Shortly after the library opened, it was noticed by a Corvallis photographer who contacted the Doyle office asking if it shouldn't be photographed. Times were hard for photographers, with their traditional mainstay of studio portraiture drying up; architectural magazines were a promising market, as, since the late 1920s, they had been turning to photographs as a less expensive alternative to line drawings. Photographs were also seen as more honest, providing a more literal representation of buildings than artist's drawings.

Belluschi agreed, provided the photographs were well composed and conveyed the texture of the materials as well as the fineness of the detailing.[34] His insistence on good photographs and concern for what he called their "pictorial quality" evinced his awareness of progressive trends in the art of photography and his experience as a juror at the Portland Art Museum. A good photograph, he was later to say, could flatter a mediocre building and "sell" it to the press, clients, city officials, and the public at large. It was often more compelling than reality itself, an insight not lost on Belluschi, who with his characteristic astuteness was quicker than most to see it as a key marketing device.

Other libraries followed the same basic plan, such as the McMinnville Library, in the town of McMinnville southwest of Portland (actually a library for Linfield College, a longstanding Doyle client), and the Willamette University Library across from the State Capitol in Salem. Though unremarkable stylistically, the libraries met the requirements of the task:

Corvallis Public Library, Corvallis, 1931
(photo: author).

Linfield College Library, McMinnville, 1935–1936 (Belluschi Collection, Syracuse).

Willamette University Library, Salem, 1936–1938 (photo: Wesley Andrews, courtesy Oregon Historical Society).

simple, efficient, well planned, spacious despite small size, amply lit with good circulation and security, all on low budgets. The buildings have proven over the years to be highly successful when measured by these criteria: all are still admired by professionals and the public alike, and in use with little modification.[35]

The libraries were significant for another reason. In their reliance on a proven prototype, in this case one of his own creation, he came closer than in the State Capitol competition to achieving his design ideals. Rather than seeking a novel architectural form for the artistic statement it might make, Belluschi believed that if a preexisting type or form worked, it should be used, adapted to fit the context and requirements of the particular situation. This was his interpretation of modernism, a restrained regional modernism in harmony with its setting.[36]

In 1936, the Doyle office received a commission for what proved to be a second major stepping stone in Belluschi's career after the Portland Art Museum, catapulting him to national attention. The quarters of the Finley Mortuary, an old, respected Portland establishment, needed remodeling and the addition of new chapel. Belluschi saw the problem as basically threefold: a difficult circulation pattern requiring the complete segregation of polite public spaces from the less decorous private operations of the mortuary on a relatively constricted site; visually reconciling the old white stucco colonial revival building with its more modern additions; and creating a new chapel that was nondenominational yet clearly bespoke a religious function.

After working out the circulation, his primary concern, he turned to the elevation, for which he relied on European, largely Scandinavian and Dutch, prototypes. Distinctly modern despite their Georgian overtones, the new portions of the building consisted of simple bold geometric forms with a pronounced horizontality, of brick with limestone trim. The chapel, sited on the corner of a busy intersection and thus requiring insulation from both noise and public view, was given visual distinction by the use of a continuous clerestory of glass brick, obviating the need for side lights and flooding the parabolic interior with natural light. The public entrance was defined by a simple, stately portico and marked by a tall rectangular tower at the far end.[37]

Recognized for its clean-swept modernity, the building drew immediate national attention. It was published in the *Architectural Forum* in December 1937 and honored by both the national AIA and the Architectural League of New York the following year. It was included in an exhibition sponsored by the American Federation of the Arts that traveled throughout Europe and England as well as the United States. The chapel and the

Pietro Belluschi

Finley Mortuary, Portland, 1936–1937, exterior (courtesy Finley Sunset Park Mortuary).

Portland Art Museum were also selected by a committee of the AIA as two of the hundred most distinguished buildings built in the United States since World War I.[38]

By this time, Belluschi had gained a reputation as one of the foremost progressive young designers in the Pacific Northwest. As the economy began to pick up rapidly in the Portland area, commissions began pouring in: a new wing of the Portland Art Museum, a new science building for Willamette University, a drive-in restaurant for Waddle's, a new Umatilla County courthouse, a quarter-million-dollar "marble palace" for the Boiler-Makers Union, plus a half-dozen retailing projects, largely stores and storefronts. There was also talk of reviving the Commonwealth/Equitable project.

A number of these buildings caught the eye of the national press. Henry-Russell Hitchcock, then one of the leading critics in the country, in an article published in 1940 in the then-highly influential *California Arts + Architecture,* singled out the new Hirsch Wing of the Portland Art Museum, which Belluschi added in 1938, calling its skylighted court "both ingenious and splendid"; its exterior sculpture court with its cantilevered travertine slab roof around the edge "recalls the purity and richness of Mies van der Rohe's finest work." He also found Belluschi's newly remodeled National Cash Register Company storefront, with its rose/gray granite exteriors and simple, elegant display windows framed in what he thought was stainless steel (it was actually aluminum), one of the best examples of the type in the country. Hitchcock saved his most glowing praise, however, for the Sutor House, "easily among the very finest in the country," a work in a wholly different vein that was to establish Belluschi as one of the leading modernists in the regionalist tradition.[39]

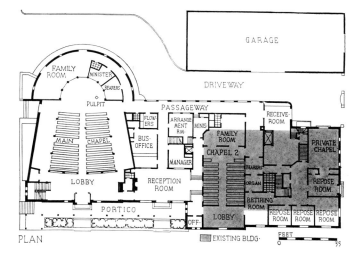

Finley Mortuary, plan (Architectural Forum, *December 1937*).

Pietro Belluschi

Hirsch Wing, Portland Art Museum,
1938.

National Cash Register Company store-front, Portland, 1939.

Pietro Belluschi

Preceding page: Coates House, Tillamook, courtyard.

Belluschi's return from Italy to the Doyle office in the late summer of 1933 coincided with the lowest point in the Depression. He filled idle time by designing a small, in-town studio-cottage for Harry Wentz, with whom he stayed until he could find quarters of his own. Like the seaside cottage Doyle had designed for Wentz close to a decade and a half earlier at Neahkanie, it proved seminal.

Based on a common bungalow type from the 1920s, it was to be a moderately priced house costing no more than $6,000. The principal aim was to maximize usable space indoors and out, and to provide full privacy on a confined, 50-by-100-foot city lot. The house was sited at one end of the lot and linked by a loggia to a studio/greenhouse at the other, with an open landscaped courtyard, pond, and vegetable garden in between. A garage and guest room adjacent to the house bordered the lot on the far end. The whole complex was shielded from public eye by a fence. Like the Wentz Cottage at Neahkanie, it was of naturally weathered wood, with clapboard run horizontally, massive stone fireplaces in both house and studio, and the characteristic Wentz Cottage roofline, a simple pitched roof that fanned out in a shed over kitchen and porch.

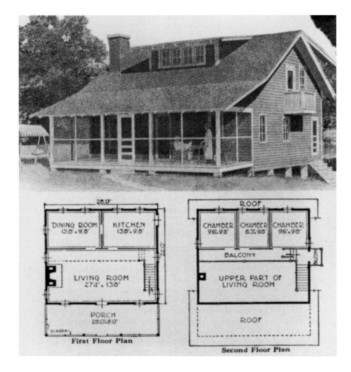

*Bungalow (*117 House Designs of the 1920s, *Gordon-Van Tine Co., 1923 catalog, Dover reprint).*

Compact in plan, the interior was opened spatially by expansive windows and the use of alcoves and partitions rather than separate rooms. The living/dining area spanned the full length of the house and looked out onto the secluded landscaped garden and lily pond through a mullioned window wall, recessed to form a protected terrace. The garage was adjacent to the kitchen, facilitating deliveries. Beyond the garage was a guest room that could be converted to a workshop, and space was provided for a small vegetable garden just beyond the kitchen area out of sight from the living room.[1]

Though it remained a project, the House for an Artist, designed with Wentz's close collaboration, provided Belluschi invaluable experience in the efficient planning of residences—efficient in space and materials as well as budget. Here in embryonic form were some of the basic concepts of his highly acclaimed regional houses of the 1940s, for which lots as well as budgets were considerably larger: open planning, garage sited next to kitchen, light sunny kitchen with view out onto vegetable garden, vegetable garden adjacent to kitchen but out of sight from the living room, zoned spaces with bedroom areas separate from public areas, living room looking out onto private landscaped garden, full privacy on all sides.

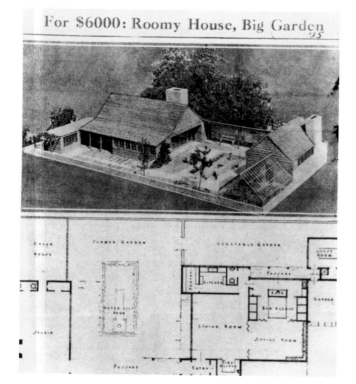

Belluschi, "House for an Artist in Town," plan and model, July 1935.

The project drew on ideas he and Wentz had been discussing for several years. While abroad, Belluschi had written Wentz long letters describing his admiration for the simple weathered vernacular buildings of old cities and towns, particularly of southern France, such as Carcassonne, Arles, Nîmes, and their "fit" with the natural surroundings. These were thoughts he developed in his Portland Art Museum lectures the following year.

The Wentz project also reflected conversations with John Yeon. Yeon had staged an exhibition at the Portland Art Museum in January 1934 in which he juxtaposed photographs of the Oregon wilderness with reproductions of old master landscape paintings and prints—a photograph of the rugged crags of the Columbia Gorge with a hundred-year-old Hiroshige print, for example, or a photograph of the misty Multnomah Falls with an ancient Chinese scroll. Pointing out the commonalities in form, color, and composition, Yeon's aim was to point out the aesthetic potential of Oregon's natural terrain. According to reviewers, the exhibition suggested the formation of an identifiable school of regional artists who focused on the local landscape in their portrayal of modern life.[2] Many of the ideas explored in the exhibition contributed to Yeon's growing notion of a regional architecture, and more specifically to the design of his pivotal, highly celebrated Watzek House two years later.

Regional concerns were an increasing force in the general climate of thought. The effort to revitalize local economies by fostering pride in an American identity was a key aspect of Roosevelt's New Deal. Communities throughout the country, after decades of looking abroad for cultural direction, were urged to return to their roots and to reestablish their regional identity. Supported by the federal government, regionalism flourished, especially in the arts. In architecture, particularly in the West, this meant a reaction not only against European influences but also against the hegemony of the architectural establishment on the East Coast.[3]

At the heart of this celebration of indigenous American culture was the Emersonian transcendentalist ideal. "We have listened too long to the courtly muses of Europe," Emerson had written; "the spirit of the American freeman is already suspected to be timid, imitative, tame." Emerson urged the young American "to plant himself indominable on his instincts," and by these alone abide. This was the Emersonian self-reliance, American instinctual energy rather than European civilized form, with the image of the American artist deriving energy straight from nature, free to set his own standards and create his own norms, that was reflected in Belluschi's lectures at the Portland Art Museum in the mid-1930s. The heavily underlined copy of Emerson's *Essays,* especially the essay "Self Reliance," in Belluschi's personal library gives a measure of its profound influence on him.[4]

Percy L. Manser, Untitled (Mountain Slope), *Portland Art Museum (undated, but published in* Oregonian, *4 April 1935).*

Exhibitions at the Museum of Modern Art in New York both encouraged and reflected the interest in regionalism, such as one on American architecture in 1933, one year after the International Style exhibition (which in fact, its later acclaim by historians notwithstanding, was neither a resounding critical success nor that well attended).[5] Another exhibition of this period focused on "Early Modern Architecture and the Chicago School Skyscraper Development," still others on Walker Evans's photographs of anonymous nineteenth-century houses and on modern architecture in California.[6]

The Portland Art Museum played an active role in promoting this pride of place. In 1932, while Hitchcock and Johnson were staging their International Style show at the MoMA in New York, in Portland popular writer Thomas Craven lectured at the museum on what he saw as the "ridiculousness" of importing art from abroad, and urged instead the development of a locally based regional art. Western Europe had little in common with America and nothing to offer the American artist, he said. Do American, be American. The following year, the Northwest painter Kenneth Callahan exhibited at the MoMA,

attracting national acclaim and focusing attention on the vitality of the arts in the Northwest. Although one of the main characteristics of the work of Northwest painters, among whom were Morris Graves, Mark Tobey, and Guy Anderson, was its diversity and lack of stylistic dogma, consistencies such as the subdued palette, mystical overtones, introspection, and the influence of Asian art were often noted. All this was not lost on Belluschi, whose own aesthetic tastes were being formed at this time.[7]

In Portland, the interest in regionalism peaked in 1934, prompted by a series of PWA exhibitions of Oregon artists. The works exhibited consisted mostly of landscapes celebrating Oregon's natural beauty: its rugged coastline, snow-capped mountains, rich agricultural valleys. Harry Wentz was a member of the organizing committee; Yeon and Belluschi were curators. Yeon's exhibition of the Oregon landscape, part of the series, was specifically designed to encourage Northwest artists to reject the tensions of the modern industrialized city with its violence, harsh lights, and smoke-filled air, then dominating modern American art, and to turn instead to the serenity of the Oregon countryside.[8]

One of the PWA-sponsored exhibitions, held in April 1934, was specifically architectural. Nine models built by local architects were displayed with the aim of showing "building trends particularly suited to the Northwest." Belluschi's House for an Artist and a project by Yeon, "House for a Mountain Setting," were among them. Yeon's, designed specifically for the view, was to face south with the entire front of the house in paneled glass, bedrooms in back staggered on different levels to conform to the natural contours of the land, the whole landscaped so that the house "seemed to have grown with the trees." Anticipating the Watzek House with the landscape an integral part of the design, extensive use of glass, and its figural conformity to the topography, it was modern and regional at once. It and Belluschi's project were deemed the best in the show, lauded in particular for expressing the specific nature of the Pacific Northwest.[9] Much of this set the stage for the emergence of a regional architecture in the Pacific Northwest a couple of years later.

Council Crest House, 1936–1937

Belluschi's personal life by this time began to settle down. With his youthful good looks and charming, flirtatious manner, he was known to be a ladies' man, indeed somewhat of a rake. Among his personal alliances, one had ended tragically and appears to have contributed to his departure for Italy in the fall of 1932, just before the opening of the new Art Museum. He was restless in Rome with his family, however, and missed his friends and the excitement of the office, and in less than a year he was back. It was clear, however, that his personal life needed stabilizing. His family, too, still without a male heir, was eager to have him settle down and start a family. In December 1934 he married Helen Hemila, a strikingly beautiful, intense, deeply intelligent Finnish woman he had known for some time. It was a passionate beginning to what proved to be a difficult life together.

They lived at first in Helen's apartment, relying primarily on the salary from her work with a property management company until jobs picked up in the Doyle office. A wedding present of $600 from his mother enabled them to acquire a lot on a steep slope near Lake Oswego on the outskirts of Portland. As it proved too steep to build on, Belluschi sold it and bought a double lot in Council Crest, a growing suburb west of Portland overlooking the Tualatin Valley. In July 1936 he drew up plans for a house; construction was begun immediately, and the new house completed by May of the following year.[10] Belluschi's principal aim was a house that fit comfortably into the naturally wooded, sloped terrain, providing views of the valley to the west as well as a secluded garden in back.[11] Drawing on ideas he had explored in the House for an Artist project, as well as some of those Yeon had incorporated in his Mountain House project, the Council Crest house was a small, single-story, U-shaped structure sited forward on the lot close to the street to leave ample space in back for a private landscaped garden notched out of the side of the slope. Like the House for an Artist, it had a simple pitched roof angling out at the eaves to form a deep protective overhang. The house was of conventional wood

Helen Hemila Belluschi, 1942.

frame, with exteriors of brick and horizontal spruce siding allowed to weather naturally to blend with the wooded surroundings. The brick consisted of a newly developed, inexpensive local earthenware tile that, when split, had long thin proportions resembling the elegant Roman brick of Frank Lloyd Wright; it was used with Belluschi's trademark wide mortar joint. This and other cost-cutting measures kept the cost of the house down to $4,100.[12]

One entered from the driveway on the north, stepping into a shallow entry hall that opened immediately onto the spacious living/dining area; the kitchen was to the north on the cooler side of the house, near the garage; master bedroom, bath, and study, which could be converted to second bedroom, were in the south wing, with early morning sun and views to the southeast. The wide eaves, filled soffits, built-in gutters, and low-pitched roof, as well as the concept of the house as a series of loose wings wrapped around an open courtyard rather than a single contained block, indicated Belluschi's familiarity with the work of Wright, especially the buildings at Taliesin, Spring Green. Large banks of windows, like those of the Neahkanie cottage but now with more Wrightian proportions, provided the living room an expansive view of the valley, and opened onto the spacious terrace for outdoor meals and entertaining.

Modern in its clean lines and simple forms, the Council Crest house was published widely.[13] A special issue on houses in the *Architectural Forum* singled it out for its specificity, designed for a particular site as well as client. Commending it for its privacy as well as expansive views, its compact plan and economy of means, *Forum* jurors found it one of the best projects submitted.[14]

Council Crest house, Portland, 1936–1937, exterior.

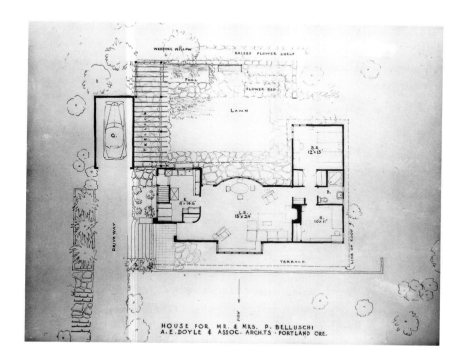

Council Crest house, plan.

Council Crest house, living/dining room
(Belluschi Collection, Syracuse).

Watzek House, 1936–1937

While Belluschi was working on the Council Crest house, John Yeon approached Aubrey Watzek with the idea of designing him a house. Watzek was a close friend of Yeon's and a prominent figure in Portland's civic and business community: director of the U.S. National Bank of Oregon, on the board of directors of the Commonwealth Trust, also on the boards of both the Portland Symphony and Portland Art Museum. An attorney with degrees from Yale and Harvard, Watzek had moved to Portland in 1919 and made a fortune in the timber industry. He shared Yeon's love of the Oregon wilderness; both were members of the State Park Commission.

Hearing of Watzek's plans to build a new house for himself and widowed mother, Yeon proposed that he design it. Watzek was receptive, so Yeon scouted for the perfect lot and found an expansive, pristine two-and-a-half-acre site on the promontory of a hill not far from Belluschi's Council Crest house, overlooking the Willamette Valley with spectacular views in three directions: Mt. Hood to the east and Mt. Adams and Mt. St. Helens to the northeast and north, with downtown Portland in the foreground. The lot was

John Yeon, Watzek House, Portland, 1936–1937, west elevation (Oregon Historical Society).

purchased in November 1936, and within a month Yeon had drawn up preliminary plans and built a model.[15]

Watzek found the design too modern and turned to an architect who specialized in colonial, whereupon Yeon intervened and suggested trying Belluschi instead. Neither Watzek nor Belluschi himself was happy with Belluschi's proposal, but by this time Watzek had warmed up to something unconventional and was ready to accept Yeon's original scheme. As Yeon was not licensed and had no office, it was suggested that he work in the Doyle office, using its technical staff and facilities. Belluschi agreed, as the office needed the income; in January of 1937 Yeon moved into the Doyle quarters.

Yeon developed the design himself, with little modification from his original version, working alone in a corner of the drafting room. The staff provided the drawings, which were extensive, with over 75 full-sized details; Kemery, the staff engineer, worked out the complicated air and heating systems.[16] Belluschi stepped in only occasionally to offer suggestions on technical problems.[17]

Watzek's requirements were simple: a two-bedroom house for himself and his mother, guest room, sleeping porch off the master bedroom, kitchen and pantry, with separate house for the chauffeur. Other than that, he requested only ample light and, being a lumberman, that the house be of wood. There was no mention of budget. With four men working on the job virtually full-time, work progressed rapidly. By December 1937, the house was ready to be occupied.[18]

Starkly modern, elegant yet frankly of wood, formal yet one with the natural terrain, it sat low on the horizon, a single-story structure roughly U-shaped in plan, of conventional wood frame construction with flush siding. Pulled well back from the main road for privacy, with access down a long private wooded drive, the house was sited on the crest of the hill to maximize distant views in all directions. The front was aloof, a formal composition of flat planes, slender columns, and gabled roofs that echoed the verticals of the firs and the peak of Mt. Hood in the far distance, a meticulously controlled formal order of clearly articulated triangulated forms and staggered roof lines balanced by slim columns and chimneys. Conceived less as a functional building than a perfect work of art, it revealed a painter's eye at work, now in three dimensions and on an architectural scale.

Under a protective portico, one entered through a door that opened onto a private, stone-paved courtyard. The informality of the Japanese landscaping, with draped wisteria, graceful flowering cherry trees, and lily pond, was in sharp contrast to the formal

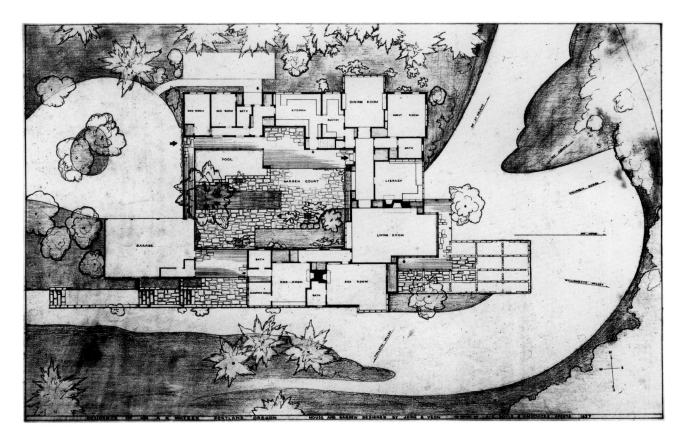

Watzek House, plan (Oregon Historical Society).

geometric order of constructed elements. Bordering the pond was a loggia defined by a colonnade of simple stately two-by-fours that formed a long formal pathway leading to the elegant, wood-paneled front door of the house.

The interior was equally formal, governed by the same exacting visual order. Spaces were disposed in a cross-axial plan, with the north-south axis running through the length of the entry hall from living room to dining room and a view through the thick forest to the north; the east-west axis ran from the landscaped courtyard through the living room out to the view overlooking the valley and Mt. Hood to the east. Like Belluschi's Council Crest house, it bears the influence of Wright, especially of Taliesin but without its informality.

The principal facade, with its stately portico reminiscent of a Palladian villa, faced east, overlooking the Willamette Valley. With thin sloped eaves carried on slender pillars, it had the demeanor of a classical temple, but now with the attenuated forms and linearity of wood: classic in spirit, modern in form. Exteriors of unpainted spruce tongue and groove siding were sanded smooth, divested of all traces of rustic texture, and stained a pale

Watzek House, courtyard (photo: author).

Watzek House, east elevation.

silvery gray. The interiors were equally fine, with walls lined of vertical-grain noble fir and floors of oak. A sunken planter just inside the glazed entry dissolved the barrier between inside and out.[19]

Rejecting the current interest in open planning. Yeon deliberately returned to traditional eighteenth-century French planning principles. He wanted the house formal, with a succession of discrete, well-defined spaces, each a unit unto itself, linked axially to a vista or visual terminus outside. Unlike Belluschi who leaned toward functionalism, Yeon's interests were purely aesthetic: lines of movement, enfilades of space, a system of formal axes and framed views combined with the modern conception of linked interior and exterior spaces. It was a very different conception of space from Belluschi's.

With its custom-designed ventilation system for Watzek, who was asthmatic, exquisite materials, meticulous detailing, and fine craftsmanship, the Watzek House was enormously expensive. The cost of the house when completed in January 1938 was $85,189. The chauffeur's house alone was $7,746, almost twice the cost of Belluschi's house in Council Crest.[20]

The Wentz Cottage, with its naturally weathered exteriors and framed views of Mt. Neahkanie, was Yeon's ultimate source of inspiration. But there was also the influence of Wright and Taliesin, with its long rough-textured flagstone walls extending beyond the house to the landscape beyond, low-pitched roofs, covered loggia, and landscaped courtyards. And there was William Wurster, whose directness, lack of pretension, and freedom from the concept of "style" Belluschi and Yeon both admired. A major factor in Yeon's thinking was Wurster's Gregory Farmhouse of 1927 in Santa Cruz, which had won a *House Beautiful* award in the early 1930s and was included in the MoMA exhibition of modern architecture in California in 1935, then featured in a *Forum* article in May 1936, several months before the Watzek House was begun. Its simplicity, composition of firm lines and taut geometries, low horizontal massing carefully balanced by the vertical of the water tower, staggered triangular roof lines formed by clean-cut gabled ends without overhangs, inner landscaped courts onto which living spaces opened widely, flush unpainted siding, most of all its blend of formality and unpretentiousness, very different from Wright's informal coziness, all appear in the Watzek House, significantly reinterpreted by Yeon's own personal conception of architecture in the Pacific Northwest.

Yeon sought a regional architecture, but from a perspective differing radically from Belluschi's. Yeon saw Northwest architecture not as a matter of local building materials or climatic conditions, factors he thought obvious, but as a deliberate aesthetic choice of forms sympathetic to the landscape, architectural forms that visually merged with the lines and planes of the natural terrain. His design approach was that of a landscape painter—like Cézanne with his sliding, dissolving planes, or the Chinese landscapists—but now working in three-dimensional space, imagining how the building would fit visually, compositionally into the whole.[21]

William Wurster, Gregory Farmhouse, Santa Cruz, California, 1927. (Architect, August 1935).

The Watzek House was immediately recognized as extraordinary. Knowing how valuable national recognition was becoming in securing jobs, and knowing how much the Watzek House would enhance the reputation of the firm, Belluschi routinely included it with other work shown the press under the firm's name. Yeon as a temporary member of the Doyle office was only incidentally credited, leaving the impression that as the office's chief designer, it was Belluschi's work. It was an ambiguity Belluschi did little to dispel.

Petty as it now may seem, the dispute about credit revealed a side of Belluschi not immediately apparent, and led to an irreparable rupture in his rapport with Yeon. Though Belluschi later explained it as an expediency he felt obliged to take at the time, the spat did not stop there.[22] The Watzek House, one of the most celebrated in the Northwest, was included in the 1939 "Art in Our Time" exhibition at MoMA in New York, published in the *Architectural Record* of December 1940, featured again in the MoMA publication *What Is Modern Architecture* in 1942, then again in MoMA's *Built in USA: 1932–1944* in 1945, typically appearing under the name of A. E. Doyle & Associate, or sometimes simply Pietro Belluschi. And so it became known to many. Years later, Hitchcock in his discussion of the Watzek House talked of the signs of Belluschi's "fine Italian hand"; James Marston Fitch in his widely used textbook on American architecture referred to its deft combination of the domestic tradition in wood and Belluschi's "sparse Italian elegance." Each mention opened old wounds.[23] But the Watzek House brought Belluschi the publicity he craved. His quest for recognition was at times ruthless, and this was hardly the last time that he would claim more credit than his due. The incident aroused bitter feelings among many in the profession that time has done little to dispel.

The Watzek affair had other consequences: it placed in sharp perspective the differences between the two architects. He and Yeon both had strong egos and a good measure of vanity. But while Belluschi was Italian, open, personable, and accommodating, Yeon was northern, introverted, moody, difficult to get along with, highly discriminating and exacting in his demands on others. He knew precisely what he wanted and how his buildings should look.

They also had fundamentally different aims. Belluschi had an office to run, and his goals were pragmatic. First and foremost, he thought in terms of the budget: what the limits were, how much office time and labor should be devoted to any one job, the cost benefit of one material or type of detailing over another. Architecture to him was not simply an art but a business, a creative endeavor dependent upon and never free from social and economic restrictions. Having the building work, getting it done on time and within the client's budget counted more, in the final analysis, than how the building looked.

To Yeon, architecture was an art. An artist and architect of considerable skill, he lacked Belluschi's public relations ability, his business acumen, his drive for fame and fortune. He neither cared about the former nor needed the latter, hence never achieved the outward success Belluschi did in the architectural profession.

Nonetheless, the Watzek House radically transformed Belluschi's thinking. Gone henceforth were the brick exteriors and white trim, with their Georgian associations, of houses like Council Crest. Belluschi learned much from the Watzek House, subsequently translating many of its ideas into forms accessible to clients of ordinary means. It marked a turning point in his career.

Sutor House, 1937–1938

While the Watzek House was under construction, Belluschi received the commission for a house for Jennings Sutor. In its freedom from tradition, now entirely purged of any lingering Georgian associations, full use of wood, porticoed front on slender two-by-four colonnade, attenuated proportions, and expansive fenestration, the house he built owed much to the Watzek House.[24]

Sutor, the editor of the *Oregon Journal,* had lived most of his life in the Arlington Club, a private men's social club in Portland.[25] Nearing fifty, and like Watzek a bachelor, he too decided to build his own house. The budget was substantial, though considerably less than that of the Watzek House; as a bachelor, his practical needs were minimal. He imposed no restrictions on design. He was, however, a collector of Asian art, which was a major factor in Belluschi's thinking.[26]

The site was near the Watzek House, and like it had views of Mts. Adams and Hood. An early study of July 1937 indicates that Belluschi initially thought of a structure that would curve around the ridge of the slope in a broad C; this proved too expensive, and the final scheme of April 1938 was for a far more compact building.[27] The plan was simple: basically rectangular, with a spacious entry leading into a cross-axial living/dining area, with views out across the valley to Mt. Hood and toward the secluded garden in back. The kitchen was just off the entry adjacent to the garage, with a room for the maid; bedrooms were at the far end for privacy. Though limited in size, the living/dining area seemed spacious, opened up by extensive glazing on both sides; the sense of space was expanded still further by a full mirrored wall in the dining room. The interior read as a series of simple rectangular modules, like Japanese tatami, some parallel and others

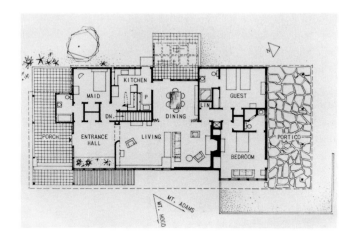

Sutor House, Portland, 1937–1938,
plan.

Sutor House, exterior.

Ise shrine (Drexler, The Architecture of Japan*).*

at right angles to the view. Construction was of simple wood frame, with exteriors of rough spruce siding run horizontally on long sides, vertically on gable ends, and treated with iron chloride and a preservative only; the roof was of rough cedar shingles. A two-car garage was tucked into the hill on the garden side, all but invisible from view; services were buried from sight in a below-grade basement.

Poised on the hillside like a simple Japanese shrine, the Sutor House indicated a new direction in Belluschi's thinking. Inspired by Yeon's use of wood in the Watzek House, and aware too of the popularity of wooden houses in the press, Belluschi, whose background both in Europe and the Doyle office had been in masonry, turned to the Japanese for design precedents in wood. The entrance hall of the Sutor House was like the vestibule of a Japanese pavilion, with modular full-length plate glass windows, mat floors, and a ceiling of woven fir slats. Walls were paneled of natural vertical-grain fir and zebrawood, or in some areas wheat-colored Japanese grass cloth. Built-in furniture minimized clutter. Textured raw linen draperies and other fabrics, as in the Watzek House, were all handwoven. But while the Watzek House was formal and aloof, the Sutor House was informal and intimate. Instead of classical grandeur created by an elegant, austere temple front, clean taut forms, and a formal axial plan, the Sutor House was low, compact, nestled into the ground, its Irimoya roofline and deep overhangs conveying a sense of shelter.[28]

Frank Lloyd Wright had of course spoken often of the Japanese in his writings and lectures.[29] But more significant in this case, it appears, was the series of lectures given by Jiro Harada, a visiting professor at the University of Oregon from the Imperial Museum in Tokyo. Harada's lectures, delivered at the Portland Art Museum in late 1935 and 1936, focused specifically on what lessons Japanese architecture offered the West.[30] Harada extolled the simplicity of Japanese architecture, the advantages of standardization, and its conformity to use. In particular, he pointed out its oneness with nature, so different, he said, from the International Style with its "factory-like rigidity," "aggressive shapes," and "uncompromising bleakness which seem to decree that it is, and always will be, a stranger in the place it finds itself. It wars with the landscape . . . , the spirit of the country disappears."[31] The Sutor House, with its compact plan, modular order, spare furnishings, and sense of quiet reticence, marks a definitive turn from historicism to a new sense of place in Belluschi's work.

The Sutor House was completed in 1938 at a cost of $14,000. With the rest of the nation still mired in tradition, it drew the attention of professionals and the public alike. The *Architectural Record, California Arts + Architecture, Time Magazine,* and *Sunset* all published it, often in conjunction with a Belluschi statement on the natural beauty of barns.[32]

The east Coast critic and arbiter of taste Henry-Russell Hitchcock, who visited it in 1939, was one of the first to recognize its distinction.[33] Given the growing interest in the work of Mies van der Rohe at the time, Hitchcock's admiration for the Sutor House, which anticipated the Farnsworth House, its analog in structural clarity, by over a decade, is not surprising. For all their differences, the comparison is telling.

Although others in the 1930s were drawn to Japanese architecture—one thinks of Greene & Greene and Harwell Hamilton Harris in California, Antonin Raymond and Bruno Taut abroad—the real wave of Japanese influence in the United States did not occur nationally until after the war, when Arthur Drexler staged an exhibition of it in 1955 at MoMA in New York. Belluschi's synthesis of Japanese elements with the forms and ideals of the modern movement in the late 1930s thus seemed prescient, and accounted for much of its appeal. The Sutor House offered what many Americans sought: a modern building that was simple, economical, and geared to human use, without the austerity of the machine aesthetic. Presenting an architecture of naturally weathered wood rather than machine finishes and materials, traditional pitched roof with its associations of shelter and protection rather than flat roof, laterally expanding forms generously opened up to the outdoors rather than taut enclosed volumetric boxes defined by thin membranous skins, an architecture integrated with the natural terrain rather than formal, white geometric blocks set against it, the Sutor House marked the emergence of a fully developed regional modernism shaped by and unique to the Pacific Northwest.

Joss House, 1940–1942

In 1939, Belluschi, recognizing a growing market in low-cost housing and wanting to broaden his image, prepared a model for a $4,500 house for exhibit in the Northwest Home Show.[34] Based on his project for Wentz of 1934 but now free of any lingering historicism, Belluschi's prototype was highly regarded and was widely published in the local press. The commission for the Joss House came shortly thereafter.

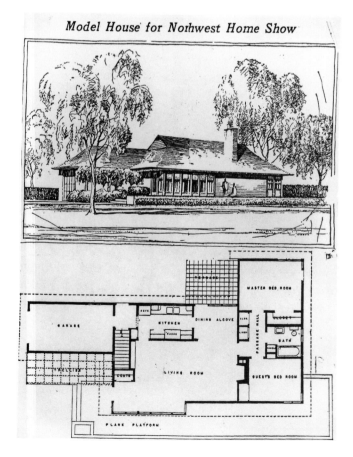

Northwest Home Show, model house, 1939.

Joss House, Portland, 1940–1942, exterior (Belluschi Collection, Syracuse).

The Josses were a young lawyer and his wife who were just starting out and had little money. Her family, however, had given them a spacious piece of property in the Portland hills, with views in all directions. Their requests were simple: a two-bedroom, two-bathroom house that was open to the views and preserved as many of the existing maples as possible. Costs were not to exceed $5,300. Mrs. Joss had also admired the small wooden Norwegian pavilion she had seen at the San Francisco Treasure Island Exposition the previous year, and requested something comparable in warmth and character.

Belluschi placed the house just below the crest of the hill well back and up from the road below, and gave it an L-shaped plan that opened out to a view of the Tualatin Valley to the southwest and the snow-capped Cascade range to the northeast. One entered from the south down a veranda to the front door, which opened into the living/dining area at the juncture of the L. The living/dining room, with kitchen at the far end formed one wing, with bedrooms and bath in another. A second story, pulled back from the front and apparent only from the rear, preserved the low contours of the house yet provided space for additional bedrooms and bath when money allowed.

Joss House, plan.

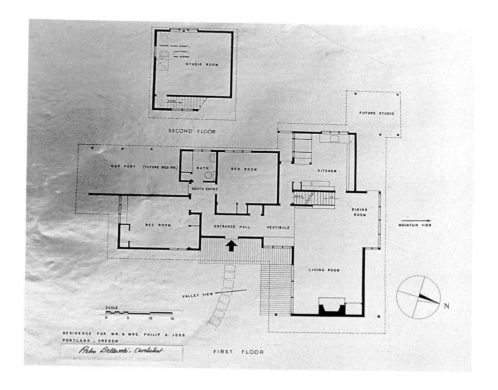

Joss House, living/dining room.

Exteriors were of unpainted rough spruce, clapboarded horizontally to reinforce the low-lying horizontality of the forms.[35] Drawing heavily on Wentz's Neahkanie Cottage, the Joss House had interiors all of natural wood, with smoothly sanded cedar walls, ceiling of hemlock, floors of random-width oak. The raised ceiling height of the living area with its exposed framing again recalled the Wentz Cottage. Broad expanses of windows on both sides opened the space to views. Dominating the living room was a large fireplace of reinforced concrete. A handcrafted bookcase was built in under the staircase; other furnishings were either designed or selected by Belluschi himself to maintain a consistent design aesthetic.

Mrs. Joss's request for a Norwegian character notwithstanding, the Japanese influence was apparent throughout. While picking up cues from Wright's Usonian houses, which had just been published as a special feature in the *Architectural Forum,* Belluschi turned even more specifically to the work of the Czechoslovakian architect Antonin Raymond, then working in Japan, whose book *Architectural Details* he had acquired in March 1939, shortly before beginning the Joss design. It provided him specific models for the flush siding, veranda, and most especially the concrete fireplace.[36] The modularity, the sense of openness with shoji-screen-like plate glass sliding doors opening onto the veranda, the L-shaped open plan, and the exposed framing of the living room thus represent a blend of ideas culled from widely varied sources. Completed in 1942 at a cost of $5,303, the Joss House marked a highly personal synthesis of high art and vernacular from both East and West, a synthesis that remained a hallmark of Belluschi's regional modernism.

Antonin Raymond, fireplace detail
(Raymond, Architectural Details*).*

Platt House, Portland, 1940, garden
facade (photo: Chas. R. Pearson).

Other Prewar Houses

Subsequent houses, such as the Myers House in Seattle, Kerr Beach House, and Coates House, all designed and begun before the war, followed the same basic concept. The Platt House, begun just after the United States entered the war, was larger in size and budget and more formal in character. The Platts were avid gardeners and wanted a house that opened widely to the outdoors, preserved as much as possible of the existing landscape, and exerted a minimum presence on the land. In Belluschi's words, the goal was to design a house "that was all but invisible," so perfectly would it blend with the terrain. On two and a half acres, part of an old apple orchard on the crest of a hill, the house like the Joss House was pressed up against the slope, with expansive windows for the views. L-shaped in plan, it had the living/dining area with master bedroom at the far end forming one axis, with kitchen, laundry room, and garage forming the other. Additional bedrooms and bath were on a second level. The use of a long curved partition of laminated cedar, terminating in a freestanding column and screening the entry hall from the living area at the inner angle of the L, suggests the influence of Mies's Tugendhat House, which Belluschi knew and greatly admired, but more likely was inspired by Alvar Aalto, whose work Belluschi had seen at the 1939 New York World's Fair and was featured in a recent *Forum*.[37] Decidedly Aaltoesque was the rich mixture of warm

Platt House, plan.

Platt House, entrance/living room (Belluschi Collection, Syracuse).

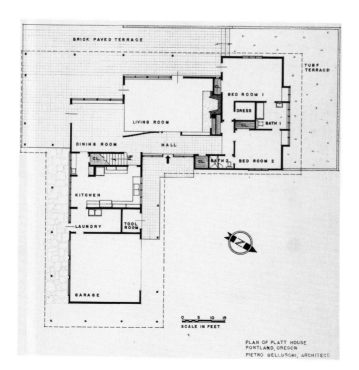

textures and natural materials: the red tile floors of the front veranda, entry hall, and dining room, oak parquet floors of the living room, richly grained birch walls, now coupled with a woven slat ceiling and handled with a characteristic Japanese restraint.

The Myers commission called for a moderately sized house in Seattle. The site was a restricted 60-foot-wide city lot, with an expansive view to the west out over the Puget Sound. Belluschi's solution here was to orient the spaces inward rather than out; with the exception of the living room and main entry hall, which faced out to the view, rooms were clustered around an inner garden court, open to the elements but sheltered from prevailing winds. Exteriors were again of unpainted wood, with textured wood ceilings on the interiors and woven bamboo screens.[38]

For the Peter Kerr vacation home on the rolling dunes of the Oregon coast, the aim was to design a house that meshed with the natural landscape and would minimize house-keeping. Drawing heavily on ideas William Wurster had explored in a beach house overlooking the ocean in California, lauded in a 1939 *Forum* article for its unpretentious-ness ("no more than a barn with a view"),[39] the Kerr House was basically rectangular in form, with low-pitched roof and shed extension over the garage. Wide overhanging eaves formed protected porches on both road and ocean fronts. Like Wurster's house, the Kerr House was closed to the road, opening out broadly by means of a bank of bay windows to the ocean on the west side; one thus stepped from the entrance hall into the living room to be greeted by a sweeping ocean view. Rooms were grouped for maximum convenience as well as views, with garage, kitchen, and dining room aligned together in one wing and maid's room and storage in a partial second story above; living and dining areas occupied a common space fronting the ocean, with bedrooms beyond for both privacy and views.

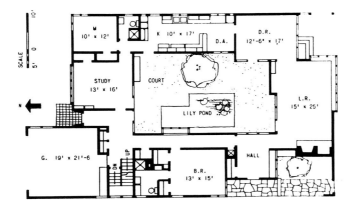

Myers House, Seattle, 1940, plan.

Kerr House, Gearhart, 1941, exterior.

Kerr House, plan.

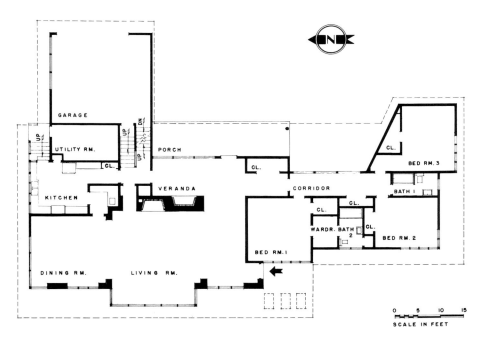

Interiors were rustic, befitting a vacation house, with walls of unfinished spruce and hemlock and a massive double-faced fireplace of randomly sized and shaped boulders. Exteriors were of stained spruce, with the flush siding run vertically to echo the tall grasses. An unfinished tree trunk formed the main support of the long covered veranda on the street side of the house, a Zen touch fully in keeping with the character of the wild dunes.

One of the most widely known of Belluschi's early houses, the Kerr beach house, despite its apparent simplicity, was not inexpensive. It was completed in 1941 at a cost of $30,000.[40]

If the Kerr House had a direct source in Wurster, the Coates House of 1941, on the beach at Netarts Bay, relied on Yeon's Watzek House. U-shaped around a landscaped court,

Coates House, Tillamook, 1941–1946,
east elevation (photo: Leonard Delano).

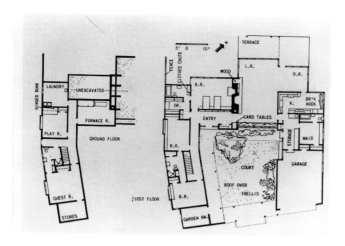

Coates House, plan.

its primary living spaces were aligned along the ocean front facing the view. As in the Watzek, one entered through the courtyard down a loggia to the front door. An entry hall provided access to the living room, dining room, kitchen, and maid's room to the right, bedrooms and bath to the left. A playroom, guest rooms, and services were in a basement below grade.

In elevation, too, the Coates House recalled the Watzek. Its low-pitched roofs and triangular, cleanly shaved gable ends, without overhangs and defined only by thin narrow eaves, were similarly composed in a series of staggered heights, though here without Mt. Hood in the distance to serve as the compositional raison d'être.

All architects cribbed, though few admitted it. But here Belluschi's source was too close for comfort, as Yeon, in a letter of complaint, made clear.[41] More importantly in the long run, Belluschi's borrowing pointed up the fundamental difference in their attitudes toward design: design skills aside, Yeon, the artist-architect, sought originality; for Belluschi, whose first obligation was to the client, more important was a building that met the programmatic requirements. If an existing form or type was appropriate, regardless of its source, he used it, reinterpreting it both operationally and artistically to fit the circumstances.

Northwest Regionalism

By the outbreak of World War II, the new modern architecture emerging in the Northwest was distinctive enough to be a recognizable trend. Rejecting historicism and embracing modern values, yet bearing little influence of the imported International Style, regional modernism was regarded by many as the most appropriate direction for American architects to take.[42]

Interest in regionalism had grown steadily throughout the late 1930s; by 1941 it was one of the leading topics in the architectural magazines. The Museum of Modern Art continued its promotion of local work, with exhibitions covering regional art, wooden houses in America, and architects such as Alvar Aalto, whose humanistic, Finnish variant of the International Style bore many parallels with indigenous efforts in the United States. In 1938, in a specific attempt to encourage regional developments, MoMA's Department of Architecture under the direction of John McAndrew staged a traveling exhibition, "Three Centuries of American Architecture," aimed at celebrating regional differences and fostering an understanding of their roots throughout the country. After opening in Paris in 1938, the show traveled around the United States, appearing in Portland in February of 1941.

McAndrew, who was also an associate professor of architectural history in the art department of Vassar, and later at Wellesley, came to Portland for a series of lectures in conjunction with the exhibition. His topics included "The Modern House and the American Tradition" and "Modern Architecture for America."[43] Other speakers lectured on American culture, Oregon architecture, the Northwest garden. Belluschi himself gave a talk on the evolution of the house, in which he traced the design process.

Leading the country in this new regional modernism, McAndrew emphasized, was the West. As architecture elsewhere stagnated, here it was exploding, fueled by the economy, availability of land and materials, and a pioneering spirit, a sense of freedom from traditional architectural values. McAndrew pointed out that for the past six or seven years the United States had led the world in architecture, and in skyscrapers since the 1880s. Now, he maintained, the most interesting work anywhere was on the West Coast. "Stay away two or three years, and you get behind."[44] Ford and Ford's 1940 *Modern House in America,* which McAndrew described as the first book devoted exclusively to the modern movement in residential design in the United States, leaned heavily on the West; Belluschi's Sutor House was included among those from the Pacific Northwest.

The following year, in response to a provocative essay by Dartmouth professor Hugh Morrison titled "After the International Style, What?," Katherine Morrison Ford published an article in *House & Garden* in which she identified regionalism as the logical alternative to the International Style, a modernism not universal, uniform, and international but inflected by regional differences. Freed from historicism by the early modernists, design was now being integrated with the best of local traditions, providing a new and welcome diversity. Characteristic of regionalism, in contrast to the earlier modernism of the International Style, was its lack of stylistic dogma, with forms determined by local environmental conditions and the use of native materials rather than a fixed set of formal characteristics. Citing the wooden Gropius/Breuer House in Lincoln, Massachusetts, a house in Pennsylvania by Kenneth Day, and Belluschi's Sutor House (which she mistakenly traced to the Coast Indian longhouse, a Washington state rather than Oregon tradition), she pointed out the strength of regional traditions. She also drew a clear distinction between California trends and those in the Pacific Northwest (a distinction later lost in the battle over regionalism versus modernism in the late 1940s, set off by an explosive article by Lewis Mumford in the *New Yorker*), pointing out the Northwesterners' particular skill in planning and use of wood and again using the Sutor House to illustrate her point.[45]

By this time the Sutor House had become emblematic of Northwest regionalism. Used yet again in a *Sunset Magazine* article in June 1941, it was likened to the barn and other naturally weathered vernacular structures in the "lasting beauty of their simple functional design" and the way they "harmonized with their setting." The barn had become the icon of the new regional modernism, the West Coast's counterpart to Le Corbusier's grain elevator: a simple, direct, regional response to a specific need. Functional in form, its shape determined by the purpose it served, and harmonizing in color and form with the site, *Sunset* maintained, the vernacular building had much to teach the modern architect.[46]

Belluschi's oft-quoted remarks about the beauty of barns and backs of buildings notwithstanding, the main sources of his regional modernism were, however, not the vernacular but high art: the Wentz Cottage, Watzek House, and the work of Wright, Antonin Raymond, and the Japanese.

An Evolving Practice: Late 1930s to 1945

The press by this time was clamoring for Belluschi material. Typical was the letter from Kenneth Reid, editor of *Pencil Points,* in June 1941, thanking him for a tour of his buildings. "I haven't had such a thrill for a long time, and I wish to salute you in complete sincerity as the author of the freshest, most stimulating, pleasing work I found during my three week trip. I did not have a chance to call on you again, but I want very much to have the honor of publishing your work." Expressing his admiration especially for the houses and churches, which he numbered "among the best I have ever seen," Reid closed his letter, "Please forgive me if my praise seems effusive. My enthusiasm is so great that I find it hard to restrain myself."[47] Belluschi sent Reid blueprints of the buildings he had admired, adding that he was sorry the Joss House had "already been promised to Hitchcock for use in one of his English publications"; two other works, a bank in Salem and a Willamette University science building, he said, were going to the *Architectural Forum. Pencil Points* replied that they were disappointed in hearing about the *Forum,* as it "was [our] intention to publish quite a collection of your work, reserving for *Pencil Points* the privilege of telling the profession how good you are!"[48]

Belluschi, aware of the growing competition among magazine editors for his work, heightened it whenever he could. He cultivated the press deliberately, entertaining visiting editors and critics in his home, giving them private tours of his buildings, and maintaining close personal contact through phone calls and letters. He rarely missed an opportunity to pass on unsolicited material of new buildings he thought might be of interest. Most were.

As activity in the office quickened in the later 1930s and early 1940s, Belluschi spent less time designing and more time with clients. Jobs were increasingly turned over to junior members of the firm who worked under Crowell's supervision. While design directives still came from Belluschi, most of the careful attention, the thoroughness in carrying out design development and construction, and the skill in detailing for which the Doyle office was known came from Crowell. He was old, however, and Dave Jack, the office's business manager, was evidently spending more time at the Arlington Club bar than securing new work.[49] Increasingly the task of drumming up jobs fell on Belluschi.

As war clouds thickened in the early 1940s and the younger men in the office were drafted, Belluschi filled their places with women. Initially only one, Ebba Wicks Brown, was licensed. Mary Alice Hutchins, who began her undergraduate work at Stanford, then transferred to the University of Oregon to get a degree in architecture, was brought in for specifications; Jo Stubblebine, whose training was in interior design and who later served as the editor of a book on Belluschi's work, joined as office help. Marjorie Wintermute, also with a degree in interior design, was hired to do drafting.

Belluschi's procedure was to meet with the client, assess the problem, then sketch a preliminary solution. Sometimes he would develop this more fully, with a "shirt front" elevation meticulously drawn with hard pencil and invariably to scale, which he would then turn over to others to pursue. A shrewd judge of skill, Belluschi assigned tasks accordingly, allowing as much freedom in design as the individual's talent warranted.[50] Always open to suggestions, he readily went with or assimilated the ideas of others if they seemed better than his own. It mattered little whether the source was an astute office boy or the latest architectural magazine: if the idea was good, he'd use it. Style for style's sake didn't interest him. On the other hand, a fashionable style sold. Belluschi knew this, and was much too pragmatic, too determined to succeed, to ignore it. Articulate about his own architectural ideals, he was also keenly aware of the contradictions inherent in the profession, and was not one to let theoretical principles impede his progress.

When war broke out and other architectural offices throughout the country closed for want of work, activity in the Doyle office continued to escalate. With the rapid expansion of the Kaiser shipyards on the Columbia River, which attracted thousands of workers and their families from across the nation, came a large number of war-related, government-sponsored shopping centers and housing developments. The Doyle office, in part because of the broad network of contacts Belluschi had cultivated, but also because of the success of projects like the low-cost model house for the Northwest Home Show and the Vista Apartments, a housing complex funded by the FHA, received a lion's share of the work.[51] It was at this time, in his words, that he "moved out from a penurious profession into a more prosperous one."[52]

As the country's commitment to the war deepened and housing for defense workers became a top priority, the architectural magazines urged those in the profession to embrace the war cause by designing low-cost, rapidly built housing. Belluschi was well prepared; the ability to grasp the realities of changing situations and respond quickly with an appropriate solution was, to a large extent, responsible for his professional success.[53]

Among the war-related jobs the office received were the Bagley Downs shopping center in Vancouver, Washington; a 2,000-unit housing development for the Housing Authority of Portland, including a community center and shopping center; another housing development for the Housing Authority of Vancouver, with 978 individual units plus 2,100 row housing units, child care centers, a theater, and infirmary; the McLoughlin Heights Shopping Center in Vancouver, a 209-bed hospital for the air base in Pocatello, Idaho; another 1,003-bed hospital in Walla Walla, Washington; and a Japanese "relocation center" in Portland. Most of these were temporary structures only, built as rapidly and cheaply as possible, and were of minimal design consequence. Nonetheless, as little else was being built, several were published. The McLoughlin Heights Center, for example, was published in the *Architectural Record* and later included in the MoMA "Built in USA, 1932–1944" exhibition.[54] Belluschi's war projects enabled the office to stay open, indeed flourish, at a time when others were shutting down; they also paved the way for future government contracts. Perhaps most importantly, they provided him invaluable experience in large-scale site planning, community development, and shopping center design. Much of this was to pay off handsomely in his career in the postwar years,

McLoughlin Heights Defense Housing, Vancouver, Washington, 1942 (Oregon Historical Society).

especially as a consultant to the shopping center developer James Rouse. They also kept his name alive in the press.

There were drawbacks, however, to this meteoric rise to fame. Throughout the 1930s, Portland architects had watched Belluschi grow under the auspices of the Doyle name, capitalizing on its reputation, clients, and experienced, smoothly operating team. Resentment grew as the city slowly pulled out of the Depression, then in the arid years of the war as, increasingly, what few jobs were available went to the Doyle firm.[55]

After Belluschi's return from Rome in 1933, he had been made a partner in the firm. In 1935 the office reorganized again and a full partnership was signed, with Crowell and Belluschi architects, Dave Jack as business manager, and William Kemery, their engineer, as partners. The office continued to function, however, under the old A. E. Doyle & Associate name.[56]

In March of 1942, Belluschi moved the office from its spacious location in the Pacific Building to new quarters on Jefferson Street, on the outskirts of the downtown. Economics may have been a factor, as the space they rented in the Pacific Building was expensive, but more likely the move was primarily for symbolic reasons. Belluschi had clearly ridden on Doyle's reputation, arousing not only resentment but legal questions as well. With his own growing prestige and the prosperity of the firm during the war, he now

McLoughlin Heights Shopping Center, Vancouver, Washington, 1942 (photo: D. W. Edmundson).

Belluschi office, Jefferson Street, 1945
(photo: Leonard Delano).

had enough clout to stand on his own. Recognized as a leading modern architect in his own right, Belluschi was eager to shed the remnants of Doyle's conservative image. The firm's new quarters were in an old, one-story concrete industrial building that had been used as a garage, which Belluschi himself acquired and modernized to fit the new image.[57] As soon as peace was declared and building permits and materials were again available, he remodeled it a second time with the help of FHA funds, adding apartments which he rented out and a private office on the second floor.

In early spring of 1943, he bought out the firm and changed the name to Pietro Belluschi, Architect. By this time, he was virtually running the office himself. Frustrated by the holdover partnership, with all financial decisions remaining joint, he wanted sole control. Despite his charming manner, Belluschi by temperament was individualistic; moreover, as an astute businessman he liked running a tight ship. The dissolution process was painful, however, especially for Belluschi who preferred to avoid conflict, and it left bitter feelings. He resolved never to engage in a partnership again.[58]

1 *Portland Art Museum, 1931–1932,*
exterior (photo: author).

2 *Sutor House, Portland, 1937–1938,*
exterior (photo: Mary Alice Hutchins).

3 *Sutor House, exterior (photo: author).*

4 Kerr House, Gearhart, 1941, west
facade (photo: author).

5 Burkes House, Portland, 1944–1948,
exterior (photo: author).

6 Burkes House, entrance.

7 Burkes House, living/dining area, facing south toward den (photo: author).

8 Burkes House, living area, facing north toward dining area (photo: author).

9 First Presbyterian Church, Cottage Grove, 1948–1951, exterior.

10 First Presbyterian Church, Cottage Grove, interior.

11 *Equitable Building, Portland, 1946–1948, exterior (photo: Roger Sturtevant).*

12 *Equitable Building, detail of facade (photo: author).*

13 Northwest Airlines Ticket Office,
Portland, exterior, 1944.

There were legal reasons, too, for changing the name. In 1935, apparently provoked by Belluschi as much as anybody else riding on inherited names, the state legislature passed a law requiring the names of architectural firms to reflect their actual constituency; it also stipulated that all partners be registered architects.[59] A grandfather clause had granted the Doyle office a grace period in which to continue using the Doyle name. With his acquisition of the firm, however, it behooved Belluschi to change the name. The new name of Pietro Belluschi, Architect, became legal in March 1943.

Meanwhile, the architectural press continued to fight for rights to publish his work. *Architectural Forum, Architectural Record, Pencil Points* (soon to become *Progressive Architecture*), *American Home, House & Garden, Time,* and *Sunset* all pursued him for photographs of his work. Competition was fierce. "Dear Mr. Belluschi," the editor of *American Home* wrote, "Mrs. Austin and I have just been looking over photographs of the John Platt house and to say that we were most enthusiastic about it would be putting it mildly. . . . We definitely want it. Do you have other houses at present which are *American Home* material? I'd appreciate having first choice at seeing them and arranging for their exclusive publication."[60] Douglas Haskell, associate editor of the *Record,* with whom Belluschi was to lock horns in the 1960s over the Pan Am Building in New York City, was eager for something in retailing. "Dear Mr. Belluschi, Is there any of your excellent work as yet unpublished and ready for publication in department stores? The *Record* is now compiling a study."[61] George Nelson, editor of the *Forum,* pleaded with him to allow them "first crack" at whatever kind of new buildings he was doing. "After all," he wrote, "you have been our favorite architect on the West Coast for a long time and we don't propose to give up [publishing your work] without a struggle."[62]

Photographers, too, played a crucial role in the process. "[Architectural photographer] Phyllis Dearborn has just shown us her pictures of the Bagley Downs Community Center and the Platt House," Henry Wright, managing editor of the *Forum,* wrote, "and we are extremely anxious to publish both jobs as soon as space permits. . . . Delano has also sent pictures of the Coates and Kerr Houses, but I understand from Phyl that these jobs have already been promised to *Pencil Points.* . . . P.S. Just learned (again from Phyl) that Delano has also submitted the Platt House to *Pencil Points* and the *Record.* Can't you get him to lay off?"[63] And the architectural magazines were not alone in wanting Belluschi's work, however minor it might have been. The MoMA exhibition "Built in the USA, 1932–1944" included the McLoughlin Heights Shopping Center, as well as the Watzek House.[64] In its review of the show, the *Forum* emphasized the importance of the West Coast contribution, of which Belluschi was a leading figure, to the development of modern architecture in the United States, as its Wright-inspired architecture of wood

Belluschi with Peter and Tony, Aloha Farmhouse.

represented a very different approach from much of the other, more "European influenced" work.[65]

Meanwhile Belluschi's family was growing. His son Peter was born in 1939, and a second son, Anthony, in 1941. Belluschi's utter absorption in his work, however, was hard on Helen, left alone with two young children. Hoping a move would change her attitude, but also to satisfy a dream of his own, in April of 1944 Belluschi bought a six-acre farm in the Aloha countryside just outside Portland. He remodeled the old farmhouse, removing interior walls and replacing mullioned windows with expansive plate glass to open up the interior into one large room; living room, dining room, and kitchen were grouped together, with bedrooms off to the side. It was a dream he had long harbored: an idyllic existence in the country, with blossoming cherry trees, a stream, goats, isolated from the concerns of the world. With its ordinary vernacular buildings modernized to fit their needs, the Aloha farmstead seemed to represent to others, too, the fulfillment of an American dream, and photographs of it, together with Belluschi and his two boys, were published widely. It was a short-lived idyll, however, as Belluschi himself was rarely there, and the countryside only exacerbated Helen's sense of isolation.

During this time jobs continued to pour into the office, and Belluschi himself became increasingly involved in professional activities on both the local and national level. These varied from serving on juries to giving speeches, on topics ranging from modernism and shopping centers to church design. He was also president of the Oregon chapter of the AIA, reelected for a second term in 1944, a member of an advisory committee in charge of planning lectures on city and regional planning, and active in the planning of postwar Portland.[66] Among the speakers he invited was Catherine Bauer, wife of William Wurster whom Belluschi had met just before the war. Now, as their interests and professional commitments increasingly overlapped, Wurster had become a good friend. It was an important contact that was to prove highly significant in determining the course of his career.

Burkes House, Portland, 1944–1948

At the end of the war, with the dismantling of the Kaiser shipyards and the drop in shipbuilding employment, Portland did not suffer the economic arrest many had feared.[67] As smaller industrial firms moved into the region, attracted by its cheap hydro-electric power and production of aluminum, the economy in the second half of the 1940s boomed. The building industry in particular took a spectacular leap, propelled by the backlog of jobs held up by the war. As other firms began the slow task of reassembling their offices, Belluschi, whose office had not had to cut back, was poised for action.[68] Throughout the war he had kept an eye on the future, maintaining contacts in the Portland City Club and the Portland Art Museum and remaining a familiar face to those in the city's power structure.

In the flourishing economic climate, the office's commercial work took on a new scale and importance. In the meantime, however, Belluschi continued to design houses and churches in the regional modernism for which he was now nationally known. Though larger and with far more substantial budgets, these were basically reinterpretations of his prewar types.

The Burkes House, which many believe to be among his finest, was long in gestation.[69] The clients, Dr. and Mrs. D. C. Burkes, just before the war had decided to sell their old colonial house and build a new one; aware of the fame of the recently completed de Graaff House by the celebrated Los Angeles architect Richard Neutra in the hills south-west of Portland, they decided that theirs, too, should be modern. Wartime restrictions on building materials led Belluschi to conceive of the plan in stages, starting with one wing that would serve as a one-room apartment for the couple and could be expanded after the war. Costs, however, proved exorbitant even for this one wing, and the project, drawn up in 1944, was shelved.[70] As soon as restrictions were lifted, in July 1947, work was resumed, and a month later construction was begun. The site was superb but challenging. At the end of a short cul de sac midway up the steep slope of the west hills overlooking Portland, it had a commanding view of the downtown, with the Willamette River Valley and and the majestic Mt. Hood beyond.

The house was designed, like his others, to take advantage of the view while preserving privacy. Facing outward to the expansive view of the city on one side, it opened onto a secluded garden notched out of the hillside on the other. The living and dining areas were combined into one long continuous space paralleling the view, with a kitchen area set off to one side by a large brick masonry core; this housed a stove, indoor barbecue unit, and rotisserie. Opposite this was a second masonry block with fireplace and hearth; this also served as a room divider between the living area and den. Beyond were master bedroom and bath.

The sense of an open, expansive space was enhanced by continuous cork floors throughout, and by the lush boards of the fir ceiling which continued uninterrupted through the glazing of the walls to form protective porticoes for terraces on both city

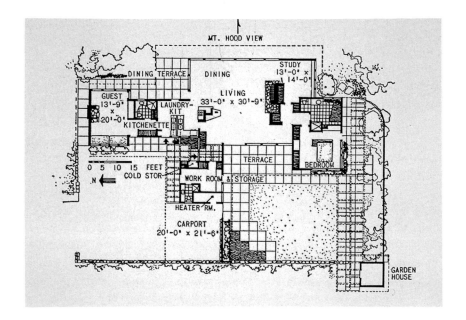

Burkes House, Portland, 1944–1948, plan.

Burkes House, living area, facing north
toward dining area (photo: author).

and garden sides. Materials were principally glass and wood, the latter left natural, with the noble fir walls and ceiling at most stained. The fireplace wall was of rough-hewn Mt. Adams bluestone, elegantly proportioned in long, thin slabs, with thick joints of darkly pigmented mortar; the kitchen block was of brick in the same long, thin proportions, soft terra-cotta in hue, subtly textured, again with a tinted mortar. Exteriors were of unpainted cedar, with smooth, flush surfaces only lightly stained and oiled.

With more than a nod to Wright, particularly the Jacobs House but now reinterpreted with a wholly un-Wrightian sense of refined elegance, the Burkes House was L-shaped in form, defined by a largely unbroken wall, with carport to one side, and a glazed, recessed entry at the inner angle. The roofline was virtually flat, with a deep fascia and wide overhangs.

Mrs. Burkes had much to do with this. A woman of independent mind and sophisticated in the arts, she had brought in photographs and tear sheets indicating what she wanted. It was she, according to Belluschi, who, aware of the International Style and the acclaim the Neutra house was receiving, insisted on the flat roof. Her frequent changes of mind meant, too, that plans kept changing, with a darkroom added at one point for her

Burkes House, living area, detail of exposed columns (photo: author).

Burkes House, bathroom with sunken bath (photo: Chas. R. Pearson).

husband, then a room for her daughter which eventually became a guest room with its own fireplace and kitchenette.

The two exposed columns in the living room were the result of one of her eleventh hour changes. Finding the space of the living area defined by the brick block too narrow, she insisted it be enlarged, which meant moving the wall four feet to the north; this exposed both the structural member supporting the main roof beam and a drain pipe. Belluschi made the best the situation by wrapping the exposed columns in hemp, which added an Aaltoesque touch fully in keeping with the overall design. It was one of many such serendipitous touches that made the Burkes House the success it was.

The house was full of ingenious ideas Belluschi culled from a variety of familiar sources—Aalto's Villa Mairea, the Usonian houses, Taliesin, Antonin Raymond's Japanese work, the Watzek House, Harry Wentz. Among them were the kitchen core that allowed the cook to work out of sight of guests, yet within earshot and but a few steps from the dining area, and with a view of Mt. Hood as he or she cooked; the series of protected terraces, such as the small courtyard just beyond the dining area for casual outdoor meals overlooking the city, or another on the garden side for more elegant, large-scale entertaining; the glazed double-paned plate glass walls on both sides of the living area that abut the ceiling plane without interruption, eliminating, fully, any sense of an enclosed space; the regular modular rhythms of the window supports, with the formidable

technical challenge they presented in working out the corner detailing;[71] the entrance with its sunken pool and translucent trellis, both slipping continuously into the interior uninterrupted by the plate glass wall; the private guest apartment in a separate wing off the kitchen, with its own entrance, kitchen unit, and bath, plus full view of Mt. Hood. The ventilation system, with screened slatted louvers below fixed plate glass panes obviating sashes and providing burglar-proof windows, with transoms just below the eaves on the other side of the room to provide a good flow of cross ventilation, represented the state of the art, as did the fully invisible radiant heating system, with copper pipes embedded in the concrete slab ensuring a continuous, noiseless, draft-free heat throughout the house, even under the sunken built-in bath. Other notable features were the skylighted master bathroom, a private Roman bath with broad plate glass wall providing a view of Mt. Hood; the tea house tucked invisibly into a corner of the garden for use as a guest house or private study; and the Japanese woven wood wall screening the garden, echoed on the ceiling of the master bedroom. It was a compendium of architectural marvels, brilliantly combining Belluschi's engineering skills and expertise in efficient planning, his paramount concern for user comfort and convenience, and his highly cultivated artistic eye. The house was completed in 1948 at a cost of $75,000.[72]

Menefee House, Yamhill, 1946–1948

Of the four or five other fine houses Belluschi did in the late 1940s, the Menefee House was his own personal favorite as well as the most widely acclaimed.[73] Elegant yet informal, private yet warm and inviting, more Japanese than classical in character, it drew upon familiar attributes of the American home—low-pitched roof, centralized chimney, exteriors of wood—yet in its clean lines and simple forms was unmistakably modern. It was also the swan song of his postwar Portland houses.

Menefee House, Yamhill, 1946–1948,
courtyard (photo: Mary Alice Hutchins).

Commissioned in 1946 by Mr. and Mrs. Percy Menefee, owners of a 1,800-acre turkey ranch in the Yamhill valley west of Portland, it was to be a highly functional, flexible, comfortable place with separate offices and a guest house, where they could run their business and entertain house guests as well as live comfortably year-round. They wanted a house that, while private, opened up broadly to the views.[74]

As was by now his custom, Belluschi aligned the living/dining areas with the view, coiling the other, more private spaces around in back so that each looked onto the sheltered landscaped court. The principal facade, seen from below, was formal, with a gabled and pillared portico like that of Watzek House, but now with Belluschi's distinctly lowered roofline, deep protective overhangs, and dark-stained wood.

The owners deferred to Belluschi in all aesthetic matters, giving him free rein in the interior design and furnishings. Everything, including materials, furniture, colors, reflected his eye. Believing that color should be used like spices in cooking, integrated with the whole but never overpowering, Belluschi picked his cues from the surrounding terrain: rich browns, bright daffodil yellows, golden tans, and a whole spectrum of greens.[75] He envisioned the project as a *Gesamtkunstwerk,* a total work of art in the old arts and crafts tradition, with all aspects governed by a single overriding design. Thomas Church, the renowned landscape architect who often worked with Wurster, was brought in from California for the landscaping; the sculptor Frederic Littman, a Hungarian emigre living in Portland, was asked to design the bas-relief copper hood of the fireplace.

The artistry of the Menefee House notwithstanding, the convenience of his client came first. Rather than an architectural statement by the architect or status symbol for the owner, Belluschi maintained that the house should provide a personal yet adaptable arena for good living, pleasing to the eye and comforting to the spirit. More than just a shelter, the house should be a private haven offering respite from the harassments of public life, a place of peace and solitude where one might refresh one's inner being and reinvigorate the soul.[76]

Final cost in 1948 was $120,000.[77]

The Menefee House was immediately acclaimed as the most progressive house in the United States, receiving, along with the Equitable Building, a *Progressive Architecture* honor award for excellence in design. It was featured in *House & Garden, Saturday Evening Post, Time,* even the Home section of the *New York Times*.[78] As emblematic of its time as McKim, Mead and White's Low House of Bristol, Rhode Island, was of its and Mies's Farnsworth House was to become a decade later, the Menefee House represented in the minds of many the quintessential American home.

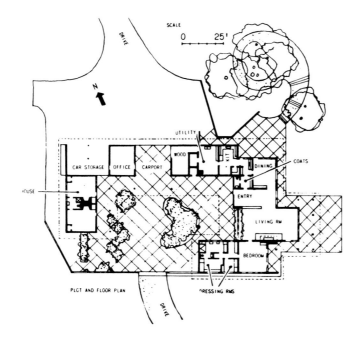

Menefee House, exterior (photo: Mary
Alice Hutchins).

Menefee House, plan.

Menefee House, living room with fireplace (photo: Ezra Stoller).

Other Residential Work

In addition to fine houses for the well-to-do, Belluschi designed a number of other residential projects of note. The Radditz House on a steep slope in the Portland hills was a small two-story, low-cost house in which Belluschi experimented with prefabricated plywood modules.[79] In a solar house project for Libbey-Owens-Ford, he explored the use of solar energy for a house in Oregon.[80] He designed a low-cost house for *Life* magazine as part of its effort to address the housing shortage in the postwar era; his plans called for a minimum house costing no more than $4,000 that could be expanded into a more substantial dwelling.[81] The plans, which sold for $100 a set, proved highly popular, and the issue of *Life* in which they were published was immediately sold out in the Portland area. The design later served as a prototype for a speculative housing development in Cedar Hills, a Portland suburb. Belluschi's concept was again used several years later by builder J. L. Eichler for a split-level model home in Redwood City, California. Passed thus into the hands of large-scale merchant builders throughout the West, it was quickly absorbed into the postwar vernacular.[82] Still other projects included a model home for *Parents Magazine;* Seaside Apartments, a private development in Seaside on the Oregon coast; and the Indian Hill project, a large-scale housing development in Tacoma, Washington.[83]

Radditz House, Portland, 1947.

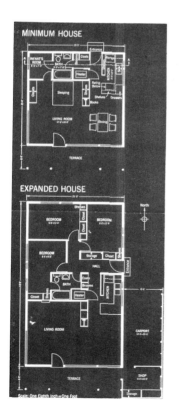

Life Magazine House, exterior
(Belluschi Collection, Syracuse).

Life Magazine House, plan, minimum
and extended (Belluschi Collection,
Syracuse).

By the end of the 1940s, Belluschi was one of the most highly respected figures in the profession. He was persistently sought after nationally, even internationally, as a spokesman for modern house design, ranging from fine individual luxury homes to small, mass-produced, low-cost units. Known for his sense of balance, Belluschi aimed at creating houses both livable and beautiful, homes his clients of whatever social class and income level would find both visually distinctive and a constant source of pleasure. To him personally, they and the churches provided him one of his greatest sources of joy.

Model House, Eichler Homes, developer, Redwood City, California (photo: Ernest Braun).

5   Modernism versus Tradition: The Churches

Preceding page: Zion Lutheran Church, Portland, interior.

Belluschi's sense of personal involvement in the design of houses was felt all the more strongly with his churches. Both building types provided contact with ordinary people, as he put it, a welcome relief from his other clients, most of whom were aggressive, high-powered businessmen. Churches, too, were for him a means of exploring architecture as an art rather than a business, an outlet for spiritual and artistic expression not possible with other building types. Though Belluschi had as a youth rejected institutionalized religion, he remained a deeply spiritual man. This was reflected in his churches, which in retrospect he felt constituted his most important work.[1] The design of the church brought new challenges. Beyond the usual site, budget, and operational requirements, there was the more subtle problem of analyzing the typically unarticulated but deeply felt emotional needs of his clients, who often came from cultural traditions and religious backgrounds different from his own.

Less compelling to him personally was the problem of style. By the early 1930s, he was fully committed to the modernist tradition, albeit an American, not European, modernism. The design of churches posed squarely the modernist dilemma: how to reconcile the modernist demand for a new, innovative architecture born of contemporary circumstances, materials, and technology, with his congregation's need for a recognizably familiar, and in that sense traditional, building?

Church architecture had not been a major part of the work of the Doyle office, which had concentrated largely on commercial and institutional work. Shortly before he died, however, Doyle had been asked to design a ceremonial entrance to the Riverview Cemetery, an old, established, parklike burial ground for Portland's upper class. Belluschi carried it out within the parameters Doyle had established, and on the basis of this connection was commissioned to do a chapel, mausoleum, and office building for the cemetery a decade later.[2] Belluschi had also designed the chapel for the Finley Mortuary in 1936–1937, a building that had brought him national fame.[3]

St. Thomas More Catholic Church, 1939–1940

Several years later, Belluschi received the commission for a small, low-budget Catholic church in the semirural wooded hills above Portland. Its site and budget, plus changing values in architecture, called for a very different formal language from that of the earlier mortuary chapels. The commission came not through a Doyle connection but from personal contact. Belluschi had met the pastor socially, at a gathering sponsored by the Italian-American Society of Portland. Finding the young Italian architect gracious and personable, knowing, too, of his Catholic upbringing as well as his growing reputation in the design of low-cost buildings, the pastor asked him to be their architect.

This, then, was Belluschi's first real church. He was convinced that it should be modern yet draw enough on tradition both to convey to the community its function as a church and to create for the individual worshiper a religious experience, which was a strictly personal affair. Though no longer a member of the Roman Catholic faith, he had been raised in a staunchly Catholic family and was thoroughly grounded in the grand tradition of classical and baroque buildings in Rome; he thus had a good sense of what architecturally contributed to a spiritual setting. It was not lavish decor, splendid mosaics, dazzling frescos, brilliant stained glass, richly carved sculpture, or elaborate gilded moldings, all of which he considered superficial, but rather the experience of the space itself. This could be created, he believed, by a simple, logical structure, humanistically scaled architectural forms, craftsmanlike use of natural materials, and most of all the skillful handling of light.

The program called for a new church building accommodating a congregation of 200, with a budget of no more than $12,000. In terms of design, the pastor requested only that it be in harmony with its natural setting.

St. Thomas More Catholic Church, Portland, 1939–1940, exterior.

Belluschi sited the building back from the street on the crest of a hill, with parking area behind and out of sight from below. The building itself was of wood and was domestic in form and scale, its form derived in fact from the low-cost house type he had designed for the Northwest Home Show the year before. Exteriors were of flush unpainted knotty pine, with boards run horizontally to reinforce the sense of a low, unimposing structure. The gabled roof was actually double sloped, flaring out slightly over the side aisles, and of untreated cedar shingles left to weather naturally to a soft, silvery gray. A building recalling the simple rural churches of Europe in its seeming naturalness, the only obvious sign of its religious function was the spire, its slender, gracefully proportioned polygonal form rising in stages on a square base over the chancel.

The exteriors were deliberately unobtrusive, with drama saved for the interior. Entering a shallow narthex through a sheltered porch, one turned into a long rectangular nave terminating in the altar. Overhead was an exposed scissor truss system of wood, with bracing members bolted together between doubled rafters to form regular repeated bays that stopped just short of the apse. The trusses were of unfinished fir two-by-eights, supporting roof planks of Douglas fir. In a characteristically subtle contrast of color and texture, walls were of cedar planking, sanded and rubbed smooth, here run vertically to reinforce a sense of loftiness in the nave; the exposed wall framing, aligned with the doubled rafters and defining the bays of the nave, was of unfinished fir. The explicit articulation of structure, bearing an obvious analogy with the Gothic church, recalled the exposed framework of the Wentz Cottage, but in fact was drawn from the recently published work of Antonin Raymond. The small wooden church of St. Paul in Karuizawa, Japan, published in the *Architectural Record* in January 1936, had the same simple massing, pitched roof with shed roofs over side aisles, raised cupola and spire over chancel, scissor trusses, and exposed framing. Seeking precedents in the use of wood,

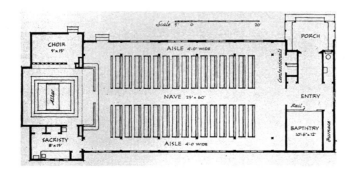

St. Thomas More Church, plan.

St. Thomas More Church, interior.

Belluschi found that Raymond's interpretation of the vernacular church of Japan, with its utter simplicity, respect for the basic nature of materials, and responsiveness to nature, suited the Oregon setting as well.[4]

Belluschi's aim was to generate by the manipulation of height and light a sense of progression down the nave, culminating in a dramatic climax over the altar. Light in the nave was subdued, filtered through the aisles from casement windows, clustered three to a bay, in the exterior walls; of small-paned translucent glass held in diamond-patterned cames, these were stained in pale hues of violet, amber, and plum, imparting a soft colored glow to the nave. The raised cupola over the altar, with three sides of clear windows at its base, poured light from overhead into the chancel. Though the forms were thoroughly modern, the symbolism of the sudden height and brilliant light from above went back to ancient roots of the religious experience.[5]

Belluschi's consummate artistic taste was evidenced throughout. A simple portico set at right angles to the body of the church in response to the sloped site defined the entry. The main portal itself, traditional symbol of the gateway to heaven, was designed and

St. Thomas More Church, portal
(photo: Jack Sidener).

executed with matched-grain cedar panels in a lozenge pattern, echoing the diamond-paned windows. All other church furnishings—pews, sanctuary lamps, altar railing, baptistery font, tapestry over the cross—were designed and executed by members of the Portland art community, in keeping with the refined, preindustrial arts and crafts sensibility of the whole. Belluschi was by then in the midst of designing the Hirsch Wing of the Portland Art Museum, and in close contact with its artistic community; he was thus able to draw upon some of the finest talent around. He also used the same contractor John Yeon had found for the Watzek House, ensuring the same high quality of workmanship. The building was completed in 1940 for $12,500.[6]

Though not novel in form, the church was seen as fresh and new, especially in Portland, and marked a clear departure from the conventional historicized church. Small, unpretentious, its distinction lay in the subtle use of simple means, a result of Belluschi's rigorously analytic mind and highly refined eye. Its merit was immediately recognized. Published widely after a feature article written by a member of the Belluschi staff in *The New Pencil Points* brought it to national attention, St. Thomas More became known throughout the world and established Belluschi as a major church designer.[7]

Church of the People, Seattle (project), 1945

With the end of the war, one of Belluschi's first commissions was for a church in Seattle. This time the site was urban, on the corner of a busy intersection across from the University of Washington campus, the budget larger, and the congregation Universalist. What was wanted was not so much a church as a meeting house, a social center that included an auditorium for movies and lectures, a library, several small one-room apartments, and a kitchen, as well as a chapel. Belluschi thus pursued a design direction very different from that of St. Thomas More. Inspired by recent Saarinen churches, the Church of the People project had the clean lines, crisp geometries, and flush walls of the European modernists, with form broken down into discrete units reflecting their different purposes: low horizontal block with long, continuous ribbon window in the residential wing, somewhat higher block housing the auditorium, tallest block for the chapel with its vertical gridded window wall, all wrapped around an open landscaped court. The only indication of its religious function was the stylized relief signifying brotherhood above the chapel's main portal. Though it remained a project, it too was published, in *Progressive Architecture* in 1947.[8]

By the time of the Church of the People project, the situation in the Belluschi office had changed. Walter Gordon, author of the St. Thomas More article, had studied architecture at Princeton, then waited out the Depression working in museums, first at the Museum of Art in Buffalo, then at the San Francisco Museum of Art, finally at the Portland Art Museum in the late 1930s, where he met Belluschi. Belluschi was looking for fresh blood in the office and eager to learn more about new trends on the East Coast; Gordon was one of several younger men who worked in the office in the early 1940s before being drafted when war broke out. He helped introduce some of the newer trends reflected in the Church of the People project into the office's work.

Though subsequent churches bear its influence, the rigorous European modernism of this project remained an exception in Belluschi's church design. Avant-garde trends in architecture were not what congregations in the uneasy, disillusioned climate of the postwar period sought. Belluschi's struggle to reconcile his own modernist interests with the more traditional ones of his clients marked his work throughout the later 1940s. This challenge, not unlike that he faced during the Depression to derive the maximum from minimum means, resulted in some of the finest churches of the era.

St. Philip Neri Catholic Church, Portland, 1946–1952

St. Philip Neri was commissioned by a lower middle-class Italian congregation on the east side of Portland that wanted a church reminiscent of those of their native land. The budget was limited, and fund-raising difficulties made the process long and drawn out. Preliminary studies were begun in January 1946 and a final solution not agreed upon until March 1947. Construction was delayed for another year, by which time costs had risen sharply and bids came in far higher than the means at hand. The design was cut back and the job again put on hold. In the meantime the postwar inflation continued and costs soared. In late summer of 1949 the job went out to bid again, with the lowest coming in at $208,000, far exceeding the congregation's funds. The contractor then proposed that he build the basic concrete structure for about a third of that cost, which could be used until the rest of the funds were raised.[9] After further cost-cutting measures brought the estimate down to $149,000, a contract was signed in the fall of 1949 and construction begun immediately, with completion set for August 1950.[10] Still in its raw state, St. Philip Neri was dedicated in October 1950, with the exterior brickwork, lighting, and furnishings carried out after Belluschi had left the West Coast to assume the deanship at MIT. The building was finally completed in 1952 by Belluschi/SOM, to whom Belluschi had sold the practice after leaving Portland.

Belluschi's aim was to find as simple and economical a solution as possible that recalled the simple vernacular churches of Italy yet did not contradict his own modernist princi-

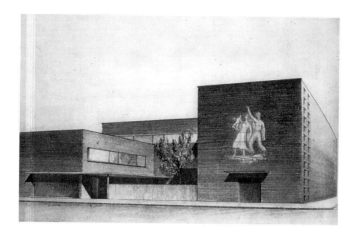

Church of the People project, Seattle, 1945.

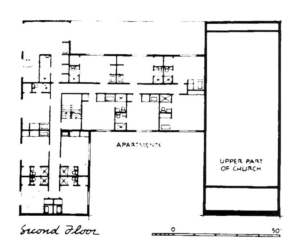

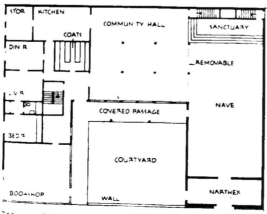

St. Philip Neri Catholic Church, Port-land, 1946–1952, exterior.

ples. Implicitly referring to the early Christian basilica, it drew more explicitly on current design precedents in modern brick churches of Italy and northern Europe.[11]

The early Christian basilica, itself an adaptation of a secular Roman building type, consisted of a large rectangular hall built of local materials and destined to house large numbers of people who met for communal worship. Conceived as a simple Christian meeting place, not a house of God, it was very different from, and much plainer than, the magnificent Gothic cathedral of later times. Recalling the basilica type in conception, St. Philip Neri was a large, unadorned building of variegated brick, simple, stark, and imposing in form. Set on an open, flat site in the midst of a working-class residential area filled with wooden bungalows built largely in the 1920s, it was without the usual trappings—soaring vertical massing, steep gables, and spire of the Gothic revival, or the pedimented, towered, and steepled colonial—then standard for churches in the Portland area. Nonetheless its religious purpose was clear. It had a simple rectangular, transept-less plan, with side aisles and flat chancel. Interior spaces were clearly legible on the exterior, with the high volume of the nave flanked by lower side aisles and narthex, a semicircular baptistery to one side and freestanding bell tower on the other. The fenestration enhanced the legibility of the form, with a large rose window in the narthex, a series of narrow slit windows defining the nave, and a stained glass window wall lighting the chancel in the east end.

St. Philip Neri Church, interior.

The interior was equally straightforward. One entered on axis, through a large narthex running the full width of the church; this was screened from the nave by removable panels so that it could serve as an overflow space during holidays. The nave itself was defined by plain plastered walls carried on a colonnade of simple, square pillars, separating it from the aisles. To relieve the severity of the white, flush-surfaced interior and to break up the hard reflective surface acoustically, the nave wall was gently pleated, setting up a regular pulsing rhythm of subtly angled surfaces in each bay, like Saarinen's Lutheran church in Minneapolis, which had also provided a prototype for the campanile.[12] The nave is vaulted by a plain wooden roof borne on shallow exposed timber trusses, a traditional feature of the early Christian basilica. A simple arching baldachino of wood framed the altar.[13]

The sheer size, plainness, and sobriety of the building exerted a quietly monumental presence in the neighborhood. The fineness of touch, sensitivity to proportions, handling of materials—here, a rough textured buff-colored brick and wood—and subtle detailing marked it as unmistakably Belluschi's.[14]

Zion Lutheran Church, Portland, 1947–1950

The Zion Lutheran Church drew on different cultural roots. The congregation of northern Europeans, largely of Scandinavian stock, needed a new, larger church building and parish hall to be built on the site of the existing church. Belluschi's first major challenge was understanding the Lutherans, a quiet, typically undemonstrative people with a cultural heritage very different from his own. Less ostentatious than the traditional Catholic church, the Lutheran church called for a simple, even plain communal space in which music rather than the visual arts played the dominant role.

The site presented another challenge: restricted, sloping, and fully urban, on the corner of a street intersection on the periphery of the downtown, not far from the Portland Art Museum. The original church, a small white Gothic revival structure of wood, was to remain intact throughout the construction process for the congregation's use; it was then to be demolished, leaving its space as a forecourt for the new church.

The biggest challenge, though, was the congregation's resistance to a modern design. Belluschi's original proposal for a starkly modern flat-roofed rectangular form was rejected out of hand, because the plain, unfenestrated block looked, in the words of the pastor, "too much like a factory." A softer but still flat-roofed second proposal was equally unacceptable, prompting the chairman of the building committee to demand a pitched roof and spire.[15] Belluschi was by this time preoccupied with the final stages of the Equitable Building and had a dozen or so other major projects on the boards as the office moved into its busiest year ever; losing patience, he turned the project over to Ken Richardson, his chief designer.

The final scheme consisted of a basically rectangular form with simple pitched roof over nave and chancel and low, wide hipped roof over the narthex, brought down low to form a protective porch; a slender octagonal spire was supported on a simple stepped square cupola, marking the juncture of narthex and nave. The longitudinal plan stepped up, from narthex to nave to chancel, conforming to the slope of the site. True to modernist principles, the three different spatial units are clearly indicated on the exterior by their setback forms.

Resolving the roofline was a problem. After Richardson grappled with it, Belluschi stepped in, deftly suggesting the addition of the hipped roof over the narthex, supported by a simple colonnade to form a porch. He also suggested locating the spire here rather than over the chancel to help hide the awkward juncture of narthex and nave, a parti evidently inspired by the work of Antonin Raymond.[16] Accommodating his client's wishes for a cupola and spire, purely symbolic features that ran counter to Belluschi's modernist

Zion Lutheran Church, Portland, 1947–1950, exterior.

functionalism, he characteristically put them to use by running the pipes of the organ up into the cavity.[17]

The simple brick exteriors of the Zion Lutheran belie the complexity of the internal structure. The structural system is of wood, with a series of great laminated arches rising over the nave and supporting the gabled roof, wholly independent of the exterior brick walls which serve as non-load-bearing, sound-insulating, privacy-providing enclosures only. Using laminated beams, a rapidly developing postwar technology exploiting the high-strength plastic glues developed during the war to enable normally rigid wood members to be molded into arched forms, Belluschi vaulted the nave with a series of pointed wooden arches that soar in a single unbroken sweep from floor to ridge line.[18] This gave a sense of loftiness to the nave and at the same time of intimacy to worshipers seated in pews.[19] The arches articulating bays are repeated in shallow piers of the brick wall that carry the roof rafters.

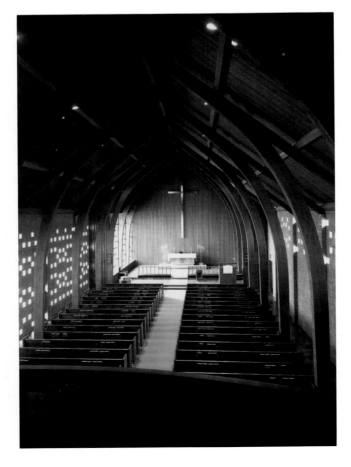

Zion Lutheran Church, interior.

Zion Lutheran Church, portal.

Light in the nave is purposefully dim, brought in by individual glass blocks set in the brick walls. Composed in a repeated geometric pattern, these relieve the otherwise plain brick wall needed to block street noise. Directional glass was used to angle light into the upper reaches of the vault rather than the eyes of worshipers; the glass blocks were also recessed on the interior, with reveals lined in a shiny reflective copper to magnify light, but kept flush on the exterior in keeping with Belluschi's desire for an utterly smooth exterior wall.[20]

In dramatic contrast, the chancel was lit by a softly stained glass window wall on the east side. A simple design of pale roses, violets, and amber glass was set in an abstract patterned wood frame. Forming a warm, richly textured backdrop for the altar, the chancel wall was of redwood battens on which was suspended a simple burnished brass cross; the grooved wood also provided an acoustically absorbent surface to counter the hard reflective surfaces of brick. Grooved fir boards were used on the ceiling and back wall, again to absorb sound.[21]

The Zion Lutheran Church, providing Belluschi an escape from the pressures of office life, brought to the fore his love of art, his sheer delight in composing nuances of colors, textures, and materials—the warm earthy tones of the rosy Willamina brick with its flush pigmented mortar playing against the rich stained redwood of the chancel wall, the subtle hues of stained glass, and restrained use of bright, shimmering brass. Deeply committed to collaboration in the fine arts, Belluschi brought in Frederic Littman, the Hungarian sculptor living in Portland who also did the Menefee House fireplace, for the design of the repoussé copper portals. These were virtually the only added art, in keeping with the restraint of the Lutheran tradition. The church was completed in May 1950 at a cost of $187,645, six months before Belluschi left for MIT.

Central Lutheran Church, Portland, 1948–1950

The Central Lutheran Church, for a more affluent congregation on the other side of town, was very different in character. Bigger, with a substantially larger budget, it was situated on a corner site in the midst of a well-established middle-class residential neighborhood studded with trees. It proved to be the largest and most complex of Belluschi's early Portland churches.

The program was demanding: a large nave with seating capacity of 750 that could be expanded to 1,000 on holidays, parish hall, administrative offices, classrooms, several meeting halls for Sunday school, mothers' room, nursery, kitchen, living quarters for

Central Lutheran Church, Portland,
1948–1950, exterior.

custodian, plus large dining hall and rumpus room—all on a tightly restricted site in a quiet residential neighborhood.

Wholly untraditional except for its bell tower and simple wooden cross, functionally the building reads with exceptional lucidity. It consisted of a flat-roofed rectangular nave terminating in a high, semicircular apse, with a tall, framed timber bell tower at the opposite end. Its main body, a long rectangular block containing parish hall and nave, was of a warm, richly textured brick below with a bonding pattern of alternating projecting and recessed crosses, surmounted by an open framework of dark wood and stained glass above; the apse, of brick alone, was both wider and taller than the nave, creating a zone of windows that cast a halo of light into the chancel within. A wing containing library, offices, and meeting rooms on two levels flanked the church on its east side. Distinctly modern, the building suggests the influence of both Aalto and the Japanese.

Central Lutheran Church, gateway.

Central Lutheran Church, interior (photo: Lawrence Hudetz).

One entered from the side through a wooden Torii gateway with its gently upcurved timbers, into a shallow narthex that opened at right angles onto the parish hall on one side and the nave on the other. Supporting the roof of the nave and defining its bays was a series of broad suppressed laminated-wood arches that spanned its full 44-foot width; these terminated at the chancel, which was both wider and taller than the nave, leaving a broad clerestory between the two. The nave was dark, lined by slatted stained fir walls with colored glass windows of deeply saturated reds, purples, and blues on the west side. In stark contrast, the chancel, defined simply by a plain plaster curvilinear wall, was brightly lit by its halo of pale amber glass. The altar itself was framed by a slatted wooden screen bearing a simple bronze cross. Other than the stained glass, this was the church's only adornment. Its emotional power, created by space, light, and the use of ordinary materials—glass, brick, wood, and bronze—stemmed from the simplicity of structural means and the rigorous discipline that controlled the whole.

Refusing to do a Gothic church, Belluschi sought a form that represented the beliefs of its own time. His aim was not novelty for its own sake, but a form that used new technology and reflected new religious attitudes. "First of all," he told the congregation,

> a religious building must create an atmosphere conducive to prayer and meditation; by using honest means it must suggest true and lasting values, give a sense of warmth and security to its congregation and inspire them to a renewed sense of community life. If there is a conscious striving for beauty it must come not from cut-rate imitations of the fruits of past civilizations developed in alien lands, but from our own methods with our own materials, and from a judicious and sensitive use of space, color, and texture.

The architect cannot force a congregation into his way of thinking:

> he must rather try to find within himself the power and wisdom to interpret their wishes and guide their decisions by logic and persuasion. He should know their various intimate problems and the scope of their activities; he must have the ability to integrate all needs into significant forms, even in the knowledge that there is no perfect answer to any problem, and that he is a fallible and limited human being.[22]

The church was dedicated August 1950 and had a final cost of $235,000, which included all fees.[23]

First Presbyterian Church, Cottage Grove, 1948–1951

The First Presbyterian Church in Cottage Grove, a small timber town south of Eugene, was commissioned in January 1948, just as the nationally acclaimed Equitable Building opened in Portland, and was dedicated in 1951, the year Belluschi left for the deanship at MIT.

The congregation was initially undecided about the kind of church building it wanted. The pastor, Reverend Hugh Peniston, fresh out of Princeton and the Union Seminary in New York, believed Gothic was appropriate; members of the congregation envisioned something colonial, of brick with white trim. The only thing they agreed on was that it have gabled roofs and a spire. To resolve the issue, they each agreed to study new currents in church design. Reconvening with eyes newly opened to modernism, they decided not to do a grand or pretentious historicized building, but rather something that drew on the materials and labor of the local community, a building specifically tailored to their own needs.

First Presbyterian Church, Cottage Grove, 1948–1951, exterior (photo: Julius Shulman).

Their primary concern was that the sanctuary be planned in accordance with the democratic spirit of the Presbyterian church. This meant a single undivided sanctuary space for minister, choir, and congregation, rather than long narrow nave with separate chancel, as was customary in the Catholic church, a communion table around which they would all gather instead of an altar, and a sense of reasonableness and fairness, family harmony, and democracy, rather than otherworldly mysteriousness.

Belluschi himself approached the job humbly, aware of how easily his polished, urbane manner might intimidate his clients. After interviewing several architects, the congregation chose him because its members appreciated his humility, his ability to listen, and his sense of understanding. They found appealing the warmth and simplicity of his other churches, his use of native woods and natural light. They were also intrigued by his idea of entering the church, which he envisioned as a quiet, sheltered place for communal worship, through a garden or landscaped court that emotionally and psychologically would prepare the individual for the religious experience, rather than entering abruptly from the street.

The commission came at an extraordinarily busy time in the office. The Equitable Building had just opened under considerable national attention, the Oregonian Building was in the final stages of construction, the Burkes and Menefee houses, as well as several other major jobs plus a score of smaller ones, were in progress. Belluschi himself was now president of the Portland Art Museum board of trustees and was increasingly being asked to lecture around the country. He was also running the entire office himself, making all business and administrative decisions, as well as supervising design. Reluctant after the lean years of the Depression to turn down any job, but also intrigued by the challenge of the Cottage Grove church, he accepted the commission with the proviso that he be granted plenty of time, as much as two or three years. He also, with characteristic shrewdness, specified his desire for "an intelligent building committee" and, tapping into the Presbyterian spirit of democracy, a good working relationship, with everybody working together until a satisfactory solution was agreed on.[24]

The site was a corner lot in a quiet residential neighborhood of common wooden cottages, dotted with large, expansive hundred-year-old black locust trees. The budget was limited. Specific demands were for a parish hall, Sunday school facilities, library, kitchen, and office spaces in addition to the church. As space was limited, a highly efficient plan was paramount. This, and saving the trees, were Belluschi's main priority. When asked by an anxious congregation how the building would look, he urged its members to be patient. A good plan had to come first; an appropriate exterior would follow, he maintained, as a natural consequence. A time-honored modernist principle not always evident in practice, with Belluschi it was always a fundamental truth.

Admitting ignorance, he hounded the congregation with questions. As this was his first Presbyterian church, he wanted to know all about their customs, expectations, and spiritual needs. Unlike the Catholic church, with its authoritarian hierarchy and its segregation of laypeople from priest—a segregation reflected in the traditional design of the church with the chancel removed literally and symbolically from the nave—Presbyterians were "truly democratic," their service more communal. This was true of the Cottage Grove congregation in particular, where the democratic spirit led to an eagerness to be involved in the church design process, backed by a willingness to work. Belluschi found this team spirit, this readiness to participate, inspiring. This, plus his own openly collaborative approach, led in large measure to the success of the building.

The design process proved highly educational for both sides. Belluschi drove down to Cottage Grove frequently for communal meetings, then would return weeks later with revised schemes. At no time, according to Reverend Peniston, did he impose his own views. He argued convincingly, but also listened; responsive to their ideas, he was also persuasive in helping them to understand his. "It was a real cooperative experience," Peniston described it later. "We were all working together. It is hard to explain the excitement involved in this experience of planning. You have to understand something of the atmosphere that prevailed in the Belluschi office, as well as the feeling in our congregation that our little church was about to do something new."[25]

It was this feeling of excitement, of a spirited collective endeavor, that Belluschi personally found so invigorating. It was the same electrifying esprit de corps that he had encountered in working with Ralph Cake on the Equitable Building, and that was to inspire the Church of the Redeemer in Baltimore a decade later.

Despite their involvement in the planning process, the congregation was nonetheless shocked when confronted with the modernity of Belluschi's proposal. In the interest of harmony, they agreed to let it sit awhile to allow them time to get used to it. "I don't really like it," Peniston recalled one of the building committee members saying, "but when you think about it, Mr. Belluschi has expressed simply those ideas we wanted him to express."[26]

The choice of contractor was another issue. With Belluschi out of town and preoccupied by other affairs, their selection of a reliable builder was critical. Their decision to use

Albert Vic & Company, a local contractor, was, to use Belluschi's word, felicitous. Vic's understanding of wood, his skilled craftsmanship, most of all his sense of personal involvement in the project contributed greatly to its success. Inspired by the same communal spirit that permeated throughout, he set a high standard, and was exacting down to the smallest detail.

Belluschi designed an L-shaped building, with parish hall in one wing, church and subsidiary spaces in another; he sited it back on the site to preserve trees and free the central portion of the lot for a landscaped courtyard, which was shielded from the street by a rustic, trellised wooden wall. The visitor entered through a sheltered gateway down a short loggia bordering the landscaped court to the church. Simple copper-paneled portals opened into the narthex, which in turn opened at right angles onto the nave.

The nave itself was small but spacious-seeming, opened by a series of clear plate glass windows along the north side facing the garden court. Rather than the dimly lit, dark

First Presbyterian Church, Cottage Grove, interior.

wooden walls of his previous churches, which focused dramatic attention on the brilliantly lit chancel, the nave and chancel here read as a single space, amply lit throughout. Walls were white, sand-plastered for texture. The high flat ceiling of sound-absorbing grooved fir undulated gently up over the chancel, uniting the nave and sanctuary in a single space while symbolically endowing the chancel with special importance. A stained glass window wall of pale rose, amber, and violet hues cast a softly colored light on the chancel wall.

The use of plate glass in the nave was new. Rather than an enclosed, mysterious, dimly lit space, the nave opened broadly to the outside, imparting a sense of unity between constructed and natural space. It came about, as was so often the case with Belluschi, at the suggestion of his client, Reverend Peniston, who was reminded of a Presbyterian church in Scotland where the sanctuary was glazed behind the altar to provide a view of the town, reminding the congregation of its obligations to the community below. Intrigued by the idea, Belluschi reinterpreted it, opening the nave along its side to the garden, with a view of the trees and rooftops of the community beyond.

Domestic in scale, the church was of conventional wood frame, with exteriors of inexpensive rough-sawn vertical board and batten of Douglas fir, a local product that was the community's main source of income. It thus served a symbolic as well as practical purpose. Belluschi characteristically put it to aesthetic advantage by leaving it untouched, staining it only lightly to blend with the hues of the surrounding trees.

The landscaped court was an integral part of the design. By now Belluschi was well versed in Japanese landscaping principles, having acquired a book that remained throughout his life one of his most prized possessions, Samuel Newsom's 1939 *Japanese Garden Construction*.[27] He had proposed a large sculptural rock just inside the sheltered gate to screen the sanctuary from the eyes of newcomers. Finding it too expensive for the budget, he suggested a simple wooden trellis instead. But having listened to his eloquent statements on the spiritual as well as aesthetic function of the stone in the Japanese garden, the congregation was unwilling to to give it up, and several of the more enterprising members took it upon themselves to find and install the great rock.

This sense of common purpose was evidenced in more mundane matters as well. In planning the kitchen, Belluschi found the ideas of one of the women in the congregation better than his own, and followed them rather than those of the professional he had intended to use.

*First Presbyterian Church, Cottage
Grove, courtyard with great rock
(photo: Julius Shulman).*

The building was completed in May 1951 at a cost of $150,000, several months after Belluschi had moved to MIT. Throughout the design process, he had been enormously busy in the office. While he drew up the plan and managed all client negotiations himself, he turned over much of the actual designing to Ken Richardson. After working out the plan, he had left for an interview with MIT officials, instructing Richardson to come up with some elevations and "get this building to work." In his absence, Richardson prepared three schemes, one with a shed roof, another pitched, and a third undulating.[28] Belluschi liked the last, its Aaltoesque contours softening the geometries of the original cubical form.

This was typical of the way they worked: Belluschi established the parameters, Richardson would take it from there. The design was further developed with the help of others on the staff, with Belluschi reviewing, critiquing, and in the end having the final say. His own forte was in matters of lighting, textures, colors, selection of materials, handling of details: all the final artistic touches he knew constituted the difference between an ordinary and a distinctive building. The church at Cottage Grove was a result of Belluschi's adeptness in dealing with others, his eye for and ability to retain talented co-workers and to draw the best out of them, combined with his ability to analyze a problem carefully and thoroughly and to synthesize the most useful of what had been achieved in the past.

The Cottage Grove church was recognized immediately in a spate of publications: *Progressive Architecture,* January 1951, and again in March 1952, and *Architectural Record,* April 1953, and again in July 1956, always superbly illustrated with photographs by Ken Richardson and by the Los Angeles-based architectural photographer Julius Shulman. "Truly numinous" was the way the theologian Paul Tillich, whom Belluschi was later to meet in a symposium on church architecture sponsored by the *Architectural Forum,* described the small, rural church.[29] Richard Neutra, though not a religious man, also found it moving.[30] It established Belluschi as one of the foremost designers of modern churches in the country and especially enhanced his reputation among the faculty and students of architecture schools.[31]

As interest in church architecture soared throughout the world in the 1950s, Belluschi was in constant demand to contribute essays, lecture, participate in symposiums, adjudicate reviews—anything having to do with the design of the modern church. Despite the fact that religious architecture remained only a small fraction of his output, by the time Belluschi began his career at MIT he was known in the profession principally as a designer of churches.[32]

Pietro Belluschi

6   The Equitable Building and the Postwar Boom

Preceding page: Equitable Building,
Portland.

When the Second World War finally ended in August of 1945, the Belluschi office was prepared for the expected onslaught of work. Portland had expanded phenomenally during the war, as thousands of workers and their families poured into the area seeking employment in the Kaiser shipyards. Since most stayed, there was an urgent need for civilian buildings of all types, commercial, institutional, residential, and religious. Wartime restrictions on materials had limited all building except that directly related to the war effort; architects thus faced a backlog of commissions as soon as restrictions were lifted. Many of these came to Belluschi, whose office was one of the few that had remained open during the war. The level of productivity he had enjoyed during the war, with workers' housing, community centers, shopping centers, hospitals, and other govern-ment-sponsored projects, rose sharply in the postwar era as commissions continued to pour in. Between 1945 and 1950, the office successfully completed close to two hundred jobs, among which were at least ten large commercial or institutional buildings.[1]

Equitable Building, 1945–1948

The Equitable was the office's first major postwar job. It was conceived, however, long before. Ralph Cake, the president of the Equitable Savings and Loan Association and longstanding Doyle client for whom Belluschi had drawn up the Commonwealth/Equita-ble Office Tower project in 1929, was eager to move ahead on a new Equitable building. In the late 1930s, Equitable had acquired the remaining portion of the half city block it occupied in the downtown business district and, with progress halted by the war, was awaiting the release of building materials to begin construction.

Meanwhile, sometime during the early years of the war, Belluschi met J. Paul Raven, head of the Bonneville Dam Administration, the major producer of the hydroelectric power on which the Kaiser Aluminum Company depended for the production of light-weight metal used in the aircraft industry. Raven was anxious to find peacetime uses for the large quantities of aluminum being produced for the war effort. With this in mind, Belluschi began looking into its potential architectural uses.[2]

Early in 1943, Howard Myers, editor of the *Architectural Forum,* then the most progres-sive of the three major architectural magazines, proposed a special issue, "New Build-ings for 194X," aimed at stimulating thinking about new design directions after the war. It was to contain proposals for a broad variety of building types destined for a hypothe-tical city of moderate size, with a specific focus on exploring new uses of existing technology. Knowing of Doyle's reputation for high-quality commercial buildings, he invited the Doyle office to submit a proposal for a postwar office building. For the project,

Myers specifically asked that the architect avoid passing fashions and think instead of long-term investment values; he also wanted him to consider designing the building so that it covered only a portion of the lot to allow ample space for light and air. The site was on a major city street, with a southern exposure, for which protection would be needed. Actual size and height were left up to the architect.[3] Among other invited contributors to the *Forum* issue were Stonorov and Kahn, Hugh Stubbins, Carl Koch, Holabird and Root, William Lescaze, Serge Chermayeff, and Mies van der Rohe.

Belluschi's project, calling for a high-rise office slab elevated on stilts and pulled back on the lot to allow for a low, two-story retailing building and landscaped court, anticipated the Lever House in its site plan, but in fact was based on a recently published proposal of Morris Ketchum's for a retail complex, and presented nothing new. More interesting were Belluschi's proposals for the use of new technology. He suggested using aluminum for both structural members and exterior cladding; double-paned, sealed windows to minimize heat loss; and individual, standardized air-conditioning units set under windows. Other ideas were for the use of acoustical paneling, fluorescent lighting, and radiant heating. Noting that the problem of cleaning the windows of new, flush-surfaced buildings had not yet been adequately solved, he also proposed a window-washing device that would be suspended from the roof, running on a track around the periphery.[4]

Belluschi sketch, Architectural Forum *office building project, 1943 (Belluschi Collection, Syracuse).*

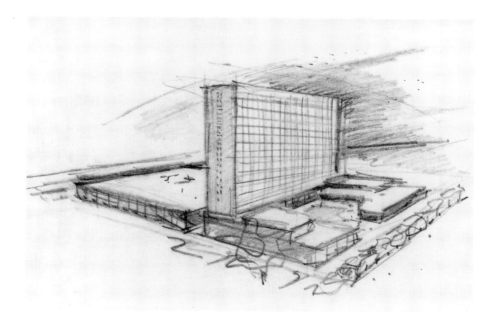

Northwest Airlines Ticket Office, Port-land, exterior, 1944.

Many of these ideas he was to incorporate in the Equitable Building after the war. Before that, however, he had an opportunity to experiment with aluminum cladding on a small scale. The Northwest Airlines Ticket Office in downtown Portland, which he had remodeled in 1939 when the office first opened, needed modernizing again to keep up with the rapidly growing commercial airline industry. Using materials recycled from the original storefront, Belluschi stripped away the existing decor, angled the display window back from the street, and opened up the front with large panes of plate glass. To suggest both modernity in general and the nature of the business in particular, he riveted thin sheets of aluminum, like those used in modern aircraft, to the baggage portal at the left of the entry, keeping surfaces sleek and smooth.[5]

Ralph Cake, meanwhile, was quietly working behind the scenes to expedite progress on the Equitable Building, and had gone to the War Production Board in Washington seeking an early easement on building restrictions; he was thus one of the first in line to gain approval of a nonmilitary use of structural materials. In January 1945, well before peace was declared, he gave Belluschi the go-ahead to proceed with preliminary drawings.[6]

Cake proved to be an all but ideal client, not only because of his enterprising mind and assertive nature, but because of his own eagerness to explore new uses of advanced technology coupled with a tolerance for risk. He and Belluschi worked well together, as both had a keen business sense as well as driving ambition and each respected the other; many of the most progressive ideas for the building were the results of their brainstorming.

By the fall of 1945, plans were set. Belluschi himself went before the Building Code Board of Appeals to request a variance for the use of aluminum facing; negotiations were begun with both Pittsburgh Plate Glass and Libbey-Owens-Ford on manufacturing the oversized glass; and Donald Kroeker, their consulting mechanical engineer, was brought in to design the innovative reverse-cycle heat and air-conditioning system. By the time the building permit was approved, construction documents were ready, though details were yet to be worked out. In January 1946, the 1931 Equitable building was demolished and construction begun. The new building was completed in January 1948, the first major high-rise building to go up in Portland since the late 1920s and the first major corporate tower to be built in the country after the war.[7]

The building was momentous. The technical advances alone made it exciting: Kroeker's experimental heat pump heating and cooling system, the specially manufactured over-sized, hermetically sealed, thermopane windows, the utterly flush, tinted glass and aluminum skin. The thrill of witnessing something extraordinary was heightened by a constant stream of out-of-town visitors, who learned of the project through regular progress reports in the press.[8] Belluschi's own exuberance was conveyed in his statement to the Appeals Board, which coupled futurist rhetoric with a Corbusian sense of moral conviction:

> *The design of this new office building for Portland is fundamentally an expression of faith in a great future for our civilization—a faith born out of a conviction that from our modern techniques, materials, and understanding of present-day architectural problems, we are able to create not only more useful buildings, but also a new kind of beauty—a beauty which is not borrowed from the past but is our own—clean, strong, and straightforward.*[9]

The new building rose twelve stories high, just short of the city's height limit, in a single unbroken plane. The rectangular slab, eleven bays wide by three bays deep, abutted the street in front but was set back in the rear, with a lower, two-story portion filling the remainder of the lot; display windows were recessed at the base, exposing structural

Equitable Building, Portland, 1946–1948, exterior.

TYPICAL OFFICE FLOOR

Equitable Building, plan.

piers as pilotis or stilts. The structure was of reinforced concrete, using a newly developed formula that enhanced its strength, thus permitted its reduction to an absolute minimum.[10] This allowed a gain of space, both in upper-story offices and on the street floor, which was used for a bank lobby and retailing; it also meant a gain of light, as interstices of the thin structural frame were infilled entirely by glass, except for a narrow concrete sill required by code. Belluschi faced the sills with dark green cast aluminum both to distinguish them visually from the silvery sheets of rolled aluminum elsewhere and so that they would read as part of the void rather than solid, thus preserving the effect of an absolute minimum structural frame. With the structural members reduced to a minimum and, except those on the street floor, all clad with a thin veneer of aluminum, the building appeared extraordinarily lightweight, as though entirely of steel. The slender two-story stilts at the base were clad in a solid, richly grained pink marble rather than with the shimmering dematerializing aluminum, both to provide warmth, texture, and a sense of human scale at the pedestrian level and to give the otherwise lightweight, fragile-looking building a sense of solid anchoring at the base.[11]

Surfaces were absolutely flush, without projecting sills, moldings, or decoration. Exploiting, but also clearly expressing, the natural properties of the thin aluminum skin, which was no more than one-quarter inch thick, nothing—no hinge, bolt, or rivet—was allowed to project more than seven-eighths of an inch. The effect was clean and smooth, like the surface of a plane.

Interiors were remarkably light and spacious. As Cake had predicted, Portland at the end of the war desperately needed office space. Belluschi aimed not only at maximizing the available rentable space to enhance his client's return on the investment but, on Cake's urging, at designing the most comfortable, desirable office space possible, in the hopes that it would remain in constant demand. Anticipating what the typical postwar tenant might want or expect, he and Cake sought to incorporate the most advanced lighting, year-round air conditioning, acoustical controls, and flexible as well as distinctively designed interiors possible. The building was planned with office spaces aligned

Equitable Building, typical office (photo: Ezra Stoller).

along either side of a double-loaded corridor, so that each would have an exterior window—indeed, a fully glazed wall—looking out over the city; the electrically powered reverse-cycle water pump ensured year-round temperature control; 8-foot low-voltage fluorescent tubes, deliberately exposed for easy access as well as a straightforward, functional look, allowed an even distribution of lighting.[12]

The sheer amount of glazing was unmatched by any building of comparable size in the country at the time.[13] To obtain the thermopane in the dimensions Belluschi wanted required special manufacturing. Libbey-Owens-Ford refused, saying it could not guarantee it in such large sizes;[14] Pittsburgh Plate Glass balked, then finally agreed after Belluschi persisted. Belluschi eventually got the panes in the proportions he wanted, but six months after the building was completed, several cracked, as the manufacturer had predicted.[15] The panes proved to be defective, however, vindicating Belluschi, and once replaced have remained intact to this day. Trained in engineering rather than architecture, Belluschi like Frank Lloyd Wright had an intuitive sense about what structurally was possible, and constantly pushed the limits of technology in his search for the perfect form. Lingering doubts about the soundness of the building were put to rest the following year when Portland was struck by an earthquake. Like Wright's Imperial Hotel in Tokyo, the Equitable came through unscathed.[16]

Belluschi also aimed to integrate the fine arts in the Equitable. In the lobby opposite the entry was a blank wall that cried out for decor. Walter Gordon, with his background in museum work, suggested a work of Alexander Calder, whose popularity was widespread as the result of a recent MoMA exhibition in New York. Belluschi wrote Calder, who responded with the sketch of a mobile, together with a cost estimate of $10,000. Recoiling at the sight of the Calder proposal, a whimsical abstraction of yellow shapes suspended from fine thin wires, Ralph Cake categorically rejected it on the grounds that "too many people would ask questions and ridicule the idea, since to the layman there's no purpose to it." Despite Belluschi's considerable prowess in the art of seduction, Cake refused to budge. Belluschi wrote Calder to apologize. "I too am sorry things have come to naught," Calder responded. "It's too bad I didn't meet Mr. Cake. I might at least have scratched his icing."[17] The office's hilarity at Calder's reply aside, the incident was revealing of the aspirations of the Equitable team: they sensed they were doing something momentous, and little seemed beyond their reach. In the end, Belluschi designed the mural himself, a combination of Mondrianesque geometries and Arp-like forms that was executed by ordinary house painters for about $50.[18]

Equitable Building, lobby with original Belluschi mural (photo: Ezra Stoller).

Technologically advanced as it both was and appeared, the Equitable Building owed much to history. Like other modernists, Belluschi spoke rarely of history except to denounce it. The legacy of Louis Sullivan and the Chicago School in the Equitable design, however, is clear. The Chicago School architects were well known in Portland, and indeed the Pacific Building, on which Belluschi had worked when he first joined the Doyle office in 1925, drew on Chicago School principles. The Carson Pirie Scott Building, included in a recent Portland Art Museum exhibition of Chicago School architecture, was an obvious progenitor, in the horizontal window proportions as well as the exposed structural framing. The simple, direct expression of the Equitable's structural grid was wholly deliberate—Belluschi's conscious continuation of the Chicago frame carried to its logical extreme.[19]

The projected cost of the building in 1947 was roughly $2 million. The final bill, in September 1949, was $3,123,287, a cost overrun resulting not only from Cake's enthusiasm for exploring new directions in technology but also from soaring inflation.[20]

The significance of the building was immediately recognized; Belluschi himself played a major role in making sure the building was well publicized.[21] The direct expression of the structural frame, sleek aluminum skin, progressive mechanical services, its enormous expanse of windows and wholly modern proportions of solid to void, all coalesced to make it one of the most widely acclaimed buildings of the time. Featured on the cover of the *Forum* in September 1948, it was celebrated as a new "crystal and metal tower," looking "the way all skyscrapers are really built but few admit," and seen as a benchmark in office building design. *Progressive Architecture* featured it in a special Belluschi article and granted it a *Progressive Architecture* award for design in 1949. Recognized as a watershed in history, the Equitable served as a point of departure for another *Progressive Architecture* article in 1950 on architecture in the United States, where, juxtaposed to the 1899 Cable Building of Holabird and Roche, it was portrayed as both the culmination of the most significant architectural development since the first of the century and the beginning of a new era of the crystalline metal and glass skyscraper, a demonstration of how far architecture had come in the expression of the structural frame.[22]

Publicity aside, the sleek, prismatic Equitable was widely acknowledged to be one of the clearest postwar expressions of the Miesian ideal. At the time of its completion in 1948, well before Harrison's Alcoa Building, the Lever House, and of course Mies's Seagram Building, it represented the cutting edge of the profession and marked the high point of Belluschi's career.

Oregonian Building, 1945–1948

The Oregonian was another large commercial building on the Belluschi boards at the time. Though it did not receive the critical acclaim of the Equitable, bearing nowhere near so striking an image, it was actually far larger in total floor area and a costlier and more complicated building.

The Oregonian Publishing Company, publisher of Portland's largest daily newspaper, needed a new building to house its operations as well as serve as corporate headquarters. Specific requirements called for fully modernized facilities for newspaper production, studio spaces for the Oregonian-owned radio station, KGW, a public relations office for home management advice, and business offices. It also wanted distinctive design.

The site was a 200-by-200-foot city block just down from the Portland Art Museum and some six blocks south of the Equitable Building in downtown Portland. To accommodate a 24-foot slope from east to west in the site, Belluschi conceived the building as a staggered six-story block, two levels of which were below grade on one side. On the opposite side, facing the street to the east, these lower levels were fully glazed, enabling pedestrians to watch the action of the gigantic printing presses inside. The main entrance was to the west facing Broadway, one of the city's principal north-south arterials. Running through the middle of the building from one side street to the other was a truckway for the loading of papers and deliveries.

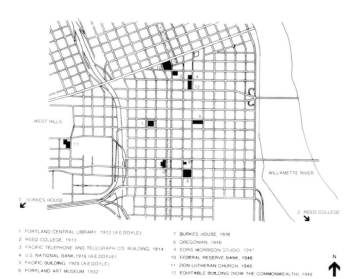

Street map, Portland, with Belluschi buildings through 1950 (courtesy Joachim Grube, Yost/Grube/Hall).

1 PORTLAND CENTRAL LIBRARY, 1912 (A.E.DOYLE)
2 REED COLLEGE, 1913
3 PACIFIC TELEPHONE AND TELEGRAPH CO. BUILDING, 1914
4 U.S. NATIONAL BANK, 1916 (A.E.DOYLE)
5 PACIFIC BUILDING, 1925 (A.E.DOYLE)
6 PORTLAND ART MUSEUM, 1932

7 BURKES HOUSE, 1936
8 OREGONIAN, 1946
9 EDRIS MORRISON STUDIO, 1947
10 FEDERAL RESERVE BANK, 1946
11 ZION LUTHERAN CHURCH, 1948
12 EQUITABLE BUILDING (NOW THE COMMONWEALTH), 1948

Based on extensive study of progressive newspaper plants throughout the country, and designed in collaboration with a New York engineer who specialized in newspaper plant planning, Belluschi's solution focused on efficiency and economy. The speedy production of newspapers required related departments to be located in close proximity. News and editorial offices were thus grouped together on the third floor, adjacent to rooms for composing, engraving, and stereotyping; plates ready for printing were then transferred to the press rooms on the first floor by automatic conveyers. Printed papers were then sent, again by conveyers, to the second-floor mailing room, then to loading platform and delivery trucks in the center of the building. The presses, weighing 600 tons each, were mounted on a 74-ton concrete slab set on a bed of sand, structurally discrete from the rest of the building to minimize vibration. Recording studios on the fourth floor were hung from the masonry structure of the building to isolate them from vibration, and a television studio was included, in anticipation of the arrival of television in Portland.

The structure was of reinforced concrete, with 50-foot steel beams spanning the open space of the pressrooms. Exteriors were of a warm rosy agate granite at the base, with a lighter Indiana limestone above. Utilizing much of the advanced technology being explored in the Equitable, the Oregonian was provided with the same type of reverse-cycle water pump for continuous air conditioning, with radiant heat panels in walls and ceiling; windows set in horizontal bands were of the same aqua-tinted thermopane held in aluminum sash.[23]

Though bearing much of the same distinctive rhythms and proportions, refined use of materials, and careful regard for detailing as the Equitable, the Oregonian did not have its compelling image. Declared the finest newspaper plant in the country by Henry Luce, Publisher of *Time, Life,* and *Fortune,* who visited it upon its opening, it made less of an impression on the architectural community, whose criteria for greatness focused less on function than aesthetics. Not perceived as a daring new design solution or dramatically creative turn, it created little stir in the architectural magazines, hence has had little impact on the historical process.[24]

Other Commercial Buildings

As the economy boomed in the postwar years, the Belluschi office was swamped by requests for new commercial buildings and remodels, from banks, the telephone company, department stores, boutiques, shopping centers, and warehouses to doctor's offices, restaurants, and coffee shops. He turned few of them down. Many were also published.[25]

Edris Morrison Photographic Studio,
Portland, begun 1945, exterior (photo:
Dearborn-Massar).

One of the most interesting of these was for the Edris Morrison Studio, commissioned in January 1946. The program called for a photographic studio with two main studio spaces, dressing room, darkroom, office/reception space, and a distinctive front. The site was a narrow but deep lot on one of the major city streets in downtown Portland, a stone's throw from the Portland Art Museum and less than a block from the Oregonian Building. Belluschi's aim was to provide functional but appealing quarters for a small outfit in commercial photography. The solution was a two-story concrete structure providing 8,000 square feet of space, dramatically set back from the street to provide area for a fully visible but shielded outdoor landscaped courtyard. This was protected from the street by an unobtrusive glazed front consisting of broad plate glass panels held in place by a narrow framing of stainless steel; mounted on this were picture frames suspended from thin wires for the display of photographs. Offering visual interest to the casual pedestrian, it also served as excellent advertising for the business, making explicit the building's purpose. Exteriors of he building were simple, even severe, of exposed concrete painted white to serve as a foil for the landscaped garden. The ground floor was glazed, with reception room looking out onto the landscaped court and darkroom in back; upstairs were the studios, lit by a single zone of ribbon windows. Recognizably contemporary in design, the Edris Morrison Studio represented a simple, creative solution to the architectural problem. It was published in *Progressive Architecture* in February 1949, where it was lauded as much for its contribution to the city as for its distinctive design.[26]

The budget figures reveal as much of the economic climate at the time as of the design process. The original estimate at the time of the contract in February 1946 was $25,000. As changes and additions were made and inflation set in, costs rose dramatically; by the time the building was completed less than a year later, the final bill was $68,000.[27]

One of many buildings and remodels the Belluschi office did for the telephone company was the main headquarters building several blocks north of the Equitable in downtown Portland. The plan, basically a series of loft spaces for the housing of equipment, was prepared by the phone company's own engineers, leaving to Belluschi the design of the exteriors and public lobby. It was to be an 11-story, steel-framed building, with six stories to be built immediately and five to be added later.[28]

The building read as a simple, clean, sharply defined rectangular block with an even, overall grid of windows, square in proportion repeating the virtually square proportions of the building itself. Each pane was divided by thin T-shaped mullions into three, with a slender horizontal rectangle above spanning a pair of more nearly squared rectangles below in a typical Belluschi proportioning. Walls were clad in a dark, richly veined

Edris Morrison Studio, courtyard
(photo: Dearborn-Massar).

Pacific Telephone and Telegraph Company Building, Portland, 1947 (photo: author).

polished granite at the street level, with fine white Georgian marble above. The paneling too was squared, with joints carefully aligned with the window openings. Thermopane glass, now standard in Belluschi's commercial structures, was clear and transparent rather than tinted and reflective, so that the windows read as a pattern of black voids against a solid white ground, rather than a continuous reflective skin. Again, as was customary in his commercial work at the time, surfaces were absolutely flush, with glazing held to the wall plane and windows articulated only by thin bands of aluminum sash. It was this meticulous attention to details, as well as the quality of materials and overall harmonious proportions, rather than a compelling form, that marked the building as Belluschi's.

The Federal Reserve Bank, a building Robert Venturi was known to have admired, located directly opposite the Pacific Telephone Company Building, was its complement: a five-story building of creamy white marble supported on a base of dark richly veined granite. Belluschi exploited the corner site by giving the building a rounded facade with entrance on the diagonal and opening up the base with regular bays of large plate glass windows. Above, even rows of squared windows continued unbroken around the corner, uniting the principal facades as one.

The curved corner entrance with smooth flush polished surfaces, and the dark, richly textured base with regularly gridded white superstructure above, recall two icons of the modern tradition: Sullivan's Carson Pirie Scott Building in Chicago and George Howe's PSFS Building in Philadelphia. Belluschi admired both of them, for different reasons, and drew from them elements he thought would work well here, transforming and synthesizing them into an aesthetic language uniquely his own.

Though high design was clearly Belluschi's main interest, he was not above taking on the ordinary. The Waddle's Coffee Shop was another Belluschi building that surely Venturi would have liked had he known it. Motels, coffee shops, and highway restaurants were increasingly popular in the affluent postwar era, as more American families now equipped with cars took to the road and the tourist industry grew, especially in Oregon. Catering to the average American family with its milkshakes and hamburgers, Waddle's was a drive-in restaurant located just outside Portland on the main highway at the approach to the interstate bridge crossing the Columbia River. It was scaled to be read from afar, with a conspicuous billboard-sized sign floodlit at night. A walkway protected by a cantilevered flat slab roof supported on a colonnade of Lally columns extended from the building itself to the parking areas, so that meals could be delivered to travelers remaining in cars; dining facilities in the coffee shop itself were available for those who preferred to eat inside. Efficient in plan, drawing on the latest furnishings and mechanical

Federal Reserve Bank, Portland, 1948–
1949 (photo: author).

equipment, and wholly modern with its unadorned form, flat roof, ribbon windows, and slender pipe columns, the Waddle's Coffee Shop became a local institution. Recognized nationally as well, it was published by *Progressive Architecture* in June 1947.[29]

Colleges and University Buildings

Most of the office's work was commercial, but Belluschi had made a point of maintaining Doyle's longstanding connection with schools, colleges, and university campuses in the Portland area. As colleges and universities in particular, after more than a decade of little or no building, faced rapidly increasing enrollments in the postwar years, many began plans for expansion. Belluschi was asked to design a number of their buildings.[30]

The principal challenge lay in reconciling modern tastes with existing campus buildings, most of which dated back to the turn of the century and were Tudor or Georgian in style. The problem on the Reed College campus, for which Doyle had prepared a plan in 1911 and designed most of the early buildings, was particularly trying. In 1936, the Doyle office had been asked to draw up a new master plan, including proposals for new dormitory and science buildings. At the time, Belluschi felt that while any new building should be practical, stylistically it ought to mesh with the existing buildings. While one might object to the Gothic as not being of our times, he argued, it had been adopted by the college at its founding, and all subsequent buildings "should respect within certain limits of reason and with sympathetic latitude its restraints." While on the one hand urging the

Waddle's Coffee Shop, Portland, 1946,
exterior.

avoidance of "too narrow a definition of style," he suggested that worse was the "inconsistent hodge-podge" too often seen on campuses and elsewhere today.[31]

By 1945, however, the situation, and his thinking, had changed. During the war, Reed College had contributed to the war effort with the training of highly skilled scientists in the development of radar and the atomic bomb. After the war, the college hoped to continue its alliance with pioneering scientific research. A top priority was thus a fully up-to-date science building, with laboratory facilities for both radiochemistry and physical chemistry.[32] By September of 1945, a month after peace was declared, the Belluschi office had schemes ready for both a $150,000 women's dormitory and a $240,000 science building.[33]

The proposals reveal clearly the conflict Belluschi himself felt between preserving the traditional character of the campus and using by now fully accepted modernist forms. The new dormitory, sited with the men's dorm and President's House at the west end of the main quad, pursued the direction of the 1936 design and was Tudor in style, albeit stripped. The science building, on the other hand, both because of its importance in the postwar Reed curriculum and more importantly because of the symbolism involved, was fully modern, unmistakably International Style in derivation. Different functional units were housed in separate wings in a dynamic, asymmetrical plan; the form consisted of a one-story, brick and glass flat-roofed building composed of broad planes of blank wall and plate glass. Other than the materials, which were as Tudor as they were modern, there was no concession to the historical character of the campus.

Values had changed; the climate in the latter 1940s was one of progress and innovation. Then, too, the situation in the office had changed. Things were extraordinarily busy, and Belluschi was off in a score of different directions. Though he continued to handle negotiations with the client (E. B. MacNaughton, who as head of the Oregonian Publishing Company had commissioned Belluschi to design the Oregonian Building before becoming the president of Reed), Belluschi turned the design over to Warren Weber, one of his new young designers and a Miesian. After Philip Johnson's staging of the Mies exhibition at MoMA in 1947, Mies had become the darling of the profession, especially popular among younger architects. Torn between preserving the unity of the campus and a "sense of rationality for what was going on now," Belluschi approved of the direction Weber had taken, arguing that one could no longer continue the Gothic, especially for a science building representing the forefront of research. Economic factors, too, weighed in favor of the modern, as Belluschi now was quick to point out; Gothic was expensive, and the craftsmanship required hard to come by in the postwar era.[34]

Reed College, Science Building (photo: Eric Stork, courtesy Oregon Historical Society).

The new building, sited behind the library building and screened from the rest of the campus by fir trees, was the first modern building on the Reed campus. It opened, with only the chemistry wing completed, in October 1949; other wings were not added until the 1950s, by which time Belluschi had moved east and had sold the practice to SOM.[35]

Other Buildings

Among several large-scale institutional buildings, one of which was the Oregon State Hospital addition in Salem published in the *Architectural Record* in October 1950, was the Marion County Courthouse in Salem.[36] Aside from his unsuccessful bid for the Oregon State Capitol Building in 1936, and an unrealized project for the Umatilla County Courthouse in 1938, this was the one major civic building of Belluschi's career.

Marion County needed a new modern courthouse to replace its obsolete Victorian building. The site was two blocks away from the State Capitol Building, amidst a complex of mostly 1930s state buildings. According to Richardson, Belluschi's design assistant, Belluschi had wanted to do a dramatically asymmetrical modern building but couldn't get the plan, with its courtroom, corridors, and sequence of office spaces, to work. After struggling with it for some time, he finally gave up the idea of asymmetry and

Marion County Courthouse, Salem, 1950–1954 (photo: author).

concentrated on coming up with a workable plan, which turned out to be a traditional symmetrical plan, with offices aligned down parallel corridors. Richardson roughed out a perspective indicating the overall massing and disposition of spaces, which was submitted to the county clerk for preliminary approval. Leaked to the press in the interest of soliciting public opinion, the drawing was published, provoking an enormous protest. An editorial in the Salem *Capital Journal* called it "an extreme example of what is called, we presume, the 'modernistic New Deal in architecture.'" Others said it was hideous. "For no extra money we could have a beautiful building, not a large packing box." "Mr Belluschi is regarded as one of the most talented architects of the day and undoubtedly has the ability to build a beautiful and impressive building," one editorial concluded. "But in an effort to be original in design, he has not hesitated to sacrifice exterior beauty for an extremity of simplification of outline."[37]

Belluschi hastily explained that the drawing merely showed the masses of the building, and that doors and windows would of course be added later.[38] The following September, a second perspective was published, this time with finished elevations. But minds were made up, and the reaction was no better. "The published sketch of the exterior of the proposed new Marion County Courthouse is a distinct disappointment to taxpayers pungling up the tax money for its construction," a second editorial read. "It looks like a glorified warehouse or an old-time morgue, with its simplified blank white walls and absence of windows or ornamentation, a frantic effort at over-simplification. There are a number of similar architectural buildings in Salem already that resemble nothing so much as marbleized barns."[39]

After minor revisions, considerable lobbying, and the support of former state governor Charles Sprague (for whom Belluschi had recently completed a vacation house),[40] the proposal was approved. Construction was to have started in March 1951, but was held up until additional cost-cutting measures were taken and more funds were secured. The building was finally begun in 1952, well after Belluschi had left for MIT, and finished in 1954 by B/SOM.

It was a five-story concrete building with marble veneers, symmetrical in design, with low projecting wings on either side. The facade was divided horizontally into zones, with different but balanced fenestration patterns, and divided vertically into unequal bays that were ordered around a central axis to establish a distinctive rhythm. While upper stories were flush, the ground floor was recessed to allow supporting members to form a simple colonnade; aligned with the bays above, the supports continued their rhythm. It bears Belluschi's unmistakable stamp in its tightly organized, exacting visual order.

Though never published, the Marion County Courthouse is significant on several counts. The history of its design tells of the resistance to European modernism Belluschi continued to face in Oregon as late as the 1950s, a hostility not apparent with the classical modernism (or modernistic classicism) represented by the Oregon State Capitol Building in the 1930s. It reveals something of the nature of Belluschi's clients, in this case hard-headed state officials more used to telling than listening, and to whom symbolism and style mattered more, at least in the design stage, than function. And it is revealing of Belluschi, who was perhaps less successful in dealing with state legislators and anonymous public bodies than with individuals. He was at his best when he could talk to and negotiate with his clients personally, hear what they wanted, and try to convince them of the appropriateness of his proposal rather than win them over with flamboyant designs.

Belluschi and the Office in the Late 1940s

Throughout the latter 1940s, the office continued to operate as it had since moving to the Jefferson Street building and changing its name to Pietro Belluschi Architect in 1943. Although by 1946 the staff had increased from four during war years to about 15, everybody continued to work in the one large drafting room, with Belluschi at the first desk. As jobs got bigger and more numerous, Belluschi moved into the file room, seeking quiet. The office remained modest: his desk was just another drafting table consisting of two saw horses and a set of drawers covered by a piece of plywood, plus a file cabinet. Equipped with two phones often both going at once and with the desk piled high with papers, he was the model of the harried businessman.[41]

As jobs kept coming in and the staff continued to grow, the office needed more space. In 1947 Belluschi took over the other half of the building, which he had been renting out. With the help of an FHA loan, he remodeled the building again, adding a second story of apartments which he rented to cover the cost of the remodel, and a second-story studio office with large, sloped plate glass windows on the north wall. This became his office, shared with Ken Richardson, who was by then his chief design assistant. The arrangement did not last long, however, as Belluschi was always running up and down the stairs to the drafting room, and he built a makeshift office in the drafting room and moved himself and Richardson in there. The upstairs studio he converted into another apartment.

By 1948, when office activity was at its peak, the number of staff reached about 28.[42] Despite its size and the astonishing number, variety, and complexity of jobs, the office organization remained loose and informal, basically that of a small firm, with everybody participating in a wide variety of jobs.[43] Maintaining this organizational pattern, Belluschi was able to oversee the design of most jobs, only occasionally letting one slip by without his seeing it. Although the office was run strictly as a business, with everybody expected to work hard, Belluschi was respectful enough of the artistic process to allow a high degree of autonomy among his designers, as well as plenty of time, especially in the early stages of design.

Belluschi himself remained in control of the business of the firm, as well as handling all negotiations with clients and supervising design. Genteel as he was, he was also a shrewd businessman who knew the value of a dollar, ran a tight ship, and liked to run it his own way. Dave Jack, the former business manager who was let go when Belluschi took over the firm in 1943, had thrown down the gauntlet, predicting that the office would not survive without him to run the business. Determined to prove him wrong, Belluschi assumed the role of archbusinessman: honest, fair, clear and straightforward in his business deals, but very careful and very smart.

Tight-fisted by his own admission, he was nonetheless not greedy and at times could be generous. He would on occasion waive fees for clients unable to pay, donate his services, or return a percentage of his fee, especially to church organizations, when he felt the situation warranted it and there was promise of payoff in some other way.

He readily delegated design. As the number and complexity of jobs increased in the later 1940s, he began turning more and more of the designing over to others, keeping tabs on the process to a greater or lesser degree. With his reputation, he attracted talent, mostly regional but not entirely so, and had a good pick of job applicants. Recent architecture school graduates were especially welcomed; he liked their new ideas and fresh way of thinking, and was willing to assume whatever risk came with their inexperience. Typically he let them each have a hand at designing before sizing up their abilities and assigning them to jobs best suited to them. Increasingly he saw himself less as a designer than as a catalyst for design, encouraging and stimulating the ideas of others, working mostly as a design critic or troubleshooter.[44]

After meeting initially with a client, he would always schedule ample time to study the problem. On a job he was particularly interested in, he typically would devote a great deal of time to thinking before putting anything down on paper, then would come in early in the morning, long before others arrived, and rough out his ideas in a quick sketch. Sometimes he would simply describe his ideas verbally to whichever designer he thought best for the job—Ken Richardson, Walter Gordon, Henry Klein, Hobart Wagoner, George Wallace, or one of the others.

He would start with the plan, working out the siting, circulation, and other operational requirements, then proceed from there. Sometimes he would put two or three designers on the same project, after which they would tack their proposals on the wall for discussion. This enabled Belluschi, who had set the general idea, to consider a range of design possibilities.[45]

The system succeeded because Belluschi was good at assessing talent, his own included, and putting it to best use. His skill was in perceiving exactly what his clients wanted, supervising the design work of others, and running the business. His priorities were clear: practicality came first, in terms of meeting the budget and working out an efficient, functional plan, with formal concerns important but always secondary. The system also worked because of the Belluschi team, by this time mostly hand-picked and trained by Belluschi himself. Loyal, drawn to him because of his values, they shared those values and respected his vision.

It also succeeded because of Portland, its size, scale, resources, and cultural sophistication. Belluschi knew the city and its resources well, from civic leaders and influential families to contractors, craftsmen, and local suppliers—L. H. Hoffman, Oregon Brass, Willamina Brick. He knew whom to call for what job, and they knew him, what he wanted, his tastes and exacting standards. He also had a core of consultants he could count on, skilled specialists such as Kroeker, for their mechanical services. With a smaller field of operation than that of New York or Chicago, he was on top of it all, a big frog in what was to prove a very small pond.

Meanwhile, Belluschi was becoming increasingly involved in professional affairs on the national level. Much of this was due to *Architectural Forum* editor Howard Myers. Through Myers, Belluschi was appointed a member of the Architectural Advisory Committee of the Federal Public Housing Authority in 1945; the following year, he was made a member of its executive committee, along with William Wurster, Louis Kahn, Timothy Pfleuger, and Eero Saarinen. He was asked to serve as a juror for the Southern California chapter of the AIA's Honor Award Program, then asked to give a series of lectures on his work in San Francisco. His reputation as well as his network of connections spread as he was invited to serve as juror on increasing numbers of national architectural competitions. In 1948, after the Equitable Building opened, he was elected a Fellow of the AIA, one of the highest honors in the profession. The following fall, he was asked to serve as a visiting critic at Yale, then to speak to architecture students at the University of Illinois, then to deliver a talk to a group of professionals in White Sulphur Springs, West Virginia. Invariably he was introduced as one of the nation's leading spokesmen for modernism.

He also carried on in local activities, particularly in connection with the Portland Art Museum. In 1947 he was elected president of the board of trustees of the Portland Art Association. The museum's exhibitions of those years, including major displays of abstract expressionism, surrealist art, and other avant-garde trends, kept him fully abreast of contemporary art. It was to a large extent his sophistication in the arts gained through the museum that Easterners found so astonishing when he moved to Cambridge. Belluschi also continued his activities in city planning with the local chapter of the AIA, and in 1945 was asked to join the national AIA committee on urban planning.

By the late 1940s, he was one of the most highly respected architects in the country. As the practice of architecture changed, with offices becoming larger in size and more complex in structure, and as competition among architects stiffened, *Progressive Architecture* devoted a series of articles to the practices of prominent architects. Belluschi was one of those selected, and in February 1949 his operations were described as a model of the successful postwar office.[46]

His success came at a time when the profession was struggling to hold onto traditional ideals while meeting new goals and the often conflicting demands of profession, client, and society at large. His buildings were not trendsetters so much as simply good, solid, and pleasing, representing to those who set the standards a sense of quality and visual order rare in the profession.

By the late 1940s, Belluschi was personally very well off. Born into an aspiring, entrepreneurial bourgeois family, he was further shaped by the struggles of his early years in the United States and his later achievements. Much as he admired, and on one level aspired to, the simple straightforwardness of Harry Wentz, by nature Belluschi was complex: deeply intelligent, quietly determined, and fiercely ambitious. What you saw was not what you got. Reticent, his manner mild and voice soft, his means subtle, he fought for what he wanted, but discreetly and often behind the scenes. He was also inclined to back off when he sensed his approach wasn't working and that he was fighting an uphill battle.

For all his affability and outward warmth, he was an immensely private man, wary of others and maintaining a certain aloofness even from close friends. Only occasionally did he engage in social affairs, often just for appearance, and typically he left early. Rather than large parties, he preferred the company of a few select friends for dinner and an evening of good conversation. Urbane, charming, discriminating in his choices of friends, books, wines, and music, he prided himself on his taste. Poised, always impeccably groomed, he was acutely aware of his public image.

Knowing what it meant to be without, he appreciated what money could bring and enjoyed being able to afford whatever he desired. He had always fancied nice cars—a Model T Ford in the 1920s when he first arrived in Portland, then a Hudson in 1929, a Chrysler and a LaSalle in the 1930s, a Cadillac, the ultimate sign of American success, in the late 1940s (which he had shipped back when he moved to the East), then eventually a series of Mercedes.[47] He enjoyed dressing well, displaying the same discerning eye in his attire as in his work. While the nonmaterialistic Wentz may have served as his alter ego, Doyle was in fact his role model; like him, Belluschi wore a smock in the old Beaux-Arts manner when he worked, partly because of its patrician image, partly to keep from smudging his good clothes.[48] Belying his quiet demeanor, he relished challenge, and rather than retreating from risk he sought it out, constantly testing himself, pushing himself to new heights. In so doing he took on some of the most important and daunting architectural problems of his times.

Belluschi and his family continued living in the converted farmhouse in Aloha until 1948, but Helen, isolated from friends and home alone with two small boys, remained unhappy. Hoping to improve her spirits, as well as ease his own commute to and from the office, Belluschi moved the family again in 1948 to the affluent neighborhood of Palatine Hill, where he remodeled an older house in anticipation of the time when he could build a new house on a piece of property he had acquired in nearby Abernathy Heights.[49] Where she lived, however, was not Helen's problem, and, increasingly despondent, she began drinking.

Whatever the couple's problems, they were not immediately obvious. The Belluschis continued to attend and occasionally give parties, which she, vivacious and outgoing, enjoyed, and he, by nature more reclusive, simply endured. They struck others as a successful couple, actively involved in high society, often photographed and quoted in the society pages of the local paper.

Regionalism and the Western Tilt

"Modern architecture must reflect the beauty of its environment, not borrowings from the past," Belluschi told students at the University of Washington in the spring of 1948. "Machines, people, climate . . . local traditions cannot be disregarded, but neither can they stand in the way of logical development. Architecture must not be dictated by the machine. It must express an emotional understanding of its environment."[50] It was a decidedly western stance.

Since the late 1930s, West Coast regionalism had been gaining momentum. It peaked in the late 1940s. The wartime economic boom fueled population increases and an expanding market, there was plenty of undeveloped land in which to grow and build, traditions were less entrenched than in the East, and clients by and large less conservative. This was where creative action was occurring and new ideas being explored, with William Wurster, Gardner Daily, and John Dinwiddie in the Bay Area, Neutra, Schindler, Raphael Soriano, and Charles Eames in Los Angeles, and John Yeon, Van Evera Bailey, Paul Thiry, and Belluschi in the Pacific Northwest. The work of European modernists like Neutra and Schindler in Los Angeles, or Gropius and Breuer in the East, was for the most part resisted; though their influence gradually spread, it remained basically limited until after the war. Not so with Wright, whose work had a profound impact, especially in the West. Scorned by the conservative East Coast architectural establishment as late as 1949, Wright was revered by younger architects throughout the country, most especially in the West.[51]

The architectural press had long played a major role in breaking the lock of East Coast biases.[52] Recognizing the fertility of new ideas across the country, editors of the *Architectural Forum, Architectural Record,* and *Pencil Points* (which became *Progressive Architecture* in 1945) periodically sent out scouts to keep abreast of what was going on. As travel especially in the prewar years was still mostly by train, this involved a sizable outlay of both time and money. Often it took weeks to get from New York to the Pacific Coast; once reporters were there, they packed in as much as they could, traveling up and down the coast, typewriters on lap, taking notes on what they saw. As telephone calls were expensive, most interchanges took place by mail or by telegram.[53]

John Entenza, editor of *Arts + Architecture* in Los Angeles, was a major figure in stirring interest in what was going on in the West. It was he who brought Henry-Russell Hitchcock out in 1940 to do a feature article on West Coast architecture, prying open East Coast doors. Howard Myers, publisher of the *Forum* in New York, was another key figure. Keenly interested in significant new developments taking place throughout the country, and with an open mind to young, unproven talent, he kept a sharp eye on the West. It was Myers, as Belluschi put it, who more than any other "brought me in on the scene" by affording him national attention.[54]

Elisabeth Kendall (later Elisabeth Kendall Thompson) was the West Coast correspondent for the *Architectural Record;* she, James Marston Fitch, and then Douglas Haskell wrote regularly on West Coast affairs. Haskell, who left the *Record* in 1949 to join the *Forum,* according to Peter Blake "knew more about the real origins of modern architecture in this country than anyone else. While everybody was taught to believe modern was

Corbusier, Gropius, Mies, and that it all came over to this country in the 1930s but because of the War didn't have any impact until the 1950s and '60s, this ignored the modernism that existed on the West Coast before the Grand European exodus."[55] Haskell was a particularly avid supporter of Belluschi, at least until the early 1960s and the controversy over the Pan Am Building in New York.

In 1947, the *Record,* under the auspices of Elisabeth K. Thompson, opened a section specifically geared to work in the West, acknowledging the differences in style and approach from those of the East, their different materials and wholly different attitudes toward space. Their cultural roots were seen as different too, the East typically more style-conscious, open to European trends, its modernism heavily influenced by the machine aesthetic of the Bauhaus and other paradigms of the International Style, whereas in the West eyes were more open to the natural environment, and architectural roots were in the bungalow vernacular, arts and crafts, Maybeck and Greene & Greene, craftsmanship, the Orient, Wright, organic theory, and later Aalto, yielding a gentler, less doctrinaire, more humanistic modernism. Especially in the postwar years, with so much construction taking place in the West, architects in the East tended to theorize while those in the West built.[56] Reflecting this activity, *Progressive Architecture* held its second national *PA* award ceremony in California, its third, in 1949, in Portland. One award and two mentions went to Portland architects, one of whom was Belluschi.[57]

By the late 1940s, the tilt toward the West was clear. As Wurster wrote in 1948, architecture in the United States had now broadened its base. No longer was there only New York; significant work was occurring elsewhere.[58] As regional rivalry mounted, Lewis Mumford fanned the fires with his "Skyline" column in the *New Yorker* of October 1947, comparing the stodginess of the East to the freshness of work in the West, which he saw as a new, promising, humanistic variant of the International Style. "That the modern house is a machine for living in has become old hat. The modern accent is on living."[59]

The issue exploded at the 80th Annual Convention of the AIA in June 1948. The AIA was "notoriously undemocratic," the July *Forum* pointed out in its summary of the meeting, with most decisions made unilaterally by its conservative leaders. Things were different this year, however, with the usually dull organizational meetings disrupted by dissension. A "rebellious younger group" of 140 delegates and members signed a petition urging next year's Gold Medal be awarded to Frank Lloyd Wright. Despite efforts to keep the resolution off the floor, it was "steam-rollered there by newly-made Fellow Pietro Belluschi," as the article put it, "and passed with only a few timid bleats of 'no.'" Belluschi had actually written planning consultant Arthur McVoy in Cambridge the previous year complaining about the conservatism of the AIA. A letter Gropius had written in the April

AIA Journal, Belluschi said, provided the reasons why younger people don't belong to the AIA. "Personally," Belluschi added, "I think it's a mistake to sit in the corner and sulk; what the younger people should do is to join the AIA, be very articulate in their demands for opportunity, raise hell in general, and kick the old gents out of their comfortable seats. Rivalry and incompatibility between the younger and older architects is a healthy sign of natural growth, and I hope that when you and Carl Koch get old and respectable, a new crop of young squirts will be telling you to hurry up and move over. . . . I'm in between, so I can sit on the fence and watch the play, and think I'm not in it—yet!"[60] Belluschi did not sit by for long, however, serving as one of the major supporters of Wright's nomination for the AIA Gold Medal, as noted by the *Forum.*

In the meantime, the western faction of the national AIA gained ground. The 1948 meeting was held, significantly enough, in Salt Lake City. Belluschi was invited to speak in two sessions, on shopping centers in a session on retail buildings, and on regional qualities in residential design for a seminar on dwellings. The latter particularly drew a large crowd.[61] Regionalism was a key subject. "There has always been a powerful need for the human race to harmonize itself with all the forces of nature which surround it," Belluschi said in his talk. "By that token, contemporary design—as all creative architectures in the past—reflects the will to create forms which are alive, and by alive I mean appropriate, in tune with the life which flows everywhere around us." Reflecting the wide interest in his regionalist perspective, excerpts from his talk were published in the *AIA Journal* in August 1948.[62] Belluschi was asked repeatedly throughout the late 1940s and early 1950s to speak on regionalism, particularly to students. His talks typically were published, either excerpted or in toto.

By the time of the next AIA convention, held in Houston, support for the West Coast rebels, coupled with disillusionment with East Coast conservatism, had grown to the point where people such as Thomas Creighton, editor of *Progressive Architecture,* actively lobbied for change. William Wurster, then dean of architecture and planning at MIT but still seen as a Westerner and a key figure in West Coast regionalism as well as representative of the radical West Coast crew, was nominated for AIA president. Running with him for vice president was Pietro Belluschi. A *New York Times* article described the "revolt" and the lobbying on both sides, "with the 'rebels' calling for defeat of the 'staid, conservative older element'" that had traditionally controlled the Institute. This was the same younger group, the *Times* pointed out, that was responsible last year for the Institute's decision to award the Gold Medal to Wright in Houston, "despite some opposition by conservative delegates who considered Mr. Wright's work 'too revolutionary and too advanced.'"[63]

The 1949 convention drew the largest attendance on record. The presidential election, pitting Wurster against the old guard's Ralph Walker, was seen as momentous, marking a "high point of vitality" at the Institute. Walker won, a victory for conservatives, but their triumph was overshadowed by the awarding, finally, of the AIA Gold Medal to Wright, a resounding victory for the regional forces.[64]

And for the West, which was seen as the mainspring of regionalism. "For [Western architects], good design is achieved simply and naturally," Buford Pickens had written, citing men like Wurster, Daily, Bailey, and Belluschi. Aline Louchheim, art critic in the *New York Times* who later married Eero Saarinen, felt much the same. In an article in the *Times* devoted to the art of the West and particularly of Portland, she pointed out that some of the best modern architecture in the country was being produced there.[65] The regional architecture of men like Wurster and Belluschi *was* modern—clean-lined, efficient, rational, functional. But it was more than that. It was an architecture in tune not just with the time but with the place.[66]

1950, the MIT Offer, and Dissolution of the Firm

As professional honors continued to pour in on both the local and national level, in the spring of 1950 Belluschi received a telegram from President Harry Truman informing him of his appointment to the National Commission of Fine Arts. Established in 1910 as an advisory body to the President on issues concerning the arts—architecture, painting, sculpture, and landscape architecture—in public works, the commission's tasks by the 1950s were largely confined to approving design proposals for government buildings in Washington.[67] It thus had a strong architectural component, and when Belluschi was appointed three of the seven members were architects: Joseph Hudnut, dean at Harvard, Elbert Peets, and himself. David Finley, director of the National Gallery, was chairman.[68]

Belluschi's name had been put forth for the position by Jed Davidson, Assistant Secretary of the Interior and formerly a lawyer from Portland to whom Belluschi had sold the Council Crest House in 1944 when the family moved to Aloha. One of Davidson's minor tasks as Assistant Secretary was to fill the Fine Arts Commission.[69] A nonpaying position that members held for four years, it demanded little and was largely ceremonial. It helped, however, to enhance Belluschi's prestige and enlarge his sphere of contacts, especially in government circles.

At this point Belluschi was at the height of his career, with his own highly profitable practice in Portland, known internationally for the Equitable Building as well as for his regional houses and churches, a leading spokesman for modernism and recognized authority in retail design, AIA Fellow and recent winner of two *Progressive Architecture* design awards, nominee for national AIA vice president, and recognized by the President of the United States as preeminent in the arts. It was all very heady for someone who started out an emigre without formal architectural training. At age 50, he had reached what many regarded as the pinnacle of success.

It was at this point that James Killian contacted him. Killian, the president of MIT, was searching for a successor to Wurster as dean of the School of Architecture and Urban Planning; he had heard of Belluschi through the Truman appointment, but more importantly through Wurster, who had specifically recommended him. In July of 1950 Killian invited Belluschi for an interview. Years later he remembered being struck by Belluschi's engaging personality, and by his grasp of the real issues plaguing the architectural profession, his concern for what he deemed important in architecture and the leadership it required.[70] The following month Killian offered him the position. With an alacrity that surprised Killian, who knew of Belluschi's successful practice in Portland, Belluschi accepted.[71]

It was a decision, according to Belluschi, that he agonized over. It meant giving up his highly lucrative practice in Portland for a salary one-tenth of his regular income;[72] it also meant assuming an administrative position in academia, a field in which he was wholly inexperienced, at one of the most prestigious institutions in the country.

On the other hand, there were drawbacks to his situation in Portland. Running the office single-handedly was ruining his health, and he had developed severe ulcers. Then, too, there were problems at home. More importantly, he had reached a plateau in Portland: there was simply not much higher he could go. He was comfortable, but merely comfortable wasn't enough; given his ambition and relish for challenge, the MIT deanship was an opportunity he could not resist. It was the same sense of adventure and love of risk that had brought him to the United States as a youth, landed him a job in the West, and launched him on his by now highly successful career. It meant change at an age when most men were thinking of retirement, but he was used to change and embraced it.

Wurster too had encouraged him, assuring him that his income could be supplemented by consulting, with as much work as he wanted. Moreover, Wurster argued, the profession needed him, needed his West Coast perspective, as, in his words, "the whole international, tight point of view of the MoMA needs healthy questioning."[73] This was a chance to change things, a chance, as Belluschi put it, "to steer young students into a more contemporary outlook."[74]

A major problem, however, was what to do with the firm. The office was in the middle of a number of big jobs, among them the Marion County Courthouse, Idaho Statesman Building, and Federal Reserve Bank, as well as master plans for the McChord Air Field and Larson Air Force Base in Washington state.[75] Until now the office had been a one-man show, with Belluschi fully responsible for the business side as well as the architecture of the practice. This included long-range pension plans and a profit-sharing system for his employees that could not be easily abandoned.

At first Belluschi considered putting the practice in the hands of four of his staff members, with him remaining as a consultant.[76] When that did not pan out, he thought of selling it to an architect in Spokane whose office was large enough to handle it.[77] Then by chance he met Nathaniel Owings of SOM. Owings wanted to expand SOM's base of operations on the West Coast; they had recently opened an office in San Francisco, and were looking to open another in the Pacific Northwest. Seattle was his first thought, but hearing Belluschi's proposal revised his thinking. As Belluschi's office was by this time the largest and most prestigious in the region, he had little hesitation, and by May 1951, by which time Belluschi had moved east, the two had signed an agreement setting up an association they called Belluschi/Skidmore, Owings & Merrill, or B/SOM. It was to last five years, long enough for the Belluschi work still on the boards to be completed, at which point they agreed to renegotiate.[78]

By then there were about 28 people in the office. After Belluschi left, however, the body lost its soul, and within months the tightly knit organization fell apart. As the Belluschi staff left, they were replaced by newcomers from Chicago and San Francisco. Belluschi himself continued to commute back and forth from Boston, with his visits diminishing in frequency as projects were completed.[79] Several jobs, such as a shopping center in Cedar Hills, a Portland suburb, the Lutheran Church in Walnut Creek, California, and the School for the Deaf in Portland, commissioned while Belluschi was still in charge, were designed almost wholly by SOM.[80]

Belluschi/Skidmore, Owings & Merrill was an unlikely union. Headquartered in New York and Chicago, SOM was noted for its consistent formal, austere, mechanized Miesian structure. Belluschi, on the other hand, was known for his styleless, warmer, more sensual and humanistic approach, with its Aaltoesque sympathies and paramount concern for comfort and human scale. The alliance, shaky to begin with, remained uneasy, and at the end of the specified time it was disbanded by mutual accord.

Reed College Honorary Degree and Address

On the eve of Belluschi's departure for Boston, E. B. MacNaughton, deeming it inappropriate for him to assume such a high-ranking position at MIT without an advanced degree, in December 1950 granted him on behalf of Reed College an honorary doctor of laws degree.

Of more lasting substance was Belluschi's convocation speech. It proved to be one the most important of his career, addressed to an educated but lay public on the ideals on which contemporary architecture was based, in terms poetic and at times prolix, his thoughts densely woven but inspiring. Having progressed beyond the narrow functionalism of the 1930s, and facing the new social and cultural conditions of the postwar period, Belluschi now expressed a mellowed and more humanistic philosophy. Architecture,

> to be significant, must absorb and give meaning to modern methods of construction, and to newly developed materials, as well as reflect the physical environment of a region and particularly the traits of its people. In this respect, the West Coast with the pioneering heritage of its people, with definite natural characteristics of its own, and with less binding ties to the past, has been able to advance more visibly towards the realization of valid contemporary forms.

Architects today could no longer rely on the past as an example and guide, nor turn to the cities of Europe for ready-made solutions. The social order that had produced those stately plazas, monuments, and fountains no longer existed. Contemporary society was conditioned by the machine and dominated by the desires of the common person. No longer willing to live in slums, but not asking for palaces, the public wanted clean houses and safe playgrounds, comfortable working conditions, cities free of traffic, smoke, and parking problems. The demand for an efficient city was just, and contemporary architects needed to heed it, putting their own aesthetic concerns aside.

The modern architect, Belluschi continued, "must come to terms with his environment; only then can he hope to become again creative, not in the anemic method of the academy, or as a fashionable hireling of the wealthy, but as a lively interpreter of the new social order and as a prophet of his age." Results thus far were mixed, he admitted. Less to blame for this than their clients and the public were the architects themselves, who were beset by their own conflicts and limitations. Grappling with bewildering new technical advances, coping with changing values and trying to discern the fundamental from those merely superficial, architects, he said, have to develop an inner discipline to protect against the seduction of fashionable but transitory forms.

Albeit successful in designing functional factories, the contemporary architect has failed to create beautiful monuments.

Today we are more honest, more practical, and quite functional, but it has been at the expense of grace and gentility. We have taken away many of the established forms, so cherished by our ancestors, and have replaced them with stark utilitarian ones, which give little nourishment to the senses. We have taken away from the man in the street all the stereotyped little ornaments, cornices, cartouches . . . , but we have not been capable of giving him back the equivalent in emotional value.

The fact is, that after three decades of rather cold functionalism, we have come to the realization that emotion is a great force in our everyday world; it pervades our actions, our political motives, our very happiness. Yet emotions have not been given the guidance they deserve; they are the very soil in which both architects and public may grow to creativeness and understanding.

Looking at our cities, it is quite obvious that we have not been the interpreters and the prophets we had wished to be; we are still shy on wisdom, but I believe our thinking has acquired a greater clarity of purpose and discovered new aspects of beauty, yet to be translated. We have also found that beauty is forever changing and eluding possession, perhaps because of the power of the human mind to perceive and to create, and that power has no end. We have rediscovered on our own terms that architecture is the art and science of organizing space and relating it to man for his pleasure and comfort, and that an architectural work really lives and shines only when it is part of a larger organization.

[A utopian vision perhaps,] but I believe that the complex events of our modern life which eventually will force us to make fundamental decisions are accelerating in their tempo. Wars, obsolescence, traffic, air travel, mass education and so on, will inevitably bring us new demands for change and from them new forms. If we are prepared, if our vision is clear, we can make each move—however small—an orderly and logical step toward the total plan.

Expressing his faith in students, he hoped that they could acquire the discipline of mind he felt was needed to replace the discipline of "styles," and hoped that they "will have enough feeling and integrity of purpose to make their work of lasting significance." But as they were winning the battle against dogma, he hoped they would also retain a respect for the symbols and forms of the past, "because people need them and live by them to a greater extent than is realized. They furnish a feeling of continuity which give them faith in their evolution. This fact architects must understand if they want to be leaders."

> *In these dark times we have a greater need of faith in the future than ever; by the symptoms of current events our civilization may commit suicide on a tremendous scale, and in a shattering shortness of time. But I persist in the optimistic view that in all events the foundations of a new renaissance are being laid now. It will not be for us to see it, and we must only reckon in terms of generations for its flowering, but I believe a better environment for a happier mankind is in the making. It is a task to excite the imagination, and it is now in the hands of our young people.*
>
> *It is for this reason and in this hope that I have elected to forgo a busy practice to take part in education. I look with great misgivings at my accomplishments of the past, full as they are of compromises, failing of their goals, yet I have never doubted that there were ideals to sustain; these I hope to transmit to the younger generation.*

Eloquent in its prose, lofty in its ideals, Belluschi's speech was compelling. Published in the *Reed College Bulletin,* it was excerpted in the *AIA Journal,* and published again in toto in the *Architectural Record.*[81]

Pietro Belluschi

7   MIT, Boston, and Change in Practice

Belluschi left Portland in January 1951 to assume the deanship of the School of Architecture and Planning at MIT. Alone at first, he found a large house on Traill Street in Cambridge, with spacious living room and kitchen suitable for the entertaining he envisioned with faculty and students. The rest of the family joined him the following year. They lived there for three years, then moved to a townhouse, a narrow, three-story brick building on Fairfield Street in Boston's Back Bay, which was more conducive to his consulting work. Here he converted a room on the second floor that had a large bay window, bookcases, and a fireplace into an office.[1] He then set up a long doubled drafting table in the basement, which was where George Wallace, a designer from the Portland office who joined him as his assistant in the fall of 1954, worked.[2]

Over the next decade, Belluschi's increasingly frenetic pace was hard on his family. In moving to Cambridge, he had hoped Helen would find interests of her own that would occupy her time. Portland, however, was where she had lived all her life, and she felt cut off in Cambridge. She resented the demands of his career and the sacrifices of the wife of an architect, especially one as ambitious and devoted to his work as Belluschi. As he took on more and more professional commitments, many of them requiring extensive travel, his long absences left her feeling abandoned with their two boys, who were now reaching adolescence and encountering problems of their own. She began drinking more heavily, affecting her mental health, and in 1953, with much anguish, Belluschi sent the boys to boarding school. It was the last time they lived at home.

Belluschi's health, too, was not good. The stomach ulcers he had hoped to cure by leaving his practice and coming to MIT worsened. In the fall of 1956, he underwent surgery that left him free of pain at last. But as his work load increased, the situation with Helen continued to deteriorate. A highly private man, Belluschi bore his domestic problems with equanimity and refused to let them intrude on his professional life, but he found no real peace or tranquility until Helen died in March 1962.[3]

When Wurster announced his intention to leave MIT for the deanship at the University of California at Berkeley, many of the younger faculty at the Institute, aware of the acclaim Gropius was bringing Harvard, wanted the new dean to be José Sert, who was, like Gropius, a European and a leading member of what was then called "the Bauhaus school."[4] Wurster, however, lobbied for Belluschi. Like him, Belluschi was from the West Coast and represented its more humanistic perspective. Killian, a close friend of Wurster's, trusted his opinion; the Institute was also seeking to fill the position with a practicing architect of national repute rather than an academician.

The Boston architectural community was leery and for the most part regarded Belluschi as a regionalist, his work a softer variant of the more intellectual and theoretically rigorous modernism of the International Style. Although Belluschi's name was well known to the faculty at MIT, he was an outsider and a dark horse. No one knew, once he was on the East Coast, what direction he might take.

Belluschi disliked the stylistic pigeonholing and tried to clarify his stance in a *Boston Herald* interview soon after he arrived. Denying any stylistic partisanship, he maintained that his only aim was "to assist in the training of young minds to be aware of their surroundings and to try to distill beauty from them no matter how grim the conditions." As he put it, his was an approach as different from Frank Lloyd Wright's as it was from the Bauhaus's, with no a priori formal determinants or style. Humanistic rather than formalistic in approach, it addressed the user and his or her experience of the building, how it felt rather than simply how it looked. While not indifferent to form, he believed form was a consequence, not a determining factor.[5] Belluschi's sensitivity to regional differences, his concern for understanding the nature of the people and the cultural context for which his buildings were intended, precluded his doing any buildings in the East, he said, until he better understood it.

Despite the reservations of some, the faculty at the Institute greeted Belluschi warmly. Shortly after he arrived Ralph Rapson, then an assistant professor in the architecture department and one of those sympathetic to his views, with the help of several others stripped him of his shoes, dunked his feet in red paint, then unceremoniously inverted him and stamped his footprints on the ceiling, alongside those of Aalto, Gropius, Buckminster Fuller—an initiation rite he never fully understood but appreciated anyway, as it helped break the ice.[6]

In his capacity as dean, Belluschi made no major changes in educational policy. The battle to shift from the old Beaux-Arts system to a modern curriculum had been fought by Wurster, and by the time Belluschi arrived the new approach was firmly established. Belluschi simply endorsed it, giving full support to the faculty.[7] In another major policy move several years before Belluschi arrived, Wurster had split the school into two departments, architecture and planning, and even though the planning program was still embryonic when Belluschi took over, administratively the work had been done. The program, one of the first in the country, had been established in the 1930s to meet the urgent need for professionally trained city planners; once in place, it expanded rapidly, in response both to the rise of city planning departments in cities throughout the country and to the urban renewal programs of the postwar years. Belluschi himself, however, had no direct role in the Planning Department, and other than personally regretting that it was pursuing a pragmatic rather than a design direction, he left the faculty on its own.

Other than the opening in 1957 of the Joint Center for Urban and Regional Studies with Harvard, another program initiated by Wurster that came to fruition during Belluschi's tenure and was implemented by the faculty on their own, his role within the Institute was mainly one of maintaining the status quo. After the tumultuous years of the Wurster regime, he established a climate of peace, allowing the dust to settle, wounds to heal, and the faculty to get their feet back on the ground. President Killian, speaking on behalf of the administration, remembered it as a congenial, serene time, and a good era for architecture at MIT.[8]

As dean, Belluschi was not expected to teach. The faculty at the Institute was solid, more familiar than he with academia, and had a formal architectural training that far exceeded his. Lawrence Anderson, for example, chair of the architecture department when Belluschi arrived, was a liberal arts Phi Beta Kappa from the University of Minnesota who had received his M. Arch. from MIT in the late 1920s, then as recipient of the Paris Prize spent three years at the Ecole des Beaux-Arts before returning to the United States to become principal design teacher at MIT in 1933.[9] Faced with credentials such as these and aware of his own lack of academic architectural training, Belluschi turned to writing and lecturing, where he felt more comfortable. An articulate, compelling speaker who consistently addressed his audience, lay or professional, on its own terms, he was in frequent demand at AIA meetings on the local and national level, specialized institutes, panels, seminars, and public functions. His energies were thus spent mainly in outreach to the community, serving, in Killian's terms, as a cultural ambassador for the Institute, which was trying to change its public image as a trade school devoted to math, science, and engineering by emphasizing its commitment to the humanities and the fine arts. It was a role for which Belluschi, with his background in engineering, understanding of architecture, and abiding interest in the literary as well as visual arts, was eminently well suited. The subjects of his talks ranged widely, depending on his audience: modernism in church design, shopping centers, urban planning and the problems of the city, the role and responsibility of the architect in modern society. As dean at MIT he was also frequently asked to serve as a panelist with other leading figures in the arts as well as academia, as a juror for awards programs, competitions, and design review boards, and as an advisor on the selection of architects and other architectural issues, a role that was to assume still greater importance in his career later.

Though Belluschi did not teach, he did from time to time serve on graduate juries as a design critic. Though his views increasingly lost their appeal as the popularity of the European modernists spread, his participation by and large was welcomed. His judgment was sound and respected, his advice good—critical but encouraging, often inspiring. He spent little time in studios, which many students resented, but felt he made up for it by being available to students individually whenever they wanted to meet. His viewpoint was consistent: rather than a formal doctrine or specific lexicon of design elements, he believed it important that students learn a general approach—how to analyze a problem fully and sympathetically, then through a process of careful thinking arrive at an appropriate form.

In one of his first addresses to MIT students and faculty late in the fall of 1951, Belluschi stressed that modern society expected the architect to be both a reliable practical man and a man of vision. To be effective, the architect had to be well and broadly educated. He had to be a businessman, with managerial skills as well as a basic understanding of economics; a planner, familiar with land use, sociology, surveying, and landscaping; an engineer, understanding structure as well as heating, ventilating, electrical systems. And he must be a liberally educated man, with a knowledge of and appreciation for the past as well as the present, and with a sincere interest in the fine arts. He must be all these, but also a sensitive, sensible man, with sufficient honesty and integrity to inspire the confidence of his client.

Most important, he told them, the architect had to be a man of vision; not a visionary, innovative form-giver, but more literally an expert in the field of visual and spatial relationships. This was the artistic role society expected of him, this was what distinguished him from ordinary builders. The seeds of such creativity were in us all, there to be nurtured in the right setting; it was this that he hoped MIT would be able to provide. The architect's role was to bring about orderly beauty where only useful disorder exists. But what was beauty and by whose standards should it be defined? Few architects today, he said, were willing to pledge blind allegiance to the aesthetic ideals proclaimed by the new leaders. One aspect of it, at least, was clear: it provided spiritual uplift. And this was something man must have, as it was his quest for spiritual substance that was at the basis of his pursuit of the arts, with architecture at the helm.[10]

Rather than a brilliant lecturer or studio teacher, Belluschi thought of himself as a mentor. Though few in the East had actually seen and experienced his Portland buildings, his work was well known and highly respected through the national press. Students revered him, at least in the early years, and he served as a guru for a whole generation of young architects.

Belluschi's status as a celebrated architect cast light on an aspect of the profession that some of the more thoughtful found troubling. For centuries, architects had seen themselves as an elite corps, guardians of a specialized field of endeavor accessible to only a few. In the course of professionalization in the nineteenth century, they continued deliberately to limit entry into the field, with only those who had gone through a specific training or passed certain tests allowed in.[11] The traditional elitism of the profession, combined with the growing power of the mass media to establish cultural heroes and determine future trends, led in the postwar era to a new sense of power on the part of the architect, and a certain arrogance. As traditional standards of taste fell away with the collapse of the old Beaux-Arts system, aesthetic judgments could not longer be based on fixed, time-honored criteria. Such judgments increasingly were made by recognized "experts," certain select architects (or occasionally architectural writers) of impeccable taste and exceptional powers of discrimination. The publication of Ayn Rand's best-selling novel *The Fountainhead* in 1943, with its headstrong, self-absorbed architect-genius Howard Roark, then its production as a film in 1949 with Gary Cooper adding machismo to the already glamorous image, had a profound effect on the architectural profession.[12] Attesting both to the growing power of the mass media to shape social values and to the American craving for cultural heroes, *The Fountainhead,* with its message of the hero-architect standing firm in his convictions, unwilling to bend to the demands of his philistine client, served as inspiration for a whole generation of young architects. *Time* magazine's series of feature articles on star architects in the late 1940s and 1950s fed this hero worship, making Richard Neutra, Eero Saarinen, and Edward Durell Stone household names. Belluschi saw the falsity of the Roarkian model and cautioned students against its arrogance. But having savored the pleasures of center stage, he, too, was not immune to the appeal of hero worship, and loved being revered

"Arise and Build," envelope postmarked 1959 (Belluschi Collection, Syracuse).

as a cultural leader and a man of exceptional taste. Unassuming as he seemed, the effect of this idolatry was simply more subtle.[13]

Succeeding Wurster, Belluschi was appointed a member of MIT's Advisory Committee on the Arts. As member, then chair, of the Central Administration Committee, he also worked closely with the administration and the Central Planning Committee, a long-range planning committee organized to advise on the campus's expansion plans and building program, and his opinions were relied on heavily on issues related to campus planning and design. His advice was always carefully reasoned, and his judgment was trusted; at a pivotal time in the expansion of the MIT campus, he thus had a great deal of influence over what got built and which architects got the jobs.

His role in the controversy over Eero Saarinen's proposals for the Kresge Auditorium and chapel might serve as an example. Saarinen had been given the commission on the recommendation of Wurster, who considered him one of the best young architects of the postwar era. Facing opposition from the administration, Belluschi urged them to approve Saarinen's schemes on the basis of their functionality, reasoning that as long as the new buildings functioned well, as they promised to do, nobody could fault them on how they looked, as that was a matter of taste. Structural engineers had assured them of the stability of the auditorium, and the acoustician, one of their own faculty members, had sanctioned its interiors. His own approval of the auditorium "as an architectural work of aesthetic value," he maintained, was

> therefore based on the supposition that it will serve its purpose well. On the other hand, if it does not, none of us will be able to defend himself successfully from the accusation that the form adopted by Saarinen was capricious, arbitrary, and based on transitory aesthetic values. I will not exclude the possibility that even if it works as well as we hope it will, the following generation will not look upon it with a feeling similar to that with which we look upon our present [Beaux-Arts] MIT domes. Creative masterpieces do not come easily or by timid approach, and even abstract ideals do change. Architecture, being a crystallization of ideas, needs to go through the same vitalizing experimentation which we're ready to advocate for the world of science and engineering. The alternative is sterility.[14]

Belluschi's ability to argue clearly and convincingly for what he felt was right won him the confidence of other high-level individuals in government and the private sector as well. As his reputation as an advisor in the arts and architecture grew, he became one of the most highly valued consultants in the country, with his advice sought, and usually followed, for the selection of architects for some of the most important buildings of the time, among them the Air Force Academy, Seagram Building, Ford Foundation Building, National Center for Atmospheric Research in Boulder, John F. Kennedy Library, and the East Wing of the National Gallery of Art.

The 1950s, an age of cultural expansion on a level the country had not seen before, was marked by aesthetic turmoil. Just as Americans were beginning to accept modern abstraction, Robert Rauschenberg and Jasper Johns appeared, challenging the abstract expressionists; John Cage's four minutes of silence shattered notions of what music was or could be; Allen Ginsberg and the other Beat poets stunned audiences with their raunchy, rebellious readings. In architecture, the free-flowing sculptural forms of Candela, Nervi, and Le Corbusier turned upside down the lucid rationalism of an earlier phase of modernism, questioning Mies just as his work was finally beginning to take hold. Professionals were as unsure as anybody of what direction art was taking or should take, insecure in their own tastes. As a Truman appointee to the National Commission of Fine Arts as well as dean of MIT's school of architecture and planning and one of the Institute's key advisors in the arts, Belluschi was perceived as an authority, someone whose artistic judgment by virtue of his position was beyond reproach.

Remarkably aware of what was going on, not just in architectural affairs on both local and national levels but also in larger societal and political matters, he was valued as a reliable source of information—on who was doing what, who might be appropriate for a job, how likely it might be that they would be interested and able to come. When asked whom he would advise as architect for a certain job, or whom he would recommend for dean or department chair, he usually responded with a list of anywhere from five to fifteen names, with specific comments on their personalities and particular skills, or personal impressions of their work. He was, for example, one of three advisors to the Secretary of the Air Force on Skidmore, Owings & Merrill's controversial project for the Air Force Academy's chapel in Colorado Springs. The proposal, designed by Walter Netsch, for a stark aluminum and glass structure in the foothills of the Rocky Mountains created an uproar when it was unveiled, and resulted in the House of Representatives' refusing to appropriate funds for construction. In Appropriations Committee hearings, the "famed architect" Frank Lloyd Wright (who coveted the job) referred to the SOM proposal as "yet another factory," and called it "a violation of nature, . . . not American in conception, and unworthy of the tradition of this nation."[15] Belluschi successfully defended the SOM project as a fine example of contemporary architecture, on the grounds that it served as a symbol of technical achievement in deliberate contrast to the natural beauty of the place. He subsequently served as design consultant on the project, reviewing Netsch's work on behalf of the client.[16]

Modernism in the 1950s: Shifts in Critical Fashion

In 1948 the Museum of Modern Art symposium "What Is Happening to Modern Architecture" focused on the question of what direction modern architecture was going to take now that the battle against historicism had been won. The issue had been raised by Lewis Mumford in his October 1947 "Skyline" column in the *New Yorker,* where he indicated the need for a richer, broader, more flexible idiom than the mechanical and impersonal functionalism of the International Style. Much as this charge "must hit hardest those academic American modernists who imitated Le Corbusier and Mies van der Rohe and Gropius, as their fathers imitated the reigning lights of the Ecole des Beaux-Arts," the West, Mumford said, was where one should look for direction, and "for the continuing spread, to every part of the country, of that native and humane form of modernism one might call the Bay Region style," which was a far more "truly universal style than the so-called international style of the 1930s, since it permits regional adaptations and modifications."[17]

This was of course the indigenous modernism—humanistic, regional, and basically styleless—that Belluschi had embraced in his Portland years and articulated so clearly in his Reed College address in 1950. He restated his ideas in a series of talks for East Coast audiences soon after his arrival, notably at the Middle Atlantic Regional AIA Conference in June 1951:

> By the forms which are derived from our own needs and devices we shall be known to posterity, and it is by such standard that we should try to judge contemporary architecture, not merely by the externals, the fashionable cliches and the package embellishments which have become the labels of modernism. It is not so much the flat roof or the sloping roof, the vertical spandrels or horizontal ones, the plastic domes or the two-story glass windows, nor even the brilliant tour-de-force that make a building truly modern, but its sense of creative inevitability in respect to its purpose, its surroundings and its people.

Exercises in external form, he said, should be neither denied nor glorified, only recognized for what they are: words, not ideas, the form, not the content of modern architecture. Finally, man must be the measure. Just like politicians, architects must listen, understand, sympathize. They must learn to interpret and lead, not impose.[18]

Participants in the 1948 MoMA symposium, however, failed to come to agreement on the direction of modern architecture, and instead got sidetracked in a discussion of style.

WURSTER AND BELLUSCHI, LACKING
ESTHETIC AND STRUCTURAL DIS-
CIPLINES, PLY THEIR HANDICRAFT
WITH UNCHECKED EMOTIONALISM

Wurster and Belluschi cavorting (cartoon, Architectural Forum, *1953).*

As progressive architects in the 1950s rejected the cold, mechanical, dehumanizing work of early modernism, they continued to splinter off in a number of different directions. In the ensuing "battle of the styles," a squabble in which Belluschi frankly had little interest, two major contestants were identified, the International Style revolutionaries, or European modernists, and the regionalists. The polarity was reinforced by Bruno Zevi's *Towards an Organic Architecture,* published in 1950 as a response to Le Corbusier's *Towards a New Architecture* of 1927, where he drew a distinction between "inorganic" and "organic" architects. The first were characterized as mechanistic, geometrical, contemptuous of nature, ruled by systems and laws rather than intuition; the second, of which Frank Lloyd Wright was the most renowned example, as exhibiting closer contact with nature, multiplicity of form, intuition in design, with dynamic forms freed from the tyranny of geometry: Arp versus Mondrian, Aalto versus Mies.[19]

Critic Frederick Gutheim cemented the dichotomy in his review of Talbot Hamlin's *Forms and Functions of Twentieth Century Architecture* in the *Architectural Forum* of June 1952. Seeing two separate architectural philosophies "struggling against and complementing each other," he saw the split as stemming from the 1932 MoMA exhibition in which Hitchcock and Johnson described modern architecture solely in terms of the International Style, a rigid, doctrinaire approach completely excluding Wright and other "romantic individualists" who also worked in the modern tradition. Defining modernism wholly formalistically, and basing it on the work of Europeans such as Mies, Gropius, and Le Corbusier, dismissing too the social and ethical thought supporting it, their definition ignored architects like Aalto, Dudok, Mendelsohn, Eliel Saarinen, as well as the group of American modernists on the West Coast—Maybeck and Greene & Greene earlier in the century and their heirs in the 1930s and 1940s such as Wurster, Vernon DeMars, and Harwell Hamilton Harris.[20] Gutheim saw Belluschi as fitting neither category. Though he was part of that West Coast tradition, Gutheim, basing his comments primarily on visual characteristics, saw him as too classical.

Fanned by the press, the debate flared into a major battle. In May 1953, the *Forum* launched a series of articles aimed at stimulating discussion of current design trends. In one of the first, Eero Saarinen, fine-tuning the stylistic codification, identified six major branches of modern architecture. He distinguished the group represented by Belluschi and Wurster, with their reverence for nature, use of natural materials, open plan, and emphasis on handcrafted architecture, from Wright and the organic group. Characterizing Belluschi and Wurster as representative of "a strong group of individuals that search for their own form in architecture by a particular responsiveness to the problem imposed by local or regional conditions and traditions," he saw them as architects with "ears close to the ground, humanistic in approach," with a "tendency toward unchecked emotionalism, which because of its lack of artistic and structural disciplines, has little future for architecture." On the other hand, he added, tellingly, there is an invaluable lasting quality to their work. Opposed to these "humanists" were the functionalists, Le Corbusier, Gropius, and Mies, followers of the International Style.[21]

The second article in the series, "After the International Style, Then What?," ironically bearing the same title as the article by Hugh Morrison several decades earlier, was by the young, thoughtful architect Robert Woods Kennedy. Arguing that the International Style had become as academic and outdated as revivalistic architecture, he saw other, more humanistic interpretations of modernism, such as that of the Bay Area regionalists, as superseding it. A similar effort to counter the mechanistic aspect and indifference to place of the International Style with a more particularized, humanistic approach could be seen in the British "new empiricists," whose work was regional rather than universal in character, emphasized anonymity rather than highly visible personalities, and eschewed theory and dogma in favor of experiment and experience—in short, "common-sensical, anti-rule, anti-style, anti-dogmatic, and careless of technique." Rooted in the present, a time between past and future, as well as in place, respectful of tradition as well as responsive to the environment, it was a direction Kennedy strongly endorsed.[22]

As the lines between camps hardened, resentment built up. In an article titled "The Threat to the Next America," Elizabeth Gordon, editor of *House Beautiful,* furiously took to task "*some* museums, *some* professional magazines, *some* architectural schools, and *some* designers" for hammering home the idea that "less is more." This definition of modern design, promoting universality, a stripped-down emptiness, a lack of storage space, therefore lack of possessions, is contrary to common sense, and, bluntly, bad. The International Style designers, she said, represented but one branch of modern, and one wholly divorced from American roots. Far healthier, she maintained, was a more indigenous branch of modernism, a "home-grown variety of modern design [that] has developed slowly and steadily along sound functional lines for well over sixty years and is in a remarkably healthy and progressive stage. This healthy, rational branch of modern is skillful enough to produce buildings that have both beauty and performance, without sacrificing either." Citing John Yeon's work as an example, she defined a different set of criteria of good architecture: does it work, will it stand up to time, does it look good?[23]

Certain museum directors, editors, and academics aside, members of the architectural profession an large were in concert with this view. The *Architectural Record,* by then perhaps the most sympathetic to regionalist concerns of the three major architectural magazines, devoted its April 1953 issue to the Pacific Northwest. This coincided with the national AIA annual convention in Seattle, which had regionalism as its major theme. Belluschi was the keynote speaker.

Immune as he had been on the West Coast to the fashionable whims of the eastern establishment—the powerful East Coast academic and publishing forces that Belluschi and his western cohorts called "the Mafia"—having moved east Belluschi was more than ever aware of the volatility of stylistic trends and the behind-the-scenes forces that drove them. In his address to the AIA in Seattle, Belluschi focused on principles rather than formal characteristics; his title, "The Spirit of the New Architecture," evoked Le Corbusier and the early theoretical stages of modernism before its stylistic features were codified. Deemphasizing form, he deliberately shunned the word "modern" as too suggestive of a stylistic label, and refused to show slides or describe new trends to avoid "the fashionable externals which may have caught the eyes, fancy, or indignation of our magazines." His focus instead was on the far more elusive, difficult problem of modern architecture's fundamental aims. As architects in the 1950s, increasingly mesmerized by hero worship, reacted against the barebones functionalism of an earlier phase of modernism and reverted to the old Beaux-Arts conception of architecture as a fine art, Belluschi reminded them that architecture was not a pure art but had practical obligations, however rapidly they were changing, that had to be met. Recognizing that one aspect of modern architecture was "the striving of a few great artist-architects" to create what he called "new aesthetic symbols" for the age, Belluschi acknowledged the importance of their work: society "needs men who can help bring about new and deeper understanding, who can help restore the relationship between form and matter in the spirit of poetry which needs continually a new language to express itself." But architecture could not ignore the realities of life, for not only "would it soon become decadent for lack of nourishment which its roots must have from life, but it would also leave a large void in the everyday physical environment of human society which is itself built of earthy motives and necessarily moves with earthy boundaries." Sketching a spectrum from buildings of necessity, such as basic shelter, to architecture of pure form, Belluschi said there must be a middle ground that is more than merely utilitarian and less than the poetry of pure form but, like it, artistic, satisfying both the needs of common sense and the pleasures of the eye.[24]

Belluschi's address, excerpted in the August 1953 *Architectural Record* and reprinted in its entirety the following October, was granted an AIA Award for best article of the year in the professional press, the first time such an award was granted.

Peaking in 1953, interest in regionalism faded over the course of the next several years. The reasons for this are complex, having, so the evidence suggests, more to do with the particular concerns of certain academics, key figures at MoMA, and the press than with an inherent shift in architectural values. Hitchcock, for one, was aware of alternatives to the inexorable dominance of the Miesian aesthetic. In an article in the August 1951 *Record,* he pointed out that modernism was more than the International Style he had done so much to launch in 1932. There were other architects, most notably Wright, who deliberately opposed the International Style but nonetheless belonged to the modern movement as much as Le Corbusier or Gropius.[25] Bay Area architect Jack Hillmer, in response to an article in the *Forum* predicting Gropius and Mies as the dominant influences in architecture of the next fifty years, spoke for many in suggesting that that seemed like a self-fulfilling prophecy. Architecture did not *have* to take that direction, and while noting that not all of Wright's designs merited emulation, Hillmer held that his basic philosophy still offered a worthy alternative. Noting too the great influence Breuer, Gropius, and Mies had had in the East Coast, he pointed out that while there was considerable objective appeal to their work, "the minute the human being is connected with it physically, he immediately seems and feels out of place."[26]

Sigfried Giedion, too, before his move to Harvard, was sympathetic. In 1954, just before his left MIT to join the faculty at Harvard, then the bastion of the Bauhaus system in the United States, Giedion published an article in which he urged architects to move beyond the International Style to a "New Regionalist Approach," which he saw as a hybrid of Western civilization and that of the Far East. The rationalistic, materialistic attitude had prove barren, he pointed out, and increasingly those in Western countries were becoming intrigued by the spiritual outlook of the Far East. That this coincided with the growing interest in Japanese architecture in the 1950s is significant, but more so, in this context, is Giedion's interest in regional variants of modernism, which he saw then as a promising trend.[27]

But by the middle of the decade, interest in regionalism, at least in East Coast academia, had all but petered out. Reflecting perhaps the broader concerns of the profession, editors of the *Architectural Record* asked Belluschi to write a feature article on it for the December 1955 issue. It was an essay of major importance, and not only in defining a design approach that, though it was rapidly losing support in academia, was still respected by the profession at large. It also indicated the direction Belluschi's work with the U.S. State Department was beginning to go in the design of United States embassies abroad.

Long, richly textured, and subtly argued, the essay is not easily summarized. Acknowledging that regionalism was currently thought of as naive and soft-headed, and that it ran counter to current trends, Belluschi warned that it was a direction architects pursued "only at their own risk." Rising above stylistic disputes and avoiding mention of formal characteristics, he focused on the larger issue: the need for a flexible response to a specific architectural problem within its particular cultural setting. He illustrated his point by describing his advisory work for the Foreign Buildings Operation sponsored by the U.S. State Department. How should the architect, using the modern materials and structural systems that make economic sense today, and with all the comforts and conveniences of modern life, design buildings in places such as New Delhi, Oslo, or Guinea, which have very different climates, terrains, building traditions, and cultural mores? How avoid the "drab, standardized, straight, no-nonsense architecture being built with appalling sameness from Bagdad to Rovaniemi," the modern, industrial-looking buildings that had provoked trenchant criticism from Congress and the public and led to the formation of the architectural advisory board in the first place? By what criteria does one assess the quality of a modern building in a regional context; what aspects or characteristics should one address?

The issue went far beyond the obvious formal relationship of the building to the land, but embraced "all that man is and believes in, as a creature of his environment." Mores, values, tastes, and traditions as well as climatic and geographical terrain, all mattered. Noting that typically buildings in the past were part of a vernacular, produced not "by a few intellectuals, but by the spontaneous and continuing activity of a whole people with a common heritage, acting under a community of experience," Belluschi admitted there was no going back to that simpler age. The dilemma was real: the State Department opposed Edward Durell Stone's design for the New Delhi embassy because it did not look sufficiently "Indian." Could, Belluschi asked, an "Indian" architecture be defined, and if so should America build its embassy in such a style? Should it also do so for all other countries where new buildings were to be erected? How would one go about measuring the regional content of architecture?

The issues were challenging, not just for work in the Foreign Buildings Operation but for contemporary architectural thought. Modern man with all his science and technology, his supremely rationalized, "efficient," and standardized building forms, had lost touch with basic human nature. Focused on economic rather than social values, formal rather than functional concerns, on being original rather than good, the modern architect was unable to relate in a human way to the needs and desires of those he designed for: architects knew much, but felt little. Architectural forms not born of the particular demands of the job, the human conditions as well as the physical setting, but derived from or determined by preconceived aesthetic theory alone, ran the risk of becoming artificial, tricky, or merely fashionable.

While respecting local customs and terrain, the architect could not, however, turn his back on modern building technology. The modern skyscraper, regardless of where it is, cannot be built by the same techniques of those of a house. While one might question the appropriateness of using vast amounts of glass in projects such as SOM's Air Force Academy buildings in the Rocky Mountains, "the juxtaposition of crisp, clean, business-like structures on a mountain landscape can be justified by sound esthetics—but more so by the strictly disciplined around-the-clock life which cadets must live while being trained in modern warfare." Answers were not simple, and the architect should expect to be challenged. The best he could do was to think the problem through carefully, and in the face of conflicting demands propose what seemed the most appropriate solution.

> An architect's creative powers need not act in a vacuum; they are nourished by the world he lives in, by the people he knows and with whom he must deal, by the things he sees and the things he has learned, and also by old symbols and forms. Thus the greater his understanding the greater scope will his creative powers have, and within such sphere his contributions will have lasting significance. Believing this, we should not attempt to formulate a rigid intellectual program for architecture. We must accept the enormous variety of situations which our age has created and try to find solace in the thought that nature has evolved the weed and the orchid, the whale and the mouse, the eagle and the hummingbird, from a wonderfully complex but orderly set of things.

> We may find reasons to hope for an improved set of social values for mankind, but our creative struggle will never come to an end because the human mind, which reflects and recreates, feeds what it touches and in turn is nourished by what it sees, will always make architecture a dynamic, expressive force which should be allowed to grow, to flourish, even to decay when need be. As an art it will strive for roots and continuity but will not deny to the man of genius the right to innovate if that is his moment and if his voice rings true.

Where a situation calls for it, Belluschi continued, a regionalist solution "can still be obtained by thoughtful self-imposed discipline, by a submission to certain traditional ways, by a humility of approach, and in rejecting show and change and experiment except for a good cause. But Regionalism at its best cannot be measured or imposed, is not a school of thought but simply a recognition within its own sphere of what architecture is to human beings, a deep regard for their emotional demands. This need not be forfeited even in the most practical demands of a project." Belluschi ended with the plea not to retreat to the safety of the past, but to embrace the future with all its challenges, facing "creatively as free spirits and in deep honesty the complexities of our modern world, never forgetting that man is the measure of all values."[28]

Acknowledged a second time for his contribution, Belluschi received the annual prize in architectural journalism for the best article published that year in the professional architectural press.

By 1958, it was clear, however, that despite resistance from large segments of the profession, the International Style with its universality and Miesian aesthetic of technological determinism had become the dominant tradition in American architecture. The completion of Mies's Seagram Building, preceded by SOM's Lever House across Park Avenue, lent impetus to the trend, resulting in a wave of sleek, glass and metal tall office buildings in cities throughout the world. Equally significant, on another level, was the changing of the guard at Harvard. Joseph Hudnut, as new dean at Harvard in 1935 and an early adherent of the International Style, had initially tried to hire Le Corbusier; when he refused, Hudnut turned to Gropius, bringing him in in 1937.[29] Over the course of the years, influenced perhaps by William Wurster at MIT who in turn had brought in the Finn Alvar Aalto, Hudnut's thinking broadened, and by the early 1950s Hudnut leaned toward a more humanistic, less rigorously technocratic architecture. His retirement in June 1953 just as interest in the regionalist tradition peaked, to be replaced by Sert, then president of the Congrès Internationaux d'Architecture Moderne, opened doors to a sweeping change in the Harvard faculty. Signs posted by students labeling the architecture school the "Graduate School of Bauhaus" and "Congrès International d'Admiration Mutuelle" said it all. Sert brought with him others of such a pronounced International Style persuasion that many of the less doctrinaire faculty members, among them Charles Burchard, Hugh Stubbins, and Jean-Paul Carlhian, resigned.[30]

Whatever the causes, the lack of interest on the part of those in power led not only to the demise of regionalism but to its virtual eclipse from histories of modernism in the United States. With these now typically construed in almost exclusively European modernist terms, a tradition was lost that many felt modernism could or should have had.[31]

The Modern Architect: Artistic Genius versus Social Architect

The role of the architect in modern society was another issue about which Belluschi felt strongly. He saw the architect as a professional in the service of a client; the art of architecture was not pure, but had practical restrictions. On the other hand, the architect was also an artist, trained in the art of visual and spatial relationships; unless he gave his buildings meaningful form and order, he would fail society's expectations.[32] The true architect, Belluschi felt, had greater affinity with the philosopher and poet than with the scientist; the latter had led society "toward a barren civilization where machines had become its idols and progress was measured in statistics." The arts balanced that, providing "the key to unlock the meaning of life, explain its unity and continuity." Art was the only medium, he felt, that could bind mankind through the generations and across barriers of language.[33]

The nature of the architect in modern society—artist, practical businessman, or social servant—was much debated throughout the decade. A symposium held at the Boston Institute of Contemporary Art in February 1952, with Gropius as the keynote speaker, was typical. Architecture was an art, Gropius asserted, but created by a team rather than an individual, a communal endeavor with social expression as its goal. Challenging members of the profession, Gropius demanded that the architect climb off his pedestal and get involved again in the actual process of building. Modern building depended on team production, with architect, engineer, scientist, and builder designing and producing together in a wholly collective endeavor. Belluschi agreed, but with telling qualifications. Teamwork was essential, but unlike Gropius who saw it as truly collaborative, with all members equal, individual players anonymous, and the decision-making process clearly a joint affair, Belluschi believed the architect should remain the leader, maestro of the whole show.

Agreeing with Gropius that creating novel forms was less important than producing good ones, and that students should be allowed to follow historical precedents once these were thoroughly absorbed and digested, Belluschi disagreed with him on the unity of design and production. The architect and builder could not be one and the same. Living in an industrial age of specialized skills and a division of labor, and given the rapidly changing building technology in the postwar years, especially on large, complex building projects (something Belluschi had had considerable experience with, as Gropius had not), the modern architect had to learn to work together with others equipped with skills he lacked, respectful of their differences. He had to understand construction techniques but could not be expected to have mastered them himself.

In Belluschi's view, the architect was like the conductor of a symphony who brought to the performance his own skills in pulling together the talents of others; as no one expected the conductor to be able to perform the role of each of his orchestra members, neither could one expect that of the architect. "No matter by what name we call the man who coordinates and guides the team, he will be the man who not only has the ability to understand the problem which faces him but also shares with others the task of solving it. He is the man who has the intuitive powers of synthesis which from time immemorial we have called the architect and who may now well be called the coordinator or the engineer-architect, or simply the best man on the team."[34]

The issue took a somewhat different turn in a symposium at Yale in 1953, later published in *Perspecta.* One of a series of "Studio Discussions" for the benefit of students, it focused on the architect, his education, practice, and responsibilities; panelists were Philip Johnson, Louis Kahn, Belluschi, Yale architectural historian Vincent Scully, and Paul Weiss, professor of philosophy at Yale. The debate between Johnson and Belluschi proved to be the liveliest part of the session. Johnson opened by stating that "architecture was an art primarily and hardly anything else." Belluschi immediately countered with a more pragmatic view. The architect, he maintained, had the task of processing the everyday material of life into superior aesthetic form. One could not simply take an abstract form and make a building of it because he thought it looked good. "The moment you do this you defeat the very idea of architecture, which is an attempt to give spiritual content to the very elements which are part of the fabric of our life." Architecture is not sculpture, and is more than visual form. "Architecture is space and form serving a social purpose beyond aesthetic satisfaction. Architecture is not a pure art, it is a social art. It has a great many restrictions and obligations, the first of which is to extract beauty from the very sources of our actions; it must attempt to process confusion into order."

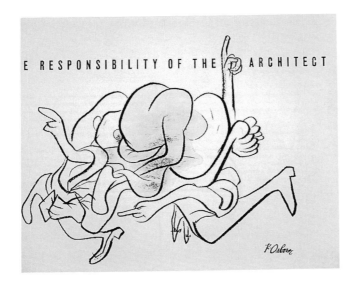

Philip Johnson and Belluschi debate
*(*Perspecta *no. 2, 1953).*

Wright's Johnson Wax Research Tower was not an example of good architecture, Belluschi contended. It was uncomfortable, inefficient, and filled with glare. "As an architect, Wright's not very good; as a sculptor, he's wonderful. But look what would happen if all egotistical architects without [Wright's] genius had their way in our cities." He shuddered at the thought of Wright's conceiving the form of the Johnson Wax laboratory long before he had a client. "Do you realize what the indirect results of that idea are? The Chrysler Buildings, the Grand Central Buildings, and finally the jukeboxes! You cannot start from the outside with an arbitrary form." Standing by his modernist principles, Belluschi insisted that form must rather follow function.

> There should be complete understanding of all the limitations of the problem and from that, with a great deal of discipline, the form will emerge, the result of both the maturity of the creative processes which will come from it and the choice of an infinite number of little things that you may or may not do in order to give aesthetic significance to that form. The best way to be original for most of us is to really follow that process of thoroughly understanding what the purpose is, not only functionally, but also psychologically, and of imparting to the work that feeling of suspense that is really part of the creative process. The real test of a great piece of architecture is one that gives satisfaction to the mind as well as the senses. It is great if it carries conviction.

Discipline was required to understand all the complex factors, Belluschi said, but it was not discipline as Mies conceived it. Mies saw discipline as years of rigorous training, after which the architect was free to let his imagination soar. Belluschi saw discipline as unending: an ongoing, open-ended, essential part of every new architectural task.[35]

The Johnson/Belluschi polarity was extended the following fall in an AIA debate on the role of the client. Johnson, by then director of the MoMA Department of Architecture and Design, answered the keynote question, Should the architect subordinate his art to the wishes of the client?, with a vehement No! Throwing out a typically flamboyant claim, Johnson persisted, "Too many times an architect takes the attitude that his client can call the tune because he's paying the piper. Often the client gets in the way of an architect's creative ability. . . . An architect's first duty is to his art." Belluschi, rising to the bait, argued the opposite. The architect's primary obligation, regardless of the job, was always to the client.[36]

The fifties was a glorious decade for architects, as the postwar building boom continued and their prestige grew in the eyes of the public. It was also an age of cultural expansion marked by a growing appreciation of the role of the fine arts in ordinary life. Throughout the 1950s, as MIT's cultural ambassador, Belluschi had been a strong advocate of the arts, proselytizing for their civilizing role in modern society. Toward the end of the decade, as worship of the heroic star architect, heightened by the mass media grew, Belluschi acknowledged the importance of the few truly creative geniuses, but continued to warn of the dangers of idolatry and of the purely formalist approach. In his introduction to the exhibition "Form-Givers at Mid-Century," sponsored by the American Federation of Arts in 1959, he wrote of their contribution in the arduous search for truth and struggle to give it form. "But truth is enormously complex and elusive; it is more than function or structure or emotional fulfillment. It is all of them, plus the imaginative spark of artistic conception. Architecture is many things, but above all it is an Art, and only as such will it produce significant forms. Modern forms are born through the experience of our own time—a fleeting moment in human history, a coming together, so to speak, of certain elements to form a crystal." But the mere invention of forms, he said, cannot be the whole of architecture. Even as art, architecture must satisfy many restrictive conditions. Above all, it must submit to an underlying discipline of logic and order; arbitrary or merely fashionable forms only add to the visual chaos already engulfing us.

> *Architecture is a complex of Art and Science. To flower in our modern climate, it needs many minds and many talents working together. In our day, the artist-architect is learning to accept technology as a great liberating tool to enhance and enrich rather than to demean man's way of life; he recognizes the importance of Man as a measure and inspiration for his Form-Giving. He realizes that even as our society is undergoing enormous changes, particularly in the enlarged scale of space and time within which mankind must operate, he never forgets that the individual remains physiologically unchanged, that his basic emotions cannot be denied, that love of color and texture and play of light have a real meaning to him, and that merely intellectual rationalizations will not satisfy him for long. We may feel that ornamentation and richness of space may again return as a part of man's long heritage. The architect is in effect the humanizer of society, the artist with the will to make the earth a fitting place to live.* [37]

Belluschi defended the capricious forms of Le Corbusier and Wright as the work of exceptional geniuses. Wright ignored societal needs, but he served as a catalyst for other lesser talents, giving an idea of the "great potentialities of architecture as an art form." "Wright's death has stung us," Belluschi wrote elsewhere, "because his vitality appeared to have no bounds. With all his irritating ways, irritating perhaps because of our own unconfessed guilt, he stood as the most precious of all symbols: that of independence of thought and action in an age of conformity." An arrogant genius always contriving for effect, Wright was "undisciplined, shallow at times, blatant, lacking in serenity, poise or maturity, the very symbol of all that is weak yet great in a man. A genius indeed, a mirror of our own humanity, a beacon to guide us perhaps, but not a light to enlighten our darkness."[38]

Foreign Buildings Operation

In January 1954, Belluschi became involved in what proved to be one of the most significant experiences of his career.[39] In the wake of World War II, the American building industry figured prominently in the United States' emerging role in foreign affairs. As its sense of responsibility to its allies expanded, new towns, dams, power plants, highways, hospitals, and housing as well as new military bases were built throughout the world with the help of American engineers and contractors. Part of the effort was aimed at accelerating the industrialization and democratization of developing countries, thus making them less vulnerable to communism. But another goal was purely diplomatic, a public relations task aimed at creating good will abroad and projecting an American presence prominently and positively as a major new world power. Other nations of the free world had accepted U.S. partnership in international economics and politics; culturally, however, Americans were still regarded as backward. As scores of new embassies, consulates, libraries, and other federal buildings were built throughout the world, American architects were thus asked to play a key role in presenting a new, progressive image of the nation, one symbolic of its new cultural as well as economic and political leadership. The U.S. was also rich in talent, having garnered most of the leading architects in the world as refugees during the 1930s and 1940s; this, too, it wanted demonstrated.[40] In 1953, the Foreign Buildings Operation, set up by the State Department to oversee the design and construction of all federal buildings abroad, underwent a major reorganization. Leland W. King, its former chief, had been a strong proponent of the International Style, which he saw as a more powerful expression of the growing strength and vitality of the U.S. as a world power than traditional, imported, and mainly classical styles. Under his forceful direction, the agency had granted commissions to some of the leading young architects of the time, among them Eero Saarinen, Harrison and Abramovitz, and SOM. The program had recently come under attack from all sides, including the U.S. Congress. Members of a House appropriations subcommittee objected to the use of the International Style, seeing, in the growing climate of the Cold War, the European-derived, technologically driven modernism as anti-American.[41] There were also veiled complaints from members of the architectural profession that a lion's share of the prestigious commissions appeared to be going to a favorite few;[42] particularly egregious in this respect was Gordon Bunshaft of SOM receiving seven new consulates as well as all the information centers and embassy housing in West Germany, especially since it appeared as if they were all to be built according to the same (uninspired, in the eyes of design professionals) Mies-derived steel and glass formula.[43] Most alarming to the State Department were the "peppery" letters from critics abroad, condemning the new modern buildings as out of character with local traditions and insensitively flaunting U.S. affluence and prestige.[44]

At issue here was the question of what an American embassy should look like, what image or character it should project abroad. The situation was complicated by the stylistic chaos within the profession itself and the uncertainty about what modernism was and what direction it should take. As Philip Johnson bluntly put it in a discussion on modernism in 1954 at Yale, no one knew what was coming next. Given the diversity of current directions, from Eero Saarinen's expressionistic thin-shell concrete domes to Louis Kahn's rough-cast, brutalist work at Yale, Johnson concluded, "Each of us likes his own kind of romanticism and disapproves of the other fellow's." Meanwhile, Bunshaft wondered what was wrong with sticking to plain steel and glass buildings.[45]

King was replaced in 1953, evidently because of his relying on the advice of one "strongly opinionated designer" and running the office as a one-man show.[46] But his policy of hiring only the "best and the brightest," effectively establishing a level of high-quality modern architecture as the norm for embassy buildings abroad, was continued after he left. To fend off further criticism, an architectural advisory committee was proposed, with the specific goal of depoliticizing the selection process. The AIA was asked to recommend panelists in the interest of obtaining a more open, balanced selection process.[47]

A five-member advisory board was set up (three architects, staff member, and veteran diplomat), with former AIA president Ralph Walker, Henry Shepley of the Boston firm of Shepley Bulfinch Richardson and Abbott, and Pietro Belluschi appointed as participating architects. Walker at age 64 and Shepley at 66 were both of an older generation, and considered conservative in their thinking; Belluschi was 54 and represented a more progressive perspective. How, why, or by whom Belluschi was suggested is not clear, but it appears that he was brought in specifically because of his lack of allegiance to the International Style and known openness to other modernist approaches.

At the close of their first meeting, Belluschi was asked to summarize the discussion in a general policy statement that would set the direction of the committee in its future work.[48] Endorsing King's policy of seeking the best talent available on the assumption that it would provide the best work, and basing their statement on the State Department's architectural policy they had been provided, which stated the need for facilities "in an architectural form representative of the United States expressing such qualities as dignity, strength, and neighborly sympathy," of high-quality design, appropriate to the site and country, economic in construction, and using American materials if appropriate,[49] Belluschi outlined the criteria they had agreed to use in the selection process.

> To the sensitive and imaginative designer, [the FBO commission] will be an invitation to give serious study to local conditions of climate and site, to understand and sympathize with local customs and people, and to grasp the historical meaning of the particular environment in which the new building must be set. He will do so with a free mind without being dictated by obsolete or sterile formulae or cliches, be they old or new; he will avoid being either bizarre or fashionable, yet he will not fear using new techniques or new materials should these constitute real advances in architectural thinking.

> It is hoped that the selected architects will think of style not in its narrower meaning but as a quality to be imparted to the building, a quality reflecting deep understanding of conditions and people. His directness and freshness of approach will thus have a distinguishable American flavor.

> If the above philosophy is adhered to, we need not fear criticism; on the other hand, if we act timidly, solely in the hope of avoiding any and all criticism from whatever quarters, we shall surely end up in dull compromises with the result that we shall have nothing but undistinguished buildings to represent us abroad. We would thereby have forfeited our opportunity to display the high American cultural achievements in the field of architecture generally recognized by architects of the more advanced nations of the world.[50]

In short, Belluschi's statement asked architects to design projects that would represent America abroad, but that were also responsive to the particular climate and site and reflected an understanding of local culture. It was a flexible, nonstylistic approach open to the use of whatever forms were most appropriate for the particular job. Simple, clear, direct, it became the cornerstone of FBO policy.

The program was widely recognized as remarkably successful, largely due to the existence of the nonpartisan architectural advisory panel, whose judgment, at least initially, was rigorously respected.[51] To ensure fresh blood in the process, members of the advisory committee, according to Belluschi at his suggestion, were rotated every two years.[52]

With architects freed from dogmatic restraints and their creativity stimulated by the challenges of adjusting to a foreign culture, the FBO's new policy resulted in an era of major architectural achievements by some of the most progressive architects in the country, among them Eero Saarinen, José Luis Sert, Walter Gropius, William Wurster, Harry Weese, Hugh Stubbins, Carl Koch, Antonin Raymond, Yamasaki, Richard Neutra, and Louis Kahn. Its success was felt around the world for years. In 1957 the New York Architectural League, in conjunction with the New York chapter of the AIA, *Architectural Forum,* and *Life* magazine, celebrated its success with a major exhibition of embassy and consulate buildings, in the hopes of galvanizing similar successes on the local level.[53] Elsewhere, as in a 1958 *Forum* article, the demand was voiced for similar guidelines for U.S. government buildings at home. Others saw still larger implications of the policy, with the spate of new buildings serving as a catalyst for a whole new direction in American architecture.[54]

The decision to involve design professionals in the decision-making process, which predated Belluschi, was the major breakthrough. To what extent the guidelines he drew up represented the results of their collective thinking, and would have been established, if less simply and eloquently, without him, is difficult to say. But the age and conservatism of the other members of the advisory committee suggest that his role was crucial. After stepping down in 1957, he remained in contact with the agency; in 1966, he himself received an FBO commission to convert the Rothschild mansion in Paris for use as an embassy residence.[55] Later, when William Slayton, former director of the Federal Urban Renewal Program and an old friend and admirer of Belluschi's, assumed directorship of the FBO in 1979 after a long fallow period, he revived many of Belluschi's open, fair, regionally based policies, and brought him in as a consultant.[56] It was in this capacity that Belluschi played a crucial role in the design of the Lisbon embassy in Portugal, which had stalled; as a result of his last-minute advice, architect Fred Bassetti changed his design to a low rather than high-rise structure, better suited to the hilly site.[57]

Pietro Belluschi, Design Consultant

In Portland, Belluschi had been a big frog in a small pond, with his own team of trained staff, knowledge of local labor conditions and available resources, and broad network of contacts in both the business and artistic communities. Boston operated on a wholly different scale. It also had different architectural traditions as well as climatic and cultural conditions. Having vowed never to run an office of his own again and wanting a practice that would not interfere with his academic obligations, Belluschi turned to associating with other firms in the capacity of design consultant. Though later a standard practice, it was then a pioneering role.

His function varied, from principal designer backed up by an associated firm, to advisor brought in primarily to act as a design critic. In each case, the degree of involvement differed. At his most fully involved, when the job was actually his, he would handle the initial negotiations with the client, establish the basic concept, then stop in to the architectural offices with which he was associated from time to time to monitor design development. His contribution in cases like these was typically confined to the initial design phase, tapering off as the job moved into production, then, if it was a project that particularly interested him, picking up toward the end with finishing touches.

In Portland, he had been revered as the leading designer in the city. In Boston, which was then the architectural capital of the country, with even MoMA in New York in effect being run from there,[58] he was measured against the likes of Saarinen and Stone, but also Le Corbusier, Gropius, and Mies. It forced him to come to grips with his own abilities as an architect. By his own admission, he was not a form-giver and defined himself in a more modest role. Relying more on his "critical sense of fitness, his sensuousness, and intuitive sense" than on his creative abilities, which, as he put it, were limited, he saw himself as one of the rank and file, those who produced "the great body of buildings forming our cities . . . , painstaking realists who by their day-to-day efforts, by their ability and willingness to be part of a team and to accept the realities of life . . . make their influence felt in the communal process of giving form to a healthier, happier and wiser society."[59] Unlike architects such as Mendelsohn or Aalto who were able to size up a situation, then sketch quickly and deftly a proposed solution, Belluschi's approach was slower, more methodical; only after studying a problem thoroughly, researching comparable situations, and rummaging around in his own vast repertoire of remembered forms, was he able to devise an appropriate solution. Typically, he would come up with several from which he would select one he felt was best. Then either he or one of his associates would develop it into workable form.

Although careful to cover his tracks, Belluschi had no qualms about using the forms of others. Not out to reinvent the wheel ("nothing new under the sun," he was quoted often as saying), as long as a solution worked, he would use it. He condemned only blind imitation, using stuff "second-hand" as he put it, without rethinking it, so that it was "not of the heart." Not disavowing the modernist aim of the new and original rather than existing form Belluschi simply redefined it in more realistic terms: architecture was a cumulative art, inevitably built upon forms inherited from the past. If an available form fit the structural and functional requirements, there was no need, nor had he it in him, to invent a new one.[60]

Churches

The fame of the Equitable Building notwithstanding, it was as a designer of churches that Belluschi was most sought after when he moved to the East. This perhaps had as much to do with historical circumstances as with Belluschi per se.

The country was in the midst of the greatest boom in church building in history, and only a limited number of architects who specialized in religious buildings were modernists. Though modernism had gradually spread throughout the past two decades and by this time was in wide use in other building types, churches because of their inherent ties with the past were slower to change. People wanted a church that looked like a church.

Belluschi's simple, unmistakably modern churches were then among the most highly acclaimed in the world. Of 18 churches granted awards for design excellence in 1956 by the Commission on Architecture of the National Council of Churches, four were by Belluschi.[61] Of the buildings built over the course of the AIA's century-long history, his Central Lutheran Church in Portland was one of the four acknowledged masterpieces in church design, sharing the distinction with Richardson's Trinity Church in Boston, Maybeck's First Church of Christ Scientist in Berkeley, and Wright's Unity Temple in Oak Park.[62] Architect-critic Peter Blake, writing on modern architecture in a 1958 *Forum,* illustrated his article with two churches: Le Corbusier's Ronchamp Chapel and Belluschi's Zion Lutheran. "Two civilizations, two kinds of modern architecture," Blake wrote of them. "Le Corbusier's Ronchamp in the Vosges Mountains of eastern France is plastic, curvilinear, white, stucco-finished—unmistakably Mediterranean in character. Belluschi's church in Oregon is angular, straight-lined, natural-finished—unmistakably the product of a wood-building, northern country. In its particular setting, each has validity, each is equally 'modern,' and each belongs to an equally ancient tradition."[63] Joseph Hudnut, in a *Forum* article on the church in a modern world, illustrated his essay with Le Corbusier's Ronchamp Chapel, Rudolf Schwarz's Church of St. Anna in Düren, Germany, and Belluschi's First Lutheran Church in Boston.[64] Feature articles on contemporary churches in the *Saturday Evening Post, New York Times Magazine, Life,* and *Time* made the Belluschi name virtually synonymous with modern church design.

"Pietro Belluschi knows how to build churches. Few architects do," wrote the *Record* in 1959.[65] After a decade of the greatest level of church building the nation had ever known, this evidently was still thought true.

Belluschi's first church in the East was Boston's First Lutheran. Commissioned in 1954, it was also the first church to be built in the Back Bay for over a generation. He had done

Lutheran churches before, but this presented a whole new set of challenges: a tightly congested corner site, in a historic neighborhood, a restricted budget, and, most daunting of all to Belluschi personally, located just across the Charles River from MIT, hence easily accessible to students and colleagues curious about the direction his work was taking.

Because the job was small and the site close, a double lot on the corner of Marlborough and Berkeley not far from his Fairfield Street townhouse, he decided to do it on his own, working out of his house with the assistance of George Wallace, a former member of the Portland office.[66] The budget of $269,000 seemed at first substantial, compared to those he had had in Portland, but as building costs on the East Coast were far higher than those in the West, and coping with the marshy subsoil of the Back Bay added an unexpected cost, it proved restrictive.

It was a difficult job: what was wanted was a distinctly modern building that would not be out of character with the mainly Victorian buildings of the Back Bay; after struggling for months to find an appropriate form, Belluschi finally turned to a scheme he meanwhile had worked out for a church for Portsmouth Abbey in Rhode Island. Belluschi had always been interested in exploring new structural systems. Here, he drew on some of the experiments being conducted at MIT in thin-shell concrete. The building consisted of an utterly simple, unfenestrated rectangular block of brick, with thin curved roof of concrete.

First Lutheran Church, Boston, 1955–1957, exterior (photo: author).

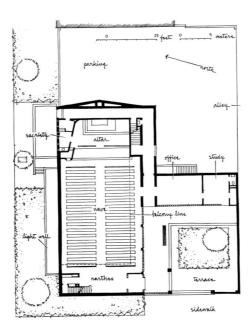

First Lutheran Church, plan.

Light was provided by a clerestory of transparent windows just under the overhanging eaves. The structure was of steel, with regular supports, buried for fireproofing in the non-load-bearing brick cavity walls, supporting a series of segmental arches over the nave which in turn carried the barrel-vaulted, thin-shell concrete roof. The plan was traditional: longitudinal with narthex at one end, apse at the other. The entrance, however, was off to the side. One entered through a vine-covered trellised gateway into a secluded landscaped courtyard occupying one portion of the lot, then to the narthex, then at right angles into the nave—a typical Belluschi progression of spaces. The building was completed in the fall of 1957, at the budgeted cost of $269,000, over twice the cost of the Central Lutheran Church in Eugene of two years earlier.[67]

Reactions to the church were mixed. Hudnut considered it a welcome relief from the historicism of the past and convincing testimony that traditional buildings like churches could be built using new technology and modern forms; others found it thin and insubstantial-looking; still others considered it stark.[68] Belluschi himself felt he had perhaps gone too far in the quest for simplicity. He also admitted that the thin, arched roof with eaves extending beyond the walls of the church to form an overhang for the window below "was an attempt to get away from the flat roof without going into a pitched one," evidence of his concern for style and the pressure he was feeling from the architectural community to keep up with current trends.[69] But his solution to the tight urban site, the secluded landscaped court providing a transitional zone between street and sanctuary, his use of ordinary materials and handling of details were vintage Belluschi, endowing the building with his characteristic quiet distinction.

For the Portsmouth Abbey church, he turned to a different design tradition. He had been asked to design a new church and monastery for the Benedictine campus, a private

First Lutheran Church, interior (photo:
Joseph Molitor).

Portsmouth Abbey, Portsmouth, Rhode Island, aerial view, circa 1950 (photo: Hopf).

boys' school in a rural setting at the south end of Portsmouth in Rhode Island, in 1952, shortly after he arrived in Boston.[70] Since its founding in 1912, the school had accumulated a hodgepodge of buildings, including several modern structures in the 1940s by the Boston firm Anderson, Beckwith & Haible. Lawrence Anderson, then a young assistant professor at MIT, had drawn up a campus master plan that included plans for the new monastery and church. Questions had been raised, however, about the appropriateness of his stark, European-inspired modernism in Portsmouth's rural setting, and when Belluschi arrived, offering an approach clearly modern but without the austerity of the "Bauhaus" work, the Portsmouth fathers decided to go with him.[71] Knowing that AB&H was familiar with the campus and to ease potential bad feelings with Anderson, one of his colleagues at MIT, Belluschi asked to associate with them.

His initial proposal, a simple rectangular structure of fieldstone capped by a shallow-arched thin-slab concrete roof with flared overhanging eaves and cupola and spire over the choir end, was of keen interest to the architectural community and published in the *Architectural Record* of 1954.[72] The Portsmouth fathers, however, felt the church needed more presence and should be taller so that it clearly dominated the complex as a whole; Benedictines were also at the forefront of the liturgical reform movement in the United States, which rejected the hierarchical arrangment of the traditional church in favor of a more unified setting, suggesting the use of a centralized rather than longitudinal plan.

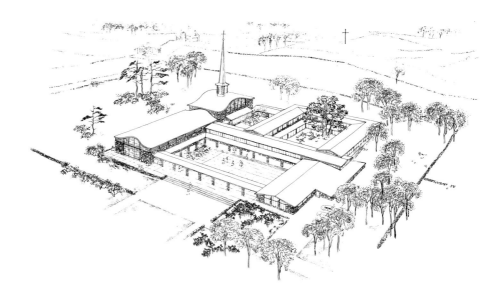

Portsmouth Abbey church and monastery, early scheme, 1954.

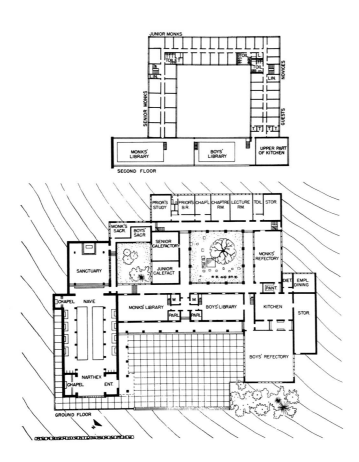

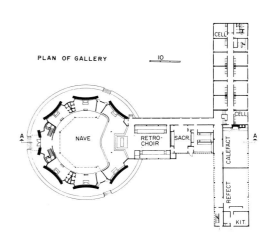

Portsmouth Abbey church and monastery, plan, 1957.

Portsmouth Abbey church, plan as built.

Portsmouth Abbey church, 1957–1960,
exterior (photo: G. E. Kidder Smith).

Portsmouth Abbey church, interior
(photo: Joseph Molitor).

By this time, Belluschi was involved in another centralized structure, a hexagonal syna- gogue in Swampscott, Massachusetts.[73] In 1957, after several trips to Italy that included a stay at the American Academy in Rome in 1954 and a visit to Ravenna where he saw San Vitale, he submitted a revised plan showing the influence of both traditional and contemporary buildings: a simple octagonal structure with radiating chapels, elongated choir behind the altar linking it to a monastic wing in back, and a refectory to one side forming an open court. An eight-sided dome rose over the centralized nave, supported on a system of freestanding radiating laminated bents; exteriors were of alternating slabs of local fieldstone and panels of redwood board and batten, with narrow slits of trans- lucent cathedral glass in between. Most light came from the dome, composed of a grid of wooden board and batten inset with stained glass.[74] Above rose a slender octagonal cupola topped by a tall spire and cross. In 1958, as the revised scheme was still being worked out, the New York abstractionist Richard Lippold, who had done a sculpture for Gropius at the Harvard Graduate Center, was brought in to design the altarpiece.[75] His ethereal, fine-wire sculpture was suspended over the altar like a baldachino, catching the light from an inconspicuous skylight overhead, shooting it down on the altar, and radiating it throughout the nave. It formed the focal point of the nave, activating the space and bringing it to life, pursuing Belluschi's theme of light and space expressed in the architecture itself. The church was completed in 1960 at a cost of $824,114.[76]

The association with Anderson, Beckwith & Haible was delicate. Anderson was chair of the architecture department at MIT, and under Belluschi administratively; moreover, he was a designer in his own right and, bruised already by losing the Portsmouth job to Belluschi, was understandably reluctant to have his office become known in a supportive role; as architect of record, his office was also legally responsible if anything went wrong. Finally, Anderson's staff was used to working in a formal language very different from Belluschi's. The association was congenial but strained, and for his subsequent work on the Portsmouth campus Belluschi went elsewhere.[77]

Church of the Redeemer, Baltimore, 1954–1958

While at work on First Lutheran, the Portsmouth Abbey Church, and the synagogue Temple Israel in Swampscott, Belluschi received the commission for a religious building of yet another denomination. This was the Church of the Redeemer for an Episcopal congregation in Baltimore. He was selected from among fifteen or so architects, among whom were Saarinen, Edward Durell Stone, Breuer, and Gropius, who had been recom- mended by the Washington, D.C., architectural critic Frederick Gutheim. Belluschi was chosen over the others on the basis of his respect for the church's existing building, a small century-old "English parish" church, and his willingness, in the words of the rector, "to struggle for a creative solution to the problem without preconceived plans and ideas. He seemed the tallest man in understanding, artistic sensitivity, and humility of spirit."[78]

What was needed was a new church that would accommodate a congregation of as many as a thousand, yet not overwhelm the small parish church which was to be left standing as a chapel, nor mar the natural beauty of the site, a spacious, wooded 9-acre lot in a semirural suburb west of Baltimore. For his associates, Belluschi turned to a pair of young Annapolis architects, Archibald Rogers and Francis Taliaferro, whose work had caught his eye as he was chairing the jury for the 1954 national AIA Honor Awards. Belluschi had by this time begun consulting for the developer James Rouse on a proposed shopping center in the Baltimore area and had become acquainted with the city and its architects, most of whom he found conservative. He was thus delighted to find Rogers and Taliaferro, who in turn felt honored to be asked to associate with so celebrated a man. Taliaferro had also long admired Belluschi's work, his arts and crafts ideals, respect for materials, and restrained, straightforward buildings, and at one point had considered leaving practice and returning to school to work with him at MIT. The association thus was based on mutual admiration and respect.[79]

Belluschi was by then busy, with his time divided between MIT and his growing number of outside professional commitments. Knowing he would need a lot of help, he was explicit about a truly collaborative relationship. This pleased Rogers and Taliaferro, who had expected to do working drawings and supervision only, by allowing them a substantial role in design.

Church of the Redeemer, Baltimore, 1954–1958, site plan.

With Belluschi working in Cambridge and Rogers and Taliaferro in their office in Annapolis, they worked out the site plan, vetoing Belluschi's first idea to site the new church back behind the original parish church on the southeast portion of the site. Taliaferro, with closer access to the site, realized that space behind the old church was cramped, and that to fit the new church in would have meant pressing it up against the street. He and Charles Lamb, who joined the office shortly after the contract was signed, proposed demolishing the rectory north of the old church and siting the new one on that side instead. Belluschi agreed.

While they were working out the site plan and beginning design, Belluschi came down to give the congregation an introductory presentation of his work. Assuming that by coming to him they wanted something modern, he presented slides of his previous work. Members of the congregation were horrified, and dubbed the occasion "Black Tuesday." Belluschi himself was not well, as his ulcer problems had worsened over the past several years, B/SOM in Portland was having financial difficulties, questions were being raised about government money he had received for Air Force work in Alaska, and there were family problems at home. But more to the point, the congregation was not prepared for modern work; some never recovered from the shock and remained steadfast in their allegiance to a traditional design.[80] Nonetheless, encouraged by the enthusiastic young rector who, once he had overcome his initial skepticism, became their strongest ally, Belluschi and his team valiantly went ahead. Working independently but conferring regularly, after several more fits and starts in May 1955 they came up with a proposal that the vestry approved.

Their proposal called for a new church building north of the old, cruciform in plan with generous transepts and room for expansion in galleries at some later time. The profile of the building was to be kept low through careful handling of roofline and scale, with roofs of the same pitch as the original, glazed gables flattened at the apex to form gambrels, and a rather squat spire over the crossing. Placed at right angles to the original 1858 church, the nave of the new church would parallel Charles Street so its principal facade would not compete with the original fronting on Charles. Set well back from the street to preserve as many trees as possible, it would be linked to the old church by a low stone and slatted wood wall, forming an inner courtyard, or cloister, between the two.[81]

At this point, with the basic concept set and design under way, Belluschi left for India on FBO affairs for a month, returning just in time for the presentation of the proposal to the congregation. Reactions were decidedly mixed. While some comments were favorable, many were bitterly opposed. "Doesn't look like a church"; "too modernistic";

Church of the Redeemer, aerial view
(photo: M. E. Warren).

"exterior is cold, is not my idea of a church building"; "just wish it didn't look so much like a cowbarn"; "couldn't there be more beauty—not so modern?" Others were more specific: "eliminate the hip"; "preserve the architectural lines of the original roof"; "drop the spire."[82]

Belluschi listened, and plans accordingly revised. But by late fall opposition had grown. Despite the rector's unflagging support, the vestry was urged to find a more traditional architect. Hoping to avoid its coming to this, Belluschi and Rogers, Taliaferro and Lamb made a presentation of the revised plans. The timing was not good, though, as new cost estimates were $975,000—over three times the original $300,000. "I am both disappointed and astonished that any recognized firm of ecclesiastical architects could present plans and designs for a church building so modernistic in character," one member said. "It looks *nothing* whatsoever like a church though it would make a perfectly wonderful camp in the Adirondacks." "The side facing Melrose Street looks exactly like an inviting hotel," another remarked. Others said they should have known, especially after his Black Tuesday presentation, that in engaging Belluschi "we were dealing with an advocate of 'Modern Radical.'"[83]

Hoping to quell the storm, Belluschi came down again to reassure the congregation. Affirming his own convictions about contemporary architecture and his commitment to its ideals, he gained just enough of their confidence that when a vote was taken whether to stay or switch to a more traditional architect, the congregation voted in his favor, though just barely.

Once the final design was approved, Belluschi came down less frequently, leaving much of the design development to Taliaferro and Lamb. He remained in touch by mail, however. In May of 1956, after arguing against holding a design competition for the main altar window in favor of an artist of his own choosing, Belluschi brought in Gyorgy Kepes, professor of visual design at MIT and a close personal friend. He then left again for a month in Australia and Japan. His visits to Baltimore by this time were intermittent, as other activities—his other churches, FBO work, a large commercial development in Back Bay, and by now the planning of Lincoln Center—severely encroached on his time.

A key concern of his was that the Kepes glass be fully integrated into the design of the whole. As work on the chancel moved into its final stages, Belluschi worried that its design was going ahead without his knowledge.[84] One of the drawbacks to the consultant role, he discovered, was that decisions had to be made regularly and work had to proceed whether or not he was there. Increasingly this meant he lost control as the design developed without him, with little he could do about it.

As news of the building spread throughout 1957 and requests to publish the work began pouring in, Belluschi insisted on holding off. He told Rogers, in response to a call from *Architectural Record,* that he had had a good deal of experience with this sort of thing, and knew the value of waiting to get good architectural photographs of the finished product before going public. "I need not tell you that photographs can make or kill even the best of jobs. Also, they can kill the interest." A master strategist when it came to the press, Belluschi had already refused the *Forum* a year earlier; knowing that *Progressive Architecture* was planning a major article on all of his East Coast work, he wanted not to steal its thunder.[85]

As the design moved into finishing stages in December, Belluschi stepped up his level of involvement, if mainly by mail, checking on details of the chancel furnishings, choice

of marble for the altar, color of the carpet, etc. It was here that his keen artistic eye, his sure sense of color values and gradations of tone and texture, coupled always with his awareness of their role in the overall composition, came to the fore.

The new church was just what Belluschi had hoped: modern yet unobtrusive, and respectful, despite its size, of the character and scale of the original church. In accordance with the wishes of the congregation, it was spireless to avoid competition with the steeple of the old church, and the pitch of its roof and gable design echoed those of the old. Rising steeply in a single sweep over the nave and transepts, the roof was brought down low, then angled out shallowly at the lower edge over the side aisles, like St. Thomas More in Portland. Low stone enclosure walls served as a visual base for the great roof above, their non-load-bearing function made clear by the continuous zone of stained glass between them and the roof. The roof itself, dominating the whole, was carried on a freestanding framework of laminated wood arches, exposed on the interior like the vaulting of a traditional Gothic church.

Characteristically, the exterior was reticent, with Belluschi's main interest focused on the interior. One entered through a loggia into an open landscaped court with pond and outdoor baptismal font, then through a short, wide narthex to the nave, a progression of spaces differentiated by variations in scale, character, and light. The nave itself was dark, defined by the richly stained, grained wood of the great roof and lit only by a narrow band of pale stained glass at its base that wrapped around the sides of nave and transepts, tying the nave and chancel visually and symbolically together. These met in an explosion of color in the main altar window.

This was the focal point of the whole. A dramatic climax to the progression of spaces, with their gradations of color, texture, and light, it filled the entire chancel. Belluschi envisioned it as an integral part of the architecture from the start, not just a decorative window but a major work of art, and had spoken to Kepes about it in the very earliest stages of the project.[86] The work, a screen lit artificially from behind to allow space for a shallow sacristy, consisted of brilliantly colored one-inch pieces of glass, each faceted to refract light, and set in a delicate lacelike mortar of concrete and epoxy held in place by a discreet metal grid. Only gradually, as the eye grew accustomed to its hues, did the image of the cross emerge from the composition, created by a subtle graduation of tone from luminous on the periphery to all but white in the center.

Church of the Redeemer, exterior (photo: Joseph Molitor).

The subtlety of the image was part of its appeal. In response to the rector who wanted a more literal cross, Kepes explained the difference between a sign and a symbol.

A sign is easy to read and forget. Part of the very nature of a true symbol is its subtlety. It cannot be encompassed in a glance, it calls upon more than eyesight for appropriation. It demands a measure of insight. It is too deep to be easy. To be found it must be entered into, and when found it keeps demanding participation from the beholder. . . . Its seeming weakness is precisely its great strength. . . .

Man can never capture the whole meaning of what he symbolizes in outward form. True symbols are therefore never exhaustive but suggestive, leaving room for the deep levels of mystery inherent in all truth.[87]

The idea of discovered rather than stated beauty, suggested rather than revealed truth, was a Zen notion consistent with Belluschi's own philosophy of art.[88] It was this common way of thinking about symbolism and meaning that united Belluschi and Kepes in their approach to the visual arts.

Its consistency with the English country parish church notwithstanding, a subtle Japanese influence pervaded the Church of the Redeemer throughout, from the great hovering Irimoya roof to the small landscaped courtyards, each a private pocket for individual meditation, scattered throughout the complex of buildings. While in Japan in the summer of 1956, Belluschi had visited the ancient Katsura Palace in Kyoto; he was also privy to many of the discussions about Eastern mysticism and the connections between Zen and Catholicism held by the fathers at the Portsmouth Abbey. Then, too, popular interest in Eastern philosophy and the art and architecture of Japan, much of it generated by the exhibition of Japanese architecture at MoMA in 1955, was at its height now.

Despite the initial fierce resistance of the congregation to his "Modern Radical" design, which almost cost him the job, the Church of the Redeemer proved to be one of the most accomplished of Belluschi's later churches. Like the Cottage Grove Presbyterian Church in Oregon, much of its success was due to the nature of the collaboration and the genuine interest of all those involved: the rector, Rogers, Taliaferro and Lamb, the landscape architects, Kepes, the lighting engineers, and a host of others. Its success played a major role in launching the Rogers, Taliaferro and Lamb firm, which became, in large part because of the Belluschi connection, one of the largest and most successful in Baltimore.[89] As for the rector Bennett Sims, it marked a profound turning point in his ministerial career, redirecting, in his own words, "my whole understanding of history and the human aspiration after truth and beauty."[90]

Church of the Redeemer, interior (photo: Joseph Molitor).

The church was completed in 1958, at a cost of $950,000, and was widely published.[91] Years later, after numerous awards including an AIA Honors Award in 1960 and the twenty-five-year award of the Baltimore chapter of the AIA in 1986, aware of the irony of the congregation's opposition to his initial proposal, Belluschi wrote them his thoughts on the true nature of the church. "People in time will come to understand that a church is much more than a building to be created from remembered images of the past. It is people coming together in a common desire to evoke the commanding vision of God's eternal harmony, which entails a continuous search for what is in harmony with our time."[92]

A Miesian Turn: Skidmore House and the Bennington College Library

Belluschi did a number of other churches and synagogues in the 1950s and 1960s, among them a proposed addition to Richardson's Trinity Church, in Copley Square, Boston.[93] But as his presence on the East Coast grew, he began receiving commissions for other building types as well. One of the first of these was from Louis Skidmore, an MIT alumnus with whom Belluschi was then also professionally associated through the B/SOM office in Portland.

In the spring of 1952, a year after Belluschi arrived in the East, Skidmore asked him to design a house in Winter Haven, Florida. Skidmore came to him, according to Belluschi, because no one in the SOM offices was able to come up with a house his wife liked.[94] In May, he and the Skidmores took a train down together to see the site: spacious acreage in a large orange grove overlooking a lake, which they had purchased for eventual retirement. The major problem, as Belluschi saw it, was the hot, humid climate. Skidmore was adverse to air conditioning and wanted the house naturally cooled.

Using a four-foot module, Belluschi designed a single-story, four-bedroom house, flat-roofed and rectangular in form, with exteriors of diagonal wood paneling. It was raised on stilts for air circulation, with a double-roof system to allow the escape of warm air above, a system inspired, Belluschi maintained, by a house lived in by Admiral William Halsey while he was stationed on an island in the South Pacific during the war.[95] The plan was square, with an atrium or open courtyard and reflecting pool in the center; individual rooms were disposed around it so that each would receive maximum cross ventilation. Belluschi also incorporated the louvered ventilation system John Yeon had used in the Watzek House, with fixed louvers below, transoms above.[96] The concept sounded good in theory, but given the amount of glazing and shallow roof overhangs, plus very hot summers, an artificial air-conditioning system was found to be needed and eventually installed.[97] Completed in 1955 at a cost of $60,000, the Skidmore House, with

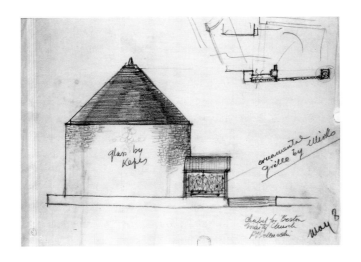

H. H. Richardson, Trinity Church, Copley Square, Boston, drawing with proposed Belluschi addition, 1960.

Belluschi sketch, Trinity Church Chapel, 1960 (courtesy Cooper Union Museum, New York).

Skidmore House, Warm Springs, Florida, 1952–1955, exterior.

its simple geometric form, industrial modularity, flat roof, and stilting, indicated a new design direction in Belluschi's domestic work. A regional response on the one hand, it also indicated the influence of a new Miesian austerity, softened by the use of natural unpainted wood and diagonal paneling. Belluschi liked the building and wanted it included in the body of work he was sending the architectural press; it was not published, however, on Skidmore's insistence.[98]

Belluschi continued this Miesian direction in the Bennington College Library, Bennington, Vermont, commissioned in 1957. Till now, his reputation in the East had been as a Pacific Northwest regionalist; the Bennington Library commission, like the Skidmore House, offered him a chance to shed that image.

Bennington specifically wanted a famous architect, "one of the great architects in the country." After interviewing several other prominent architects, the architectural selection committee, "enchanted" by Belluschi, recommended him to the trustees.[99] Belluschi had not only a well-known name but long experience in designing libraries, including those for Reed, Willamette, and Linfield colleges and several public libraries in Oregon in the 1930s and 1940s. More recently he had served as a consultant for the Seattle Public library system as a design critic for their new downtown library.

Bennington College Library, Bennington, Vermont, 1957–1959, exterior (photo: Ezra Stoller).

The problem at Bennington was familiar: they wanted a distinctly modern building that at the same time maintained the character of the small rural New England campus. Originally built in 1932 with white-clapboard colonial buildings modeled after Thomas Jefferson's University of Virginia, on a 350-acre site in the gentle rolling mountains of southern Vermont, the Bennington campus had changed little since then except for the addition of some converted farm structures on the outskirts of the central quad and several other random buildings. The Bennington community was very specific about the kind of building it wanted: one that "belonged to the land and to the character of Vermont and its buildings—those lean stone houses and mills in town, the big barns high on the hills." Not interested in "being stately," nor in having a building that stylistically mimicked the old, they wanted a modern building that nonetheless fit in gracefully. "Harmony isn't all a matter of style," the head of the building committee said in stating their desiderata, "it's a matter of scale and attitude, the way of life a building presupposes." The qualities they sought were warmth, informality, "and a kind of forthrightness," rather than style or "outward show."[100] Destined to serve the research requirements of the faculty as well as student study, it was to provide space for a 75,000-volume collection, within a relatively restricted budget.

Belluschi asked Carl Koch and Associates, with whom he had collaborated on the Swampscott synagogue and with whom he was also working on a large commercial development in the Boston Back Bay, to associate. Brought in at the outset of the project to help resolve a dispute among faculty, students, and administrators concerning the site, Belluschi also asked the landscape firm of Sasaki Associates for advice in site selection as well as planning, grading, and landscaping.

Belluschi aimed at a building that would be practical, tailored to the particular needs of the Bennington community, and fully modern, yet would harmonize with existing buildings and with the natural setting "so that it would seem to grow naturally and convincingly." He wanted it friendly and inviting, "visually satisfying without being forced or sophisticated." And finally, detailing was to be simple, refined, and easily maintainable.[101]

Belluschi went abroad over the summer of 1957 but returned in the fall. Working rapidly once the site was determined, even with an unexpected reduction of the budget that perforce changed their plans, Belluschi, Koch, and Sasaki had drawings prepared and approved by January 1958. Begun the following September, the building was completed by fall of 1959, at a cost of $420,000—on time and on budget.[102]

Bennington College Library, louvers
(photo: Ezra Stoller).

Located in the center of campus between the student dormitories and the classroom "Barn," with expansive views to the south and east, the new library consisted of a simple rectangular, two-story, flat-roofed building with modular bays defined by projecting, non-load-bearing fins of wood, painted white to blend with the white-clapboard colonial dorms. Horizontal wood louvers were used both as sunscreens and to relate the building visually, as the architects explained it, to the other clapboard buildings on campus. The regular row of vertical fins of the porch recalled colonial pilasters, and the brick, stone walls, and other paving were similar to those elsewhere, tying it in visually, according to the architects, with the rest of the buildings on the campus. The scale of the building was kept low by sinking a third story into the slope of the hill to minimize its visual impact.

The program specified that the building be designed to be run by a minimal staff. With the assistance of Keyes Metcalf, former librarian of Harvard and one of the country's leading experts in library planning, the Bennington Library was designed with a single entrance that opened into a lobby, with circulation desk on one side and catalogue room beyond; broad stairs to the right provided access to stacks and reading rooms on upper and lower levels. Sound booths for language training, a study room with its own outside entrance so it could remain open after hours, acoustics, lighting, ventilation, with thermopane windows and air conditioning throughout, were all fully contemporary. One of the most appreciated touches was the secluded landscaped courtyard on the south side of the building, where students and faculty could sit and read outside in warm weather.

A simple, white, rectangular building with a structural frame of reinforced concrete, cantilevered floor and roof slabs, and regular modules defined by projecting fins, it bore obvious analogies with buildings such as the Farnsworth House and was squarely in the Miesian tradition. Belluschi's associates, the SOM offices in New York with the Skidmore House, Carl Koch and Associates of Boston with the Bennington Library, may have had something to do with this. But, as one of the associates on the library pointed out, Belluschi was unquestionably "a one-man architect." It was he who called the shots, with his associates working strictly as a backup team. Moreover, Belluschi had brought in the design, complete with dimensioned plans, at the start.[103]

The use of modular forms, fins, screens, and louvers and the overall lightness of structure and delicate patterning were widespread at the time, suggesting the influence in particular of architects such as Stone, Yamasaki, and Saarinen, with whom Belluschi was working at the FBO. But in fact Belluschi's design for the Bennington Library was based on the recently completed Tucker-Mason School for the Deaf in Portland by B/SOM, on which he was only tangentially involved: same Miesian structural form, modularity defined by projecting fins, and same system of louvers, though there run continuously rather than in asymmetrical panels.[104]

The new library proved controversial. For all the talk of a regional fit, not everybody saw it that way. Douglas Haskell, editor of the *Forum* and a Belluschi loyalist, liked it and published it in the February 1960 issue. But a reporter for the *New York Times* was not alone in seeing it as standing "in radical contrast" to the wood and brick colonial campus.[105]

Then, too, Belluschi's prototype, the School for the Deaf, was a wholly different building type, designed for a wholly different climate in a wholly different part of the country. The design proved less appropriate for a library in Bennington, Vermont. While the structural system worked in Portland, with its light rains and little snow, in Bennington it had problems. The cantilevered terraces sagged under the weight of ice and snow, the flat roof was unable to hold up under heavy rains, and there was a problem with glare on the south and west sides. Belluschi was clearly in foreign territory, and under pressure not only of time but more subtly of style. The Miesian tradition was by then thoroughly established in progressive architectural circles on the East Coast. The informal, pitched-roof buildings of unpainted wood he was accustomed to in Oregon in the 1940s seemed now, to use his own word, "quaint." As one of his associates in the Koch office bluntly put it, *nobody* did pitched roofs any more.[106]

Formalist criticism and design sources aside, the library was deemed one of the best undergraduate libraries of its size in the country at the time,[107] and one of the four libraries—at a time when libraries, like school buildings and churches, were being built by the score—to receive top honors in the First Library Buildings Award Program sponsored jointly by the AIA, American Library Association, and National Book Committee.[108]

B/SOM, School for the Deaf, Portland, completed 1953, exterior detail (photo: author).

Mondawmin Shopping Center, Baltimore, 1952–1956

One of Belluschi's first major consulting jobs after moving to the East Coast was for the Mondawmin Shopping Center, a $8 million retail complex in Baltimore and one of the largest in the country, by the developer James Rouse.

In March 1952, just over a year after Belluschi had assumed the deanship at MIT, Rouse contacted him on the recommendation of the architect Kenneth Welsh, a specialist in retail design whom Belluschi had befriended in 1948 when both had participated in the retail seminar at the AIA national convention in Salt Lake City.[109] Belluschi had a long, wide experience in retail design going back to stores and department stores he had worked on in the late 1920s under the auspices of Doyle and the small shopping centers he had designed during the war; two of his recent stores, the Nordstrom Shoe Store in Portland and Esther Foster Shop in Salem, had just been published in the *Forum* in 1950.[110] As a recognized authority on shopping center design, he had been asked to write the chapter on the shopping center for Talbot Hamlin's four-volume *Forms and Functions of Twentieth Century Architecture,* published in 1952.[111]

The Mondawmin Center was a project on a wholly new scale. On 46 acres of land three miles from downtown Baltimore, it was to include two anchoring department stores, a 10-story office building, and 40 to 50 stores and shops on two levels facing inward around a pedestrian mall, with parking on the periphery.[112] Drawing on many of the concepts espoused by Victor Gruen, particularly on the Southdale Center outside Minneapolis, and those used by John Graham, architect of the highly successful Northgate Shopping Center on the outskirts of Seattle, the Mondawmin Center was planned for compactness, both in the interest of reducing long walks for pedestrian shoppers and to enable it to be enclosed as an atmosphere-controlled mall.[113] One of the key features of the Mondawmin Center was its scale: despite its actual size, which was gargantuan, it seemed small. Designed around a series of small courts and pedestrian passageways, it was aimed at breaking down the sense of a vast, alienating mall. Deliberately geared to the pedestrian rather than the car, and patterned on the open markets of Europe with their congeniality and small scale, it was to feature short walking distances, maximum visual variety, and a minimum of dead areas—designed, in Rouse's words, as a place people would want to be. Seeking the most qualified help available, Rouse, a highly intelligent, thoughtful young entrepreneur who was just beginning a lifetime career as one of the largest, most successful developers of commercial centers in the country, brought in as consultants Kenneth Welsh, landscape architect Dan Kiley, Stewart Mott, former director of the Urban Land Institute, and Belluschi, all top figures in their respective fields.[114]

Belluschi was brought in primarily for his background in site planning and wide experience in retail design. Rouse consulted him regularly on a broad range of issues. It was Belluschi, for example, who suggested incorporating an underground service tunnel, used with great success by John Graham in the Northgate Center in Seattle, then by Gruen in his Fort Worth Center. Belluschi stressed the importance of not cutting corners on quality, insisting that the time and money spent at this stage would pay off in the long run. Belluschi, too, benefited from working with leading figures in large-scale retail design. Much of what he learned—about large-scale commercial development, marketing, traffic control, and other urban design and planning issues—he was to draw on in his work in the Back Bay.

Back Bay Center Project, Boston, 1953–1955

Shortly after the Mondawmin Center, Belluschi became involved in what would have been one of the largest urban real estate developments anywhere in the country: a $75 million commercial complex of hotel, stores, and office tower on 28 acres of by then obsolete railroad yard in the middle of Boston.

Early in the spring of 1953, Belluschi, Carl Koch, Walter Bogner, Hugh Stubbins, and Walter Gropius met to form the consortium of Boston Center Architects. Their purpose was to provide architecture and planning services for R. M. Bradley and Company, Inc., a real estate development group headed by New York developer Roger L. Stevens, owner of the Empire State Building. Recognizing the magnitude of the project and its enormous financial risk, the architects agreed to assume a share in the gamble by receiving no renumeration in the planning stage beyond operating costs, on the understanding that if the project did proceed they would be retained as its principal architects. In drawing up the joint venture contract, the members of the group, following Belluschi's suggestion, were scrupulous in setting down its terms. A harmonious working relationship among them was essential, and anticipating the obvious sources of discord—the splitting of labor, responsibility, profits—they set up a separate office with an independent staff. Accurate bookkeeping was essential, with a meticulous recording of all costs.[115] Gropius was designated chairman, Stubbins vice-chairman, Belluschi (whose business acumen was immediately apparent) was administrator and treasurer, Bogner and Koch deputy administrators. Their contract with Stevens was signed in May.

252

It was a big, highly publicized project. On the former site of the Boston and Albany railroad yard in the tightly congested Back Bay area, with a plot twice the size of Rockefeller Center, it was to include a 750-room hotel and convention hall complete with helicopter landing, department store, shops, supermarket, drug store, restaurant, and post office, a total of 11,000,000 square feet of office space plus 850,000 square feet of store space.[116] On Belluschi's urging that they hire leading specialists, Wilbur Smith from Yale was brought in as a traffic consultant and Kenneth Welsh for store placement and layout. Belluschi himself served as spokesman for the team, in charge of making presentations, drawing up copy for press releases, and other public relation roles.

Functioning as a collaborative team, with all of them participating in the design process to a greater or lesser degree, they met in June to work out a basic concept. Belluschi, Gropius, and Bogner then left for the summer, leaving the design mainly to Stubbins and Norman Fletcher of The Architects Collaborative, Gropius's office in Cambridge. When they reconvened in the latter part of August, Stubbins and Fletcher had drawings well along and a large-scale model under way for a public unveiling September 10.[117]

As Belluschi described the project in the *Architectural Forum,* it was a daring piece of architectural economics. Their principal aim was to draw shoppers, lured away by the convenience of suburban shopping centers, back to the city with the promise of easy vehicular access and ample parking. Geared specifically to a clientele equipped with cars, it was to provide accommodations for 5,000–6,000 vehicles in a below-grade parking structure, with a 28-acre platform of office and retailing space "floated" above. Drawing on the concept of the suburban shopping center that had proved so successful in the postwar era, the Boston Back Bay Center promised to add "big city excitement and power," with the addition of a 1,400,000-square-foot office building, 7,500-seat convention hall, 750-room hotel, and 116-room motel. The complex as a whole was to be carefully planned around open-air plazas and promenades—in effect, a city within a city, all in the center of Boston's small-scale, highly congested, historic Back Bay.

One of its key concepts was the circulation system, which was to be vertical rather than horizontal. Unlike the usual one-to-two-story suburban shopping center, one would enter from the three-level parking area below grade and progress upward. A subway station on either side of the site, plus a railroad station run diagonally under it, linked the center with the city's public transit systems. The project was to be funded entirely privately, needing only the compliance of the city government to proceed.[118]

Back Bay Center project, Boston, 1953–1955, model (photo: Robert D. Harvey Studio, Boston).

Recognizing it as momentous, not only because it was one of the most ambitious commercial developments of the time but also because of the famous names involved,

Progressive Architecture, the *Record,* and the *Forum* all fought for publication rights.[119] It was finally decided, on Belluschi's advice, to go with the *Forum,* but only if certain conditions were met: that the project be given the cover in color, that BAA be given the right to review all copy prior to going to press, that the layout be done in close collaboration with the BAA office, that illustrations be in color, and that reprints be made available to them at no cost.[120] In December, the project was awarded a *Progressive Architecture* award for the most outstanding project of the year, and in March 1954 the Museum of Modern Art, spearheaded by Philip Johnson (who cautioned the architects to keep their focus on it as architecture, not as a business venture), staged an exhibition of the model and drawings, to be followed by a reception for the architects.[121]

The mayor of Boston, who considered it "the best thing that could ever happen" to the city, endorsed it,[122] but it was staunchly opposed by inner city retailers, organized labor, and political leaders who feared the competition,[123] and in the end it was aborted by a Supreme Court decision not to allow the tax easement needed to make the center financially viable.[124] Stevens, who had had a three-year option on the land, sold the option to the Prudential Insurance Company, which eventually developed it into the Prudential Center, with Charles Luckman as architect.[125]

Though it remained a project, the Back Bay Center constituted an important stepping stone to two of the biggest jobs of Belluschi's career: the planning of Lincoln Center and the Pan Am Building in New York.

Lincoln Center, New York, 1955–1970

In the late fall of 1955, John D. Rockefeller III called a meeting to begin planning what was seen then as the biggest and boldest complex devoted to the arts ever attempted in the United States. Meeting with the heads of the Metropolitan Opera Company and Philharmonic Orchestra, plus several key figures from the architectural profession, one of whom was Pietro Belluschi, they planned a conference to explore the possibilities of a new musical arts center. The Metropolitan Opera Company, still housed in its original 1883 building, long recognized as obsolete, had been looking for a new home ever since the collapse of the real estate deal in the late 1920s that later developed into Rockefeller Center;[126] the Philharmonic was also about to lose its lease for Carnegie Hall. Apparently at the instigation of Wallace Harrison, partner of Harrison and Abramovitz and longstanding architect of the Rockefeller family, it was proposed that the Metropolitan combine forces with the Philharmonic to form a joint center. The chance arose in the early 1950s, when a site became available as part of Robert Moses's large Lincoln Square redevelopment project. The idea gradually expanded into the concept of a cultural center including all the performing arts—dance, drama, and film in addition to symphony and opera—to be subsidized by federal funding under Title I of the 1949 Housing Act, a portion of which in 1954 was made available to the arts.[127] The decision to include music educational facilities as well as a library/museum of the performing arts was also made early on to form a center embracing scholarship and education as well as performance.

A two-week conference was held in October 1956 to discuss the planning of the proposed center with a group of "the world's most noted architects and acoustic engineers."[128] Among them were the Finn Alvar Aalto, noted Swedish architect Sven Markelius, who was a member of the board of design consultants for the United Nations Building and head of city planning in Stockholm, Viennese architect and stage designer Walter Unruh, Marcel Breuer of New York, Henry Shepley of Shepley Bulfinch in Boston, Philip Johnson, then architect with Mies of the Seagram Building and affiliated with the Department of Architecture at the MoMA, and Pietro Belluschi.

The proposed $75 million center on a three-block site in Manhattan's Lincoln Square was celebrated as a symbol of the flowering of the arts in the United States, and publicized with the hopes that it would serve not only as a stimulus to the performing arts in New York City but as a catalyst for similar cultural centers throughout the country. It was also seen as an exceptional architectural opportunity, as never before had such a group of buildings wholly devoted to the arts been built in this country on such a scale. It was, in sum, one of the biggest, most challenging urban projects of the time.

Spearheading much of the architectural thinking was Wallace Harrison, who had been affiliated with the Metropolitan Opera since the late 1920s, when the original plans to

Lincoln Center planning team. Seated, left to right: Marcel Breuer, Pietro Belluschi, Wallace K. Harrison, Alvar Aalto, Philip Johnson; standing, left to right: Max Abramovitz, Hope Bagenal, Hugh Ferris, Herbert Graf, Walter Unruh. Presenting is Sven Markelius. (Architectural Forum, November 1956.)

build a new opera house on the site of what was later to become Rockefeller Center fell through; Harrison was also the architect to whom the Philharmonic turned later when it began thinking of a new home. When land became available through the Lincoln Square Urban Renewal program, a corporation was set up with John D. Rockefeller III as president, Anthony Bliss of the Metropolitan Opera, and Wallace Harrison as coordinating architect. It was thus under his advice and in consultation with the heads of the constituent organizations that architects were selected for each building, to work under his leadership as part of the Center's team. Harrison himself was to design the Metropolitan Opera House, his partner Max Abramovitz the Philharmonic Hall, Philip Johnson the Dance Theater, Belluschi the Juilliard School of Music, Eero Saarinen the Drama Theater, and Gordon Bunshaft of SOM the library-museum.[129]

A joint office was set up where the planners and representatives of Lincoln Center held meetings. After three years of planning, reflecting continuous shifts in their thinking, the site plan was set, several large-scale models made, and ground rules for the actual design and construction of the buildings laid. Among them was the agreement that a more or less uniform architectural style would govern exteriors.[130] Harrison would be chief, with the understanding that each of the architects involved would work not only on his own building but with Harrison in charge of coordinating the center as a whole. Given the number of top-heavy egos, as music critic Harold Schonberg poignantly put it in the *Times,* it was a touchy situation.

> *Suppose six great pianists—Horowitz, Rubinstein, Novies, Serkin, Richter and Backhaus, say, all mighty executants, all overpowering personalities—were locked in a room and ordered not to come out until they had decided on the correct interpretation of Beethoven's "Hammerklavier" Sonata. How many eons would pass? How many wounds would be inflicted? How much blood would be shed? Yet in another field, much the same thing is actually going on. Working on the site plans and the buildings for the Lincoln Center of the Performing Arts on New York's West Side, are Wallace Harrison, Abramovitz, Johnson, Bunshaft, Saarinen, and Belluschi—six of America's most prominent architects, six notable temperaments, each with strong ideas about design.*[131]

It was Harrison's lot, with his experience in negotiating the collaborative effort on the United Nations Building, to coordinate their thinking before they turned their attention to the design of the buildings proper. A delicate act, because, as Schonberg's article pointed out, though they had all grown up in the International Style (an honest but mistaken assumption on Schonberg's part, as Belluschi, albeit a modernist, had not), their work by this time was no longer doctrinaire. It was not that long ago that Philip Johnson, at the Yale symposium on the future of modernism, had declared that there was no consensus on a design direction, and that as far as modernism was concerned it was each man for himself. Harrison himself detected two different schools of thought governing their work: those (surely Johnson among them) who advocated a more formal, symmetrically ordered scheme with the Metropolitan Opera House in the center and other buildings arranged in a balanced composition on either side, and others (Belluschi among them) leaning toward a freer, more informal approach. "The six of us may have different ideas," Schonberg quoted Johnson as saying, "but we're united. After all, we're all on the same side of the fence. We have come up through the Modern Movement together and we're looking away from the Puritanism of the International Style toward enriched forms. I would say that we have extraordinary agreement on the direction our plans will take." Belluschi put it more bluntly: "We hang together or we hang separately."[132]

Involved in the project from the first, Belluschi had been brought in by Harrison, who knew Belluschi through their work with the FBO. As a member of the advisory committee for the selection of architects, late in 1957 William Schuman, president of the Juilliard School of Music, consulted Belluschi on whom to retain for the design of their new building. Belluschi provided a list of six of the leading young architects at the time whom

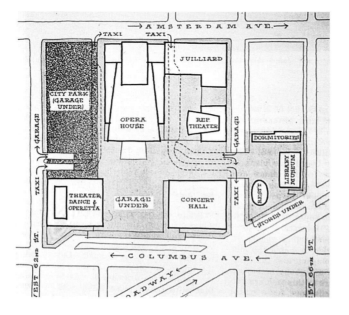

Lincoln Center, New York, original site plan, 1958 (Architectural Forum, August 1958).

Lincoln Center, model of original complex, 1963.

he thought should be considered: Stone, Pei, Saarinen, Yamasaki, Hugh Stubbins, and Eduardo Catalano. He also included his own name on the list, with the understanding that were he selected, he would work in association with another firm. After Schuman and he talked it over, in a turn of events not at all uncommon with Belluschi in such situations, it was agreed that he, Belluschi, would be the architect. He was to associate with Eduardo Catalano, a young Argentine architect whom Belluschi had brought to MIT as a professor of architecture in the early 1950s, and Helge Westermann, a former student of Catalano's who had established an office in New York.[133]

As a member of the planning team, Belluschi was highly respected for his astuteness and seriousness of purpose, his comments always welcomed. According to Mark Schubart, dean of the Juilliard School who attended the meetings intermittently, Belluschi "always seemed to bring a humanistic point of view, reminding the others they were creating buildings that were destined to be used by people rather than merely monuments." He fondly recalled meeting Belluschi in Venice one summer during the planning stages and, over drinks in the piazza facing the Palazzo Ducale, musing how splendid it would be to do something comparable at the Lincoln Center.[134] European precedents were part of Belluschi's thinking as one of the "informalists" using a smaller, more intimate scale and less grandiose approach to the design of the Center's buildings and spaces, a plan focused on use and pedestrian circulation rather than the formal, classical scheme eventually adopted.

Not all of Belluschi's recommendations were followed, nor were all of them, in the long run, good. It was Belluschi who, again with Italian precedents in mind, suggested the use of travertine as a veneer throughout Lincoln Center as a means of visually tying the buildings together and uniting the whole. Though adopted, it later proved unwise, as the travertine did not fare well in the extreme temperatures of the New York climate.[135]

The design of the Juilliard School itself got off to a slow start, delayed by frequent changes of site, directorship, and program. By 1959, when the final negotiations on the planning of the Center were taking place and work on the first of the buildings, Abramovitz's Philharmonic Hall, was under way, Belluschi, working with Catalano, had prepared preliminary designs for Juilliard.[136] These were placed on hold, however, as decisions on site, budget, and program continued to change. This marked the beginning of a 15-year process that left Belluschi and Catalano both drained.[137] Lincoln Center formally opened in 1962, without Juilliard.

Pietro Belluschi

Pietro Belluschi

The sixties combined both blind optimism and a growing frustration in American society. Optimism stemmed from startling advances in science and technology, borne out by the fulfillment of President Kennedy's promise to put an American on the moon by the end of the decade and by the growing use of mainframe computers in finance, education, and government bureaucracies; it flowed too from an unprecedented flowering of the arts and humanities, and an explosion in higher education. Yet these changes were accompanied by frustration, as much of the social idealism of the 1950s was wearing thin. Signs were inescapable: continuing poverty, civil rights unrest, the destruction of the environment. Developers more interested in personal profit than the common good were converting thousands of acres of rural countryside into new suburban communities, freeway interchanges, and large-scale shopping centers. This had been going on since 1945, but by the 1960s the massive scale and destruction could no longer be ignored. At the same time, continued population growth, coupled with postwar affluence, meant more Americans than ever were buying cars, and the two-car family was becoming standard. This compounded problems of parking, traffic, and pollution in already congested cities.

Cities throughout the world were transformed, increasingly filled with standardized high-rise office buildings, steel and glass Miesian derivatives, either slabs or blocks. Demands for more stringent controls over the height and densities of downtown growth became strident; the laissez-faire expansionism of the 1950s took a new turn as public interests increasingly collided with private concerns, launching an era of confrontation and social activism in urban development.[1]

The trend toward bigness in American economic life begun in the postwar era continued, with marked repercussions in architecture. A gradual shift took place from individual clients to impersonal corporations, from the private homeowner to the merchant builder, and from small community shopping centers to gargantuan regional centers 75 to 100 or more acres in size. Huge office towers reached heights hitherto unseen in most cities, symbols of the new, big, 1960s scale.

Federal support of the arts that had made possible new cultural centers such as Lincoln Center continued, given impetus in 1963 when President Kennedy set up a permanent office of Special Consultant on the Arts, whose duties included setting high standards in the building of new federal buildings, and established a federal Advisory Council on the Arts. With Kennedy's assassination in November, however, much of this momentum was lost, and concerns started shifting away from the arts toward more pressing social issues. Museum construction, much of it begun in the 1950s, nonetheless continued unabated.[2]

The plight of cities demanded immediate attention. No longer could architects ignore urban issues by focusing on the single building alone, isolated as a self-sufficient, self-contained monument. The context now demanded equal concern. As *Architectural Record* editor Emerson Goble described it after an urban design conference at Harvard in 1962, the city was *the* major problem facing architects in the 1960s.[3]

Its dimensions were frightening. Urban renewal programs planned for Boston alone over the next decade were expected to comprise over one-third of the area of the city and affect over half the population. The architectural profession, Goble said, was wholly unprepared; neither architects nor planners were sufficiently knowledgeable about the staggeringly complicated objectives and procedures involved, or had clear ideas about their architectural goals. As goals remained nebulous, cities were dying, increasingly sold out to unscrupulous developers building feverishly without guidelines or control.

The urban renewal program itself was under question. The Housing Act of 1949 had finally given substance to the longstanding national commitment to provide decent housing for all Americans, granting federal subsidies to local municipal agencies willing to clear, resell, or lease substandard or undeveloped land for residential uses to private developers or public housing agencies. In 1954, Title I of the act was amended to broaden its terms so that 10 percent of federal funds could be used for nonresidential projects. The program was expanded still further in 1959, with 20 percent allowed for nonresidential uses. As a result, large numbers of cheap rooming houses, residential hotels, rundown rental units, and other dilapidated buildings typically used for low-cost housing were being replaced by large office buildings and high-rise apartments, with reliable relocation programs not implemented until later, and then only under mounting pressure.[4]

One of the chief concerns of the architectural profession was design, and the lack of control over quality or aesthetics.[5] After the optimistic launching of bold urban renewal programs in the 1950s in New York, Baltimore, Philadelphia, Boston, San Francisco, Los Angeles, New Haven—with Belluschi involved in all but the last (perhaps not uncoincidentally the home of Yale, and Vincent Scully)—attitudes changed. After the publication of Jane Jacobs's *The Death and Life of Great American Cities* in 1961, then Martin Anderson's *The Federal Bulldozer* in 1964 denouncing urban renewal and advocating the program be dropped, criticism of public housing projects, especially those like Pruitt-Igoe in St. Louis designed by name architects, became widespread.

The postwar boom in the building industry continued into the 1960s. In 1960, construction over the next decade was expected to exceed all that of the past 35 years.[6] Corporate clients—most notably Ford Motor Company, IBM, Lever Brothers, Pepsi Cola, and Seagram—got bigger and more numerous, and with them the demand for large corporate towers and industrial parks grew. As inflation began to take hold in the later 1960s, interest rates rose, and as money grew tight, clients pressured their architects to turn to cost-saving measures, often at the expense of quality.

Historic preservation was another concern, as the thoughtless demolition of historic buildings continued in the name of progress, often at the hand of the federal government.[7] This in turn raised new questions about design integrity, the blending of old and new, and the value of preserving existing urban fabric, which was sometimes comfortable, pedestrian-scaled, and charming, but more often dilapidated and unsafe. Books like Jane Jacobs's proved prophetic in warning of the need for human scale. The revolt against the scale of the big city culminated in riots, demonstrations, and back-to-the-earth movements toward the end of the decade.

Architects were directly affected. As more and more of their clients were planning multimillion-dollar real estate investments like Roger Stevens's Back Bay Center, architects were forced to contend with economic issues. This added a new dimension to the question of what the architect was: creative artist and revered cultural hero, professional man like doctor or lawyer whose primary obligation was to the client, or a businessman whose principal concerns lay in securing new jobs and protecting economic interests, including his own.[8]

The question of modernism was directly related. As the social utopianism espoused by the European modernists in the 1920s and 1930s waned in the unfettered expansion of the postwar era, modernism in general was attacked.[9] Weakened by splintering and loss of focus in the 1950s, modernism's belief that history should be rejected, modern technology should be the point of departure for design, and architecture should play a revolutionary, reformist social role, was challenged. Architects such as Philip Johnson were now proclaiming purely artistic aims: architecture as art, never mind about function. The lean functionalist tradition together with much of its rationalist philosophy was seen as sterile, replaced by a new concern for the richness of symbolic form, associations, and meaning.

By the early 1960s interest in modernized white classical temples, expressive thin-shell concrete forms, and decorative structure, which had resulted in the plethora of screens, grilles, brise-soleils, and other shading devices of the latter 1950s, subsided, and de-sign-oriented architects turned toward more muscular, heavy, sculptured buildings in-spired by Le Corbusier and Louis Kahn.[10] Leading academics especially at Yale and Princeton, picking up the scattered shards of the 1948 MoMA symposium on modern-ism, staged another at Columbia in 1964, resulting in an outright rejection of modernism, particularly of the principle that function should be the rationale for form, with the body of social idealism that underscored it. Instead of a practical means to an end, architec-ture was embraced as an end in itself, a matter of intellectual, formal, theoretical dis-course.[11] This resulted in a split between theory and practice, thinkers and doers, those who talked about architecture and those who built.

Philip Johnson, mastermind behind much of the new thinking, seized the opportunity several years later, in a review of Australian architect Robin Boyd's *Puzzle of Architecture,* to outline what he saw as three major phases of modernism. First was the International Style, emerging in Europe in the 1920s and resulting in an architecture based on struc-tural honesty, repetitive modular rhythms, clarity, ample use of glass, thin walls and flat roof, the simple box as paradigmatic form, and no ornament. This, according to Johnson, was the rallying cry of intellectuals in the 1920s and 1930s, and became the formula for speculative builders in the 1950s and 1960s. The second phase in the 1950s was a reaction against that, because "all of us were bored." Pure design came back into favor, so too historicizing and decoration. Functions were stuffed into preconceived forms— geometric volumes, warped forms, symbolic forms, whatever. Form was primary. The third phase, which Johnson saw architecture currently in, was perforce less clearly defined; it was easier to say what it was not than what it was. It was not rectangular, skin-enclosed boxes (first phase), nor interesting but arbitrary shapes (second phase). A synthesis of unity and diversity, clarity and complexity, it often had a functional element, or space, picked out and exaggerated in the interest of a visually engaging form, as in Kahn's Richards Medical Laboratories. Whereas, in the second phase, space was clothed in a single significant shape, in the third, different internal spaces, i.e., the functional parts, determined form, now vigorously expressed. Both second and third phases used history, albeit very differently, in contradistinction to the first, which had rejected it. The third was contemptuous of careful finishes, of meticulous detailing and craftsmanship, characteristic of the first phase (since, as Johnson put it, the era of handicraft was gone anyway). The point of departure for the third phase was Le Cor-busier's La Tourette monastery, "which spoke to us all."[12]

With regard to Belluschi, aside from the fact that he attended neither of the two sympo-sia, several things might be noted. In discussing the history of modernism in America, Johnson made no mention of the American modernist tradition predating the International Style and represented by the Chicago School, Louis Sullivan, and Wright. Nor did he mention regionalism, or the role of West Coast architects. This in effect sidelined Belluschi, who was from the Pacific Northwest and still regarded by many as a major spokesman of the modernist creed.

Johnson, whose review appeared in 1966, the same year as Robert Venturi's *Complexity and Contradiction in Architecture* (published, significantly enough, by the MoMA with which Johnson was affiliated), was one of the driving forces behind the "eastern architectural establishment," the elite body of academics, museum directors, and publishers who dominated the architectural scene, affecting who and what got published, hence what direction architecture was taking—in short, architectural values, or taste.[13] Johnson's review is thus important in revealing prevailing attitudes among the reigning powers, and putting Belluschi's 1960s work in perspective.

By this time the Miesian tradition, monotonous and debased as it had become in the hands of lesser talents, held little interest. Gone too was the interest in Japanese architecture, with its refinement and elegance, its technical finesse, fine craftsmanship, and small-scale detailing. Reacting against this, as well as the shallow glittery cultural "jewels" of the 1950s, the pristine, purified classical buildings poised on pilotis and isolated from their settings by spacious plazas, was the work of the brutalists, with buildings such as the Boston City Hall or the Yale Art and Architecture building—bold, large-scale sculptural forms in raw concrete with a deliberate disregard for fine detailing.[14]

As winds of fashion shifted, driven by the East Coast intelligentsia, interest in the monumental, space-defining structural solids of Kahn, Rudolph, Roche, Birkerts, and Breuer rose as the reputations of Aalto and other regionalists, with their gentler, less assertive forms, waned. The larger social concerns espoused by Lewis Mumford, Clarence Stein, Henry Wright, and Catherine Bauer Wurster came under particular attack. As Wurster caustically put it at the 1964 Columbia symposium on modernism several months before her death, the rational, socially conscious approach of the modernists was abandoned "because it would have required open minds and a real kind of collaboration and teamwork; architects working with engineers and social scientists, continuously trying to find better solutions, making experiments, and testing them. . . . This," she said, "is exactly what did not happen in the main line of 'International Style' modernism. What did happen was that the famous innovators reverted to the old prima donna role: papa has all the answers, and personal aesthetic expression is paramount."[15]

Unwavering in his commitment to his modernist principles, and uninterested in their books or lectures, Belluschi was increasingly at odds with these new academic trends. Pragmatic and professional in his approach, he became aligned in their eyes with crass business interests and the rise of corporate modernism.

Architecture must serve man rather than represent an exercise in sculpture, Belluschi contended in a 1964 article in the *National Observer*. "People will be in it. They may get in the way, their habits and behavior may be unpredictable, but there they are. Architects have to take basic human needs into account." Even emotional or irrational factors in human experience can't be ignored. In the East bedrooms are always on the second floor, and to Easterners a second story means bedrooms; it's a fact hardly rational, he pointed out, but architects could hardly defy it.[16]

Belluschi was often called a "social architect." To him this meant a concern for the human values of the individual, not society at large. He weighed his concern for how a building would affect its users against the demands of his client, fiscal, aesthetic, or whatever. If they conflicted, Belluschi yielded to the client, to whom he owed his primary allegiance. Larger social concerns to him were an abstraction; like world affairs and politics, unless they directly affected him, he was, for the most part, disinterested.[17] He thus remained allied with the business interests of his client and the sophisticated world of high art and "culture," a world increasingly out of sync with the larger social concerns of the 1960s. The disjuncture, appearing in his work in the later 1950s with developments such as Lincoln Center, an elitist cultural enclave subsidized by federal funds in the name of the public good, and the gargantuan Boston Back Bay Center, which had it been realized would have meant the loss of housing for the sake of private commercial gain, became glaringly obvious in his large-scale work in the 1960s, most conspicuously with the Pan Am Building. As private interests continued to clash with those of the public throughout the decade, Belluschi became emblematic of an exploitive establishment.

But then, too, his clients now were different. Alert to the changing nature of the profession, from a gentleman's calling, designing large mansions and luxury hotels in the affluent 1920s, to the fiercely competitive climate of the postwar era, offering the new, lucrative potential of the mass market and corporate client, Belluschi, an archopportunist, was quick to adjust. He was aware, too, of the changed nature of the building industry as costs, especially of labor, rose and the careful craftsmanship of the prewar years became prohibitively expensive.

As increasingly the large-scale work of corporate clients and big developers came under attack, Belluschi defended them, pointing out the nobility of their contribution to the common good. At the ground-breaking ceremony of the Equitable Center, a new head-quarters building for the Equitable Savings and Loan Association in Portland in 1963, a formalist columned templelike form set in an isolating plaza based on mid-fifties proto-types such as those being used in Lincoln Center, Belluschi praised his old friend and client Ralph Cake for his willingness to hold out for talented architects capable of quality design, as it set an important standard in the American city. Enlightened clients found that good design paid, he noted, "not only in greater financial returns but even more in lasting values and delight to visitors and neighbors." Casting it as a selfless, philan-thropic gesture, he continued, "The City of Portland is in debt to Mr. Cake for his wisdom and for the example he has set for a whole series of well-designed buildings, which now do honor to the city and the Pacific Northwest. The new building for which we are now breaking ground will be a memorable milestone in this quest for quality, and a real symbol of civic responsibility."[18]

Whether in fact the new Equitable proved to be "a memorable milestone" is, in this context, beside the point;[19] what does pertain is that given these priorities, it is clear why Belluschi appealed to corporate clients and developers. If their principal aim was a building that would maximize profits at the least cost, Belluschi accepted that. Con-versely, he remained convinced of the important civilizing role of the arts, especially in a time of rampant materialism, and urged businessmen and civic leaders to support the finer things in life that gave it meaning or significance.[20] But while seen as a cultural high priest, a man of impeccable taste, Belluschi was also a shrewd businessman whose first obligation was always to his client. It was this, plus his realistic acceptance of the constraints of the job and the confidence clients had in his commitment to their cause, that lent Belluschi his unique appeal.

Belluschi and Changes in the Architectural Profession

In the 1960s, Belluschi's architectural work was conducted in the capacity of associated architect. As the celebrity designer, he always received a substantial portion of the architect's fee;[21] he was also spared the pressures and expense of running an office. Introduced each time to a new staff, he quickly took the measure of the situation and made the most of it. There were advantages, too, for his associates: they learned from him, profiting from his vast body of experience, and were given an opportunity to do major projects—St. Mary's Cathedral in San Francisco, the Juilliard School of Music in New York, Meyerhoff Symphony Hall in Baltimore, the University of Ancona in Italy—that they otherwise would not have had. In many cases the association with Belluschi launched their careers, establishing their credibility and paving the way for other commissions, as in the case of RTKL and the Church of the Redeemer in Baltimore. Whatever the particular nature of Belluschi's role, projects on which he was involved typically turned out for the better.

The drawbacks of the situation were equally clear. When the process broke down, as it did increasingly in the later 1960s and 1970s, it was when Belluschi sensed a competing ego or, for whatever reason, lost control. Sometimes his manner of suddenly sweeping into the office struck people as imperious, or his infrequent presence was resented, and his directives were subtly boycotted by withholding information or delaying sending him drawings until it was too late to change. Often there were problems simply because he was not around and the project had to go forward without him.

As he often depended on staff he had just met, from different parts of the country with different backgrounds and training, his work with associates became less pure. Each job took on the attributes or formal language of those he was associated with, for better or worse: Skidmore, Owings & Merrill, Carl Koch and Associates, Eduardo Catalano. Sometimes this meant that the very qualities for which he was sought—subtleties of scale or proportion, handling of materials or fine detailing—were lost in unfamiliar hands.

Among friends, he gloatingly described his role in the design process as like the cat who skims off the cream, leaving the milk to others; elsewhere, he described it as like making love to a lot of ladies without having to wait around nine months for the results. Belluschi obviously relished the situation, doing what he loved most without the real work of carrying out his projects, and avoiding responsibility for whatever went wrong. But in so doing, he incurred not only the resentment of many in the field but also their lack of respect.

More troubling still was the issue of credit. Despite his frequent disclaimers, credit mattered immensely to Belluschi. Whether this was a result of his driving ambition, his own quest for fame, or the celebrity system at large and the desire to see every new building as the brainchild of "the architect," rather than of a collective body, is hard to say. In any case, Belluschi's reluctance to share credit wasn't new, as is clear from his early years in Portland. The issue in the late 1950s and 1960s was stickier, as the architectural procession as a whole grappled with the collision between the old, post-*Fountainhead* superstar system, with its single attribution, and the new collective team approach of the bigger offices. Pioneering the new role of design consultant, Belluschi's association repeatedly raised questions of credit and attribution; because his name was known, regardless of how minor his role he typically received credit for the building's authorship. And while Belluschi himself could have clarified the situation, stating the extent of his role and giving credit where credit was due, knowing it was to his advantage not to do so he often left it unclear.[22]

Apart from his designing, one of Belluschi's most powerful positions in the architectural profession was as a juror. Because of his sound judgment as well as vast experience, not as a competition entrant, as he himself had entered only one, and that unsuccessfully, but as a practicing architect who had worked in a broad range of building types, he was in frequent demand. He was excellent in this role: fair in his assessments, balanced in his views, conscientious in his thorough study of all entries. Given the time entrants put into their work, he argued, the least he owed them was the courtesy of a measured evaluation, and he always attempted to explain the reasons for his choices, while acknowledging that sometimes they couldn't be reasoned.

He served on an astonishing number of juries, among which were some of the most important of the era: for the U.S. Embassy in London (1956), Toronto City Hall (1959), the Hawaii State Capitol (1960), Boston City Hall (1960), Franklin D. Roosevelt Memorial (1960), Lawrence Hall of Science, Berkeley (1962), UC Berkeley Art Museum (1964), Copley Square in Boston (1966), National Football Hall of Fame (1967), and later the Chiang Kai Shek Memorial in Taiwan (1975), the INTELSAT Building in Washington (1980), the Vietnam War Memorial (1981), and the National Aquarium addition in Baltimore (1983).

Because of his interest in them and the architect selection process in general, Belluschi was often solicited for advice on the advantages and pitfalls of competitions, and played a crucial role in redefining the terms of architectural competitions after decades of disuse. Speaking on behalf of the jury in the Boston City Hall competition, for the advisory committee for the National Center for Atmospheric Research in 1962, or in reply to Senator Edward M. Kennedy who sought his advice on a memorial in honor of his brother, Belluschi conscientiously spelled out in detail the pros and cons of the system. He stressed the importance of having a good professional advisor to set up the competition, a clear, complete program, and a competent, fair-minded jury. Recommending architectural competitions as a way of offering an open, equal opportunity for young, unproven architects, and an excellent means of discovering fresh new talent, he pointed out their appropriateness in some situations but not all. He spelled out their drawbacks in terms of time and cost, how critical the makeup of the jury was, given the biases that could occur, and what a competition meant in terms of the client's abdicating his power ultimately to pursue his own choice. He pointed out a fourth, perhaps less obvious, drawback: however brilliant the winning entry, its creator might lack the necessary practical skills and facilities to carry the project to completion.

Recognized by the 1980s as one of the most experienced jurors in the country, Belluschi continued to be sought out long after he had retired from the MIT deanship and moved back to Portland. He was, for example, the only architect from the U.S. to serve on the jury for the International Telecommunications Satellite Organization (INTELSAT) Headquarters Building competition, headed by Paul Spreiregen, in Washington, D.C.[23]

Belluschi had perhaps an even greater impact on the architectural profession as an advisor. Consulted by individual patrons, private developers, design review boards, urban renewal agencies, corporate bodies, university administrators, city fathers, and other government officials, Belluschi became one of the most powerful behind-the-scenes players in the profession. Suave, articulate, experienced, his aesthetic judgment trusted implicitly, he was called upon over and over for recommendations on key decisions—from which architect to choose for a major commission, to specific advice on improving a design or plan. As a design critic he was excellent, typically spotting immediately whatever problem there might be, as in the case of Bassetti's proposal for the U.S. Embassy in Portugal, and tactfully recommending another solution; in designs further along, he was good at suggesting improvements such as a more graceful fenestration pattern or finer material; as a project neared completion, he was excellent at recommending finishing touches—better choice of hardware, finish of a surface, color of rug—cosmetic, perhaps, but often the final touch that made the difference in an otherwise banal building.

From the time of his appointment to the National Commission of Fine Arts in 1950, he was in constant demand: as an advisor to Phyllis Lambert on the Seagram Building, Jacqueline Kennedy on the Kennedy Library, the U.S. government on the Air Force Academy in Colorado Springs as well as foreign embassies abroad; to colleges and universities such as MIT, the University of Washington, University of Colorado, Princeton, and University of Massachusetts; to corporate clients such as the Ford Foundation, CBS in New York, Pacific Gas & Electric in California, and other electric power companies building nuclear plants such as Portland General Electric in Oregon, and Orange & Rockland Utilities Company and Central Hudson Gas & Electric Corporation in New York; to developers such as the Perini Corporation, Cabot, Cabot & Forbes, Beacon Companies, and Rose Associates; to museums such as the Everson Museum in Syracuse and the National Gallery in Washington. Sometimes he served simply but importantly as an insurance policy for a chary client reluctant to entrust a major commission to a young, inexperienced office. Bringing them jobs with his reputation, then functioning as a senior advisor, he helped launch a number of embryonic firms, such as RTKL in Baltimore, Sasaki & Associates in Cambridge, Zimmer Gunsul Frasca in Portland, and Jung/Brannen in Boston.

In this role he exerted enormous influence. As chairman of the Advisory Committee of Deans charged with selecting an architect for the new National Center for Atmospheric Research in Boulder, as a member of the committee to select an architect for the proposed John F. Kennedy Memorial Library in 1963, on the advisory panel for the architectural development of the city of Columbus, Indiana, Belluschi was successful in getting younger, less-known architects like Catalano and Pei some of their first major jobs.

I. M. Pei is perhaps the most prominent of his protégés. When they met in the early 1950s, Pei was still working for the developer William Zeckendorf. It was Belluschi who encouraged Pei to break away and start an office of his own, and instructed him exactly how to go about it.[24] Once Pei was on his own, Belluschi was instrumental in getting him the commission for the Earth Sciences Building at MIT in 1959, then was one of the jurors awarding Pei the Arnold Brunner Memorial Prize in Architecture in 1962, then recommended him for the NCAR commission in Boulder, the Kennedy Library in Cambridge, the Everson Museum in Syracuse, the Portland Museum of Art in Portland, Maine, and most importantly of all the East Wing of the National Gallery in Washington, the commission that secured Pei his international reputation.[25]

Urban Planning: Baltimore

Urban planning was another area in which Belluschi's impact was profound. As cities across the nation struggled to cope with problems of the postwar era—public housing, mass transit, decentralization, and deteriorating downtowns—Belluschi was called upon repeatedly by city officials or planning commissions for advice, and was involved in the postwar planning and implementation of urban renewal programs in cities across the nation, from Boston and Baltimore to Portland, Los Angeles, and San Francisco.

In late fall of 1956, Belluschi was asked to advise the Greater Baltimore Committee, a group of local businessmen and developers representing some of the key industries in the Baltimore area. The well-connected Archibald Rogers, with whom Belluschi was associated on the Church of the Redeemer, was chairing the committee (of which James Rouse, with whom Belluschi was also working on the Mondawmin Shopping Center, was also a member); Rogers had suggested bringing in Belluschi as an informed but objective outsider to help resolve a dispute on the location of the new civic center. Mayor Thomas D'Alesandro, Jr., of Baltimore had selected a park site, which had aroused their concern because it would consume valuable open space and, more importantly, was located at a considerable distance from the downtown, thus would drain its business.[26]

Once involved, Belluschi found the problem was more than just a choice of sites. He suggested that what was needed was the stimulation of more life in the downtown, with buildings such as sports and cultural facilities that could serve as a community center, and amenities that would sell the public on the idea of returning to the downtown.

A decision was imminent, but with the help of local architects and city officials to secure the specific information he needed, and with Catalano in Cambridge to do the drawings, Belluschi, drawing on some of Kenzo Tange's recent town planning ideas for Tokyo, specifically his proposal for filling part of the bay, as well as those of Victor Gruen for the revitalization of inner cities by means of new downtown retailing centers, quickly prepared a proposal. It called for locating the civic center on a 10-acre site formed of new land created by filling the south end and western edge of Baltimore's inner harbor, putting the main building, a large sports arena, there, and siting the other buildings along the waterfront to the north. This would put the civic center close to the downtown, easily accessible by foot to the functions and services provided by downtown merchants, and, in Belluschi's words, would serve as a source for the social intercourse people seek and

Baltimore Civic Center proposal, January 1957.

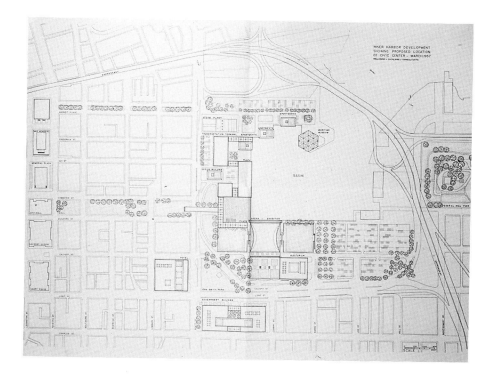

expect in a city center. Linked directly to the main traffic arteries and transit routes, it would cut down congestion and facilitate access. Parking space would be distributed so that it could be used jointly by regular downtowners as well as visitors, thus assuring full occupancy day and night throughout the year. Located adjacent to the financial district of the city, it would serve as a stimulus to future development by private enterprise in the downtown area. And finally, the new civic center, placed in a dramatic setting and located so as to be seen at a distance, would serve as a proud symbol of the city at large.[27]

Belluschi's plan, set up to be implemented incrementally as funds accrued, met each of the specific stipulations established by the mayor's civic center committee: cost not to exceed $6 million, provision of adequate space for parking, and construction that could begin immediately. As his proposal was only tentative, Belluschi stressed the importance of a thorough long-range comprehensive study analyzing traffic patterns, off-street parking needs, and land use priorities before a more concrete plan was drawn up.

Described as "somewhat breathtaking" in the local press,[28] Belluschi's proposal was reviewed by the Department of Public Works, and with its suggestions based on specific engineering and economic factors, was revised and resubmitted to the mayor the following month. Despite what were widely recognized to be strong arguments, its generally favorable response locally, its endorsement by the local AIA chapter as well as by both the Committee for the Downtown and Greater Baltimore Committee, Belluschi's Inner Harbor plan was rejected by the mayor, who went with the park site.

The principles Belluschi outlined, however, established a model, and not just for Baltimore. Philip Stedfast, director of city planning in Columbia, South Carolina, requested Belluschi's permission to cite the Baltimore proposal in his department's proposal for a downtown civic center, adding his regret that Baltimore, in rejecting it, had missed a chance to be a real leader in civic design.[29]

The proposal to develop a site in the Baltimore inner city as a means of catalyzing the revitalization of the downtown was pursued by private interests, however, the following year. Under the auspices of the Greater Baltimore Committee led by James Rouse, an ambitious $128 million urban renewal program combining federal and private funds was established. Called the Charles Center, the large-scale commercial development was to cover 22 acres of Baltimore's downtown midway between the main shopping district and the office building area. Because of his experience on the abortive Baltimore Civic Center project, plus his connections with people such as Rouse, Belluschi continued to be involved as a member of Baltimore's Architectural Design Review Board in charge of reviewing and approving all plans and proposals before the city. The Charles Center, which by 1969 had grown to 33 acres in the heart of Baltimore, was recognized as a major success, no mere "symbolic shot in the arm" or monumental government center but a live, working, economically feasible and productive center devoted largely to commercial use. At the end of ten years, it was firmly established as the urban center it was meant to be, both a center of activity in itself and a catalyst for further downtown redevelopment. Although as an article in the *Architectural Forum* pointed out, not all the buildings in the Charles Center were of the same level of quality, all served well their urban roles.[30]

In 1969, Belluschi himself was given the commission for the IBM Building on the pivotal site facing the Inner Harbor on Pratt Street. Completed in 1975 in association with Emery Roth & Sons, it consisted of a long, low, 10-story rectangular block with a two-story colonnaded base, of reinforced concrete with exteriors of precast exposed aggregate, harking back to a standard late-fifties type.

Despite occasional questions of conflict of interest,[31] Belluschi remained on the architectural review board, a position he held initially with deans G. Holmes Perkins from the University of Pennsylvania and Joseph Hudnut of Harvard from 1959 to 1975, at which time he asked to resign in the interest of age and distance, as by this time he had moved back to Portland. An obviously highly valued member of the board who had played a crucial role in setting high design standards for the project, renowned for his ability to deal with both conceptual and practical problems before they were locked up in working drawings, and for his skill in unraveling seemingly insoluble problems with feasible solutions, Belluschi was asked to continue on a nonobligatory, consulting basis, attending meetings only when his time and interest allowed.[32]

San Francisco

Belluschi served a similar role in San Francisco. In 1959 as a consultant for the Perini Corporation, a Boston-based development company, he was involved in advising and counseling his client on proposals for both the Golden Gateway, an urban renewal project in San Francisco, and the Santa Monica urban renewal project in southern California. In both, but particularly in the San Francisco project, Belluschi's participation was significant. With his storehouse of ideas and wealth of experience, plus wide range of contacts and interests, he was in a position to advise not only on larger conceptual and design problems but also on small practical issues. He would frequently come up with useful ideas gleaned from his experience elsewhere, such as using a bronchoscope,

IBM Building, Baltimore, 1970–1975.

a small tubular medical instrument like a periscope that enabled them to simulate the experience of actually walking through the elevated streets of the Golden Gateway model.[33] By opening up avenues and stimulating thinking, he got the team of architects, planners, and developers beyond impasses, moving the project ahead at moments when it bogged down. With his vast resources of information, his quick analytic mind, plus his generosity in sharing ideas, Belluschi frequently played a critical if low-profile role.

Working with the San Francisco Redevelopment Authority on behalf of the Perini Corporation in the early 1960s, then negotiating with the agency several years later on his own proposal for St. Mary's Cathedral, which was located on urban renewal land, Belluschi became well acquainted with it. In 1966, shortly after the St. Mary's plans were approved, he was asked to become a member of the Redevelopment Authority's Architectural Advisory Committee. The appointment came at a critical juncture, as major upheavals in basic values were taking place not only among architects and planners but society at large. Nowhere were those upheavals more apparent than in San Francisco.[34]

One of these occurred in 1967, during Belluschi's tenure on the Advisory Committee, pitting him against his colleagues in the profession. It was precipitated by the proposal of Atlanta architect-developer John Portman for the "Gateway World Trade Center," which eventually became the Embarcadero Center. Occupying one of the finest sites in the city, 8.5 acres by the waterfront facing the spans of the Bay Bridge from the west, Portman's proposal consisted of a tough, assertive, highly sculptural stepped form of rough exposed concrete; facing onto Market Street to the south, it was to have a wind-protected open place behind it, sited to catch southeast sun. Approved by the Architectural Advisory Committee, chaired by Belluschi, on the grounds that it showed an "enlightened attitude" on the part of the developer, the Portman proposal was vehemently opposed by the local architectural and planning community, the AIA, American Institute of Planners, and American Society of Landscape Architects, who saw its monumental brutalist form as creating a visual wall out of scale with the fragile fabric of the city; its proposed pedestrian mall they found excessively large and of doubtful amenity to the city, its parking garages gross and unacceptable at the pedestrian level—in short a bold, dramatic concept perhaps, but wholly inappropriate for San Francisco's humanistic scale. Accusing the Architectural Advisory Committee of not upholding the public interest, the project's opponents demanded a reevaluation. Among the chief opponents was Marc Goldstein of SOM, with whom Belluschi was then involved on the Bank of America Building.[35]

Belluschi's statement in defense of the Portman project, which despite the opposition was built as planned, left no doubt that he was on the side of large-scale growth and development. Published in the *San Francisco Chronicle* and subsequently quoted in an editorial, "The City's Growth to a New, Larger Scale," it did little to enhance Belluschi's popularity in the Bay Area.[36]

Boston

The situation in Boston was somewhat different. This was home territory for Belluschi, hence he was at once more involved and more detached. Involved, in that he knew the issues and their history, who the key figures were and their political connections; detached because, as his work so often overlapped with that of friends, clients, and professional colleagues, he was unable to speak as freely as he otherwise might.

Belluschi had served as a member of the Cambridge Planning Board, a civic group aimed at working with city government on city improvements, in the mid-fifties, but it wasn't until 1958 that his role in city affairs became of real significance. In anticipation of the Government Center then in the process of being planned, the Boston City Planning Board asked the Boston Society of Architects and Massachusetts State Association of Architects jointly to select a body of five men to serve as an advisory group for the center. Acting as spokesmen for the profession, the group was to consult and advise the City Planning Board on all architectural matters specifically related to the new civic center planned for Scollay Square. Recognized, in the words of the president of the Boston Society of Architects, as an exceptional opportunity for the profession to make an outstanding permanent contribution to American architecture, they sought the services of a distinguished group of men "who consistently stand for the very highest ideals of the profession and whose past achievements are a matter of proud record." The five-member committee was expected to offer the City Planning Board concrete suggestions as well as criticism, and to contribute to the negotiations with the various agencies and architects responsible for the various buildings in the project area. Invited to serve were architects Nelson Aldrich, José Luis Sert, then dean at Harvard, Henry Shepley, Hugh Stubbins, and Belluschi. One of their first tasks was advising the Planning Board on the pros and cons of a competition as a means of selecting the most qualified architect for the new Boston City Hall. Belluschi continued to be involved in the development of the Government Center, serving as head jury member in the Boston City Hall competition itself.[37]

In 1961, when Edward Logue was brought in by newly elected mayor John Collins to set up the Boston Redevelopment Agency, Logue, holding high-quality design to be a major

14 *Oregonian Building, Portland, 1945–*
1948, exterior (photo: author).

15 Portsmouth Abbey church, 1957–
1960, exterior (photo: author).

16 Portsmouth Abbey church, interior
(photo: Joseph Molitor).

17   Church of the Redeemer, Baltimore, 1954–1958, exterior with existing church at right (photo: author).

18   Church of the Redeemer, interior (photo: author).

19 *Wellesley Office Park (photo:*
author).

20 *Pan Am Building, New York, 1963.*

21 Rohm & Haas Building, Philadelphia, 1962–1964 (photo: author).

22 *Boston Company Building, Boston,*
1966–1969, exterior (photo: author).

23　Juilliard School for the Performing
Arts, New York, 1963–1969, exterior
(photo: Ezra Stoller).

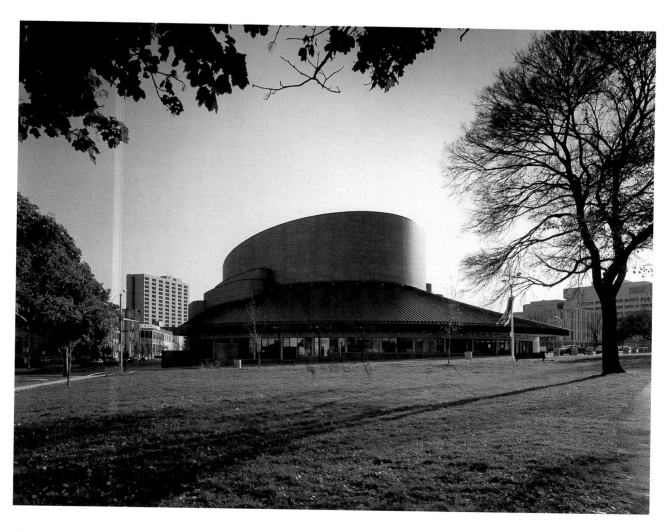

24 *Meyerhoff Symphony Hall, Baltimore, 1972–1982 (photo: Richard
Mandelkorn).*

25 United Hebrew Congregation Synagogue, St. Louis, preliminary study,
dated 4 February 1987.

26 United Hebrew Congregation Synagogue, St. Louis, preliminary study.

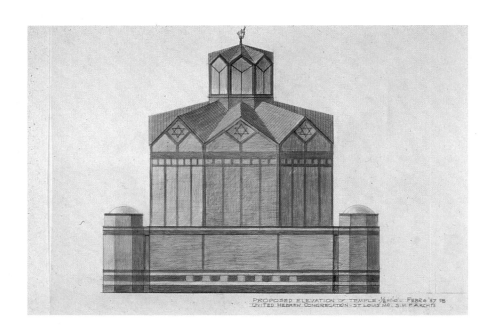

27 *United Hebrew Congregation Syna-gogue, St. Louis, preliminary study.*

28 *United Hebrew Congregation Syna-gogue, St. Louis, preliminary study, dated 15 June 1987.*

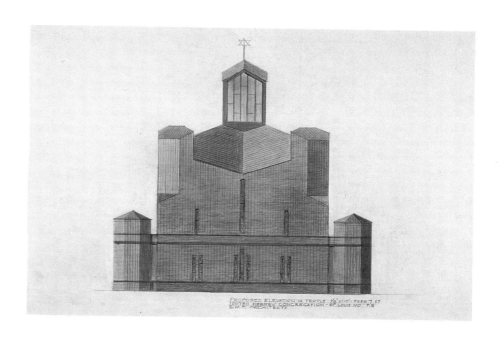

29 *Portsmouth Abbey student library
and classroom building (photo: Warren
Jagger).*

priority, reestablished the advisory committee to review and evaluate all major proposals submitted to the BRA, as well as advise on related architectural issues.

As architectural watchdogs, the committee played an important, often delicate role. In 1961 Belluschi sent other members of the committee a letter urging them to go on record as opposing the new State Office Building designed by Emery Roth & Sons, with whom he was currently associated on the Pan Am Building and three years hence would be involved again, briefly, on the Bank of America Building in San Francisco. As a result of their letter to the governor stating their opposition, progress was halted and the design restudied.

Brought on at the outset, Belluschi remained on the Advisory Committee to the BRA throughout the 1960s, playing a low-profile but significant role in determining what buildings should be saved, which demolished, and in establishing a level of quality to be aspired to. It was a critical period in Boston's history. The city was seen as a laboratory for the urban renewal process, having suffered decades of stagnation with little or no new construction in the inner core. Beginning in the early 1960s under Collins and Logue, who used the urban renewal process to inject massive doses of federal funds into downtown redevelopment, Boston experienced a building boom that lasted well into the decade, making it the most active of urban renewal cities in the nation. Familiar with the politics of urban renewal in the planning of Lincoln Center in New York, then in Baltimore, Philadelphia, and San Francisco, Belluschi was in a position to contribute a great deal.

Occasionally his contributions were pivotal, making the difference between a proposal that was unacceptable and one that was approved. One of the most striking examples of this was his assistance on the Center Plaza Building opposite the new Boston City Hall, designed by Welton Becket and Associates for the Beacon Companies. The project, being done in Becket's New York office, had stalled. While respecting the guidelines for height and overall massing set in the Government Center master plan, the 900-foot-long, curved facade of the building was simply too ordinary for such a crucial site. Commenting on the weaknesses of a colleague's design took considerable tact, but Belluschi could handle it if anyone could; volunteering to work with the Becket team, he was able to suggest a few simple but critical modifications—adding some texture to the surface, adjusting the proportions of the windows, introducing a break in the fenestration to set up a particular rhythm—all surface features, or "cosmetics," to use Belluschi's word, but beauty enhancers that made the critical difference. With his modifications, the Becket building became not simply acceptable but in the eyes of many one of the finest buildings in the Government Center complex. Purposefully discreet, conceived as a backdrop for Kallmann, McKinnell and Knowles's Boston City Hall, it complemented rather than competed in form, color, and texture, while at the same time meshing harmoniously with the existing brick buildings in the Scollay Square area. More Belluschi than Becket in its quiet distinction, the building serves as a bridge between old and new, the fabric of the existing city and the bold, muscular brutalist City Hall.[38]

Given the tight network of practicing architects and developers in Boston of which Belluschi was an integral part, there was bound to be some crossing of roles. Handling the situation skillfully and sensitively, Belluschi was careful to make known his connections with the architects, clients, and developers whose work the committee was reviewing to avoid questions of conflict of interest. He refrained from personally sending or signing letters on behalf of the committee that might compromise his working relations with his colleagues or clients. When, for example, Charles Hilgenhurst, director of the design review process to whom the Advisory Committee was immediately responsible, asked Belluschi if he would sign a letter granting only a qualified endorsement to a proposed design submitted by the developer Gerald Blakeley of Cabot, Cabot & Forbes, Belluschi replied that he would rather not as he himself was doing some work for the "ubiquitous Blakeley," and felt the signing of the letter might place him in an equivocal situation.[39]

Sometimes these relationships got complicated. When Mayor Collins asked Belluschi to serve on a special seven-member blue ribbon panel to select a developer for Parcel 8, one of the critical plots in the Government Center plan, Belluschi at the outset of their meetings disclosed not only that he owned stock in one of the competing development companies, but that he was involved professionally with virtually every one of the principals of the competing firms—Cabot, Cabot & Forbes on Technology Square, Pier Luigi Nervi on St. Mary's Cathedral in San Francisco, the construction consultant Carl Morse on the Juilliard School in New York, and the Perini Corporation on the Golden Gateway housing development. Although he felt he could retain an impartial view, Belluschi acknowledged that in a tie vote, his objectivity might be questioned, and to avoid any accusations of conflict of interest, he offered to resign. Both the mayor and other members of the panel rejected the suggestion and assured Belluschi they wanted him retained, not only because of his long-standing familiarity with the development of the Government Center but because, in their words, they considered him one of the most distinguished architectural jurors in the country and a valuable member of the team.[40]

When one of his own buildings, such as the Boston Company Building or 60 State Street, came up for deliberation, Belluschi simply left the room.[41]

Belluschi's work on advisory committees and design review boards was respected not only by city officials but by developers who valued his judgment, fair-mindedness, and sensitivity to the economic realities of their situation, as well as his connections with public officials on both the local and federal level. His name carried considerable weight. It also opened doors to his receiving major commissions from developers in cities throughout the country. It was his adroit solution to the problem of Becket's Center Plaza Building, for example, that brought him to the attention of Norman Leventhal, head of the Beacon Companies, who subsequently proved to be one of his most loyal clients in the latter 1960s and 1970s.

Campus Planning

Belluschi had excellent credentials as an advisor to universities and colleges—a leading modernist yet not a prima donna, aware of the need to balance a distinctive design with respect for existing tradition, experienced in planning a design, with college libraries, dormitories, and science buildings as well as master plans dating back to the 1920s.

The administrators at MIT were among the first to recognize Belluschi as a valuable resource. The campus had the legacy of a Beaux-Arts plan that at one time had given the campus both grandeur and homogeneity; this, however, had been lost with the postwar glut of returning veterans, and new buildings had been added without long-range planning. In the late 1940s, under Wurster's impetus, Aalto and Eero Saarinen had been brought in; their work had not been coordinated, however, and when Belluschi arrived the campus was still without an overall plan. In 1958 Belluschi was asked to work with the newly established planning office at MIT; he in turn engaged Hideo Sasaki, a young professor of landscape architecture at Harvard whom he had befriended, for site planning. Out of this came a new vision for the campus.

One of the key issues MIT officials wanted addressed was the humanizing of the campus, softening the school's image of being too industrial and austere. Another problem was the harmonizing of the various architectural languages represented by new "landmark" buildings, such as Aalto's Baker House dormitory and Saarinen's auditorium and chapel. Belluschi suggested assigning whole areas of the campus to different architects, each of top quality, and, in Belluschi's words, giving each his head with only a light hand on the reins. Upon his recommendation, Walter Netsch of the Chicago office of SOM was brought in to do the new buildings on the north of campus, I. M. Pei those on the east, Bunshaft for the Karl Taylor Compton Laboratories, and Catalano for the new Student

Center after Saarinen died. Serving as the chairman of the Long Range Planning Committee, Belluschi was charged with not only selecting architects but coordinating their efforts in the interest of avoiding the visual hodgepodge evident at Yale, where every commission, in the words of one of Belluschi's colleagues, "generated an ad hoc decision in favor of the star of the moment, the result being stylistic chaos."

As the pressure to expand colleges and universities mounted in the early 1960s, Belluschi was called upon by a number of other colleges and universities around the country to serve in an advisory capacity. More often than not, when the situation called for it, he brought in Sasaki Associates, planners and landscape architects, as co-consultants; sometimes the situation was reversed, with Sasaki receiving the commission and bringing Belluschi in for design.

As a newly appointed professor of landscape architecture and planning at Harvard in the early 1950s, Sasaki was eager to bridge the gap between the departments of landscape and architecture that had widened over the course of the years,[42] and had helped sponsor a national conference to further understanding between the two fields. Architects, then as now, were disdainful of landscape architecture. Inviting the new dean to the conference along with other faculty at MIT, Sasaki was pleasantly surprised when Belluschi was one of the few who actually came. The two men found they had much in common, sharing similar views on the integral relationship of buildings and landscape. As Sasaki put it, at a time when architects were doing striking, individualistic buildings, Belluschi refused to conform. His buildings fit the landscape, always showing a concern for the greater whole.[43] After their initial meeting, Belluschi reciprocated by inviting Sasaki to participate as a studio critic at MIT, and when in 1958 he was asked to be involved in the planning of the MIT campus, he called in the Sasaki office for assistance. It was the beginning of a long, mutually rewarding association.

Of their many joint endeavors, the University of Colorado at Boulder was one of the more important. The university had retained Sasaki Associates to draw up a new master plan; knowing several new buildings were to be added and wanting the commissions, Sasaki included Belluschi's name to lend stature to their design division. Thanks to the Belluschi connection, both the Engineering Center and Married Student Housing were done in their office, with Kenneth DeMay designer.

Retained by the university throughout the 1960s to advise the planning staff and critically review all proposed buildings, the Sasaki/Belluschi association provided a consistent outlook rare in college campuses of that era. Lauding their collaboration, John Morris Dixon in the *Architectural Forum* noted that by the time all the development projected in the 1960 master plan was completed, the university would have more than doubled in physical size from the time Sasaki and Belluschi were brought in. "It might have been possible in 1960 to initiate a visionary departure from the existing pattern—a single-structure campus or a plug-in-system that might have accommodated 20,000 students more efficiently. Instead, the design consultants saw and grasped a larger opportunity to create a harmonious environment and a visible continuity with the past. How many other universities can offer as much?" Much of this was unquestionably Belluschi's doing.[44]

Work with Corporate Clients and Developers: The Beacon Companies

As corporate clients began to eclipse the smaller-scale, single client in both number and importance, Belluschi was quick to see the trend developing. Here were the largest building resources, the most significant building programs, in short the architect's most valuable customers. As social pressure grew in the late 1950s and early 1960s, forcing developers and corporate clients to raise the standards of their design and to think beyond mere dollars, and as developers themselves recognized that architecturally distinctive corporate towers like Lever House or the Seagram Building paid off in profits as well as prestige, they began seeking the services of architects, especially those with well-known names.[45]

Investment builders shied away from "prize-winning architects" with cutting-edge designs because their work was prohibitively expensive and typically required time-consuming code variances, a message the Johnson Wax Building and the Seagram vividly brought home. Commercial architects like Emery Roth & Sons, on the other hand, relying on standardized types, promised speed and reliability. Belluschi offered a compromise: a renowned architect but not a prima donna, not interested in creating striking designs or setting new trends, and first and foremost respectful of his client's requirements and budget, someone who brought in as much artistic quality as time, budget, and his clients' tastes would allow. With his business acumen and ability to listen, both rare among design architects, he understood their problems, looked at the situation from their perspective, and specifically sought solutions that were best for them. They trusted him personally and professionally, respecting him as an honest, fair person and man of integrity and most of all trusting his judgment.

Belluschi was also cheaper. Because he worked basically as a one-man operation out of his home, with his MIT secretary and later wife Marjorie functioning as his personal secretary, accountant, librarian, and press agent (as well as hostess, housekeeper, and cook), his overhead was low, often nothing more than office supplies and the hours of a draftsman. Engaging him as a design consultant in association with an attractively priced commercial architect such as Emery Roth & Sons, the cost-conscious corporate client could get the best of both worlds: a name architect plus the efficiency and reliability of a standard commercial office.[46]

Belluschi's work with developers and corporate clients usually took one of two forms. Sometimes he served as an advisor working directly for the client, as he did with the Perini Corporation, advising them on the selection of architects and working on their behalf to ensure they got exactly what they wanted from their architects. At other times he was engaged as a design consultant to the architect, serving as the principal designer on their building in association with an established firm. It was in this latter capacity that he did some of his most conspicuous work in the later 1960s, especially in Boston.

Over the course of the 1960s, Norman Leventhal grew to be one of Boston's biggest developers. Born in Boston, Leventhal attended MIT where he studied building engineering. After the war, he and his brother formed the Beacon Companies construction firm. Aware of the growing potential for suburban development, they acquired a plot of land in Wellesley, about 20 minutes outside Boston, and established a small office park. Meanwhile, they heard of investment opportunities beginning to materialize within Boston's urban renewal program, and in 1962 they submitted a proposal for the Central Plaza Building, with Welton Becket of New York as their architect. Boston was still moribund economically, and with the Collins-Logue campaign to lure private investment into downtown building just getting started, theirs was the only proposal submitted. The Architectural Advisory Committee, consisting of Belluschi, Harry Weese, and Vincent Kling, however, was not happy with Becket's proposal, which left them all in a bind. The Beacon Companies, still small and struggling, doing mostly construction jobs for the federal government, was eager for the opportunity to expand, and Logue and the BRA needed Leventhal's money to start the development ball in the downtown rolling. Belluschi's help in improving the Becket proposal saved the day.[47]

Leventhal had known Belluschi previously through his contacts at MIT, but was thoroughly impressed by seeing him in action at BRA meetings. His eyes newly opened to design quality and its importance in gaining official sanction, Leventhal saw the shortcomings of their buildings in the Wellesley Office Park and subsequently asked Belluschi his advice in upgrading them. The two men struck a bond, Leventhal with his quick mind, plus background in construction and engineering, Belluschi with his stature and close ties to public officials, plus sound business sense and artistic eye. It was a good working relationship based on respect and much give and take. Their contact remained, even after Belluschi began turning over their projects to his former assistant, Robert Brannen, who by then had opened his own office.

As fledgling developers, Leventhal and his brother learned a great deal from Belluschi, not only about architecture and urban planning in general but also specifics on inexpensive ways of designing better buildings. They learned from an insider the art of diplomacy, and how to deal effectively with architects, public officials, and design review boards. They also gained access to Belluschi's network of contacts throughout the Boston area, which provided them resources they would not otherwise have had. Initially brought in simply to improve the looks of their existing buildings, Belluschi expanded Leventhal's thinking on such things as site planning, pointing out the public relations value of respecting the natural site as well as relating design to other buildings in the area. The original buildings in the Wellesley Office Park complex were Corbusier-derived

Wellesley Office Park (photo: Steve Rosenthal).

monuments in white concrete. Belluschi convinced Leventhal that buildings could be distinctive without being avant-garde, and that particularly in their suburban situation, with a heavily wooded site of considerable natural beauty, an eye-catching building was inappropriate. For subsequent buildings, Leventhal went straight to Belluschi, who brought in Robert Brannen as an assistant. They added four more buildings to the complex, all of high-quality design. Brannen then took over, adding buildings to the complex on his own, with Belluschi associated. Proving highly successful, the Wellesley Office Park helped launch what was eventually to become Jung/Brannen Associates, one of the largest and most successful firms in downtown Boston.

The Wellesley buildings designed under Belluschi consisted of four- to five-story multi-tenant office structures, of warm reddish brick and rust-colored Corten steel to blend with the wooded terrain. Corten steel was still experimental then, dark in color like bronze but far more economical. Belluschi also recommended Michio Ihara, a young sculptor at MIT's Center for Visual Studies, for some art. Ihara's aluminum wind sculpture at the entrance of the main building set the high artistic tone of the park as whole.

Under Belluschi's guidance, the park was transformed from an ordinary 1950s office park into a complex of extraordinary beauty. Its success was obvious, winning recognition from Boston architectural critic Robert Campbell as well as an award of excellence from the American Institute of Steel Construction, and was a major turning point in the growth of the Beacon Companies.[48] Not only did it create a threat to Boston's downtown by drawing financial services and other vital tenants from there, but it was a building complex Ed Logue found "alarming because it was so damned attractive."[49] Architecturally, it was considered the finest office park around.

The Beacon Companies henceforth retained Belluschi as their design consultant, working in association with the architect Samuel Paul, who specialized in large-scale housing, much of it for HUD, and Jung/Brannen on a series of federally subsidized low- to moderate-cost housing projects mostly around Boston: Chatham West, Oak Street, and Pine Grove Housing in Brockton, Blake Estates in Hyde Park, Whittier Terrace in Worcester, and Blue Ridge Estates in Richmond, Virginia. Belluschi's involvement was limited, basically to establishing the overall concept and reviewing progress, but critical. It was the buildings' design quality, the sensitive site planning, with units each given their own private courtyard and garden, and the landscaping, with the buildings clustered in a spacious parklike setting, that made them exceptional. As Leventhal described it, Belluschi's fee for the projects was larger than other architects', but it was a difference offset by the soundness of his advice and, at least as importantly, by the weight his name carried in getting federal funding.[50]

Century 21 Project, Philadelphia, 1968, and the Founding of Jung/Brannen Associates

The Century 21 complex, had it been built, would have been one of the biggest developments Belluschi was wholly responsible for in his career. Proposed in anticipation of Philadelphia's 1976 Bicentennial Exhibition, it was to have consisted of a $200 million complex of hotel and convention facilities, the largest downtown development since Rockefeller Center in New York City, on a 7-acre site over the Penn Central railroad yard at the west end of Kennedy Boulevard by the Schuylkill River in downtown Philadelphia. Belluschi initially thought of bringing in as a consultant John Portman, then the leading figure in the country in luxury hotel facilities, whose proposal for the Embarcadero Center Belluschi was meanwhile defending as chairman of the Architectural Advisory Committee in San Francisco. The Sasaki office (then Sasaki Dawson DeMay Associates) was brought in for site planning, and Brannen for the architectural drawings. Belluschi was to be architect in charge.[51]

Though Portman was evidently consulted, it was only after the concept drawings were done. The Century 21 complex nonetheless bears clear influence of his formal approach. Modeled on the Hyatt Regency in San Francisco, the Belluschi hotel was to have been a bold, sculptural building of structural steel forming the railroad enclosure and reinforced concrete, with its 30 floors stepped back to form a dramatic 106-foot-high skylighted atrium on the interior. On a triangular site, with the base of the building aligned with the railroad tracks, the structure was to have included a hyperbolic paraboloid, its plane twisted so that rooms faced out onto views. It was also to include three restaurant areas, banquet facilities for 2,000 people, and exhibition space of 17,000 square feet; like Portman's Hyatt Regency, it was to be crowned by a revolving tower restaurant.[52]

What made the project extraordinary, apart from its sheer size and complexity, was its integration with the redevelopment plans of the central city. At the outset of their thinking, Belluschi had called on Edmund Bacon, then director of Philadelphia's City Planning Commission, whom he knew through his work on the Rohm & Haas Building in that city in the early 1960s, for firsthand advice. Bacon recognized the potential of the project as an important stimulus for the development of the entire area, and urged Belluschi and his backers, a consortium of Philadelphia businessmen, to develop their plans in association with the owners of adjacent parcels. Bacon also indicated that the city would be willing to assist in coordinating the private ventures. He suggested they hire a Philadelphia traffic consultant for assistance in linking the complex to the high-speed commuter train system, subways, parking, and other elements of the city's transportation network, and assured them that the city would cooperate in building access ramps off Kennedy

Century 21 Urban Complex, Philadel-phia, model (Progressive Architecture, July 1968).

Century 21 Urban Complex, site plan, 1968 (Oregon Historical Society).

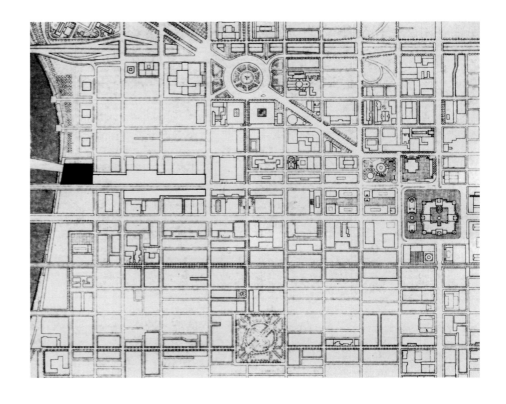

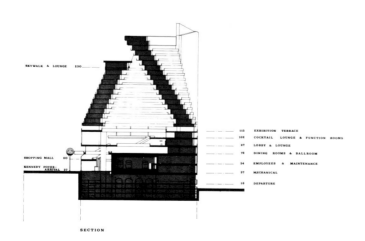

SKYWALK & LOUNGE   230

SHOPPING MALL   60
KENNEDY FOYER-
ARRIVAL   37

SECTION

115   EXHIBITION   TERRACE
102   COCKTAIL   LOUNGE & FUNCTION ROOMS
87   LOBBY & LOUNGE
72   DINING   ROOMS & BALLROOM
54   EMPLOYEES & MAINTENANCE
37   MECHANICAL
16   DEPARTURE

CENTURY 21 HOTEL
PIETRO BELLUSCHI AND JUNG/BRANNEN ASSOCIATES INC. ARCHITECTS

MARCH 27 1969

Century 21 Hotel, model.

Century 21 Hotel, section.

Boulevard and vacating minor streets if necessary. Bacon was particularly excited about the concept of the long multilevel enclosed pedestrian mall forming the main circulation spine, which he suggested be linked to the riverfront and other surrounding activity centers.[53]

As the large-scale commercial project developed, it became clear that it was not something Belluschi could handle alone, even with Brannen's assistance. The young, ambitious Brannen, however, was reluctant to give it up, and as there were advantages to working with him rather than associating with a larger office, Belluschi agreed if a third party, Yu Sing Jung, were brought in. Jung was a former Catalano student then teaching at MIT who had impressed Belluschi with his organizational skills. He agreed to join them.

The Century 21 project was huge, complicated, and demanding, the team skeletal and inexperienced. Belluschi himself at this point was frantically busy—ensnarled in negotiations with the Juilliard School of Music in Lincoln Center and St. Mary's Cathedral in San Francisco, which he had begun in 1963, still working on a corporate tower for the Boston Company and about to begin the Keystone Building in Boston, involved in the Blossom Center for Performing Arts in Cleveland, Clark Art Institute addition in Williamstown, Massachusetts, and University of Virginia School of Architecture and Fine Arts in Charlottesville, starting work on the Sacramento Convention Center, plus myriad other projects across the country. The Century 21 project advanced to the stage of working drawings, then was abandoned when their clients' partnership fell through.[54]

The Century 21 project nonetheless served as the point of departure for the Jung/Brannen office. Incorporated in March 1968, with Jung and Brannen as principals, Jung/Brannen Associates, with offices in Boston, worked as Belluschi's backup team until the mid-1980s, doing well over 150 buildings and projects that ranged widely in type and scale, from small churches to some of the largest corporate office towers in Boston at the time.

Belluschi's association with Jung/Brannen, with Belluschi as design consultant and Jung/Brannen the architect of record, or sometimes working in joint venture, was as close to a partnership as Belluschi was to come after leaving Portland. Off to a rocky start after the Century 21 project folded, the office was kept alive by other Belluschi jobs: more buildings for the Wellesley Office Park, the Ethel Walker Performing Arts Center in Connecticut, a Presbyterian church in Albany, Georgia, Douglass College at Rutgers University. Founded on Belluschi's philosophy and initially fed by his jobs, Jung/Brannen Associates gradually moved into projects on their own, expanding over the next two decades to become by the 1980s one of the biggest and most productive offices in Boston.[55]

RTKL Associates, Baltimore

Belluschi liked associating with young, not yet established architects whose minds were open to new ideas and who were still struggling to compete against older, established firms for jobs. Rogers and Taliaferro, both from Annapolis, were newcomers to the area; their association with Belluschi on the Church of Redeemer was their first major project in Baltimore and paved the way for future jobs.[56] Belluschi continued to pass jobs their way, recommending them, for example, to the FBO for the Embassy Building in Ciudad Trujillo and the Governor's Residence in the Panama Canal. As professional advisor to Goucher College just outside Baltimore, he was able to secure for them a job on the President's House. In 1959, he was asked to submit a list of architects for a new College Center. Among those on his list were Rudolph, Yamasaki, Johnson, Stone, Saarinen, Stubbins, and Weese. But after hearing Belluschi's thoughts on the program and his ideas about the kind of building he felt should be built, committee members were unanimous that he himself was the most appropriate person for the job.[57]

Goucher College Center, Towson, Maryland, 1959–1963, exterior (photo: Klara Farkas).

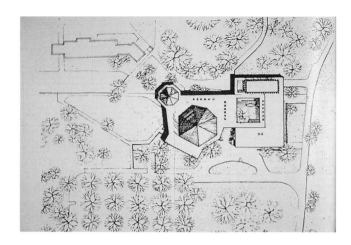

Goucher College Center, plan.

As one of the two-member advisory committee to the college charged with recommending an architect, Belluschi was very aware of the delicacy of the situation. But he also wanted the job. Despite his increasingly busy schedule, he found it hard to say no ("If I were a woman, I'd always be pregnant," he was often quoted as saying). He accepted the commission, bringing in what was by then Rogers, Taliaferro, Kostritsky, Lamb, or RTKL, as associates; he also brought in Sasaki, Walker and Associates, whom the college had retained in 1958, again on Belluschi's recommendation, to draw up a new master plan.

The new College Center, providing a symbolic entrance to the college on the south end, was to be distinctly modern yet fit in with the rustic, informal character of the campus. It was a low, asymmetrical building of local fieldstone, warm rich wood, and copper, integrated both in massing and materials with other buildings on campus. Administrative offices, student lounges, exhibition spaces, post office, and bookstore were aligned in a single-story U-shaped wing that angled around an open interior landscaped court, visually anchored by the raised polygonal form of the main large auditorium providing facilities for music and theater productions. A second smaller hall was available for lectures and recitals, with soundproof practice rooms below grade. Of reinforced concrete with ashlar exteriors, its geometries were softened by wood sunscreens stained to give a rich mix of warm tones and textures. The building was sited on the major axis of the campus, forming a natural passageway from main parking lot up the hilly slope to the campus. The main stairs fanned out at the base and leading up to the inner courtyard, like those of Aalto's town hall at Satnatsalo, completed several years earlier, and provided an informal, welcoming entrance to the campus very much in the Aalto tradition.

In the Church of the Redeemer, Belluschi had served as the principal architect, with Rogers, Taliaferro & Lamb his associates. At Goucher their roles officially were reversed, with RTKL Associates designated architects and Belluschi their design consultant. The design process, however, appears to have been very much the same. Belluschi established the parameters, then left them to work it out, reviewing the project more or less regularly as drawings were sent to his Cambridge office.

The association worked well. Belluschi brought them his name and stature, a vision, and the breadth of experience they needed to get started; RTKL provided him an eager, receptive, capable staff he could count on to carry out the work. Like Jung/Brannen Associates in Boston, the launching of the firm was based largely on the initial Belluschi connection. Grounded in his philosophy, the firm went on to become one of the most successful in the country, with offices in Los Angeles, Dallas, Washington, and Fort Lauderdale as well as Baltimore, and known particularly for its work in inner city redevelopment, downtown shopping centers, and other aspects of urban design.[58]

The Pan Am Building, New York, 1958–1963

Dean of architecture and urban planning at MIT and one of the leading modernist architects in the country at the time, in 1958 Belluschi became involved in the design of what was then to be the largest corporate office tower in the world. The building, and the controversy that swirled around it, marked a turning point in his career.

In June of 1958, New York developer Erwin S. Wolfson, head of the Diesel Construction Company and developer of more corporate towers than any other single investor in Manhattan, asked Walter Gropius to assist as design consultant on a proposed 59-story office building spanning Park Avenue in the air rights over the by then obsolete railroad

Grand Central City design team:
Gropius, Belluschi, Roth, Wolfson.

Pietro Belluschi

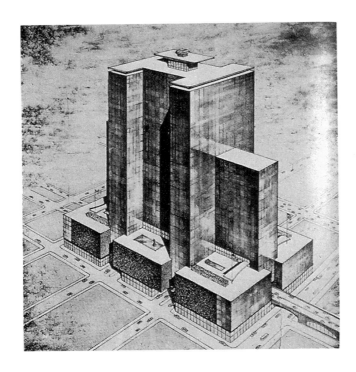

Grand Central City, New York, Fell-heimer & Wagner scheme, 1954.

Grand Central City, Roth proposal.

294

Grand Central City, Gropius/Belluschi
proposal, December 1958.

tracks behind Grand Central Terminal. An earlier proposal by the New York architectural firm of Fellheimer and Wagner, in 1954, had called for the demolition of the old Beaux-Arts Grand Central Terminal, built in 1913, and aroused a national protest. Wolfson's architects, Emery Roth & Sons, a well-established New York architectural firm noted for its reliable but uninspired high-rise office buildings, had come up with a proposal for an inoffensive Miesian rectangular block of steel and glass, set back behind the Grand Central Terminal to preserve it. They too, however, were under fire for the proliferation of undistinguished "rothscapers" that were lining Park Avenue.[59] To allay further criticism, Wolfson had asked Richard Roth to draw up a list of renowned architects whose participation might quell the storm. Walter Gropius, former head of Harvard's Graduate School of Design, was at the top of Roth's list; also on it were Sert, Stone, Bunshaft, and Belluschi. Gropius coveted the job, having wanted to do a skyscraper ever since the Chicago Tribune Tower competition in 1922, but was inexperienced; meeting with Wolfson that June, he suggested collaborating with Belluschi, with whom he had worked on the Boston Back Bay Center. Though 15 years Gropius's junior, Belluschi was far more experienced both in designing office buildings and in dealing with corporate clients. He agreed to join them, on the condition that in associating with the Roth office, whose less than sterling reputation he was well aware of, he and Gropius would have full control of design.[60]

Two days later the two men met in the office of The Architects Collaborative in Cambridge to draw up a contract. As Belluschi felt it was good business practice to have design decisions in the hands of one person, it stipulated that Gropius would have the final say on design; it also stated that should the owner and his architect Roth make a decision damaging to their design, they would have the right to remove their names from the project.[61] The division of labor was clear: Emery Roth & Sons, experts in space planning of the large office building, were responsible for the structure of the building itself, including interiors, working drawings, and execution; Gropius and Belluschi as "design experts" would handle the public spaces and the skin.

The project was ground-breaking all around. It was Wolfson's most ambitious project ever, presenting the toughest public relations problem he had ever faced as a developer. On structural grounds alone it was challenging, as the 830-foot tower had to span the several levels of below-grade tracks of the railroad terminal. For Emery Roth & Sons it was the first time they would work in an associate role, taking orders from celebrated, ego-involved designers. For Gropius, it was a chance finally to do a major tall office building. And for Belluschi, it was the opportunity to do something momentous in New York, in size and location far beyond anything he had ever dreamed.

Joint meetings began in July, one month after signing the agreement, and continued almost weekly in the TAC office in Cambridge, with material sent to and from Roth in New York. By December, after less than six months of concentrated effort, they had established the basic design. Going with Wolfson's suggestion of siting the tower north of Grand Central Terminal,[62] they had the task of working out the complicated circulation system linking the tower via pedestrian promenades to the terminal, coordinating it with city streets, traffic patterns, and transportation systems, and designing the exteriors of the complex as a whole.

Straightaway, Belluschi, aware of the criticism yet another view-blocking Miesian rectangular box would bring, thought of the newly completed Pirelli Building in Milan as well as the tower they had proposed for the Boston Back Bay. He suggested slimming down the tower and reducing its bulk by beveling the corners, which meant cutting down the amount of rentable office space from 3 million to 2.4 million square feet but offered a more sculptural, hence publicly acceptable, alternative to the plain rectangle. A second suggestion, this one Gropius's, was to shift the orientation of the tower from north-south to east-west, so it would span Park Avenue rather than follow its axis. A third idea was to use precast panels of a concrete aggregate hung on a structural system of steel instead of a flush skin of steel and glass, which would enliven the surface of the building.

The building was to consist of a broad, lozenze-shaped 56-story tower rising from a low, 8-story, site-filling base, whose main cornice was aligned with that of the Grand Central Station but visually set back from it to allow it a sculptural presence of its own. Gropius wanted the tower prominent, so that it served not just as a corporate emblem but as a significant new monumental landmark in the city at large. Not only was it to serve as its central transportation node, with a complex, multileveled, interconnected network of various means of transportation—trains, cars, subways, buses, pedestrian traffic, and helicopters—but as a sign of the cultural hegemony as well as economic power of the new, progressive, vibrant, postwar New York. The broad sides of the tower spanning Park Avenue would provide a dramatic visual terminus as one looked down the boulevard, as well as reduce the air-conditioning load, so it was argued, on the east and west facades; the prismatic form, with its angled sides catching light, would give it sculptural interest, while also accommodating the large bank of 67 elevators at the core; the two horizontal bands across the facade dividing it into thirds, behind which were mechanical equipment, would add visual relief from an otherwise monotonous wall. The row of mullions at the crest of the tower was to be uncapped, without a cornice that would visually terminate the building and arrest the unbroken vertical movement they sought at the summit. And finally, it was to have been enhanced by a single, unobtrusive spire, set to one side.[63]

Grand Central (Pan Am) Building, site

plan.

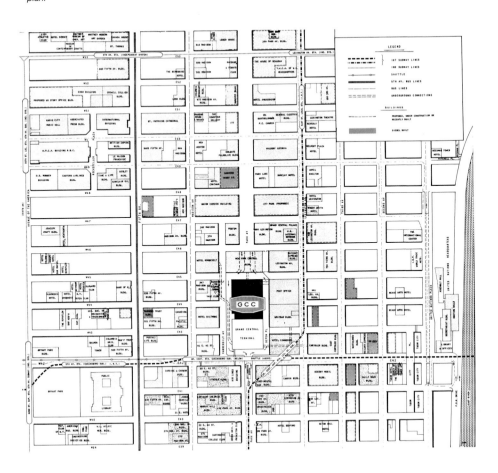

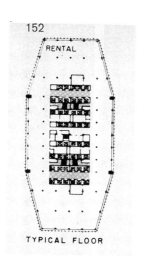

Grand Central (Pan Am) Building, plan.

Grand Central (Pan Am) Building,
model in section.

Except for the roofline, which was changed when a heliport was added, the spire eliminated, and a cornice with upswerving edges added to generate air currents, and the Pan Am sign, added when the Pan American World Airlines company became its principal tenant, the building was built as the designers conceived it.[64]

According to Gropius, the design process was truly collaborative.[65] Belluschi, however, felt slighted. Unaggressive by nature and overpowered by Gropius's more forceful presence, Belluschi offered his comments, then backed off. He would make a point simply and clearly; if it was not picked up he would rarely pursue it, avoiding confrontation and moving ahead to keep the project on track. Gropius respected Belluschi's opinions, and when he spoke, Gropius listened. In the initial stages, when the basic concept was being worked out, they functioned as coequals with decisions made jointly. As the project moved into later stages, however, Gropius, in whose office the work was being done, gradually assumed the lead; Belluschi, feeling shoved out, dropped back. The circulation system and lobby design, including the art work, were all Gropius's doing, with Belluschi only occasionally checking in.[66]

Despite Wolfson's efforts to squelch it by commissioning big-name architects, public criticism, begun long before Gropius and Belluschi were brought in, nonetheless continued. In late fall of 1954, 235 architects from around the country, among them many of Belluschi's colleagues at MIT and Harvard, had signed a letter protesting the demolition of the Grand Central's great concourse proposed in the initial Fellheimer & Wagner scheme.[67] As support for saving the Grand Central grew, press coverage fanned the issue, with many of the critics, including *Architectural Forum* editor Douglas Haskell, insisting that the space be left open to give the city needed breathing room.[68] The site, recognized as one of the choicest in the city, had already passed through the hands of several developers, including both William Zeckendorf and Roger Stevens, before ending up with Wolfson. From the beginning, then, the issue was seen as one of big real estate investors against defenseless citizens of the city: private versus public interests. As criticism mounted, arguments shifted from saving the concourse to the problem of traffic. By the time the Roth proposal was unveiled, the key issue was congestion. "The area in the vicinity of the Grand Central Terminal is already intensely developed. To add another building of the size sketched by Roth would impose still further upon an already over-taxed system," one critic wrote. "From a planning point of view, the addition of so vast an increase in building bulk in the Grand Central area is indefensible. We already have too much," added New York city architect and planner Robert Weinberg.[69] As Haskell, quieter in his manner but just as fierce an opponent of the development, put it, it was a clear case of public versus private rights. The notion that building owners are immune from criticism is obsolete. "Such a viewpoint ignores that building, so intended or not, is an act that takes place in public. It is not a wholly private affair. The public is the builder's and architect's captive audience. Escape is possible from a bad play by simply walking out or choosing not to walk in; but an ugly structure across the street is in sight virtually unavoidable."[70]

At the same time as Gropius and Belluschi, touted as "two of the world's most distinguished architects," were brought in, tempers were being inflamed by articles of Jane Jacobs and others decrying the boom in office towers, the plethora of deadly dull buildings filling American cities, and the loss of human scale. By the time their new scheme was published in December of 1958, nerves were raw. Gropius, who was quoted as having written in *Scope of Total Architecture* that "the sickness of our chaotic environment . . . has resulted from our failure to put basic human needs above economic requirements,"[71] was taken to task for defying the social ideals he had only recently espoused. "We believe Gropius is too great a man to have doubts on the meaning of his words," a letter to the editor in the January 1959 *Forum* said. "Never discouraged, he has always adhered to his ideas and convictions, and has followed all his long life the call of his social consciousness. However, what result, what kind of value or improvement, can we expect from his collaboration in this 'biggest office building in the world,' a $100 million colossus for 25,000 office workers, on top of Grand Central?"[72] Even more vehement was the rebuke from Sibyl Moholy-Nagy, widow of one of Gropius's colleagues at the Bauhaus and professor at the Pratt Institute, who maintained that those who attempt to justify the proposed building by saying it was bound to be built anyway, with or without the pedigrees of Gropius and Belluschi, are blurring "the lines of ideal and compromise," flushing standards down the drain. Calling the situation "where an architect of fame is willing to sell out to a promoter" a profound tragedy, she again chided the architects for turning their backs on their social ideals.[73]

In an attempt to stem the tide of public opinion, in January 1960 a panel discussion was held at the New School for Social Research on the question "What Is Good Design and Planning in New York?" The debate, with Wolfson, Roth, Gropius, and Belluschi on one side and Victor Gruen (then recognized as one of the leading urban designers in the country), Thomas Creighton (editor of *Progressive Architecture*), Peter Blake (associate editor of the *Forum*), and Paul Zucker (city planning historian and professor at the New School), on the other, focused on the Grand Central proposal. Seen as exemplifying one of the era's most pressing urban problems, it raised such questions as whether New York was in danger of overbuilding, whether aesthetics could be balanced with economics, how much responsibility the architect should bear for his role, at what point civic consciousness should influence building design—all key moral issues that were to dominate the decade of the sixties.

The debate was a farce. As Ada Louis Huxtable, architectural critic of the the *New York Times,* described it, the panel was "modest to the point of apology," and, awed by the presence of Gropius and Belluschi, the challengers were merely polite "in the interest of avoiding professional humility."[74] Walter McQuade in *The Nation* noted that even with aggressive questioning from the floor, the evening "could not be pulled back from the gently negative morass into which it had sunk."[75] Huxtable's despondent conclusion was that the building was just too big for the site. Despite the presence of the two highly respected architects, the result was a compromise, "and compromise is rarely art." McQuade was more blunt. Rather than focusing on the main issue, the "increasingly desperate subject of New York's decline as a place to live," the discussion was all about money and the plight of the beleaguered businessman. The two prominent architects were but packagers, he concluded, brought in to sell the product. Even Gropius admitted that it was only the best they could do under the circumstances. And those circumstances? Almost everyone on the panel implied the same thing: they shouldn't let us do this kind of building, make this kind of money. "But so long as there isn't a law. . . ."[76]

The discussion eventually came around to a delicate issue: How much of the responsibility fell on the architects? Defensive at best, the two eminent modernists evaded answering. Finally, a "bold young lady" paraphrased the question. Belluschi, never one to ignore a lady, attempted a reply. Deftly skirting the issue, he turned it around, using it as an opportunity to put in good word for congestion, which he said was of the nature of the city, the excitement found only in New York. Admitting that congestion sometimes led to disease and decay, he nonetheless professed to prefer Times Square to the broad open spaces of Central Park, with its daily murders and muggings.[77] His response struck listeners as lame.

The barrage of criticism continued. Yale professor Vincent Scully called it a "fatal blow to the street," a building that "in any terms other than those of brute expedience, should not be there at all."[78] Washington's more sober architectural critic Wolf Von Eckardt described it in the *New Republic* as "conspicuous for its ugliness and arrogant disregard of its surroundings."[79] John Burchard, dean of humanities and social sciences and a colleague of Belluschi's at MIT, saw it as "disastrous, . . . a monstrous denial of urbane urbanism."[80] Carl Condit, historian of the Chicago skyscraper (who, it was noted, spoke with some authority of such matters), predicted that it would transform the corner of Park Avenue and 42nd into "the first intersection rendered permanently impassable by traffic."[81]

The building had few defenders. Emerson Goble, editor of the *Architectural Record* and a longstanding Belluschi proponent, applauded the concept of the vertical city that concentrated rather than scattered people and traffic; Edmund Bacon, executive director of the City Planning Commission of Philadelphia, with whom Belluschi was by this time involved in the redevelopment of Independence Mall, found it a distinguished addition to the city, "remarkably successful in giving a visual background to the great historic vistas of Park Avenue."[82] These were the exceptions. For the most part sentiment was opposed, and the Pan Am Building continued to be seen as "a dam-like impediment," a "symbol of greed of real estate speculators in dark collusion with city hall," and "a moral lapse on the part of Drs. Gropius and Belluschi."[83]

The whole affair was profoundly damaging to Belluschi's reputation. Students lost respect and intensified their increasingly strident objections to his outside consulting work; his academic colleagues, who increasingly were turning to hermetic, formalistic design, evading the urban design issues represented by the Pan Am Building, sided with the charismatic Scully. Architectural critics around the country condemned Belluschi for selling his soul, becoming involved in a project that morally as well as aesthetically was "simply bad."[84]

Completed in 1963, the $100 million Pan Am Building turned out not to be the unmitigated urban calamity many had predicted, and proved to be an outstanding business success, with 92.5 percent of its space leased and the building fully financed by the time it opened.[85] But in virtually all other respects it was seen as a colossal failure. According to Huxtable, it shared with Morris Lapidus's glittery Summit Hotel the "dubious distinction of being the largest, most spectacular failure that New York has seen in years." Its bulk, overscale, indifference to its surroundings, and blocking out of sky, light, and views, topped off by the attempts of distinguished architects Gropius and Belluschi to "smooth up" its overbearing profile, struck her as particularly misguided.[86]

Although it remains today one of the most hated buildings in New York, the Pan Am Building, renamed the MetLife Building in 1992, might conceivably in the long run become accepted as a familiar landmark—like the Eiffel Tower, which, too, was reviled when first erected.[87] But in the meantime, the Pan Am Building became a heavily loaded symbol of everything that had gone wrong with modernism, urbanistically as well as architecturally, and a favorite target of attack throughout the 1960s. As the architectural community itself polarized, Belluschi found himself caught between opposing forces: between the urbanistic values of James Rouse and those of Jane Jacobs, and between architectural technocrats such as Gropius and aesthetes such as Philip Johnson and Vincent Scully. The choices for him were clear.

Bank of America, San Francisco, 1964–1969

In February 1964, barely a year after the Pan Am Building opened, the Bank of America, then the largest bank in the country with headquarters in San Francisco, announced its intentions to erect "one of the great architectural achievements of the modern world." It was seeking "the world's greatest architect" to design what was hoped would be a respected landmark worldwide. Already San Franciscans, inhabitants of that most self-conscious of American cities, were wary, their hackles raised by rumors of "some monstrous structure" that would overwhelm the city's sensitive scale. Bank officials were debating whether to hold an international competition, following the precedent of the recent Boston City Hall competition, or to have a committee of "top architects" select one of their own.

Wurster Bernardi & Emmons, the most highly respected firm in the city, with the possible exception of SOM which had just opened an office there, had been the bank's unofficial architect for a number of years, responsible for a series of mostly two- and three-story branch banks throughout the state. In 1958 WB&E had drawn up a proposal for a $13 million, 8-story building, which would then have been the second largest in the city.[88] As bank officials negotiated for a better site, however, the scale of the enterprise expanded. By 1964 when plans resumed, the city's self-awareness had grown, to a considerable extent because of articles in the popular press calling attention to the mostly negative impact of new large-scale building projects on the skyline.

Thinking a celebrity architect would help mollify criticism, the bank asked WB&E to draw up a list of well-known names. Though including current standbys such as Mies, Le Corbusier, and Gropius, WB&E warned the bank that working with a European would be difficult and time-consuming, as they stemmed out of a different architectural tradition and were unfamiliar with the formal language prevailing on the West Coast, particularly in San Francisco. Accepting this argument, the bank came back to WB&E and offered them the job on condition that they associate with a well-known architect who was experienced in high-rise buildings, as WB&E was not. Belluschi was brought in on Wurster's recommendation at that point. Belluschi in turn recommended Emery Roth & Sons, with whom he had worked on the Pan Am, for working drawings and supervision.[89]

Designing began immediately. The site was several blocks from the center of the downtown financial district, at the base of Nob Hill on Kearny Street between Pine and California streets and bounded on the east by Montgomery Street, San Francisco's equivalent of Wall Street. With the design team of Wurster, Emmons, and Ralph Butterfield of WB&E and Belluschi, plus landscape architect Lawrence Halprin who joined

Pan Am Building, New York, exterior, 1963 (photo: Joseph Molitor).

them soon after, the initial concept was quickly developed: a 52-story building with faceted sawtooth facade, its angled bays staggered in a series of setbacks as they ascended to break up the building's enormous bulk. Wurster had pushed for several small low buildings instead of the single tower to fit the scale of San Francisco; others, including Belluschi, felt a more monumental statement was called for.

The problem they faced was one with which Belluschi was by now familiar: how to create a large landmark building without overwhelming the humanistic scale of the city and without blocking views. Reviewing the WB&E proposal at their first meeting, he expressed many of the same concerns he had had on the Pan Am Building: the heavy feeling of large-scale bays and precast concrete panels, light colors that emphasize mass, the importance of keeping the building in scale with the surrounding buildings, at the same time creating a distinctive monumental form. With recent buildings such as Saarinen's CBS Building in New York in mind, Belluschi stated that he would like to see a building with vertical ribbing, without overhanging cornice or capping to stump its vertical rise, in a uniform dark tone to minimize the patterning and gridlike relationship

Bank of America Building, San Francisco, Belluschi drawing, May 1964.

Bank of America Building, wooden model.

Basaltic outcropping, Sierra Nevada (snapshot, Belluschi files).

of window to wall, and with a smooth and highly polished skin to reflect the sky, clouds, and surrounding buildings, thereby minimizing its bulk.[90] He suggested a bronze-tinted glass and dark bronze aluminum cladding, like that of the Seagram, as possible materials. Presenting them studies done in his Cambridge office, he showed his reworking of the group's original scheme, with bay size reduced from 39 feet to 20 feet and intermediate staggered setbacks at different levels in the interest of creating a monumental sculptural form at once delicate and crystalline in scale. Meeting regularly, at one point several times a week, with Belluschi attending most of the meetings at this stage, they worked out the basic concept using an adjustable wooden model made in the WB&E office.

It was brainstorming at its best, the ideas of one catalyzing those of others. Fearing criticism of their "Manhattanizing" of the city and holding out for a regional solution, Wurster kept pulling for a light-colored building to maintain the continuity of San Francisco's traditionally white buildings. Others agreed with Belluschi that it should be dark to minimize the bulk. All agreed it should be rectangular in form, with somewhat narrower sides on east and west to preserve views from Nob Hill. All took shots at experimenting with the wooden model, which consisted of triangular shafts bundled together in such a way that they could be shifted up and down in different configurations. The idea of faceting the facade vertically was well received, as the angular bays not only introduced a plasticity that architects in general were seeking at the time, but also, as Wurster pointed out, played into the San Francisco tradition of bay windows. Halprin's suggestion to stagger the vertical piers at different levels, like the dark, rugged basaltic outcroppings of the Sierra, prompted Butterfield to retrieve an Ansel Adams photograph of the Devil's Post Pile, which they all agreed served as a fitting source of inspiration. Belluschi then returned to Boston to work the idea out. The aim was to come up with a building with the informal, irregular silhouette of a natural basaltic outcropping indigenous to the West, and with the prismatic surfaces creating bays consistent with the San Francisco tradition of bay windows.

At 779 feet the building would be the tallest building in the West at the time. The bank wanted the principal entrance on the south so as to have a Pine Street address. In acknowledgment of Anshen & Allen's International Building across Kearny Street, they sited the tower back from California Street on the north, creating a generous plaza. This was in keeping with current theories of urban design, based on the model of the Seagram Building, that favored open spaces for light and air as well as creating spatially isolating forecourts for tall monumental towers. A smaller branch bank separate from, but connected to, the main tower was located on the northeast corner of the lot, bordered by California and Montgomery. A three-level parking garage was below grade. Total cost of the project was estimated at $85 million.

Plans for the building were published in the *San Francisco Chronicle* in July 1965. Construction was to begin at the first of the new year, with completion set for 1969.[91] It was at this point that Skidmore, Owings & Merrill was brought in. Wurster had had doubts about working with the Roth office in New York, primarily on the basis of their uneven record in design; he also anticipated difficulty in their handling of working drawings and the supervision of construction from New York. He persuaded the Bank to go with the local office of SOM instead: it had an outstanding reputation nationally; Wurster knew them personally; moreover, they were already doing work together on plans for the San Francisco Civic Center. Belluschi was more apprehensive, having had a minor falling out with John Merrill, Jr., over work they were to do together on a new wing of the Portland Art Museum, and had already experienced SOM's heavy-handedness in design decisions. Accommodating by nature, he acquiesced.[92]

Stemming out of a Miesian tradition in the East, hence with a very different design philosophy from WB&E's, and strong designers in their own right, those at SOM were unwilling to come in simply as associates in charge of production. They agreed to accept the tower design basically as the Belluschi/WB&E team had established it, but only if the design were allowed to undergo further development. The team, now composed of Belluschi, WB&E, Halprin, and SOM, thus gave it a second go-around before committing it to working drawings. A joint venture was set up, with a lower floor of the WB&E office serving as their work space. Charles Bassett was the SOM principal in charge, with Marc Goldstein as project director; Ralph Butterfield was project director for the WB&E team. The three seniors in charge thus were Belluschi, Wurster (later Emmons, as Wurster was already suffering from Parkinson's disease), and Bassett. They met regularly to review the work as it progressed in the hands of the design team.

With two highly divergent architectural perspectives, the one informal, low-profile, and thoroughly West Coast, representing the legacy of the Bay Area regional tradition, the other the highly rationalized Miesian-dominated SOM of the Midwest and East, differences arose immediately. SOM wanted the building squared up, regularized, more symmetrical to make it a simple rectangle, with shallow bays and a simplified top; WB&E held out for their original concept of a more organically disposed, informal, asymmetrical sculptural massing. As disputes came up, Belluschi, West Coast in heritage but now living in the East, served as mediator.

The issue of the sculpted top was a major point of contention. Goldstein had cut his teeth on Mies and had the Seagram Building "etched," as he put it, in his mind.[93] He wanted a simple systematized building with squared-off top, setbacks on all four sides ordered symmetrically around a centralized axis. The others insisted on retaining the random irregularity of the original. Faced with this clear-cut dichotomy, Belluschi, who had participated in the formation of the original concept and was loyal to Wurster, sided with the latter.

As dean at MIT, codesigner of the famed Pan Am Building, and the celebrity name, Belluschi was the unofficial leader. It was agreed beforehand that in conflicts he would be the final arbiter. Handling disputes in a fair, judicious, diplomatic manner, he was the glue that held the group together. Bassett, however, more forceful in personality, continued to pressure on behalf of SOM's design preferences; with the working drawings in their hands, he knew that ultimately they had control. Once the project was out of the conceptual stages and had moved into production, SOM's presence grew. While Belluschi's other professional commitments pulled him aside and he was there less and less, Bassett and Goldstein were around daily, monitoring and making decisions where and when they saw fit. Midway through the process, seeing what was happening, Belluschi voiced his concern about the loss of much of the freshness of the original concept. The setbacks in particular had in SOM's hands become reduced and regularized.

With pushing and shoving on both sides, the final design was arrived at with the original concept more or less intact, albeit simplified and ordered in SOM's interest of straightening up the form. SOM was also given full responsibility for the two-story branch banking pavilion on the northeast corner; this was developed as a freestanding structure connected by a below-grade concourse so that visually the building would read as a separate but complementary entity, with the open plaza in between. As the design moved into final stages, excavations were begun in August 1966, and by the following summer construction was under way. The building opened in October 1969.

Critical reaction was hostile at best. In the growing antimonumental climate that was already pervasive, especially in San Francisco with its fear of "Manhattanization," the new Bank of America Building was termed an arrogant obscenity, a tasteless big black monument to money, its elegant black granite abstract sculpture by the artist Masayuki Nagare in the plaza dubbed the "Banker's Heart." Charles Moore, a leading figure of then embryonic postmodernism and about to leave his chairmanship at Berkeley for Yale, reviewed it in *Architectural Forum*. Bemoaning it as the "great new shaft going up at the foot of Nob Hill (how great it would have been on top of it)," he felt "the spirit that thrusts it up at least gives us enough strength to keep our fingers crossed. The press release grants it the strength of the High Sierra. That's hard to see; but if it has (and it just might), . . . then reason be damned, and let the frontier triumph."[94] Other local critics were less gentle, seeing it as overscaled, its dark color contrary to San Francisco, and the plaza cold and inhospitable. Even members of the participating firm denounced it. Nathaniel Owings attacked the building publicly at a UNESCO conference on urban quality, calling it inhumane and lacking in public amenities, not a "people's place."

Moore's irreverent review in the *Forum* aside, reception in the architectural press was considerably warmer. Tired of standardized Miesian forms, many in the profession welcomed the discreet yet interestingly sculpted building. It was seen as fitting in well with the city, its vertical striations and setback forms echoing in fully modern terms the more richly embellished surfaces of the older Beaux-Arts buildings of the teens and twenties. The bays projecting above, indented below, added a new, welcomed plasticity to the surface. The dark color, a deep carnelian granite of Belluschi's choice, with glass of the same bronze hue as in Saarinen's CBS Building to preserve the continuity of surface, added a subtle texture to the smooth polished surface of the building. Also applauded was the superb craftsmanship and meticulous Miesian detailing for which SOM was known.[95]

Within a year, the tide of local resentment began to turn. Alexander Fried, art critic of the *San Francisco Chronicle,* was one of the first to stick his neck out, calling it an immensely thoughtful work of architectural sculpture that he enjoyed walking around, watching its configuration modulate as his perspective shifted or the light or weather changed, and he admitted to the thrill of high-rise cityscapes.[96] By 1976 critics were raving, commenting on how much they liked getting up early so they could watch the shifting patterns of light both near and afar on this now admired addition to the San Francisco skyline.

By this time, of course, each member of the "team" claimed it as their own, Belluschi along with the rest. But the building was simply not anyone's, as Butterfield aptly put it.[97] Given their customary language of form at the time, it was clearly not an SOM building, nor was it a WB&E, nor a Belluschi. Nor was it simply a compromise among the three. Rather, it was the fruitful meshing of very different architectural philosophies— East and West, international and regional, the search for a universal solution tempered by the concern for the temporality and particularities of a very specific place.

As it is typically identified as an SOM building, however, it seems important to establish the chronology of events, and to note that, claims to the contrary, the initial concept of the building was well established before SOM came in. Wurster, a strong designer in his prime, was increasingly incapacitated and had little to do with it except in the initial stages. Belluschi, on the other hand, soft as his voice was especially in a room of booming Bassetts and Goldsteins, clearly played a major role. As minutes of their meetings attest, his opinions were listened to and his experience in the design of large office buildings, from the Equitable to the Pan Am, both landmark buildings in their own right, was respected. After SOM was brought in and he became the mediator between two highly divisive factions, he was also the man with the final say, his opinions backed unequivocally by the bank.[98]

Rohm & Haas Building, Philadelphia, 1962–1964

Of the several low office blocks Belluschi was to do in the early 1960s, among them 565 Technology Square in Cambridge, the new Equitable Center in Portland, and the Northern States Power Building in Minneapolis, the Rohm & Haas Building in Philadelphia was perhaps the most successful.[99]

Under Edmund Bacon, Philadelphia had established itself as one of the leaders in the urban renewal program, and by the late 1950s the process of clearing and redeveloping the historic Independence Mall area was well under way. Already, however, tempers had been roused by the wanton demolition of nineteenth-century buildings of distinction and

Rohm & Haas Building, Philadelphia, 1962–1964, exterior (photo: Ezra Stoller).

the insensitive intrusion of "modern" buildings, most particularly the sheer-walled, steel and glass Mies-inspired corporate towers transforming cities across the nation. Seeing this as contrary to the spirit of recently passed ordinances designed to protect the integrity of historic structures such as Independence Hall and the old Customs House, members of the local AIA and City Art Commission, as well as other prominent local officials, had begun to protest.

The Rohm & Haas Company, manufacturers of plastic products, had decided, instead of moving out of the city, to stay in the downtown to take advantage of federal funds available to private investors on urban renewal land, and were planning a new headquarters building on Independence Mall. In 1959 they had commissioned a design from the Philadelphia firm of the George M. Ewing Company, whose proposal met with only a lukewarm response from the Art Commission. Deciding that the situation called for a leading architect, the company contacted Belluschi in May of 1962 to serve as design consultant.

In a meeting with Ewing and several of his staff in Belluschi's office in Cambridge the following June, equipped only with photos of the area and a couple of renderings of Ewing's original proposal, the team—Belluschi, Ewing, and his staff—then and there worked out the site, size, and character of the new building and its urban implications.

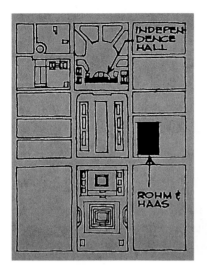

Rohm & Haas Building, site plan (Architectural Record, *January 1966).*

Rohm & Haas Building, lobby with view of Independence Hall (Architectural Record, *January 1966).*

Rohm & Haas Building, louvered screen (photo: Ezra Stoller).

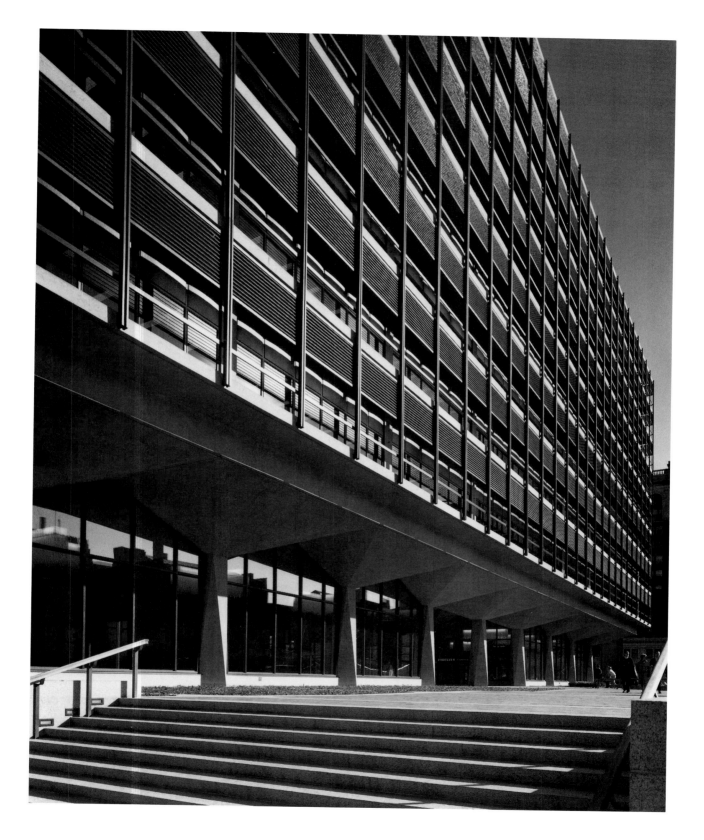

The site was on the north side of the Mall, two blocks down from Independence Hall. Belluschi's first move was to suggest a low, horizontal rectangular block rather than a high-rise slab or tower, in deference to the scale of the Mall. He then recommended turning the building on axis 90 degrees so that it paralleled 6th Street, with its principal facade facing the Mall; as this introduced the need for air conditioning, he proposed solving the problem with sunshades of Plexiglas, Rohm and Haas's principal product.[100] With buildings in mind like Raymond & Rado's new office building in Tokyo, with its low horizontal massing and louvered exteriors, and Saarinen's office building for John Deere & Co. in Moline, Illinois, with its continuous bronze-hued sunlouvers, Belluschi suggested a screen of Plexiglas held in a projecting metal framework. This would also introduce a finely textured pattern, minimizing the building's bulk. He urged the use of dark hues— brown spandrels, bronze-colored translucent corrugated panels for the sunshades, and a bronze anodized aluminum lattice for the supporting framework—again to minimize the effect of size.[101] For the landscaping he recommended they get Dan Kiley, and as a safety device suggested their asking G. Holmes Perkins, dean of the architecture school at the University of Pennsylvania, to review the project before it went up for approval.[102] Once Belluschi had established the basic concept, the Ewing staff developed the design, meeting Belluschi regularly either in Cambridge or in Philadelphia. In a matter of months, the design was accepted by the Rohm & Haas Company and approved by the Planning Commission, Redevelopment Authority, and Art Commission.

The building consisted of a 9-story, reinforced-concrete-framed building, set back from the street on a wide landscaped podium and poised on a recessed colonnade of flaring concrete piers. Broad monumental steps led from the sidewalk on 6th Street to an open walkway extending through the center of the building. Opening onto a plaza with sculptured fountain and a small pool, the passageway provided a public access to the alley along the western side of the building. Belluschi's discerning eye was evident throughout, from the execution of the poured exposed concrete to the furbishing of the lobby with its view of Independence Hall, 22-foot-high ceiling, wood-paneled walls, and Kepes light sculpture of acrylic plastic. The building was completed in 1964 with a construction cost of about $10 million.[103]

Representing the first private investment on the Mall, the Rohm & Haas Building was highly regarded by Philadelphia's city planners, who hoped it would serve as a stimulus to other private investors in the Mall area and set a standard for subsequent redevelopment buildings. Applauding its sensitivity to the site and the way it related not only to the fine texture and small scale of Independence Hall but also to the expansive landscaped Mall, architectural critic Wolf Von Eckardt of the *Washington Post,* who had only recently decried the Pan Am Building, acclaimed the Rohm and Haas structure as "probably the most handsome building in Philadelphia."[104]

Other Corporate Towers

Despite the success of Belluschi's low-profile office blocks, corporate clients throughout the sixties preferred the high visibility and landmark status of the tall office building. By the latter part of the decade, however, the criticism of corporate towers had become a crusade. Douglas Haskell, editor of the *Architectural Forum,* was a leading opponent. His editorial "Washington Needs Another Monument," in the summer 1968 *Forum,* was accompanied by a heartrending photograph of a bedraggled child standing on a trash-strewn street in front of a run-down tenement.[105] Scores of other articles set forth a litany of ills of the forgotten city: failure of urban renewal, plight of the urban poor, transformation of the cityscape into a sea of static, unyielding, inhospitable corporate monuments at the expense of cherished small-scale historic buildings, loss of traditional open spaces, neglected needs of pedestrians, and lack of low-cost housing. Coupled with this was a backlash against "good taste" and the concern for the refined, elegant, overtly expensive corporate office buildings that had dominated mainstream architecture in the wake of the Seagram Building in the late 1950s.[106]

Hardly oblivious to this antimonument sentiment, Belluschi remained unsympathetic. As the problems of cities worsened, Belluschi spoke out on the importance of maintaining a balanced view. He was aware of Americans' love-hate relationship with the city, hating it for its vulgarity, its denial of nature, its congestion, but craving its fertile social encounters, lively commerce, and rich cultural rewards. Pointing this out, he stressed the need for accepting the bad with the good, advanced technology for its reduction of costs, tall towers for the urban sprawl they helped to avoid.[107]

Upon retiring for MIT in 1965, Belluschi embarked on a series of tall corporate towers. Given their prestige, and assuming that his time would be freer, he wanted now unquestionably to be principal designer. As he put it, he saw the challenge as one of humanizing the tall office building, of reconciling the big scale demanded by the modern city with the human scale of the pedestrian. Sometimes his solution was to break down the mass and bulk of the tower with small-scale, delicate patterning of the surface, as in the Pan Am and Rohm & Haas buildings; at other times the approach was larger and more sculptural, as in the Bank of America.

In his speeches he continued to urge that the design even of large corporate towers be discreet. Asked by a student at a talk at the University of Michigan in 1967 what was so unusual about his buildings, Belluschi responded that buildings shouldn't necessarily be unusual; rather they should be "part of their environment. Architecture shouldn't stand out just for the sake of standing out."[108]

Gerald Blakeley, president of Cabot, Cabot & Forbes, one of Boston's largest commercial real estate developers, had begun building small suburban industrial parks in the 1950s. In 1960, as the Boston Redevelopment Agency became active and Boston began turning around economically, Blakeley moved the company into the city and turned to investments in the downtown.

Blakeley's first downtown investment was the New England Merchants Building by Edward Larabee Barnes, a 40-story rectangular building with smooth granite exteriors,

Boston Company Building, Boston, 1966–1969, exterior (at left center).

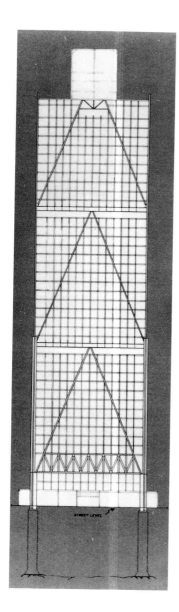

Boston Company Building, structural
diagram.

located across from the new Boston City Hall. For his second building he wanted
something with more character, something other than a plain rectangle with a flat top.
After going first to Gordon Bunshaft of SOM, who refused to comply with his aesthetic
prescriptions, late in 1965 Blakeley turned to Belluschi, who had done the 565 Technology Square Building in Cambridge in 1961 for Cabot, Cabot & Forbes with Eduardo
Catalano. Over the years, Blakeley had seen Belluschi in action as a member of the
Design Advisory Committee for the Boston Redevelopment Agency, and he appreciated
Belluschi's respect for the businessman. Faced with rapidly rising building costs and
wanting an efficient yet distinctive building, Blakeley sensed that Belluschi understood
and sympathized with the economic realities of the situation. Belluschi was, of course,
delighted to be approached, and suggested their bringing in Emery Roth & Sons, with
whom he had worked on the Pan Am Building, as associates.[109] What Cabot, Cabot &
Forbes needed was a 41-story office building, which would be Boston's tallest, on a site
at the head of State Street, directly opposite the diminutive Old State House, between
Court and Washington streets. In addition to a sculptural top, Blakeley wanted a
column-free interior.

Belluschi's initial idea, based on the newly completed 47-story Place Victoria Towers in
Montreal of Pier Luigi Nervi and Luigi Moretti and other recent structural developments,
was for a tube structure, with the loads borne by a structural core and four large tapering
columns on the exterior, rather than the usual column-and-beam frame. This, however,
called for a lot of steel. The structural engineers, from the New York office of James
Ruderman, who had also worked on the Pan Am, proposed a new system that would
cut the amount of steel, hence reduce costs: a triangular bracing system on the periphery
that would provide both column-free interiors and wind bracing. Belluschi developed the
idea architecturally so that the cross bracing formed by a series of three inverted V's
would be expressed clearly on the exterior of the building. Rather than having the bracing
members on the exterior, as in the newly completed Alcoa Building in San Francisco,
they were to be enclosed within the glass curtain wall, but expressed on the exterior by
means of staggered solid panels of anodized aluminum.[110]

Completed in 1969 as planned, the building was of bronze-colored anodized aluminum
with bronze-tinted windows. Above a two-story base sheathed in granite, irregularly
shaped to accommodate the tight, awkward site, was a zone of bronze glass, slightly
recessed, forming a clerestory for the lobby. A six-story penthouse housing the cooling
tower and other mechanical equipment was set back from the facades of the tower,
providing Blakeley the visual distinction he requested. Belluschi also extended the corner
piers of both tower and penthouse beyond the roof planes to form tiny finials, again in

the interest of providing visual interest. Completed at a final cost of $20 million, below what was originally projected, the Boston Company Building was highly praised, at least by engineers, for its advanced structural system.

Architects and Bostonians were less pleased. Belluschi himself was unhappy with the decision to lop three stories off the top, a measure suggested by Cabot, Cabot & Forbes's project director who feared they would exceed the amount of rentable office space the city could absorb; this truncated the uppermost triangular brace, and destroyed both the proportions and the logic of the structure. He also admitted a problem with the base, acknowledging that his interest was more in exploring the new tubular structural system than in relating the building urbanistically to the street.[111] Asked several years later what his aims had been in doing the building, he replied,

> As architecture moves away from the formal symbols of other ages, we find that visual satisfaction proceeds more from enlightened structural economy than from arbitrary superficial fashions of the moment. A great engineer will not hide the clarity of his solutions behind phony expressions, and a good architect will derive his best solutions through a sympathetic dialogue with the engineer. The most enduring contribution we can make to good architecture today is intelligent directness of purpose and clarity of structure. We believe the Boston Company Building gives a good example of this philosophy.[112]

Belluschi's sentiments were noble, but out of sync with the times. Both the architectural profession and the general public by then were tired of merely rational structural solutions, and wanted something more. Edward Logue, ordinarily a Belluschi proponent, had opposed the building from the start, arguing strongly against it on the basis of its color and material. Only reluctantly, and then out of principle, did he endorse the Design Advisory Committee's approval of the building. Given the tight site and low budget, the committee had felt that it was a good building, and more importantly the city's tax base needed it.

Other critics were less charitable. Sibyl Moholy-Nagy described it in an *Architectural Forum* article as "the latest product of the Belluschi-Roth team which gave to New York its Pan Am."[113] Others considered it yet another watered-down copy of Mies; still others found its proportions disturbing, its surface detailing trivial, the base indifferent to bypassers, and the sculptural top merely silly.

Its most fiercely attacked feature, however, was its impact on the city: the historic monuments it dwarfed, its awkward relationship to the site, its callousness to human scale. The solid blank granite base with deeply recessed entrances defined by a shadowy void offered little warmth or visual appeal. But it gave the client what he wanted: an economical building built on time and within budget, distinctive at least by its sheer size.

The Boston Company Building was only one of several large corporate towers Belluschi designed for downtown Boston in the late 1960s. The 60 State Street project, commissioned by the Cabot, Cabot & Forbes Company in 1968, got caught in a shift in the Boston power structure with the election of a new mayor. As Blakeley tells it, when Logue was ousted as BRA director and replaced by Robert Kenney, Belluschi too fell from political favor. His proposal for the 60 State Street Building, a simple glass and steel slab set on a low block-filling base, was rejected, whereupon Blakeley went to Marcel Breuer.

60 State Street Building, Boston, Belluschi sketch, 1968.

*60 State Street Building, first version,
Belluschi, 1968.*

Blakeley was not happy with the Breuer proposal, dismissed him, and after a million-dollar lawsuit went back to Belluschi, who came up with a second proposal, this time of brick. Destined for a site adjacent to the Quincy Market, the 40-story, indented building, with a lower level of shops, arcades, and a 5-story parking garage, aroused a storm of protest, pitting Belluschi against architects, preservationists, and the public alike. In 1972, shortly before Belluschi decided to leave Boston and return to the West Coast, Blakeley brought in Bruce Graham of the Chicago office of SOM, and the design process started over. Belluschi was retained as a design consultant, or, in his words, "dumped."[114]

The Keystone Building, a 32-story, reinforced concrete building with facades of light, cream-colored travertine, Belluschi felt would be a welcomed change in Boston. Rose Associates of New York was the developer, with Emery Roth & Sons in charge of layout and general plans. As it was little more than a standard office building, Belluschi's responsibility was limited to the skin and public lobby. The roughly trapezoidal site between Congress, High, and Purchase streets, some distance from the Government Center, suggested a shape other than a slab or straight rectangle; to accommodate it, Belluschi used a grid of flattened tripartite bay windows to round the corners of an otherwise standard block form, creating a rippling effect on the facade. The Italianate travertine, a material Belluschi had advocated for use on both the Juilliard School in New York and St. Mary's Cathedral in San Francisco, proved not to be a good idea in Boston, as the seasonal contraction of the concrete frame caused a crushing and cracking of the travertine stone at the base. Completed in 1971 at a cost of $30 million, "the cloud," as it was called, opened with little fanfare. Neither it nor the Boston Company Building was published.[115]

There were other corporate towers of the late 1960s, among them the Kerr-McGee Building in Oklahoma City, in association with Frankfurt Short Emery McKinley; Dewey

60 State Street Building, second (post-Breuer) scheme.

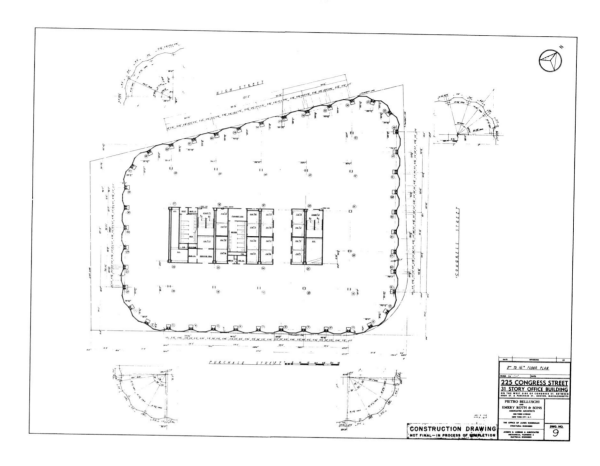

Keystone Building, Boston, 1967–1971,
exterior (photo: Gorchev and Gorchev).

Keystone Building, plan.

Square in Boston (later, One Financial Center), a joint venture with Jung/Brannen for the Rose Associates developers; the Motion Picture Building in Washington, D.C., with Vlastimil Koubek; the Pacific Gas & Electric Building in San Francisco, with Hertzka & Knowles; the Seattle First National Bank Building in Seattle, with Naramore, Bain, Brady & Johanson; and the Magsaysay Building in Manila, the Philippines, with A. J. Luz Associates. In all but the first, Belluschi's role seems to have been limited to that of a design critic or advisor.

Juilliard School for the Performing Arts, 1963–1969

Besides corporate office buildings, Belluschi at this time was also involved, on one level or another, in a wide range of other building types: schools such as the Tobin Elementary School in Cambridge; university buildings such as the University of Virginia Architecture and Fine Arts Building in Charlottesville, and the MacGregor House dormitory on the MIT campus in Cambridge; museum buildings including the Clark Art Institute addition at Williams College, Williamstown, Massachusetts, and another wing for the Portland Art Museum; performing arts centers such as the Blossom Center in Cleveland and Ethel Walker Center in Simsbury, Connecticut; the Sacramento Convention Center in Sacramento; nuclear power plants such as the Diablo Canyon Nuclear Power Plant near San Luis Obispo on the coast of California; plus numerous churches and synagogues. In some, his participation was critical; in others he appears to have lent no more than his name.[116]

One of the most important of these later projects was the Juilliard School. It was also the most complex building he'd ever done. By the time he and Gropius were brought into the Pan Am project in the summer of 1958, Belluschi was already involved in the planning of Lincoln Center on the other side of the city, and had just received the commission for the design of the Juilliard School of Music. The Pan Am Building was the more momentous, especially in its impact on his reputation, but Belluschi himself had far more to do with Juilliard.

William Schuman, president of the Juilliard School, had selected Belluschi because he felt comfortable with him personally. Rather than telling him about everything he had done, Belluschi had listened. When asked what kind of building he envisioned, Belluschi had replied straightforwardly that he could not begin to think in terms of form until he understood the situation, the emotional as well as physical climate of the school. Schuman liked this, making it clear to Belluschi that while he might associate with another architect, Juilliard would look to him and him alone as the person in charge.[117]

For the job, Belluschi associated with Eduardo Catalano, with whom he had worked on several other projects, mostly in Massachusetts.[118] Recognizing his strength in design, Belluschi had brought Catalano to MIT in 1956 to teach in the architecture department, and in time the two became close friends. Temperamentally they were very different, Catalano as resolute about his likes and dislikes as Belluschi was conciliatory. But they shared an appreciation of aesthetic values and both demanded high standards in their work. Not long after Catalano arrived in Cambridge, they began associating, with Catalano setting up a small office attached to his house and relying on former students for help. One of their first jobs was a housing project for the New York developer William Zeckendorf, which was not built; then came the Baltimore Civic Center, which again did not go through. The Juilliard commission followed shortly thereafter. All working drawings, production, and supervision was done by the Cambridge office. Helge Westermann, a classmate of Catalano's at Harvard who had a large, well-established office in New York, served as their local liaison.

After several abortive starts, the Juilliard project was put on hold until final decisions on site and budget could be made, then came to life again in the early 1960s. By this time, the Catalano office was involved in the design of the MIT Student Center, one of several jobs Belluschi helped Catalano, initially neither licensed in the United States, nor, out of principle, a member of the AIA, to obtain.[119]

Their initial studies, like others Belluschi was doing at the time, drew on mid-fifties prototypes and related comfortably to the white classical temple image being adopted in the other Lincoln Center buildings. As studies progressed, however, the site was changed from the original northwest corner of the Lincoln Center block to across 65th

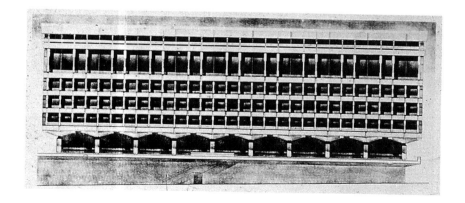

Juilliard School for the Performing Arts, New York, preliminary sketch, 22 August 1959.

*Juilliard School, 1963–1969, exterior
(photo: Ezra Stoller).*

*Eduardo Catalano, MIT Student Center,
Cambridge (Architectural Forum, November 1965).*

Street to the north. When the project finally went forward in the fall of 1963, a new contract was drawn up, with the understanding that Belluschi would provide the basic concept to be developed in the Catalano office.

A change of guard in Juilliard's administrative personnel brought the young composer Peter Mennin in to replace Schuman, who became director of Lincoln Center as a whole. In addition to replacing both the theater designer and the acoustical consultants Belluschi had been working with, Mennin revamped the program and expanded the curriculum.

By the time their work on the project resumed, Belluschi was involved not only in finishing stages of the Pan Am Building but also the Bank of America Building and St. Mary's Cathedral in San Francisco. After years of program changes and budget restrictions, and with still some uncertainty about whether it would actually go ahead, he and Catalano had both gone stale. In the hopes of generating fresh ideas, Catalano turned over several schemes he and Belluschi had proposed earlier to three men in the office—Robert Burns, who later left to become head of architecture at the University of North Carolina, Frederick Taylor, and Frederick Preis—to develop, based on the new site and revised program.[120]

Burns's solution was ultimately used. Drawing heavily on Catalano's MIT Student Center, on which Burns had worked, it was based on the disposition of main performance spaces on either side of a centralized vertical circulation system, which served as the core of the building. The structural system was to be of steel clad in concrete, using a regular structural grid; exterior massing was to consist of a symmetrical, heavily canti-levered upper portion, with recessed lower stories and projecting terraces, the whole design uncompromisingly orthogonal.[121] The plan was particularly challenging, as a great variety of different types of spaces and activities had to be compressed into a tightly knit single volume. Public access had to be provided to the auditorium of Alice Tully Hall, independent of the school proper; performance spaces had to be integrated with instructional facilities for dance and drama as well as orchestra rehearsal rooms, small chamber music halls, and individual practice rooms, plus a library and administra-tion office spaces, with acoustical insulation both from adjacent rooms and from traffic outside. Complicating the problem still further was the need to relate the building stylistically to the other buildings in Lincoln Center.

Burns worked on the Juilliard project for the next two years, with Taylor, another former Catalano student, serving as liaison among those in the Cambridge office, the consulting

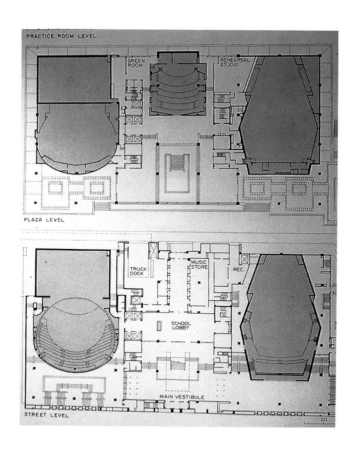

A. Juilliard Theater
B. Drama Workshop
C. Lila Acheson Wallace Library
D. Orchestra rehearsal and recording studio
E. Paul Recital Hall
F. Alice Tully Hall

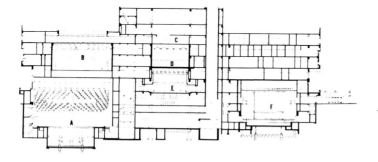

Juilliard School, plan, street level (Architectural Record, January 1970).

Juilliard School, cross section (Architectural Record, January 1970).

engineers, and members of the Juilliard staff, then, as the project moved into the fast track, with the contractor. William Pedersen, who left after a year, developed the Belluschi design for the opera theater; Austris Vitols, another MIT graduate, worked on Alice Tully Hall. Brannen was in charge of overall coordination and working drawings.[122]

Catalano was the one constant throughout, his presence always felt, providing regular guidance and criticism. Belluschi was around only occasionally until later when, as the design took shape and it appeared that the project was in fact going ahead, he began coming in to review their work. As the project neared completion, he stepped in with specific suggestions on the proportioning and detailing of the fenestration and treatment of the travertine veneer, refining, as Burns put it, their "somewhat brutish forms." Belluschi was also closely involved in the working out of the public spaces, especially the foyers and lobbies of the main performance halls, which would be a key concern of donors.[123]

Although he stopped in from time to time to review the work as it developed, Belluschi played a largely behind-the-scenes (or, from another perspective, the most publicly visible) role, negotiating with the client, donors, and consultants and balancing the needs of one against the demands of the others. The project was immensely complicated, with the architects under constant pressure to adjust to continuous changes in the program, conflicting requirements, an increasingly stringent budget as building costs continued to rise, as well as a rigid schedule. It was a highly demanding, frustrating task, which sapped much of Belluschi's zeal.

There were also distractions in his own life, first the death of his wife Helen in March 1962, then his retirement from MIT and remarriage to Marjorie Bruckner, his former MIT secretary, in 1965. By 1968, as the Juilliard building neared completion, he was busier than he had ever been, involved in major projects including St. Mary's Cathedral in San Francisco, the Century 21 project in Philadelphia, three corporate office towers in Boston, and the Ambassador's Residence in Paris for the FBO. At this point, problems with Juilliard were as much as anything a source of aggravation.

As built, Juilliard bears evidence of the rapidly shifting trends in architecture at the time. The initial studies of the late 1950s reflected then-current interest in monumental classicism, and the delicately patterned, decorative structures that dominated Lincoln Center as a whole. As admiration of Le Corbusier's recent work, such as Chandigarh and the Eveux monastery, grew in the early 1960s, and the brutalist reaction to the lightweight, fragile structures of the 1950s set in, they affected architects young and old, especially in the Boston/Cambridge area. The impact of this new interest in boldly sculptured, massively cantilevered forms is clear in the design of the new Juilliard, which was wholly antithetical to Belluschi's former formal language, though tempered by his preference for understatement and sense of refinement.

Initially conceived in 1955 as the education wing of Lincoln Center, the Juilliard School finally opened in October of 1969. It consisted of four performance halls, including the 1,000-seat Alice Tully Hall, Drama Workshop, and 800-seat Opera Theater (the stage alone of which was larger than that of Philip Johnson's New York State Theater). Its enormously complex yet highly efficient system of interlocking classroom spaces, rehearsal rooms, practice rooms, theater and drama workshop, and chamber music halls, as well as offices, lounges, and library, represented, as Mildred Schmertz put it in the *Architectural Record,* an "incredible effort on the part of Belluschi and his team."[124] Connected to Lincoln Center by a footbridge across 65th Street, sheathed in Roman travertine donated by the Italian government, and furnishing the facilities of an entire campus in a single urban structure, with four stories below grade, six above, it was a monumental achievement, the result of close to 15 years of coordinated work on the part of architects, special consultants, structural, mechanical, and acoustical engineers, as well as administrators of both Juilliard and Lincoln Center.

Belluschi was the architect in charge, establishing the basic concept, setting strategies, building consensus, reconciling, balancing, coordinating the show. Disheartened by years of battle, he put the design in Catalano's hands, who turned it over to his team of trained designers. By the time the Juilliard building was completed, everybody felt drained. LaGuardia High School, a companion project across the street, was left entirely to the Catalano staff, with Belluschi having little to do with it other than in name.

Juilliard was greeted with indifference by the movers and shakers in the architectural profession, whose basis for critical evaluation was the visual image—form rather than function, which was never Belluschi's interest. By 1969, when the building was completed, the stylistic concerns of the cutting edge had passed through their brutalist phase and were, in the wake of Venturi's 1966 *Complexity and Contradiction in Architecture,* gathering momentum for postmodernism. Nonetheless, the Juilliard School was acclaimed an outstanding success by the Juilliard administration and by critics in the general press. Seen by many as the best in Lincoln Center, architecturally as well as functionally, its acoustics, especially in Alice Tully Hall, far surpassing the others, it was warmly described as the high note of the complex. "You can't hit sour notes all the time,"

Huxtable wrote of it, finding the school remarkably free of the "uncertain pretensions and pomposities" of Lincoln Center's other buildings.[125]

The school facilities proved less successful, with students finding its labyrinthian circulation system confusing. The 65th Street entrance, supposed to be the principal one, was dank and inhospitable, buried under the pedestrian overpass, and rarely used, with most people finding the service entrance on 66th Street more convenient. On the other hand, given the challenge of fitting together the four concert halls, dance studios, theater facilities, some 67 practice rooms, office spaces for faculty and administration, with long spans superimposed upon short spans, two-story spaces dovetailing between one and three, the whole structure a closely interlocking puzzle of spaces tightly compacted into a container of set dimensions, from an operational point of view perhaps it was the best that could be done.

Remaining within its restricted budget, the final cost in 1969 was $29,500,000, compared to the almost $20,000,000 each for the Philharmonic Hall and the New York State Theater of some seven years earlier, neither of which was nearly so complex a structure, or the $47,000,000 of the Metropolitan Opera, completed three years before Juilliard.[126] Huxtable, loyal apologist of modernism, saw the building as a "marriage of form and function in terms of rational simplicity and bare-boned solutions," not avant-garde but bearing the classic simplicity and refinement of Belluschi's work.[127] It was awarded the Bart First Honor Award for Excellence in Architecture by the City Club of New York in recognition of its contribution to the city.

Mounting Criticism

Despite occasional acclaim, more often than not Belluschi's work of the late 1960s aroused criticism. His hands-off consulting style was seen as unreliable and irresponsible, often resulting in a lack of consistency or carry-through in the later stages of a project. If things went wrong, Belluschi wasn't around. Instead of a tightly knit organization, an inspired, coherent working team, often things didn't get done or got done badly.[128]

His work with large-scale developers rubbed many in the profession the wrong way, especially social activists and those in academia. Seeming to contradict his lofty statements, which increasingly sounded like empty rhetoric, he was regarded as an effete elitist, following big-time money-makers rather than safeguarding the public interest. Accepting commissions from the very developers whose work he was adjudicating as a design review board member continued to raise questions of conflict of interest, despite his efforts to avert them.

In his advisory work where, to nonprofessionals, his judgment seemed infallible, his endorsement of personal favorites to the exclusion of others, the Peis and Rudolphs rather than Giurgolas and Venturis, was seen less as a matter of discriminating taste than of abuse of power. Architectural values had changed, and Belluschi had not kept up.

Still more rankling to critics was what they saw as his cashing in on his reputation, selling his name at a high fee. Using it to get jobs that he then turned over to others earned him the disrespect not only of other architects but of disgruntled clients. Increasingly used as a marketing device, his name lost its sheen; he came increasingly to be seen as without standards or professional integrity, willing to work with anyone on any project for a price, and yielding to market values rather than holding out for artistic quality. His earnest-sounding claims to be improving the quality of what was going to be built anyway came to sound like rationalizations for sheer greed. Credit was another source of rancor, as the list of "Belluschi buildings" grew, in many of which he was only marginally involved.

One might argue that Belluschi was simply caught in the backlash of the times, the negativism of the late 1960s and the reaction against big buildings, large-scale development, the dehumanizing aspects of the city, and the whole "establishment" of which by then he appeared so much a part. But to a large extent, criticism focused directly on questions about the quality of his work, or what at best could be identified as his work. Throughout the 1960s, this showed increasing evidence of Belluschi's not being fully at home with the stylistic changes in the profession, the new values and new formal language then in favor. His own work, or again what could confidently be seen as his, was considered fussy and overwrought, too refined, too suave, his attention focused on surface articulation rather than on the larger issue of the architectural form itself, the design of which he typically left to others. The work lacked conviction, there was a loss of intensity that comes from the daily working out of the problems that inevitably arise, with the program, the client, one's own draftsmen. Some of this was inherent in the design consultant's role, but much of it was Belluschi himself. When things got rough, his schedule got busy, or he lost interest, he simply withdrew, and things fell apart.[129]

To some extent, Belluschi got caught in changing fashions. He had risen to the top of the profession when regionalism was in favor. As the tides of fashion began to change, first with postwar European modernism, then with brutalism, Belluschi's approach to architecture based on regionalist values—humanistic scale, simple reticent forms, careful craftsmanship especially in the handling of materials and detailing—fell from favor.

As taste turned in the early sixties to big gutsy sculptural forms, he tried to keep up. But design on a large scale never came easily, he was never really comfortable with the manipulation of form. His work with city officials, key people in government, corporate clients, and big developers absorbed more of his time and interest, and he lost touch with those in the profession, those grappling with the day-to-day problems of running a practice, as well as those in academia, the beacons of the profession. As new ways of architectural thinking spread in academic circles, Belluschi stayed away, preferring to pursue his own goals.

Pietro Belluschi

Preceding page: Pietro Belluschi, January 1972.

After a decade of turbulence, attitudes in architecture by the early 1970s had changed radically. The optimism of fifty years before, and the conviction that architects could play a fundamental role in reshaping the world, had been eroded by the overt failure of modernist schemes. *New Directions in American Architecture,* published in 1969 by New York architect Robert Stern, a former student of Vincent Scully at Yale and one of the more vociferous of the younger East Coast academics, reflected some of these new attitudes. Following Venturi's lead, Stern rejected modernism and its elitism, focusing his attack, among other things, on Lincoln Center, in which the Juilliard had just opened, as a glaring example of the failure of modern architects to solve social ills.

Stern's book, despite its oversimplified historical picture, rigid stylistic codification, and perhaps most telling its omission of any mention of the humanistic, regionalist tradition in his discussion of the development of modernism in America, nonetheless carried considerable weight in shaping the understanding and perceptions of the profession, especially among students.[1] Belluschi and others like him who were instrumental in the development of the regionalist tradition were simply ignored. Stern represented the new body of avant-garde academic architects/theorists/historians who, with their reawakened interest in history, were rewriting it to fit current theoretical views. Often this led to a lopsided, misleading perspective on what had actually happened.[2]

Venturi's *Complexity and Contradiction in Architecture* of 1966, and his later publications with Denise Scott Brown and Steven Izenour in the 1970s and 1980s, while making no claim to be historiography, catalyzed much of the new architectural thinking. Much had been lost by the modernists, they pointed out; the quest for purity, for an architecture derived solely from the desiderata of function and structure, had divested it of much of its richness—its symbolism, its associational values, its iconography or meaning. Citing as an example the Crawford House of Paul Rudolph (one of the architects Belluschi particularly admired and had often recommended for jobs) as emblematic of the modern movement, they criticized it not on the grounds of dishonesty—its materials and structural elements were, after all, clearly expressed—but of barrenness. Rejecting ornamentation, connotative expression, the role of past experience and emotional associations, it ignored broader cultural values that traditionally enriched architectural form, yielding it dry, empty, and boring.[3]

Many of the changes in architectural values were reflected in a new interest in theory as a guide to practice. The highly respected Robert Geddes, dean of the School of Architecture and Urban Planning at Princeton, indicated a growing rejection of modernist ideology in academia, at least in the East, and of the simplistic belief that the solution to an architectural problem could follow from the problem itself.[4] Marking another architectural trend in the 1970s was the work, largely residential, of Richard Meier and others of the New York Five.[5] They too rejected the modernist "form follows function" dictum, emphasizing form as an end in itself rather than the result of functional desiderata. They *began* with form, conceiving buildings less as functional spaces than as abstract, sculptural objects on an architectural scale, cool, formal, isolated in space, unsullied by constraints of structure or use or context—the very antithesis of Belluschi's informal, humanistic, responsive approach to residential design of his earlier years.

Still other trends marked a reaction against the optimistic celebration of progress and the technological determinism that had driven much of Belluschi's commercial work in the postwar era. The interest in architecture without architects that had emerged in the early 1960s, the celebration of small-scale, informal vernacular urban forms on the one hand and the nostalgia for country life and simple rural values on the other, indicated the strength of the reaction against unrestrained large-scale development.[6] Nonetheless, grandiose buildings and complexes continued to be built, outsizing their predecessors and proving Belluschi's contention that this scale of growth, like it or not, was inevitable.

Aware of these changing attitudes, Belluschi remained steadfast in his basic convictions—born not of European modernism but of the indigenous modernism that had developed in the Midwest and West prior to the MoMA International Style show of 1932. By the 1970s he was in his seventies, retired as dean of MIT but still an active member of the profession. Out of touch with academic theory, he was nonetheless still highly acclaimed professionally, recognized as one of the doyens of modern architecture. His entry in the 1970 AIA directory was one of the longest cited, with an extensive list of degrees, awards, honors, and service both governmental and educational, as well as principal works.[7]

Although the number of professional speaking engagements he was asked to give dropped, Belluschi remained highly respected, even revered, by the general public, and was often asked his opinion on current issues. He offered it freely. On issues of preservation, he acknowledged that he was less interested in preserving the past than building for the future; while older buildings were important in providing a sense of history and continuity with the past, once functionally obsolete they should be demolished to make room for new, urgently needed modern ones. "I'm not a great advocate of keeping and preserving," he said bluntly. "I'm much more interested in keeping the city alive and building."[8]

His architectural philosophy remained fundamentally humanistic. Simply put, he sought a solution that was satisfying from a practical, economic, and human point of view. While an engineer could solve problems, the architect was expected to add an artistic dimension, to solve the problem aesthetically. Always aware that he was designing for human use and experience, a concern that set him distinctly apart from the abstract, intellectually oriented theorists such as Venturi or Meier, he noted that few people acted fully rationally, that most actions were governed by emotions; thus the importance of the architect's understanding these emotions. Particularly in church design, it was important to understand what moved people emotionally, as design from a purely rational standpoint ignored the very dimension that made a religious space successful. "If you try to rationalize religion," he explained, "you never really get a satisfactory answer. The first thing you must do is to define the space that will make it possible for the worshipper to realize himself in the state of emotion which is religious."[9] While Venturi and others focused on a broader, more abstract cultural level, Belluschi's concern remained immediate and personal, geared to the individual, emotional, experiential dimension of architectural form. And while this is more readily apparent in the design of houses and churches, it nonetheless held true in the best of his designs for commercial buildings and corporate towers as well—hence the concern for the progression of spaces through lobby to elevator cab, for the ceiling height of a corridor, for the angle of light in a typical office space.

Asked his views on user-built housing, Belluschi recalled an example of what one might call user-built housing during the Depression, when the unemployed scrounged for wood and other materials to build their own shelters; while not much to look at, he said, their work evinced an exemplary, intuitive understanding of scale. Instinctively occupants sought a comfortable house. Their work "had an element that architects usually don't have. The human feeling that you build a house for, what it contains rather than as an object you see at a distance." He noted with regret the tendency among current architects to see architecture as a sculpture, an image to be looked at, "something to be seen or published," rather than experienced. Rarely was there a concern for what went on inside, how the spaces work, what people felt like when they used them. He advocated less concern for perfect exteriors, and more for making interiors interesting places to be.[10]

This was not mere talk. Tenants of the Beacon Companies' housing development on the outskirts of Boston appreciated the simple reticent exteriors, but it was the interiors, with visually interesting as well as comfortable spaces, and the site planning, with each unit provided with its own private courtyard, that they were most pleased with.[11] But then, the interiors—use, function, space, and its light—had always been more important to Belluschi than exterior form.

This was true of churches as well. "A church has to look well from the outside," he said, "but the dimension, the proportion, height, quality of light, source of light, materials, the scale for the human being to worship—the whole atmosphere you create should be conducive to worship. *These* are the important things. It doesn't make too much difference if outside it doesn't quite fill the role." Tellingly, he added, "A good architect does both, however."[12]

Commenting elsewhere on competence in architecture, he wrote, "If the architect knows himself, he'll keep his work within the limits of his abilities and not go beyond them. It's part of the eternal wisdom of knowing yourself."[13] Belluschi knew himself as few individuals did, and was honest with himself, at times brutally so. It was perhaps the recognition of his own limitations that made him turn so readily to other people, strong form-givers like Eduardo Catalano, for collaboration, knowing that buildings like Juilliard would be finer with their contribution. On the other hand, he was no saint, aggressively competitive and as hungry for fame and fortune as any man with a healthy sense of his own worth.

Because Belluschi typically addressed some of the toughest issues in the profession, he was often seen as hypocritical. Not always was the criticism warranted. Usually he believed in the principles he espoused, and strove to maintain them within the givens of the situation. But he was basically a realist, and accepted the limitations of client demands, his time, or whatever, aiming for the best he could do within them. "An architect should not be afraid to vary his philosophy to suit a particular project," he wrote in *Architects on Architecture*. "We must accept the enormous variety of situations that our age has created, and try to find solace in the thought that nature has evolved the orchid and the weed, the whale and the mouse, the eagle and the humming bird, all from a wonderfully complex yet orderly system." He believed the attempt to formulate a general theory of architecture futile, as it seemed impossible to draw laws and conclusions that could not somehow in another circumstance be challenged.[14]

A modernist through and through, Belluschi deplored deception. Architecture he felt must have integrity and honesty, must be based on what was possible. Structure was fundamentally important, not only the way in which a building was put together, or the simplicity of its structural idea, but how this idea was expressed. Structure that was concealed, twisted, or polluted as an idea seldom produced good architecture.[15]

Emphasizing the importance of researching all aspects of the people one designed for, their emotional wants and psychological needs as well as habits and traditions, Belluschi pointed out how difficult this often proved to be. The design of the MacGregor dormitories on the MIT campus in the mid-60s, for example, was based on a study that showed students favoring the cluster concept, with the building block broken down into a series of small, closely knit, family-sized units. By the time the dorms were built, however, student attitudes had changed; instead of 1950s-inspired protective familylike situations, they sought a less restrictive, more openly communal situation reflecting the values of the 1960s. Herein lay the problem: how design wisely for the future when the future—attitudes as well as circumstances—changed so unpredictably and fast? Again Belluschi was grappling with, rather than shying away from, the real issues, some of the most basic dilemmas facing the architectural profession at large.

The "advocacy" approach, another trend of the late 1960s and early 1970s, was one that Belluschi recognized wouldn't work, however sympathetic he was in theory. Having seen the public in action in Boston, Baltimore, San Francisco, and Portland, obstructing the progress of city planners, architects, and their clients, he maintained that bringing the public in on all decisions was mostly obstructive. The public simply didn't know enough about the situation, had no real sense of the difficulties, no understanding of the long-range implications. Reacting emotionally out of ignorance rather than rationally as a result of careful study, the public was untrained and, he felt, should leave such issues to design professionals whose lives were devoted to resolving them. Knowing it was an unpopular view, and that he would be condemned as patriarchal and elitist, but nonetheless convinced of its truth, Belluschi opposed with increasing impatience the notion of participatory democracy, where every voice had equal say.[16]

Belluschi was in Portland frequently in these years as an advisor both to the Portland Development Commission and to the U.S. National Bank on a proposed high-rise corporate headquarters building. In a talk to the Portland chapter of the AIA in April of 1972, he stressed, as he had throughout the years, the importance of visual amenities in city planning. Solving the specific social, economic, and political problems—low-cost housing, circulation, traffic, parking—was vital, but the urban designer should go beyond that. City planning in the last analysis had to be concerned with human beings, "and with the search for what gives them pride and delight." Parks, fountains, squares and open spaces that offer the common man spiritual uplift and respite from the tension of city life were thus vital. While one could not, given the hard realities of the current social and political world, redesign whole cities, could not, as Haussmann had done in Paris or Robert Moses more recently in New York, wipe the slate clean and start anew, one could nonetheless within the limits of the existing situation provide room for aesthetic expression.[17]

At the same time, Belluschi opposed too much control, too many restrictions in the planning of cities. Just as he insisted on allowing the artists or architects with whom he collaborated as much artistic license as the situation warranted, so too in city design. Especially in cities, one needed to allow for a certain randomness and unpredictability as the city grew. Anticipating the rigor mortis that was beginning to set in in cities like San Francisco, beset by design guidelines that were too restrictive, Belluschi pointed out how easy it was to kill a city by limiting access or insisting on too many open spaces, interfering with natural growth. "Common sense has never been an enemy of aesthetics. The city can be a work of art only if it is free to express the life which animates it."[18] Design strictures were important, but should be used with caution. High-rise buildings, for example, were not in themselves bad: the city had to have a certain density, but uncontrolled they could throw off the city's scale. His main point, that design guidelines were good but rigidly imposed often did more harm than good, was vintage Belluschi: hard to pin down, considering both sides of the issue, flexible and nondoctrinaire.

Belluschi's opinions continued to be sought throughout the decade, his words at least on some level still ringing true. When in 1973 Wright's Taliesin West was threatened by government plans for an 80-foot-wide canal and flood control dike, and a 124-unit development proposed west of the entrance, editors of the *Architectural Forum* quoted Belluschi, who'd spoken earlier that spring when Taliesin was granted an AIA 25-year award. "The years have not diminished its elemental quality. More than other works by this master it shows how to grasp the mood of the land and transform it into a place of harmony and beauty. Here one understands the magic of man's primeval relationship to nature."[19] Few others at that time could have spoken with such empathy—not Venturi, Stern, Meier, Philip Johnson, or others of the self-styled leading progressives—of Wright and his legacy in American architecture.

But if Belluschi's views on man's (sic) rapport with the land were out of sync in the formalist climate of the 1970s, his attitudes on women were even more so. Italian male to the core, his comments on women architects in the wake of the 1973 national AIA convention, which had raised the issue of integrating women into all aspects of the profession, did little to endear him to the younger generation, women in particular. Acknowledging there was room "for girls" in the profession "if they were good" (that mattered less for men), he recalled warning women in the 1950s not to pursue architecture because "it would be difficult."[20] Though he cavalierly joked about it later, tickled especially about being called "a chauvinist pig," the issue was hardly as light as he saw it. Yet again Belluschi became emblematic of much that was wrong with the system.[21]

The AIA Gold Medal

After decades of accomplishment and acknowledged as one of the most influential architects in the country, Belluschi was awarded the AIA Gold Medal, the highest honor in the profession, at the 1972 annual convention in Houston. Lauded for his contribution as an educator to students and colleagues alike, inspiring them to higher levels of achievement, and as advisor to public agencies, significantly advancing the cause of public architecture and elevating the quality of the environment overall, he was primarily honored for his pioneering work on the West Coast, for his houses and churches, for the respect for the demands of function and the discipline, structure, and material his buildings evoke, and their unrivaled sense of purpose as well as place.[22]

Marjorie and Pietro Belluschi, AIA convention, Houston, 1972.

Belluschi's acceptance speech, long and nuanced, was published in the July *AIA Journal.* At once proud of his accomplishments and repentant, he questioned his work and the issues it raised. His talk began with a mea culpa, disarmingly expressing his own doubts about deserving the AIA's highest honor and questioning the wisdom of their choice (false modesty, some said), then admitting an uneasiness about his new method of practice, which handed over all administrative responsibility to his associates. He also acknowledged receiving at times more credit than he deserved, and apologized. Then moving to a less personal level, he conveyed his concern about the current generation gap, noting that the lively exchange with students that he had enjoyed in the past no longer seemed to exist; he regretted this, as he felt he still offered much from which they could learn. But that was life, change, growth, which he accepted. Aware of progressive undercurrents in the profession and his own distance from them, he questioned whether he himself hadn't relied too heavily on reason, not allowed enough room for sheer fantasy in his work. Addressing the accusation that modern architects had not lived up to their goals, Belluschi said, in essence, enough of sweeping generalizations: he was skeptical of oversimplified answers, intellectual abstractions, and theories, and relied instead on his humanistic instincts, as it was "the living experience which in the end counts." The problems architects faced today were complicated, and the help of others was needed to solve them; but it was the architect who was society's torchbearer responsible for bringing grace and civility to the human environment, and it was his task to provide that extra, the *art* in architecture, that satisfied the soul. This came about as a result of an understanding of man, of others, not from theoretical abstraction.

Belluschi characteristically concluded inconclusively by saying there were no ultimate solutions, "only systems of change, doors that open and close, lights that illuminate and darken." They were in a time of change, but the architect's task remained the same: to fulfill the human spirit.[23]

It was primarily Belluschi's early West Coast work that drew recognition. In his feature article on the Belluschi award in the *AIA Journal,* westerner Marion Dean Ross, professor of architectural history at the University of Oregon and long-time promoter of his work, emphasized the eloquence, simplicity, and sense of place displayed in such buildings as the Portland Art Museum, the houses and churches, and the Equitable Building. A photograph of the 1939 St. Thomas More church graced the cover. In another article by Elisabeth K. Thompson, former West Coast editor of the *Architectural Record,* the later work was illustrated by the Rohm & Haas Building, Bank of America, Boston Company Building, and Keystone Building (photographs Belluschi had sent in, and wanted included), but was not discussed. Neither St. Mary's Cathedral nor the Juilliard School, both of which were newly completed, received comment.[24]

The Belluschi nomination was contentious. He had in fact been nominated several times before, once in 1954.[25] His 1972 nomination came at a time when few other architects were seen as eligible, and was spearheaded by a small group of former staff members and friends from his old Portland days. AIA board members, however, had questions about the quality of the later work, about his modus operandi, and whether as a "consultant" one could really call him "the architect." Doubt was cast on his claim to have "designed" over 1,000 buildings.[26] The question hinged, according to one of the board members and a former colleague of Belluschi's at MIT, on how one defined the author or architect of a building: perhaps in Belluschi's case "design guided by Belluschi" would better describe his role. John Burchard, another colleague of Belluschi's at MIT, voiced outright disapproval of the nomination and refused to support it, saying he admired none of Belluschi's work from the Pan Am Building on and had even less respect for the way he operated professionally.[27] The Belluschi nomination was endorsed by neither the Northern California chapter nor the Boston chapter.[28] It was troubled, transitional time in the profession, with stylistic directions fluctuating rapidly, and no one was sure how to measure quality or what was good. The AIA was then also under attack for its predominantly white male constituency, with few women and virtually no African-Americans represented, and hard questions were being raised about what the criteria were, or should be, for recognition in the profession. After Belluschi, the Gold Medal award was suspended for several years, according to Archibald Rogers, the incoming AIA president, because of a lack of consensus on a qualified candidate. In retrospect, it seems apparent that the issue was not so much a lack of qualified candidates as a lack of consensus on appropriate criteria for judging them.[29]

The Return to Portland

A long feature article in the Sunday *Boston Globe* of 14 May 1972 caught the gist of the Belluschi controversy. Written in honor of his receiving the Gold Medal and listing his many accomplishments, the article nonetheless focused on the criticism his later work had roused, criticism "so harsh it rocked the whole profession."[30] The article repeated the now familiar view that he yielded too often and too easily to the demands of the marketplace, putting profits ahead of architectural values. In the minds of many, architectural success should not be measured by getting the maximum number of jobs and putting them through with a minimum of friction. There was other criticism as well. With full-time help from his wife and former secretary, he ran his office at home, enabling him to keep his fees significantly below those of his peers. Free to charge virtually whatever he wanted, he set his rate on a given job, as he readily acknowledged, according to his

Cover, Boston Globe *magazine, 14 May 1972.*

level of interest in it. In short, the *Globe* portrayed him as more interested in budgets than beauty, less an architect of real integrity than a shrewd businessman.

Boston had become uncomfortable. Belluschi was in Portland for some advisory work with the city on a glorious warm, sunny day in the spring of 1973 when, hearing that the Burkes House he had designed in 1947 was on the market at a bargain price, on the spur of the moment he bought it.[31] Tired of being maligned, he was eager to return to the tranquillity of Portland where he was lionized, known as "the venerable Pietro Belluschi" and "the patriarch of American architecture" rather than a self-serving exploiter.

He had made a point of maintaining his professional connections in Portland after he left for MIT. He kept up with old clients and sustained several important jobs there, initially in association with SOM, then with other local firms. He also served as advisor to the Portland Development Commission throughout much of the 1960s and early 1970s, and he clearly enjoyed returning to see old friends and reestablish ties. Drawn to the Oregon country, whose natural beauty and serenity had initially inspired him, he had found its quiet harmony lost in the din of Boston.

Belluschi had never really been comfortable in the East, ill at ease in academia and not truly at home designing large-scale buildings in situations culturally and climatically unfamiliar. His return to Portland, precipitous as it was, surprised few who really knew him.

He stayed active nationally as a design consultant, maintaining his association with the Jung/Brannen office in Boston as well as professional ties in Baltimore, San Francisco, Philadelphia, and elsewhere. He took part in a wide range of projects, among them the World Bank Building and Pentagon City in Arlington, Virginia, with Vlastimil Koubek architect; the Cuyahoga County Justice Center in Cleveland, with Prindle, Patrick & Partners; a master plan for the University of Jeddah, Saudi Arabia; the Parliament Building in Seoul, Korea; the University of Ancona, in Ancona, Italy, with Jung/Brannen Associates; and the Davies Symphony Hall in San Francisco, with SOM. Nonetheless as his activities diminished and he gradually fell into the role of senior advisor rather than kingpin, he became melancholy. An interview in 1976 quoted him as saying that he had never believed he was going to conquer the world, only survive in it.[32] More likely this was a rationalization, a recognition, in the wake of what must have been a major disappointment over professional indifference to St. Mary's Cathedral, that at age 77 he stood little chance of attaining, much less surpassing, the height of success he had achieved with the Equitable Building in 1948, when he was at the top of the profession. His move back to Portland seems to have been an admission to himself of that, a realist acceptance of the fact that he had accomplished most of what he was going to. Whatever the disappointment, it was tempered by the satisfaction of knowing he had at least survived very well.[33]

Later Work in Portland

In 1951, when Belluschi accepted the deanship at MIT and moved to Cambridge, the economy in the Northwest had already begun to slump with the onset of the Korean War, and it remained flat throughout the decade. The Belluschi/SOM office held its own but struggled. Toward the end of the 1950s things began to revive. SOM's Standard Insurance Building, begun in the late 1950s and finished in 1963, was the first new office building built in downtown Portland since Belluschi's 1948 Equitable Building. By that time B/SOM had dissolved, and the Standard Insurance was by SOM alone.

After Belluschi left for the East, he remained in contact with Ralph Cake, head of the Equitable Savings and Loan Association, for whom he had served as architect since the late 1920s, advising him on a series of branch banks being done by SOM. In the spring of 1962, when the Equitable decided to sell the award-winning 1948 building and build a new headquarters in another part of town, Cake wanted Belluschi to be the architect.[34] Belluschi was of course pleased; knowing Cake had not been happy with SOM, he turned to the small, relatively young Portland firm of Wolff-Zimmer as associates.[35] It was the beginning of a fruitful collaboration, comparable to the one he was to form later with Jung/Brannen in Boston, though with telling differences.

As the Equitable needed its new quarters immediately, Belluschi had to move fast. Cake also wanted another landmark building. The new site, a self-contained 200-by-200-foot city block, was located at the south end of the downtown, opposite the Oregonian Building and several blocks east of the Portland Art Museum. Well before starting, however, Belluschi and Cake had been exchanging ideas and information by mail and phone, developing plans together, as they had on the earlier Equitable Building.[36]

Belluschi's proposal used as a model recent office buildings like Saarinen's just completed London Embassy or SOM's Banque Lambert in Brussels, then under construction. It consisted of a classical rectangle, a low four-story structure with recessed pilotis forming a colonnade at the base, a glass-enclosed ground floor surmounted by three stories of office space above, the whole set on a podium in a broad plaza. Exteriors were

Equitable Center, Portland, 1962–1965, exterior.

to be of textured precast aggregate panels like those used on the Pan Am Building in New York.[37] The building, with its deliberately sensuous rather than cerebral appeal, marked a self-conscious stylistic departure from the austere postwar, Mies-inspired, flush-surfaced glass and metal language of the 1948 Equitable. Following the Seagram paradigm with its spatially isolating plaza, by then a cliche elsewhere in the country, Belluschi proposed setting the pristine monument in an open square, landscaped with pools and fountains to provide the public a congenial open space. The Wolff-Zimmer office was brought in at this time.

Belluschi brought the preliminaries with him, having had them drawn up in Catalano's office in Cambridge, and left it to Zimmer and his associates in Portland to work out the problems with the then still new structural system.[38] A fast-track job, with design development proceeding at the same time work on foundations was begun, the building was up in less than two years, opening in spring of 1965.

In response to his client's sense of urgency as well as his own busy schedule, as he was then in the throes of the Northern States Power Office Building in Minneapolis, the Rohm & Haas Building in Philadelphia, and the B'rith Kodesh Synagogue in Rochester, New York, and just getting started on St. Mary's Cathedral and the Bank of America building in San Francisco, Belluschi drew heavily on the ideas of others. Rather than novelty he aimed at quality, in design and execution. Promising his client an economical structure, he concentrated on scale and proportioning, the handling of materials, and careful detailing, plus finishing touches such as the design of the pools and selection of trees for the public terrace.

Belluschi also promised another landmark building, "a memorable milestone in the quest for quality."[39] It was, in the language of the time, a handsome building—good, solid, well functioning, and, like the 1948 Equitable Building, technically progressive. But it broke no new ground, formally or otherwise, and its design was in fact already behind the

Portland Art Museum addition, 1968–1970, site plan.

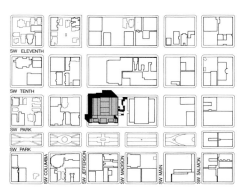

*Portland Art Museum addition, exterior
(photo: author).*

times. It drew on the classical temple image popular in the mid-1950s just as tastes elsewhere were moving into more sculptural, Corbusian-inspired brutalist directions and public sentiment began to turn against monumental, spatially isolated buildings. Stylistically dated by the time it opened in March of 1965 at a cost of more than $3.25 million, it was of little more than regional interest to the architectural profession.[40]

However marginal the Equitable Center proved to be in Belluschi's career, it was an important job for the Wolff-Zimmer office. Still small in the late 1950s, it grew in size and stature as a result, establishing a reputation as a reliable, progressive young firm. The office also learned a great deal from Belluschi, less in design than in operations, and how to go about doing a building of that size and complexity. The association paved the way for future work, as had Belluschi's association with RTKL in Baltimore, and constituted a major step in the eventual success of the firm.[41]

Belluschi continued to associate with Wolff-Zimmer, which eventually became the Zimmer Gunsul Frasca Partnership, for a series of other Portland jobs in the 1960s. Among these was a new school wing for the Portland Art Museum, a job Belluschi had begun in the early 1960s with SOM, then carried out in the late 1960s with ZGF.[42] Robert Frasca, a graduate of MIT who had joined the Wolff-Zimmer office in 1959, was largely responsible for its design, tailoring it to the earlier Belluschi work.[43]

A second job the two men were involved in bore more of Frasca's own stamp. The Oregon Historical Society needed a new building, and donors, revering the now nationally celebrated Belluschi, wanted him. The director of the Society, however, who was familiar with the problems of Belluschi's hands-off approach which left him gone most of the time, and was aware of the resentment generated by his "skimming off the cream," preferred going with a local firm. After interviewing several offices, he chose ZGF, retaining Belluschi only as an advisor.[44] It was a difficult moment for Belluschi, who had expected the job and met the news of its going to Frasca, ZGF's designer, with stunned silence. Frasca designed the building himself, a muscular exposed concrete sculptural form in the brutalist vein, with minimal Belluschi involvement.

Belluschi in association with Frasca received a number of jobs in the following years, among them a small Catholic church in Roseburg, Oregon (1964–1968), Oregon Graduate Center (1968–1970), the Trojan Nuclear Power Plant (1970), the KahNeeTah Lodge in Warm Springs (1970–1972), an addition to the Oregon State Capitol in Salem (1977), the Pacific Gas & Electric Headquarters Building (Willamette Center, 1977), and the Portland Justice Center (1978–1980). All appear to have been gotten largely on the basis of the Belluschi name, with his participation varying from design advisor to virtually none at all.

Initially the association worked to the benefit of both parties. ZGF got jobs, some of them substantial, that they would not have otherwise; Belluschi was paid handsomely, often for very little work. But after he moved back to Portland in 1973, he had more time and wanted greater involvement in, and more control over, design. By that time, Frasca had become an accomplished designer in his own right and was eager to move on in his own direction. As differences emerged, Belluschi felt pushed aside, both excluded from the design process and ignored in areas where he felt his experience would be useful. He began now to resent his name being used as a means of getting jobs.[45]

ZGF, too, squandered a valuable resource. There was much they might have learned from Belluschi, about planning, circulation, lighting, scale, and detailing if not design. Belluschi knew the Pacific Northwest—its resources, unique sensibility, its mores, its people—as few people did. On the other hand, Frasca was in touch architecturally. Belluschi was not, as the course of events would tell.

Continued Work with Jung/Brannen

After moving back to Portland, Belluschi continued his association with Jung/Brannen in Boston, usually in the form of joint venture.[46] Typically Belluschi received the commission which was then carried out in the Jung/Brannen office, with his level of involvement varying. On some jobs, such as the One Post Office Square Building in Boston (1978–1982) for the Beacon Companies, and One Financial Center (Dewey Square) (1970–1984) for Rose Associates of New York, his contribution seems to have been limited either to

One Post Office Square, Boston, 1978–
1982 (photo: author).

One Maine Savings Bank, Portland,
Maine, 1972–1975, exterior.

the very early conceptual stages or to the very late, with suggestions on siting and massing on the One Post Office Square Building and the presentation of the final project to the city on One Financial Center. In other jobs, such as the One Maine Savings Bank in Portland, Maine (1972–1975), his role seems to have been handling client negotiations and establishing the basic design parameters, which he then turned over to Robert Hsiung, Jung/Brannen's designer, to develop. Hsiung, who joined the firm in 1972, was a former student of Catalano's at MIT and a skilled designer whose work as one of the finalists in the Boston City Hall competition had caught Belluschi's eye. Hsiung respected Belluschi, listened well, and functioned comfortably, not unlike Ken Richardson in the early days, as the formal interpreter of Belluschi's ideas. After years of working in Catalano's office while Belluschi was there, he was familiar with his approach, able to grasp quickly the thrust of Belluschi's ideas and then realize them quickly in graphic form.[47]

The Meyerhoff Symphony Hall in Baltimore was commissioned in the same year as the Maine Savings Bank, the year Belluschi received the AIA Gold Medal. Joseph Meyerhoff, a wealthy Baltimore developer, knew Belluschi through his work on the Architectural Advisory Committee for the Charles Center. By this time Belluschi had had considerable

Meyerhoff Symphony Hall, Baltimore, 1972–1982, exterior (photo: author).

experience in concert hall designs, having been associated on performance halls for Goucher College, Douglass College at Rutgers, and a newly opened, highly acclaimed concert hall in Sacramento, California, as well as Alice Tully Hall and another auditorium in the Juilliard School. For Meyerhoff, president and chairman of the Baltimore Symphony board and major donor of the proposed Symphony Hall, there was only one architect he was interested in. His request was simple: he wanted acoustically the best designed symphony hall modern technology allowed.[48]

Belluschi met with Hsiung and Brannen for a preliminary brainstorming session, as they had on the Maine Savings Bank. Belluschi outlined the program, specified the client's major demands, described the site and budget, and set forth his initial thoughts on the direction design might take. Hsiung sketched. Brannen was in charge of directing the project, as he had been on the Douglass College theater for Rutgers, working with the symphony people, city officials, and contractors. Belluschi, who had moved to Portland shortly after the job started, kept tabs on it largely by mail.

The budget was adequate, though not lavish, and later cutbacks necessitated major cost-cutting measures in midstream; the site was tight, an irregularly shaped island bounded on all sides by streets in the Mount Royal area of Baltimore. Given its strategic location, at the focal point of converging streets with long vistas from several sides, a prominent, sculptural form seemed called for. Belluschi's overriding concern, however, was not form but designing the finest possible environment for orchestral music. To this end he brought in Bolt, Beranek and Newman, acoustical experts from Boston, with whom he had often worked.

Design proceeded from there, with the basic form developing out of one of Hsiung's initial sketches: an elliptical, egg-shaped form tilted on edge, with a fanned apron or skirt at the base. It was determined by and evolved from the concern for ideal acoustics and the constraints of the site. The question of form for its own sake, other than the need for something with presence, never came up.[49]

Described as a "near perfect example of function dictating structure and design,"[50] the hall consisted of crisp, lean, ovoid forms of warm, rust-colored brick. Bold, monumental, yet unpretentious, it had presence but with more of Aalto's reticence than brutalist aggression. Aaltoesque too was the clear legibility of interior spaces on the exterior: entrance with ticket office opening onto a spacious lobby, which was fully glazed on one side to provide an expansive view of a park, with a simple winding monumental stair providing access to the large 2,500-seat hall. Ancillary spaces, including a two-story

Meyerhoff Symphony Hall, lobby (photo: author).

Meyerhoff Symphony Hall, auditorium (photo: author).

rehearsal room, some 18,000 square feet of office space, music library, and storage space for instruments, were tucked around the base of the raised elliptical drum at the rear. Materials on the interior of the steel-frame structure were principally brick, wood paneling, and acoustical plaster.

As other new symphony halls opened in Minneapolis, Denver, and San Francisco, all with mixed reviews, they proved the field of acoustics more an unpredictable art than an exact science. As critics continued to point out, no matter how handsome or compelling these new halls looked, no matter how comfortable and commodious they felt to audiences and performers, if the acoustics failed the buildings were flops. On this count, the Baltimore symphony hall, opening in fall 1982, proved remarkably successful, receiving nothing but high ratings from music critics. As an editorial in the *Baltimore Sun* put it, the new hall was "one pudding the proof of which is in the hearing. Both planners and architects got the priorities right." Other halls may have been grander, with dramatic exteriors and more elegant lobbies. But the Meyerhoff Symphony Hall, exerting a quiet presence without overwhelming its neighbors, was designed for the quality of its sound.[51]

Belluschi's role was like that in the Juilliard building: he received the commission; because of his stature and reputation in the community he served as a major draw in fundraising; and as a recognized authority he was able to pull off a distinctly modern building in otherwise architecturally conservative Baltimore. He assembled the team, established the basic direction, guided the design. At the time, Jung/Brannen Associates was still fledgling, and Hsiung, their principal designer, had never done a performance hall. Working in an atmosphere of mutual trust and respect, drawing on Belluschi's wisdom and experience and with his set of architectural values, the team proved highly successful.

In the wake of Belluschi's AIA Gold Medal, Camillo Gubitosi and Alberto Izzo, professors of architecture at the University of Naples who were also associated with the Architects Design Group in Cambridge, in May 1974 staged an exhibition of his work at the university's Istituto di Analisi Architettonica.[52] Belluschi, giving a lecture in conjunction with the exhibition, happened to meet the mayor of Ancona and mentioned he was from there. Whereupon the mayor, who happened also to be both president of the University of Ancona and a professor of architecture there, and later a state senator, invited Belluschi to be the architect of the new facilities for the university's College of Engineering. There had been talk of a national competition, but in the interest of time it was determined (though evidently not agreed upon by everybody) that Belluschi should do it.[53]

University of Ancona, engineering complex, aerial view.

On his return to the States, Belluschi stopped off in Boston to meet with Hsiung and Brannen to discuss the program and suggest a general direction. They took over from there, keeping Belluschi informed by mail. Preliminary drawings, revised after a change of site, were sent to Ancona in 1976. They then heard nothing and assumed the project dead, until 1985 when they were invited to the opening.[54] Though billed as the architect "della massime," Belluschi's role was primarily that of getting the job. Jung/Brannen provided the preliminary design, which was developed and carried out by a local architectural firm.

Based on the success of its association with Belluschi, the Jung/Brannen firm continued to expand throughout the 1970s and 1980s, with their joint buildings and projects numbering well into the hundreds. By the late 1980s, with offices in New York and Hartford, Connecticut, as well as Boston and a staff of close to 200, it was among the nation's top 200 architectural firms.[55]

In 1986, Belluschi dissolved his association with the firm, except for one longstanding project: the Portsmouth Abbey School. He did so in part because the cost of liability insurance was becoming too great, in part because he no longer wanted to travel, but also, and perhaps largely, because his conscience was beginning to dog him about receiving such hefty fees for so little work. A note in his hand, "A total of $20,000 for a few lousy sketches!!!" on a bill sent to the Portsmouth Abbey, conveyed as much.[56] He was also dismayed at the size to which the Jung/Brannen firm had grown, and still more importantly at the direction their design in the late eighties was taking, with gabled roofs, multicolored exteriors, and other postmodernist clichés.[57]

SOM, Charles Bassett, and the Davies Symphony Hall, 1973–1980

A year after receiving the AIA Gold Medal and commencing the Meyerhoff Symphony Hall, Belluschi became involved in a second major performing arts center project. Bay Area architect Vernon DeMars, who had recently completed the Zellerbach Auditorium on the University of California, Berkeley, campus, had been asked informally to do feasibility studies for a possible new major symphony hall on a site behind the Opera House in the San Francisco Civic Center.[58] The DeMars & Wells office drew up a proposal, but in the meantime public awareness had grown, and Samuel Stewart, president of the Bank of America, had assumed sponsorship of the project. DeMars recognized that a small local firm located in the East Bay would need more clout to compete for the job. At the AIA convention in San Francisco in May 1973 he approached Belluschi as someone of national reputation, experienced in symphony halls, and whose architectural approach was in sympathy with his own West Coast concerns. Moreover, DeMars had worked with Belluschi on the Golden Gateway Competition and other projects for the Perini Corporation, and—another plus—Belluschi already had well-established ties with Stewart as a result of his work on the Bank of America Building. In proposing the association, DeMars assumed that Belluschi would function as their advisor, reviewing designs prepared in his office as he had on their Golden Gateway project.[59] Belluschi was thrilled by the idea; having just moved back to the West Coast and already feeling somewhat out of things, he envisioned it as an opportunity to do a major building, with him as principal designer and the DeMars & Wells team as backup associates. Immediately he began sending DeMars scores of sketches proposing solutions.

The following fall, wholly independently, Stewart asked Belluschi to serve as advisor to the client, in much the same capacity as he had on the Bank of America Building. After discussing the project with Belluschi, however, Stewart decided that Belluschi himself should be the architect in charge.[60]

While fund raising and negotiations with the city over the site took place over the next couple of years, Belluschi and DeMars traveled to Europe to study some of the new symphony halls there, in particular Hans Scharoun's new symphony hall in Berlin, which

Seiji Ozawa, director of the San Francisco Symphony, particularly admired. A new plan based on the Scharoun model was worked out in the DeMars & Wells office. Belluschi, working independently out of his home in Portland, turned his attention to the elevations. At the request of Sam Stewart, he also began fund-raising efforts, giving presentations and meeting with potential donors in the San Francisco area.[61]

In November of 1974, when it looked as if the site were going to be on the Civic Center esplanade at Marshall Square, directly opposite the 1916 classical Public Library, the Belluschi/DeMars & Wells team put out a brochure with drawings of their proposal. The principal problem, as DeMars saw it, was coming up with an exterior that would harmonize with the grand, monumental character of the turn-of-the-century Beaux-Arts Civic Center. Their scheme called for a simple rectangular form, like that of the Zellerbach Hall, but enclosing a fan-shaped auditorium plan based on the Berlin Symphony Hall.

Several months later, a new site was proposed on the corner of Van Ness and Hayes, diagonally across from the monumental dome of Arthur Brown's 1914 Beaux-Arts City Hall. With the new corner site, Jack Hillmer, then working in the DeMars office, suggested shifting the axis to the diagonal, with the entrance facing directly onto Brown's monu-

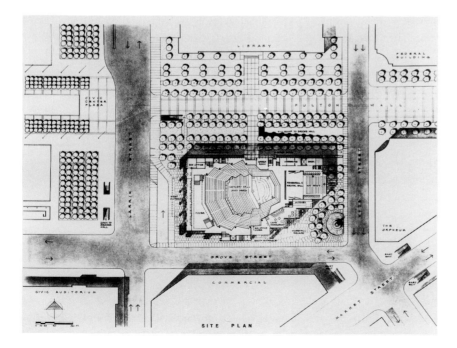

San Francisco Performing Arts Center,
Marshall Square site, November 1974
(Oregon Historical Society).

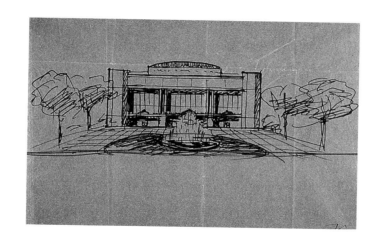

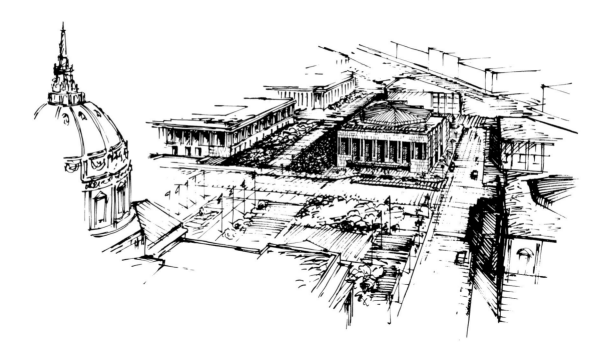

San Francisco Symphony Hall, Belluschi sketch (undated, but sometime
in fall of 1974; Oregon Historical Society).

San Francisco Performing Arts Center,
preliminary sketch, Marshall Square
site, drawing by Jack Sidener of
DeMars & Wells (Oregon Historical Society).

mental dome.[62] This not only gave the building more room on the site but helped to unify the Civic Center as a whole, focusing buildings inward onto City Hall rather than merely stringing them along independently on Van Ness Avenue. The parti of the glazed corner, providing a dramatic view of City Hall, followed from there.

Major fund-raising efforts then got under way, with Belluschi billed as the architect, and in July of 1975 one of his preliminary schemes was published in the *San Francisco Chronicle*. Described as a stark, minimally ornamented structure, it was more brutalist than classical in character and sharply different from the DeMars scheme, though the fan-shaped plan of the auditorium remained the same.[63] Belluschi developed the concept of a diagonal axis with a scheme calling for bold geometric forms framing a glazed central portion that would display a multistory lobby with a grand monumental stair. His proposal, recalling Philip Johnson's initial project for the Lincoln Center theater, most likely was inspired by the newly opened concert hall in Akron, Ohio, with bold solids alternating with expansive glazing to allow the interior lobby spaces to be seen from outside.[64]

The Belluschi scheme published in the *Chronicle* was accompanied by an article warmly endorsing it by the respected music critic Robert Commanday, one of Belluschi's strongest allies, who knew him through his work on both St. Mary's Cathedral and the concert hall in Sacramento. Commanday quoted Belluschi as saying, on behalf of the architects, that they were determined "not to allow any architectural, structural, aesthetic or economic compromise to affect even minimally the quality of the sound." Factors such as comfort, intimacy of the space, visibility, sense of warmth, quality of light, tone and mood of color, were deemed next in importance, in addition to the problems of circulation, safety, seismic strength, and other basic programmatic concerns. Finally, for the exterior, Belluschi said in his characteristically lofty prose that they sought to develop within the

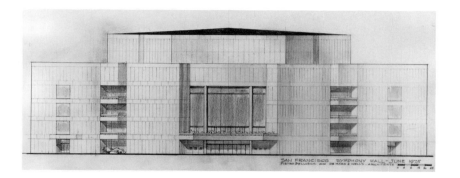

San Francisco Symphony Hall, elevation, Belluschi drawing, June 1975 (Oregon Historical Society).

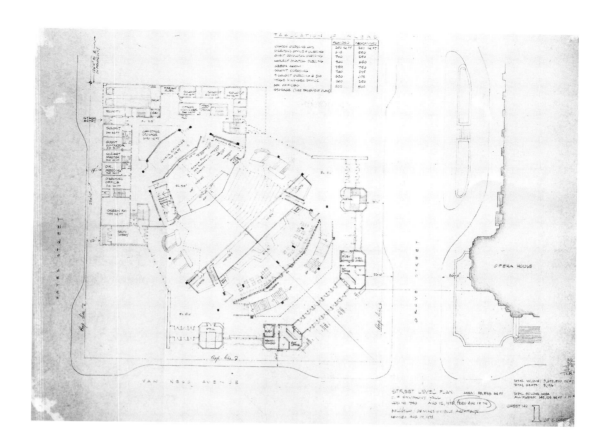

San Francisco Symphony Hall, street-
level plan, 19 August 1975 (Oregon Historical Society).

San Francisco Symphony Hall, model,
June 1975.

constraints of the budget and site "an architectural expression embodying contemporary values" that would also provide the lasting aesthetic quality needed to satisfy the eyes of future generations.[65]

The site itself, adjacent to the Beaux-Arts Opera House as well as the richly embellished and domed City Hall, presented a challenge of its own. The exterior needed to fit, yet proclaim itself distinctly modern and express an appropriate character. The architects leaned toward a simple architectural statement in which landscaping would provide both gentility and human scale. "What we have called a landscaped solution could serve," Belluschi put it, "as a suitable foil to the noble grandeur of the civic structures, related more to the gardens of the Center than to its buildings." And the transparent facade, allowing a full view of the lobby with its grand monumental stair, would enable concert-goers themselves to become part of the building's display.[66]

For Belluschi, the problem was familiar. Born and raised in Italy amid the unchanging classical forms of the past, he grew up in an era when architectural forms were drawn from a repository of basic types, and visual interest was generated not by novel form but by the skillful handling of materials, proportions, scale, and details. In later twentieth-century America he faced a very different problem: how to create a wholly new architectural form while avoiding formalism and the trendiness of "in" styles, which he saw as stemming from an ill-conceived emphasis on novelty for its own sake. In his proposal for the San Francisco symphony hall, Belluschi hoped to avoid an overbearing, pretentious form by minimizing the drama of the architectural form and allowing the hall's function to determine the form. Visual impact, he maintained, would come not from a compelling form but from the activities generated by the building, with concert-goers mingling in the grand ceremonial foyer and ascending its monumental stairs.[67]

By fall of 1975 a final decision had to be made on the selection of architect. Stewart, as president of the Sponsors of the San Francisco Performing Arts Center, wanted Belluschi to open an office of his own in San Francisco; Belluschi refused, wanting to remain independent as a design consultant. Stewart consented, stating his preference for SOM as the associating firm. This left Belluschi uneasy, as he knew SOM's way of working, its rigidity on design issues, and most importantly its very different architectural philosophy that placed formal concerns above operational. He proposed the DeMars office instead, pointing out that he and DeMars had in fact been working on the project for several years, thus had much of the groundwork done. Stewart reluctantly agreed to interview both parties.[68]

Knowing that as a small, east-side office the cards were stacked against him, DeMars called Gerald McCue, on the faculty at Berkeley and later to become dean at Harvard succeeding Sert. In December 1975 McCue Boone & Tomsick in association with DeMars & Wells interviewed for the job, as did SOM, on the understanding that in either case Belluschi would remain the primary design principal. Stewart was set on SOM, believing that as a bigger, more politically connected office based in San Francisco it stood a better chance of attracting donors. Conciliatory by nature, Belluschi did not fight.

SOM was brought in the following January.[69] From then on Belluschi became, in effect, an advisor only. Charles Bassett, chief designer of the SOM office in California and an architect with a strong sense of conviction, saw little merit in the Belluschi/DeMars scheme and insisted on starting the design process over. Belluschi, recognizing the strengths of their original proposal, argued for retaining the substance of it, at the very least on the basis of cost. SOM got its way, but after months of attempts on its own and close to $600,000 later it returned to the Belluschi/DeMars concept. Belluschi henceforth served as mediator between Bassett and the client, working on behalf of the latter to keep further costs down.[70]

As the design of the SOM scheme progressed, the tension between Bassett and Belluschi increased. Knowing his presence wasn't wanted in the SOM offices, Belluschi spent his time with the client, who consulted him frequently. Only occasionally would Belluschi intervene directly in design decisions, and then only when the situation absolutely demanded it—for example, on the "ears," the projecting semicircular terraces on the principal facade, which he strongly opposed.

When cost estimates of the SOM scheme came in late in December at $7 million over budget, an exasperated Belluschi, working alone at his drafting table in Portland, drew up a counterproposal. Called the "Christmas 1976 scheme," it represented a far less expensive solution, proving one could be done.[71] SOM dug in its heels; Belluschi responded with a "position paper" in which he acknowledged irreconcilable differences between him and Bassett, and in the interest of avoiding further conflict offered to resign.[72]

The foyer had been a major point of contention. Belluschi had envisioned a monumental, multistory ceremonial space that would provide San Franciscans, as he argued it, a spatial experience comparable to Garnier's splendid Opera House in Paris, or, in San Francisco, the famous glazed garden court of the Palace Hotel. One would enter on the diagonal, on axis with City Hall, then proceed up monumental stairs on either side to the upper reaches of the auditorium. Bassett argued against this as it would mean patrons would enter with their backs to City Hall; he wanted visitors to enter from low entries on the sides and ascend stairs through a progression of spaces that would open onto an expansive view of City Hall. Belluschi predicted serious circulation problems with this. By this time, spring of 1977, with time and funds running out, the client had little choice but to go ahead with the SOM scheme. Stewart, who had initially endorsed the SOM team, expressed his disenchantment in a blunt letter to John Merrill in May. He was not pleased with SOM's official letter to the Symphony Association stating that critical issues such as the configuration of the hall, exterior design, layout of lobbies, ingress and egress, and circulation "were no longer negotiable," thus blocking the consideration of other solutions.[73]

Belluschi had predicted as much. First, there was the legacy of his own strained relations with SOM, not only with Bassett on the Bank of America but also with Merrill in Portland, with Graham in Chicago, and with the SOM office in New York. Whereas Belluschi was open, accommodating, a listener, flexible in matters in design, an architect whose first responsibility was always to the client and budget, Bassett demanded complete design control; once fixed on an idea he stuck to it, regardless of the client, believing as a matter of principle that no competent architect let cost compromise design. More fundamental still were their conflicting views on the goal of the building itself. Belluschi's main concern was for acoustical excellence and the experiential quality of the interior spaces. Bassett's concern was for the exterior form and the role of the building in the larger urban design. Given Bassett's design abilities, which Belluschi readily acknowledged, plus Belluschi's experience in symphony halls, a building type SOM had never worked with, it could have been a rewarding collaboration. Instead, not only was it a painful situation all around, but the building, and ultimately the city, suffered for it.

The project was a particular disappointment for Belluschi, who had initially entertained high hopes, as he had for St. Mary's Cathedral. He remained as consultant throughout the project, but his advice—on circulation, handling of the entrances, cost-cutting measures, and so on—was, as the design progressed, largely ignored.[74]

As finally realized, the Davies Symphony Hall, named in honor of its principal donor, was a bitter compromise. Belluschi brought to the project the concept of the interior, the basic shape and volume of the hall worked out in the DeMars office, and the diagonal disposition on the site; he also passed on much of his experience in planning, offering advice primarily in the early stages of design on matters of size and disposition of spaces, how to get everything to work smoothly and efficiently, plus specific technical considerations such as lighting, sight lines, size and number of practice rooms. He and the DeMars team were thus largely responsible for the basic plan, with the exception of the lobby.

Davies Symphony Hall, San Francisco,
exterior, 1980, Charles Bassett, SOM,
designer.

Bassett was responsible for the design of the exterior form, how the building looked as a sculptural entity, and its role in the urban design of the Civic Center as a whole.[75]

The budget, which had been firmly set at $21 million in January 1977 after the initial SOM scheme came in substantially over the original budget, was exceeded by over twice that in the end. The final cost of the building, which opened in 1980, was $43.5 million.[76]

Koubek, Washington, D.C., and the Miami Center project, 1979–1981

Appeasing Belluschi's disappointment was a far larger, potentially far grander project, the biggest of his career: a $116 million development in downtown Miami. In 1967, Washington, D.C., architect Vlastimil Koubek had contacted Belluschi to ask his help in arguing his case against local authorities over a historic mansion that he wanted demolished to make room for a new headquarters building for the Motion Picture Association. Belluschi agreed, testified in favor of demolition, the case was won, and the Koubek building built. The two men remained in touch, with Belluschi serving as a design consultant in association with Koubek on a number of other major jobs in the Washington area, among them the World Bank Building (1977–1980) and Pentagon City Office Buildings (1979).[77]

In 1979, Theodore Gould, a large-scale developer with grandiose visions, began planning a huge, multiuse urban complex on 15.8 acres of prime waterfront property in Miami's downtown, with Koubek, who had done several buildings for him earlier, as the architect. As Gould hoped to attract major tenants such as the Southeastern National Bank for the complex's large office building, Koubek suggested bringing in Belluschi, whose name

Miami Center project, 1979–1981,
aerial photomontage.

Miami Center, model.

would lend stature to the team. Gould met Belluschi and immediately sensed a kindred spirit; when later Gould and Koubek did not see eye to eye over a choice of materials, Gould dropped Koubek and retained Belluschi as the principal architect. Belluschi was to be paid amply, some half a million dollars over the next five years.[78]

For the project, which promised to be huge, Belluschi agreed to set up an independent office, but only under certain rather extraordinary conditions. The office, Pietro Belluschi Associates, Inc., was originally in Arlington, Virginia; later it was moved to Miami and the name changed to Pietro Belluschi & Associates, Inc.[79] Staffed at various times by from three or four to twenty of Gould's own architects, planners, and interior decorators, the office was to serve under Belluschi's direction. Belluschi himself, however, was not legally a part of it. He remained an independent consultant functioning in Portland under the name of Pietro Belluschi, Inc. Pietro Belluschi & Associates, Inc., a wholly owned subsidiary of Gould's Holywell Corporation, were the architects of record and legally responsible for all work. Under this setup, Belluschi was able to work out of his home in Portland, without the normal administrative and legal responsibilities of actually running the office himself. He provided the preliminary designs, which he sent to the Pietro Belluschi & Associates office to have developed. Gould entrusted Belluschi implicitly, placing him in full control of the design. Belluschi by the same token accommodated Gould in whatever he wanted, which, in his own thinking, absolved him of whatever faults there might be in the final result. Gould had access, at least initially, to a great deal of money; thus the budget was for all intents and purposes unlimited. Local observers gasped as the money flowed.[80]

The proposed center, located on an expansive site between Biscayne Bay and the Bayfront Park, was to have consisted of a 42-story office town, a 630-room luxury hotel, and two condominium towers all rising above a site-filling, six-story podium providing parking for 4,500 cars plus 48,000 square feet of retail space. As their key marketing device, AIA Gold Medalist Pietro Belluschi was billed as the architect of the new center.[81]

Belluschi conceived of the project in terms of three basic issues: defining an appropriate character, that is, a type of urban environment that would be most appropriate for Miami's new downtown; incorporating the amount of parking Gould wanted and minimizing the amount of traffic the Center, catering solely to motorized customers, would generate; and reconciling the Southeastern Banking Corporation's plans for their own development of a critical portion of the site that they refused to sell.[82] As their thinking changed, Belluschi's proposal expanded, adding several more tall office buildings, an athletic club, retail galleria, theater, and gambling casino to the original plan.

They thought big. Koubek had originally envisioned exteriors of a a light Spanish pink granite. Belluschi convinced Gould to go with travertine, which he argued had more character. Together they flew to Italy to select the stone from a quarry belonging to an old friend of Belluschi's that had also supplied the travertine for St. Mary's, Juilliard, and the Keystone Building. As Gould's visions expanded, so did Belluschi's aspirations for the best money could buy. Upon his recommendation, Sasaki Associates were brought in for the landscaping, and Henry Moore, among others, for the art.

The huge development, like so many of Belluschi's later projects, was greeted by nothing but negative publicity from the press. Some of it was generated by Gould's manner, perceived as arrogant and highhanded; comments such as "Nobody's going to step on me" and "We'll be doing this our way" did little to endear him to the hearts of locals. But most of it stemmed from Belluschi's design proposal itself. Beth Dunlop, former associate editor of the *AIA Journal* and architectural critic of the *Miami Herald,* called the towers "monumental, somber capitalist's cathedrals," clumsy, ponderous, and overbearing in design. The entire complex was virtually "shrouded" in a dark brown Italian travertine, which she pointed out was not a tropical building material no matter how rich-looking and beautiful, and anyway could not compensate for mediocre design. It amounted to little more than a lot of marble camouflaging a multitude of architectural ills. Particularly critical of the fortresslike podium, she described it as a massive 60-foot-high structure filling the entire site, a monolithic barricade that, unless there was some yet undiscovered genius at work, promised to be ugly as well as pedestrian-repellent. In sum, she saw the project as anti-pedestrian, anti-urban, and anti-aesthetic.[83]

When the first phase of the project, consisting of the Edward Ball Office Building and Pavillon Hotel, was completed several years later at a cost of $1.1 billion, the comments of architectural critic Paul Goldberger of the *New York Times* were equally trenchant. However engaging the new skyline might be from a distance, he maintained, the new downtown center was hostile to the pedestrian, the towers themselves dull and flat, lacking in interest or life. Less critical than Dunlop of the hue of the travertine, he found its use nonetheless excessive, noting that it seemed to have been treated as "something sacred," covering everything from the insides of the showers in the hotel rooms to the Henry Moore sculpture in the hotel's "vast and empty" lobby. The effect struck him as more numbing than impressive.[84] A number of years later, after dust had settled and landscaping taken root, *Art in America* ran a feature article on Miami of the 1980s. Among the notable new buildings in the downtown were those by Charles Bassett of SOM, I. M. Pei, and Philip Johnson. No mention was made of Belluschi.[85]

The Miami Center, touted as a multibillion-dollar dream and "the most important urban development of the past 50 years whose plan and design was prepared by AIA Gold Medalist Pietro Belluschi, who designed the Pan Am in New York as well as Bank of America in San Francisco," ended dismally.[86] The extravagantly luxurious affair, with principal office tower offering "Office Spaces of the Future," and elegant triangular Pavillon Hotel with palatial decor in travertine, green Brazilian granite, teak, English oak and walnut, with Belgian tapestries, Donegal rugs, Murano chandeliers, antique and modern landscape paintings, specially designed china, crystal glassware, silver flatware (much of this selected by Gould with Belluschi's help, the two flying the Concorde to Europe together often accompanied by Belluschi's wife), collapsed in 1984, with a $194 million foreclosure suit, the largest in Miami's history.[87] Belluschi, in his position as an outside consultant independent of Gould's organization, was one of the first creditors to be paid off. The two remained friends, with Belluschi subsequently designing several private houses for Gould in Virginia.[88]

Exciting as the Miami Center project must have been, offering Belluschi an opportunity to realize some of the urban planning schemes he and the others in the Boston Center Architects had devised for the Boston Back Bay project in the mid-1950s, but on a far grander scale with unlimited budget and now under his name and under his full control, it did little to enhance his reputation. The project had promised a breakthrough in urban design, with open vistas to the bay and ample green space; instead people found it barren and inhospitable. Belluschi's apparent indifference to pedestrians and the human scale seemed hypocritical, given the humanistic ideals in urban design he had long promulgated. The inflated claims of his having designed the Pan Am Building and Bank of America only irritated people further.

With its clear-cut confrontation between Gould's right to build whatever he wanted and the city's right to reject what it found offensive, the Miami Center was a clash of public and private interests at least as egregious as the Pan Am. Whose side Belluschi was on was equally clear. His primary responsibility was always to the client.[89]

Pietro Belluschi

Preceding page: Immanuel Lutheran Church, Silverton, interior.

Rooted in the philosophical, aesthetic, and architectural milieu of Yale and Princeton and backed by Philip Johnson at MoMA, postmodernism had slowly been gaining momentum since the publication in 1966 of Venturi's *Complexity and Contradiction in Architecture*. The pace picked up in the 1970s as the tenets of modernism were challenged by critics such as Peter Blake in *Form Follows Fiasco* (1974), Brent Brolin in *The Failure of Modern Architecture* (1976), C. Ray Smith in *Supermannerism: New Attitudes in Post-Modern Architecture* (1977), then, on a more popular level, by Tom Wolfe in *From Bauhaus to Our House* at the end of the decade. Cultural values at large, too, shifted from the social concerns and political activism of the 1960s toward the narcissism of the 1980s.[1]

Architecture was among the first of the arts to reflect these changing values. By the later 1970s, orthodox modernism was thoroughly discredited among leading designers. The simultaneous appearance in 1978 of I. M. Pei's East Wing of the National Gallery, Rogers & Piano's Centre Pompidou in Paris, and Philip Johnson's AT&T Building in New York, and the proliferation of catchy new stylistic labels—historicism, high tech, contextualism, allusionism, ornamentalism—revealed the turmoil in the profession and the groping for a sense of direction.[2]

A two-day AIA design conference late in 1977 (which Belluschi, significantly enough, neither spoke at nor attended) focused on how the profession would replace the restrictive and by now discredited tenets of modernism and move on to something new. At the center of the storm was Philip Johnson. Endowed with a keen eye and restless mind, his fingers always on the pulse, Johnson celebrated the chaos as healthy and creative, and personally relished it as an alternative to modernism's restrictive moralism and austerity, promising "an experience of pure exuberance, . . . very much like sex and eating."[3]

The award to Johnson of the AIA Gold Medal in 1978 was a clear sign of the times. The profession was facing a revolutionary shift, he told the audience in his acceptance speech, difficult to discern because they were in its midst. Dismissing the modernism they'd all been taught (a modernism he defined in wholly International Style terms), they were headed toward "something new, uncharted, and wholly delightful." Johnson summarized the changes in terms of a new respect for history, symbolism, and the *genius loci*.[4]

Ada Louise Huxtable, with her sharp eye and penetrating mind, saw things differently. Reviewing Johnson's latest design for the Pittsburgh Plate Glass Building in the *New York Times* in May 1979, she described the current situation as a game, of which the master "hands and pediments down" was Philip Johnson. His "vastly overpublished, unceasingly controversial" Chippendale-topped AT&T Building, which had put architecture on the front page of newspapers and the cover of *Time,* offered smashing new visual effects if not good architecture. Disney kitsch out for shock value, it represented an excess of style. As the age of heroic modernism waned, she saw the profession moving, for better or worse, into a selecta-style architecture, a free-for-all age of fun and games wholly in tune with the "new morality" of total abandonment, complete licentiousness: in fact, she recognized, it might be an art "acutely right for the times." She also acknowledged its merits, noting that architecture had never been freer, its access to technical resources opening up unlimited potential for stylistic development. However stimulating and intellectually titillating it might be, however, the danger of this approach was that it could lead quickly to a lot of very bad buildings. Compared to any truly great building, "and particularly one with the disciplined restraint and powerful esthetic impact of a consistent ideal maintained throughout the artist's whole body of work," this architecture of appearances came up short. Denying the values that make building a complex social esthetic, it lacked depth and vigor and was fashion, not art.[5]

Huxtable's article, a well-underlined copy of which Belluschi had clipped and filed, provided the substance for many of his thoughts expressed in his address at the Convocation of Fellows at the 1979 AIA convention in Kansas City, where once again he squared off against his old nemesis Philip Johnson.[6] Aware that he was there as a representative of the arrière-garde, Belluschi refused to relinquish those old modernist principles that had sustained his practice for the past fifty years.

> We are now being told that a striving for order and clarity is an old soporific tenet believed only by platitudinous architects. We are also told that discipline and integrity in the search for excellence are but legacies of our Puritan past. I have read that a new, historical watershed has been proclaimed with great tolling of bells—where visual delight impatient with social, technical or moral restraints is declared to be the only goal worth pursuing. This well-advertised hedonistic binge has revived in new ways the old conflict between those artistes-architects who believe that only a precious vocabulary of pre-invented forms (the Beaux-Arts syndrome updated) permit free and pure esthetic expression and those architects who believe that life in all its variety and richness is the true generator of lasting forms.[7]

The situation was obviously not simple, nor the polemic new. Picking up and developing the points Huxtable had made, Belluschi acknowledged and welcomed the reality of change and diversity in architecture. But change for the sake of change was destructive of greatness. True, they lived in a society that emphasized the superficial, where the frivolous got attention, where modern advertising and the mass media fed on fads, fashions, quick turnover; true too that change for the sake of change was an ingrained human trait. "But when fashion in the art of building, as in other arts, is allowed to prevail in its most ephemeral forms, it tends to become a parasite feeding on what is legitimately new to make it profitable, soon draining it of its true worth by substituting fictitious images for substance, eventually rendering us incapable of distinguishing the phony from the real, the juke box from the simply crafted object."

There are a few great artists, true poets among architects, Belluschi said, whose work reflects, not always in obvious ways, an understanding of the human condition. But life is complex and demanding, and not all of us can be poets. He wondered if an addiction to contrived forms and styles didn't undermine our best instincts, and acknowledged the difficulty of distinguishing between the contrived and the allegorical. The challenge was to balance novelty with clarity and order. Architecture, he concluded, "is a living art that changes and moves on, but that is also permanent, leaving its mark. It is this by which posterity will know and judge us."

Belluschi's speech was widely quoted in popular sources such as the *New York Times* and *US News & World Report,* as well as in the *AIA Journal.* Paul Goldberger saw it as a spirited defense of orthodox modernism; others saw it as the gloomy dirge of an aging skinflint. Was architecture "careening along a 'hedonistic binge' after decades of sober modernism?," Robert Campbell asked in the *Boston Globe.* He attributed the awarding of the AIA Gold Medal to Philip Johnson as the catalyst "unloosing the Post-Modernist froth."[8]

Earlier in the year, a former editor of the *Architectural Record* chided the short memories of postmodernists "who think they have discovered the relevance of 'history' and 'meaning' to contemporary architecture." She suggested that they look up the work and essays of people such as Wurster, Belluschi, Wright, Hitchcock, and Mumford in the *Record,* especially around the early 1950s. As postmodernists were turning architecture into a media happening, the historical record needed to be set straight. Architects born before 1925 wouldn't be taken in, but younger architects, their clients, and the public were likely to be. Philip Johnson, of course, knew better, she concluded, "but he won't talk—he's having too much fun."[9]

Huxtable took up the issue again a year later in a long, penetrating essay, "The Troubled State of Modern Architecture," a copy of which again Belluschi had read, underlined copiously, and stored. Architecture was at a crossroads, she wrote, and modernism was under attack; but lest people forget, the changes the modernist revolution brought about were unparalleled, for the benefit of us all. Once hailed as an instrument of social salvation, modern architecture was now being denounced as a failure, and architects today were backing away from sociological and environmental concerns and returning to the realm of pure art. Though the "revolution against the revolution" was at this point generating more heated talk than actual building, she was concerned about its effect on what would be built in the future.[10]

Huxtable spoke of the current stampede to renounce modernism in the profession, the vogue of "revisionism" in academic circles, and the endless talk, which she found tiresome, pretentious, small-minded, and lacking in historical understanding. To proclaim modern architecture as "dead" when it was so clearly still alive and vital, or "failed" and a total mistake, made little sense in light of both its longevity and the common good it had brought about. Something important might come of the revolution, but she found it difficult to see what. What was going on was strange and ambiguous, forcing critics to rethink their architectural values. What made it all especially difficult was having to read what architects and theoreticians were writing. In the climate of intellectual trendiness, architectural writing went beyond permissible ambiguity. Obscure, arcane, "borrowing freely from undigested often questionably applied philosophy or skimmings from other fashionable disciplines," with its endless semiology, typologies, half-baked aesthetic Marxism, delivering small ideas in large words, weighed down with private, esoteric references and bogged in "pretentious, glutinous prose," she found merely having to read it punishing.

A term coined by a splinter group, postmodern was interested in reviving the history and vernacular discarded by modernists. Citing Robert Stern, she listed historical allusion, contextualism, and ornament as among its distinguishing characteristics. Tradition was now in, the use of history and historical styles hitherto taboo was respectable again, kitsch was fashionable, and ornament no longer a crime. In fact, "anything goes—provided it breaks modern strictures, and the more shocking the better." Alas, she pointed out, shock value was short-lived.

Philip Johnson she found hard to take seriously. The AT&T and Pittsburgh Plate Glass buildings, both postmodern flags, were clever but glib; both were "eclectic," the dirtiest word of all to the modernist, which Johnson was relishing like a forbidden toy. Rather than drawing on the real lessons of other cultures and the past, they "divorced form from content for easy decorative effect" or an instant unconventionality that denied architecture as "a difficult creative business of resolving problems of purpose, structure, space, spirit, and style."

Venturi's work, she found, had more substance, representing a difficult rather than easy eclecticism. In *Learning from Las Vegas* he and his coauthors drew on pop culture, but this was theory passed through Venturi's refined, sensitive eye. Charles Moore's work was more of a calculated stage set: eclecticism replete with symbolism, with several layers of meaning. Both were architects who commented as well as built.

Michael Graves she found the most esoteric of all. His sources were private, his art was hermetic, his eye that of a painter, a colorist, or collagist. His drawings were beautiful, but they were art, not architecture. And as an architect, his work was difficult to judge, as only one of his buildings had ever been built.

Mentioning others—Peter Eisenman, Richard Meier, James Stirling—Huxtable said that what unified them all was a sense of exploration, a search for forms and sensations denied by the modern movement; as a result doors were being reopened. This was exhilarating but also dangerous, as in the backlash against purism and functionalism the vital relationship of architecture to society was being severed. Architects were pursuing their own pure designs at the expense of social needs, suggesting an alarming trend away from truly significant sociological to exclusively esthetic concerns.[11]

James Marston Fitch was equally disturbed. Long-time affiliate of the *Architectural Record* whose memories of the development of modernism in America extended beyond the perspective of younger East Coast academic theorists, Fitch wrote an article in the January 1980 *AIA Journal,* one of the magazines Belluschi read religiously, on what he perceived as a crisis in contemporary architecture. For half a century the profession had been committed to helping society with rational solutions to its architectural needs; now it was being asked to abandon course, as postmodernists attacked the entire theoretical structure of rational response to the world as it was known and experienced. Fitch saw the problem stemming from a small but influential group of architects and critics who had seized upon modernism, the International Style, above all the Bauhaus, as the source of all that was wrong. Tracing the evolution of modernism, Fitch noted the rejection of historicism among revolutionaries of the late 1920s, their search for a new language of form, their work informed by the polemics of Sullivan, Wright, Loos, Gropius and based on the proposition that form and function were indissoluble. Yet from the moment of the 1932 International Style exhibition at MoMA, form began to split from function. And since then, the profession had continued to celebrate the formal at the expense of the functional.[12]

Belluschi, Johnson, and the Portland Public Services Building

As the polemics grew sharper, Philip Johnson, with his exquisite sense of timing and rapier-keen wit, stepped in with a deliberately calculated, precisely aimed stroke. In 1978 Portland city officials, after waiting years for a new government building, began negotiations with the county for a site between City Hall and the County Courthouse across a small park from a projected new Justice Center. Deciding on a limited design/build competition as the most appropriate means of obtaining the best, most distinctive design at the least cost, the city set up a citizen committee to solicit proposals. It was chaired by William Roberts, a friend of Portland's mayor, powerful real estate investor, and influential donor to the Portland Art Museum, whose wife was a collector of contemporary art. Roberts persuaded the others to think big and, rather than a local architect, to retain as their professional advisor Philip Johnson, who had just received the AIA Gold Medal and was much in the news.[13] Johnson was eventually to play a crucial role in the selection process, as in effect he was the jury's sole source of advice.[14]

In July of 1979, one month after Belluschi's highly publicized squaring off with Johnson on postmodernism's "hedonistic binge" at the AIA convention in Kansas City, Johnson met with the jury and persuaded it to include Michael Graves, an academic from Princeton known primarily for his architectural drawings, among the finalists, despite his limited building experience. Dismissing other proposals better equipped to meet the practical

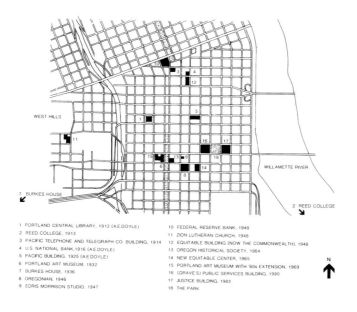

Street map, Portland, 1980s, with Belluschi buildings (courtesy Joachim Grube, Yost/Grube/Hall).

1 PORTLAND CENTRAL LIBRARY, 1912 (A.E. DOYLE)
2 REED COLLEGE, 1913
3 PACIFIC TELEPHONE AND TELEGRAPH CO. BUILDING, 1914
4 U.S. NATIONAL BANK, 1916 (A.E. DOYLE)
5 PACIFIC BUILDING, 1925 (A.E. DOYLE)
6 PORTLAND ART MUSEUM, 1932
7 BURKES HOUSE, 1936
8 OREGONIAN, 1946
9 EDRIS MORRISON STUDIO, 1947

10 FEDERAL RESERVE BANK, 1948
11 ZION LUTHERAN CHURCH, 1948
12 EQUITABLE BUILDING (NOW THE COMMONWEALTH), 1948
13 OREGON HISTORICAL SOCIETY, 1964
14 NEW EQUITABLE CENTER, 1965
15 PORTLAND ART MUSEUM WITH '60s EXTENSION, 1969
16 (GRAVES) PUBLIC SERVICES BUILDING, 1980
17 JUSTICE BUILDING, 1983
18 THE PARK

Pietro Belluschi

Belluschi with model of Graves's Portland Public Services Building (North-west Magazine, 13 April 1980).

requirements of the competition document, Johnson in effect narrowed the competitors to three: Michael Graves, the less trendy Mitchell/Giurgola, and, stylistically the most conservative of all, Arthur Erickson from Vancouver, British Columbia. In his advice to the jury just before its final decision, Johnson argued that of the three competition entries, Graves's was the most extraordinary: it borrowed historical elements from adjacent civic buildings, the arcade at street level met the requirement of providing a commercial area without detracting from the public entry, it contained the most floor space at the least cost, giving the city "the most bang for the bucks," and most importantly, as the most imaginative of the three, it would "prove a landmark for the city, in the eyes of the public as well as architects around the world."[15]

In the second go-around, Graves, craving the chance to build something big and knowing that the odds were against him, given his limited experience and controversial design, redoubled his efforts to make sure his proposal met all technical requirements. As a result, his was the only one that came within budget.[16] Despite lingering reservations, the jury, leaning heavily on Johnson, chose his project.[17]

As expected, Graves's proposal sparked heated controversy and was opposed by the majority of local architects. Leading the opposition was Pietro Belluschi, who spoke out strongly against the Graves design on behalf of the Fellows of the AIA Portland chapter.

Arguing in his testimony to the Portland City Council that the jury had been swayed by the seductive Philip Johnson, whom he described as the "high guru of a coterie of gifted young people who earnestly believe visual chaos is their reality of today's world," Belluschi acknowledged that the building was the least expensive of the three finalists, but that in this case other factors, such as its lack of respect for the spirit of the place, were more important.[18] The issue squarely pitted him, former AIA Gold Medalist and Portland's grand old man of architecture, against the faction of younger, mostly East

Coast progressives. Among the latter was Robert Frasca, who had been a classmate of Graves at the University of Cincinnati. Complicating matters, the Zimmer Gunsul Frasca office, with Belluschi as design consultant, had in the meantime received the commission for the new Justice Center located directly opposite the site of the proposed Public Services Building. A young, ambitious architect of growing stature in the Portland community in his own right, Frasca was one of but two Portland AIA Fellows to defend the Graves submission.[19]

Despite Belluschi's impassioned testimony and his predictions that Graves's "oversized beribboned Christmas package" would soon be dated, the Graves proposal was approved. Several weeks later Belluschi was sent, at his request, a set of the plans Graves had submitted to the City Council.[20] After looking them over, Belluschi again denounced the building as no more than "a personal search for an unusual solution." Shock value may be important in other arts where failures can be hidden in the dustbin of time, he maintained, "but you cannot hide a building; and if it does not answer the many constraints imposed by use, structure, and custom, and if it is not woven into the fabric of its city, as Philip Johnson in another mood has told us it must, it has little chance of surviving the test of time. Today's shock value may well be tomorrow's drag, soon to be in jarring competition with other drags from the same fanciful factory, perhaps conceived by less gifted men—and future generations will suffer." Belluschi spelled out in detail the questions he had about the choice of materials, given Portland's climate, and the numerous shortcomings in the plans, the most glaring of which was the street floor with service entrance fronting onto the park.[21] Despite Belluschi's objections, the City Council accepted the Graves proposal, with certain revisions, the following May.

The Portland building, one of the most discussed of the decade, proved a historical watershed, as Johnson predicted (and helped assure) it would be, both fascinating and outraging architects, critics, and the public at large. With the most organized opposition coming from former AIA Gold Medalist Pietro Belluschi, the battle was recognized by many for what it was: a clear showdown between Belluschi and modernism (or the "corporate modernism" for which he was known in the East; his project for the gargantuan $1.1 billion Miami Center was under way at this time), and Philip Johnson representing the more progressive postmodernism.[22]

Shortly after the Portland building opened, by which time it had attracted international acclaim and Graves had been lionized throughout the world, complaints from occupants began pouring in. The windows were found irritatingly small (though as built, they were larger than Graves had originally wanted), ceilings too low, ventilation hot and noisy, circulation poor, and public spaces mean. Celebrated as a new architectural star elsewhere in the country, Graves, as a local reporter put it, "is sure to be ducking tomatoes here in Portland for a long time to come."[23]

Vindicated as he felt by these and other similar reports, Belluschi was deeply hurt at being snubbed by city fathers who had for so long idolized him and by the city into which he had poured so much of his life's work. His pain was exacerbated the following year when Graves's building was granted a national AIA Honor Award, the highest citation the profession bestowed. Nor was it eased by knowing that Robert Frasca, former protégé with whom he was still professionally involved in the design of the Justice Center, was a member of the design awards jury.

The whole affair was a humiliating defeat for Belluschi. Casting him as a diehard modernist, a humorless moralist, out of touch with progressive thinkers and a major obstacle to their getting commissions, a shrewd operator and behind-scenes manipulator who, as highly respected doyen of the profession, still wielded tremendous political power, Johnson's brilliant *coup de grâce* gave Belluschi what many in the profession felt was a well-deserved dethroning.

Moreover, Belluschi's outspoken opposition to the Graves proposal and his attempts to block it, urging the City Council to reject the verdict of the very jury they had appointed, only served to discredit him further in the eyes of the profession.[24] More than a few viewed it with a certain irony, remembering the sanctimonious tone of his address as chairman of the AIA Honor Awards Jury in May 1973, when he expressed diffidence about saying anything, suspecting his views were those "of a crotchety old man who should make room for younger ones who may speak more convincingly for their own generation."[25]

It was a bitter lesson for Belluschi, but one from which typically he learned. Forced to reassess his own values, if anything it strengthened his former convictions. Belluschi had always approached architectural design rationally, as a problem-solving process rather than simply an intuitive pursuit. His main objective was doing what made sense for the people who were to use the building, keeping in mind the client and the cost; beyond that, he sought a solution that moved the spirit, a visual order sustained by logic. The finest artistic solutions, in his eyes, expressed this rationality, this logic. He found nothing, as he put it, more satisfying than an aesthetically moving work behind which one could sense the logic—the purpose for which the building was erected, why a certain material or form was employed.[26]

His thought, informed by philosophers like Alfred North Whitehead and Jacques Maritain, whose writings he found more convincing than those of contemporary architectural theorists, emphasized the intellect in art. Without a logical, reasoned idea, the expression of which was clear to the penetrating mind, the work was like a bad painting: empty, lacking content, without conviction. Belluschi conceived of the design process as, in effect, a quest for truth; likening it to the sciences, he saw it at its most fundamental as a statement or expression of the architect's conception of reality, which was somehow deeper, clearer, more penetrating than the norm. Just as scientists like Galileo, Einstein, and more recently Stephen Hawking (whose *Brief History of Time* he read) challenged common assumptions about the nature of the universe, so too the thinking architect analyzed changing data, questioning common conceptions about the way buildings were being designed and what people really wanted or needed. This was what Belluschi, not a philosopher but a man of probing intellect, wanted to think of as a unified theory of creativity, which, like the unified theory of relativity, constituted a search for reality in all fields of creative endeavor—music, fine arts, literature, as well as architecture. Beauty, or aesthetic pleasure, served as a catalyst for this fundamental search, and was not an end in itself, in architecture any more than in art or science. The architect was thus a *form-seeker,* his process of artistic concern like that of the scientist pursuing an analytic process of discovery, rather than a *form-giver,* who more simply conceived a beautiful form in the abstract purely for its aesthetic delight. Beauty, or a spiritually uplifting form, was just as important to Belluschi as to architects like Philip Johnson, but unlike them he saw it as a means to an end, an adjunct to the creative process and the search for a higher truth, rather than an end in itself.[27]

The Portland Public Services Building, albeit visually interesting, lacked a convincing idea, according to him, and was simply surface, a formal exercise. While proving its point as a rejection of the old and a beginning of something new, thus establishing its place in the annals of history, its purpose was novelty for its own sake, shock value, which quickly loses interest. He found the building emotionally unmoving, its decorated form already passé, and lacking the longevity that distinguished the great from the ordinary work of art.[28]

Throughout the 1960s, as progressive architects challenged modernism and its belief that function generated form, Belluschi built rather than talked. Aware of their theories, he found them of little interest, their solutions too general, too universal, inappropriate in any particular real situation. Architectural design was not abstract theory, could not be done in a void. As an advisor for the city of Baltimore, he had tried to get Louis Kahn's Inner Harbor proposal to work, and knew firsthand the practical problems posed by the arbitrary use of pure sculptural form. He recognized the importance of Venturi's *Com-*

plexity and Contradiction as an intellectual discourse and the impact it was having on the profession, but he was unable to get through it, finding it not so much boring as simply irrelevant. It reminded him of the scores of faculty members and students in postwar Italy who wielded words for want of work.[29]

As architectural values shifted in the 1950s and 1960s from structural expression to sculptural form, then in the 1970s and 1980s to historically inspired, decorated form, Belluschi's primary interest remained the character and disposition of space; form, whether from conviction or his own lack of talent, was simply the result.[30] Hence his relative indifference to the Catalano-derived exterior of the Juilliard School, or the Tange-influenced form of St. Mary's.[31] On the other hand, he recognized the design skills of architects like Richard Meier and Frank Gehry, whose work he felt had integrity, and where the strength of the artistic purpose, its logic or raison d'être, came through.[32]

He hated stylistic categorizing, hated being called a regionalist, modernist, or any other "-ist." The labels simply didn't fit. (MLC: "Well, if you're not a 'modernist,' what are you?" PB: "Just an old guy.") To his mind, they not only oversimplified but falsified the picture. Spanning the century, his career began at a time of the Beaux-Arts, predating the acceptance of modernism, and continued well after its demise in the 1970s. Fundamentally modern in his approach, he was never simply a "modernist," or what "modernism" had come to mean in the hands of Philip Johnson and others. He was and always had been aware of the need for tradition in architectural form, for some continuity with the past, for associations and symbolism, the "richness" and "meaning" Venturi, Stern, Graves, and others talked about but typically interpreted in literary rather than architectural terms. He had always insisted on the *genius loci,* his very name synonymous with regionalism and respect for place. Never doctrinaire in his approach, Belluschi worked within whatever language of forms the particular situation called for—the startlingly fresh flush-surfaced glass and aluminum Equitable Building, suggesting modern technology at its most advanced, simultaneously with the equally modern, structurally innovative brick and wood Zion Lutheran Church, with its traditional longitudinal plan, pitched roof, and spire, just blocks away.

For all the consistency of his basic convictions, Belluschi changed with the times, adjusting not only to new building technology and structural systems but to shifts in architectural values and styles. The machine aesthetic in the 1930s, technological determinism in the 1940s, precast concrete classicism in the 1950s, structural expressionism in the 1960s: he was affected by them all. But fickle though his forms might seem, they were never adopted arbitrarily. Conceiving of architectural creation in fundamental rather than formalistic terms, he borrowed forms frequently and freely if they fit. Since often these forms were determined or at least influenced by ephemeral fashion, they mattered least; what counted in the long run was what would last: how well the building functioned and the quality of its space.

Quality, Belluschi admitted, was difficult to define. It was something a trained eye and penetrating mind instinctively sensed. Ultimately, he felt, time alone would prove the judge. He distinguished between works he found of integrity and mere "period pieces" like the Chrysler Building, which initially made a big splash, then quickly waned in popularity and was seen as artificial and contrived, then was revived in the rewriting of postmodernist history and deified.[33] Having experienced the broad swings of the pendulum, Belluschi was leery of fashionable trends. While change was healthy and good, uprooting entrenched habits and breaking routine, opening eyes to new ways of doing things and new ways of seeing, the dangers were obvious. Buildings had to be designed to satisfy the aesthetic as well as practical needs of generations, not only the aesthetic of the individual designer. The difficulty lay in distinguishing ephemeral values from those more enduring—temporary fashion from lasting quality. It was Belluschi's lifelong quest.[34]

By the 1980s, the profession, or at least the faction of it that dominated the media, was caught up in a rush of theorizing and new fads—the primitive hut, Soane, Lutyens, Palladio, Beaux-Arts, semiology, Heidegger, Derrida. "Discourse" was rampant about meaning, *genius loci,* contextualism, humanism, all qualities purported to be lost in modernism. Meanwhile, Belluschi himself was quietly at work on the Dante Alighieri

Dante Alighieri Building, Cambridge, 1978–1985 (photo: author).

Building in Cambridge, a cultural center devoted to the promotion of Italian language and culture, where he confronted directly the problem of context, place, and meaning in the design of a distinctly modern building—Italian in character and expressive of Italian cultural values, yet related visually, socially, and culturally, to its Bostonian milieu.[35]

Short-lived fad as many thought it would be, postmodernism did not go away, and a year after the completion of the Portland Public Services Building the editors of the *AIA Journal* asked Belluschi his views on what was by then a recognized trend. In a characteristically thoughtful, somewhat uncharacteristically vehement essay, Belluschi expressed his surprise at the "unexpectedly large and almost euphoric" reception of postmodernism by the younger generation, especially students, and attributed its success to its "coming at a time when shock and fashionable images have become handy tools for selling the goods." No longer restraining his feelings toward Philip Johnson, a man but seven years his junior, who had not only dealt him the ultimate indignity in his own home town but had been less than kind in pinpointing him as the main obstacle to the Graves commission, Belluschi now opened fire. "When Philip Johnson proclaimed from the mountaintop that the profession was on a new watershed, I was slightly amused. Now, I thought to myself, everything goes: the good with the bad, serious with the frivolous. I am no longer amused; as always, Philip was right on course. In his natural role of guru he did much to manipulate and push his *coup d'état*." Johnson, with his astute sense of the historical perspective, knew the timing was right, seized the moment, "and he was the witty guy to pull it off. . . . So [his followers] rejected the hated glass box in favor of the enlarged jukebox." Belluschi hoped it was a short-lived phase that would soon run its course, and was pinning his own hopes on signs of a return to good planning and architecture based on human use, real rather than fictive humanistic values.[36]

Several years later in March 1985, Belluschi was again asked to address the issue at an annual Association of Collegiate Schools of Architecture meeting in Vancouver. The postmodernist controversy, though no longer new, had raised a number of questions he felt were still unanswered. Acknowledging his increasing skepticism about all the talk, theory, polemical combat in postmodernism, given how seductive words could be and how easily the distinction between truth and rhetoric could be blurred, Belluschi tried in his thoughtful, probing way to get at what he felt was the main issue: the popularity of a stylistic fad brought on by a handful of academic theorists, versus more fundamental values in architectural design. Noting the gap that had developed between the generations, and that his own was now on the defensive, he thought it important that they speak to each other with the aim of understanding rather than condemning.

He recalled his own past and the formation of his architectural principles, reminding his audience of the Beaux-Arts system that held sway in the 1920s and its repository of accepted forms that freed designers from having to invent them anew; the Italian futurists who rejected history and opened his eyes to seeing the world in a new, fresh way; the influence of modernists such as Mies but also men like Harry Wentz, who aroused in him a response to the natural beauty of Oregon and showed him the merit of an architectural tradition that responded simply and directly to nature rather than mimicking styles of the past.

Belluschi explained the principles of the modern movement that had guided him and his generation, quoting Marcel Breuer whom he saw as one of the wisest and most gifted of its protagonists: the fresh perspective and freedom from prejudices of the past, the direct contact with the problem at hand, the use of elemental forms to create aesthetically pleasing architecture, the analogies between the forms of the modern movement and those of vernacular architecture in both their impersonal character and their tendency to develop along rational lines unaffected by whims of fashion; finally, the aim not to create something new but something suitable, intrinsically right, and as perfect as it can be.[37] In recalling Breuer, Belluschi focused on the principles of modernism, not on form. Nowhere did he mention the formal characteristics of European modernism that had been the focus of attention of the 1932 MoMA exhibition, the flush white walls, flat roofs, volumetric forms, and so on: to him they were of little concern.

Belluschi recalled his Reed College speech of 1950, when he stressed the importance of a humanistic architecture that stretched beyond the starkly utilitarian or functional to nourish the spirit. He recalled a speech of 1954 in which he pointed out the limitations of the modern movement, all the dimensions of architecture it was leaving out. While he himself was struggling to reconcile the demands of modernism with those of tradition in the design of the church, his colleagues elsewhere were using Mies as the standard of modernism, defining modernism in mechanistic terms and denigrating him and his West Coast colleagues for their "soft" humanism, their traditionalism, their conciliatory stance between modernism and the past. To Belluschi, Mies's celebrated IIT chapel exemplified both the good and the bad: its stark beauty, elemental means, ability to accomplish so much with so little, but also the loss of any sense of a church. It underscored the importance of retaining traditional features, and the public's need for continuity with the past.

What he found most shocking, however, was the form "humanism" was taking in the hands (or words) of the postmodernists. Hardly humanistic in the sense he and others

Award ceremony, University of Notre Dame, with Belluschi and Philip Johnson, 9 April 1985.

had conceived it, this was a literary fabrication, built up of words and linguistic analogies, metaphors and similes that made little sense to the public. Belluschi quoted Graves to illustrate his point: "If I articulate a window in a wall which frames a view, it says to us that our bodies are not limitless." Possibly true, Belluschi said, but the windows Graves designed in the Portland building were so small that they obscured the great panoramic view of the Cascade mountains, frustrating occupants immured inside. "The tallest basement in town," Portlanders called it. Graves's explanations represented a kind of empty theoretizing, high-sounding rhetoric designed to sell the building and dupe the public. This kind of "humanism" had, Belluschi pointed out, no effect whatsoever on the experience and use of the building by human beings.

In his eyes, the Portland building represented the antithesis of what he considered good architecture; it was little more than a whimsical stage set playing into the forces of commercialism, designed solely to catch the media eye. The best Belluschi could say about it was that it would bring the city a certain notoriety and that it would not, *could* not be repeated.[38]

Belluschi and Johnson, two courtly gentlemen by then in or close to their eighties, fenced again in a final duel at the University of Notre Dame a month later. Both were there to receive honorary degrees; both were invited to speak. Characterizing postmodernism as a revolution of "brilliant young hedonists" against old-guard "self-righteous bluenose moralists," Belluschi pointed out that the basic polemic was not new, that he and Johnson had fought the same battle over thirty years ago, and that while he admired Johnson's wit and sense of humor, he disagreed with virtually everything he said. With a wit every bit the equal of Johnson's, but softened by his own willingness to poke fun at himself, he said he felt obligated to earn his honorary degree somehow, and didn't mind "going down with all his feeble guns blazing away."

In proclaiming the Portland building a watershed, Belluschi said, Johnson opened a permissive floodgate. All customary restraints—of standards, taste, social responsibility, the necessary discipline that distinguished architecture from the pure arts of painting and sculpture—were suddenly swept aside to embrace "a future full of delightful toys." This was not the appropriate message, he said, for the rank and file architect "trying his best to interpret the pressing needs of a confused restless changing society." Fearing this was an attempt to legitimize novelty for its own sake, he stressed his own conviction about architecture as something of more essence, deeper significance, ultimately a search for reality. Repeating now for a larger, broader audience the same concerns he had expressed in Vancouver, he again acknowledged the importance of fashion and change in uprooting entrenched ideas, and noted that the postmodern fascination with images might legitimately be seen as a reflection of contemporary social values. But recalling Plato's means of judging artistic quality by distinguishing among different levels of artistic creation, from the mere appearance of reality to reality itself, Belluschi feared that postmodernism represented the outermost circle of superficial appearances only. He ended on a peaceful note by calling a truce with his venerable opponent. He promised for his part to retire henceforth into silence, but—and here was Belluschi at his gentlest, wittiest, but also his wisest—only after symbolically joining the Navaho Indians in their great dance ceremony "Beautyway," a spiritual invocation of the order of the universe, that "holy complexity that manifests itself in all things changing through time in accordance with a persistent principle of disarray." Vintage Belluschi: a realistic acceptance of the world as it is, not as he would like it to be.[39]

Work in the 1980s

During these years Belluschi's role of consultant and advisor gradually diminished. He remained associated with Zimmer Gunsul Frasca in Portland, Jung/Brannen in Boston, Vlastimil Koubek in Washington, the Gould-owned Pietro Belluschi & Associates in Arlington, Virginia, and others, on buildings such as the Seattle Convention Center (1982–1988), One Financial Center, Boston (1983), University of Kentucky Business School (1984), and Fillmore Housing Development in San Francisco (1984).[40] Typically he was little more than design critic, often nothing more than a name. His own work was confined to small, local projects, mostly houses and churches, which, though the bigger jobs paid better, he actually preferred.

As a result of questions raised publicly about the ethics of his professional practice, Belluschi began cutting back on these professional associations. In March of 1980, as the Graves storm raged, the *Willamette Week,* a Portland weekly, asked him if he wasn't concerned about his name being used to lend credibility to buildings he didn't think much of. It used to concern him, he replied, but no longer did: if the association proved unrewarding, as long as he was paid, he didn't let it bother him.[41] Later, however, as others raised similar questions, Belluschi began feeling embarrassed about receiving such handsome fees for virtually no work.[42] After the Justice Center was completed in 1983, he stopped working with ZGF in Portland; in 1984, Pietro Belluschi & Associates folded with the collapse of the Miami Center; and in 1986, except for their work on the Portsmouth Abbey campus, he terminated the association with Jung/Brannen in Boston.

The article in the *Willamette Week* raised other uncomfortable questions. Asked whether he was concerned that younger architects were losing out on jobs because of his bigger name, Belluschi pointed out that the situation worked both ways, that sometimes younger, inexperienced architects *got* jobs because of his name. He cited the example of a state office building project in southern California by a firm of young black architects who received the commission on the basis of his name. Asked about situations where he was brought in simply as an advisor but was credited with the building's design because of the fame of his name, Belluschi pointed out the injustice on *his* side, where an office got a job on the basis of his name, then ignored him in a design process he wanted to be part of.[43] The situation appeared awkward, and the portrait of Belluschi was not good.

He nonetheless missed the excitement of being in the center of things, and when new opportunities arose, he found it hard to turn them down. Again, his role varied, from contributing valuable advice on the $92 million Seattle Convention Center, to serving as a name only for the $140 million retail and residential Fillmore Center development in San Francisco, where he was brought in largely for the weight of his reputation with the San Francisco Redevelopment Authority.[44] He went after the large condominium-retail tower project behind Juilliard in Lincoln Center in association with Jung/Brannen, and a $50 million convention hotel project in Charleston, South Carolina, with the developer Theodore Gould, neither of which he got. Other large-scale prospects that remained projects only were several office towers, among them the Stimson Center, a $200 million, 46-story office tower in Seattle with John Graham Associates, and the 46-story Provident Tower in Baltimore for Seattle developer Richard Hadley. One of the biggest of these jobs that did not go through was the 121-story U.S. Grant Tower in association with his son Anthony Belluschi, who had an architectural office in Chicago that had specialized in shopping centers but had had virtually no experience in high-rise buildings; commissioned by the developer Harry Grant in Newark, New Jersey, had it gone through as planned, according to Belluschi, it would have surpassed the Sears Building as the tallest building in the world.[45]

Although Belluschi professed to take no particular pride in the large volume of work he was involved in, he rarely turned down a project, as long as it did not require his traveling and he was assured of full liability protection. But by the late 1980s, these large jobs had dwindled, and Belluschi turned instead to small-scale projects, mostly houses and churches in the local community.

Among several houses he designed after returning to Portland was the Packard House. Like his others, it marked a return to his familiar language of form: simple, unadorned, reticent, of wood, with pitched roof, informal massing, and light, open, spacious interiors. His philosophy of house design, too, remained unchanged, aimed at an enclosure of space reflective of the innermost self, a place of privacy and repose where one could escape the pressures of the outside world. Invariably he included a small enclosed garden as an inner atrium or private courtyard, a contemplative landscaped space like the Japanese garden that ultimately inspired it.[46]

The Packard House, designed for an architect in the ZGF office and his family, was a distillation of Belluschi's long experience in house design, incorporating ideas and elements from his past—from the massive fieldstone fireplace and fixed pane/louvered windows of the Burkes House, to the design of the balcony parapet of the Wentz Cottage—adapted to new circumstances and refined. Here he used a tight, compact rectangular plan for a steeply sloped site comparable to the one that he had drawn up for the Radditz House in the 1940s, with principal entry and communal living spaces above, private bedrooms below, combining it with the thin-eaved, pitched, overhanging roof, prominent chimney, open plan, and expansive views of the Joss House.

But the differences are telling. Most of the materials and finishes that Belluschi would have liked to use in the Packard House were, by the 1980s, no longer available or prohibitively expensive. The metal roof and window frames, the design of which Belluschi worked out personally with the contractor, for example, were a cost-saving measure. Then too, Belluschi's clients were a young couple both of whom worked; they enjoyed informal entertaining and wanted a large, spacious, fully modernized "Yuppie" (or "Yew-pee," as Belluschi pronounced it) kitchen, with built-in microwave oven, gas stove, and two sinks—three to four times the size of the Joss or Radditz kitchen of the 1940s, open to the living/dining area but with a measure of privacy, and easy to maintain.

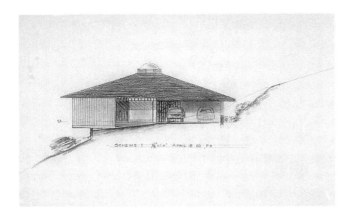

Packard House, Portland, preliminary
study (Belluschi drawing), April 1986.

Packard House, exterior, 1989.

Another sign of the times was the hot tub, not to Belluschi's taste but very much to theirs, submerged in the otherwise undated, secluded Japanese garden. The Packard House was completed in 1989; though submitted, it was not published in the national architectural magazines, as editors, focused more on image than use, found it unexciting.[47]

Late Churches and Religious Buildings

Belluschi conceived of the church in much the same terms as he did the house, as a quiet space for the soul. His overriding aim was to create a contemplative space at once private and communal, intimate yet uplifting in its clear expression of a spiritual purpose.[48]

The design of his later churches was governed by two factors: the need for a centralized plan reflecting the concern for greater integration between congregation and clergy; and the meshing of innovation and tradition with the use of contemporary architectural forms that nonetheless maintain continuity with the past. The centralized plan suggested a domed structure, which Belluschi typically conceived in segmentalized or polygonal terms rather than hemispherical for acoustical as well as economic reasons, to break up the reverberation of sound waves on the interior.

His architectural language returned to the basics: simple, elemental forms, natural materials typically brick or wood, steeply pitched roofs sheltering lofty, inspiring interior spaces, and a judicious but rich use of art.

The first of a series of later churches was the small Lutheran church in the town of Silverton south of Portland, where Belluschi had redone the interiors and added a parish house in 1947. In 1966, the congregation had asked him to remodel the building to provide a wheelchair entrance and add library and office spaces. Then in 1975 a fire destroyed the old church, and Belluschi, now back in Portland, was asked to design a new one. The site was on the crest of a hill, steeply sloped in several directions and fronted by a busy street on two sides. The building consisted of a simple pyramidal form surmounting a broad and deep base. Distantly inspired by Norwegian stave churches with their bold elemental forms and richly carved surfaces, but drawing more specifically on more recent churches such as Saarinen's North Christian Church in Columbus, Indiana, the Silverton church continued the same general direction he had pursued in the 1960s with several churches in the East.[49] The tall conical vault sat directly on the base, which was broader than Belluschi would have liked, in order to accommodate the requisite amount of floor area in the sanctuary, a problem he had also encountered in

Pietro Belluschi

394

Immanuel Lutheran Church, Silverton,
1975–1979, exterior (photo: Ed
Hershberger).

St. Mary's Cathedral in San Francisco. The base itself extended two levels below the sanctuary to provide quarters for the social functions that the church, serving also as a community center, required.

One entered through a richly carved wooden arch, which Belluschi envisioned as a visually arresting jewel set against the plain walls of the base, into a narrow narthex, followed by the sanctuary, not unlike Richardson's Trinity Church in Copley Square, Boston, which Belluschi admired.[50] A self-contained, intimate, yet lofty space surmounted by 100-foot-high wooden vault, it was lit by a zone of softly colored stained glass above the base, with an oculus of plain translucent glass in the form of a Greek cross in the vault overhead. Light washed down the angled walls of the vault, accentuating the geometries of its exposed framing. Inspired by the wooden vaults of Norwegian

Immanuel Lutheran Church, interior.

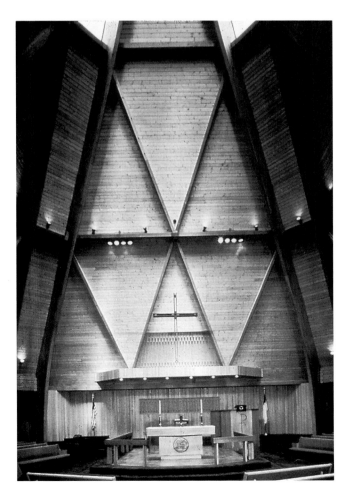

medieval churches with their clearly articulated structure, the steeply pitched roof of spruce decking was borne on four laminated bents of Douglas fir that rose freestanding from the corners to meet in the cross overhead. The materials, red cedar on the exterior, Douglas fir laminated beams, hemlock paneling, and spruce decking, were all left natural, their differences in texture and hue combining with the geometries of the exposed structural framing to form the visual richness of the whole.

The Silverton church was a small project, exquisitely crafted, with stained glass and wood carving by well-known local artists, for a congregation Belluschi had worked with for over three decades. It was done in the Boston office of Anthony Belluschi, in association with the Salem office of Settecase Smith Doss, and completed in 1979 at a cost of $800,000.[51]

Very different in nature from his small, finely crafted, wooden Northwest churches was the United Hebrew Congregation Synagogue in St. Louis. In July of 1986 a young architect with Stone Marraccini and Patterson in St. Louis, who had worked with Belluschi on St. Mary's in San Francisco, called him to see if he would be interested in associating with SMP on a new synagogue. It was to consist of a large temple, administration and education building, plus long-range master plan on a 15-acre site, for a well-to-do Reformed Jewish congregation, with a substantial budget of $4–5 million for the first phase alone.[52] Thinking that at age 87 this might be his last major job, once his concerns about insurance coverage were allayed he readily agreed (because of mounting premiums, he no longer carried liability insurance), and immediately began producing a steady stream of brilliantly colored drawings representing a broad range of possible solutions.

In going after the commission, SMP faced stiff competition from Hellmuth Obata & Kassabaum, which was just completing a $4.5 million synagogue nearby; knowing his presence would enhance their chances of getting the job, SMP wanted him to appear at their initial interview. In accepting, Belluschi had made it clear that he was no longer traveling and would not come to St. Louis; as a result, several members of SMP flew to Portland to film a 3-minute video of Belluschi for the presentation to be held that fall.

In the carefully orchestrated media show, Belluschi outlined his thoughts about synagogues on behalf of the architectural team, describing his long experience in synagogue design dating back to the Swampscott synagogue of 1956, and what he believed were the basic functions of this building type.[53] Belluschi's thoughtful, deeply felt remarks, revealing his attentiveness to the congregation's particular problem as well as understanding of synagogue design in general, were characteristic, the kind of persuasive statement that had consistently won him the confidence of clients in the past. The strategy worked again, and in January of 1987 SMP was awarded the job.

Well before this, however, though he had not yet received a copy of the program or information on the site, Belluschi had begun work on the design. He had always loved drawing, though rarely had had time to engage in it since his early Portland days. He was well aware, too, of the acclaim architectural drawings were now receiving, after decades of disfavor in the modernist era, in the wake of the exhibition of Beaux-Arts drawings at the MoMA in 1976; still more significant was the notoriety Michael Graves's drawings were currently receiving. Now, with time on his hands, Belluschi began producing scores of drawings, typically meticulously drawn, straight-edged elevations and sections in soft colored pencil.[54] In response to his hounding, SMP finally sent him information on the site: spacious, on rolling terrain with steep ascent to one side and a 10-year-old one-story brick school building on the other. The new synagogue was to relate visually to this building as well as to the congregation's old temple, a large, imposing 1903 revivalist Byzantine building of brick. With this new information, Belluschi turned in a wholly different direction, inspired, so he said, by the domed synagogues of Rome but in fact based on a source closer to home: a revivalist 1927 synagogue in Portland, in Belluschi's hands its form abstracted and given almost Kahnian force.[55]

He continued sending the SMP office in St. Louis sketches, drawings, and memos, by phone, mail, or Federal Express, throughout the year, growing increasingly apprehensive about losing touch and irritated with their unresponsiveness. It was obvious, however, that given his distance from the home office there was only so much he could do. Despite his frequent requests for more information and pleas to return calls, much of the work proceeded without him. Given his high ambitions for the project, he found it a constant source of frustration.

By March 1987, he had come up with a solution that pleased him: a simple, direct, economical structural system and remarkably compact plan. It consisted of a domed, monumental building with exteriors of brick, with well-lit, spacious interior, the centerpiece of which was to be a sculpture of the burning bush.[56]

The proposal was presented in a ceremony attended by both Belluschi and his wife, an exception to his no-more-travel rule. It was approved, and design development commenced shortly thereafter. Given his determination to have the job carried through as he envisioned it, the amount of time, labor, and mental energy he was pouring into it, and the exhilaration he felt with the solution they had developed, his anguish was palpable

*United Hebrew Congregation Syna-
gogue, exterior, 1989.*

when in December SMP called to say the congregation was $500,000 short of the budget, and the side balconies—an integral element of Belluschi's design—would have to be eliminated. Devastated after coming up with what he saw as a perfect solution, economical yet both beautiful and logical, "now to see its strength so diminished in such a casual manner . . . I wonder whether the congregation realizes how much we struggled." Knowing that the elimination of the balconies, which had provided the overflow capacity demanded by the original program, would destroy the purity and logic of his original concept, Belluschi, true to character, swallowed his pain and sent "a sort of Damage Control solution, acceptable but flawed," which involved, since the congregation liked the exteriors and wanted them retained, transforming what was hitherto logical and consistent into purely arbitrary form. The rounded stair towers, originally providing access to the balconies, he thought could be used as lounges or some other auxiliary space. Though he knew that this kind of formal manipulation was a common practice among architects, especially in the postmodernist climate it nonetheless bore heavily on his conscience.[57] Two weeks later he sent four more possible solutions, none of which he liked. The project henceforth moved ahead quickly, and throughout construction Belluschi remained in as close touch as he could, selecting the brick, advising in the selection of art work, making final decisions on the choice of wood, all by mail. As the building moved into final stages he was sent snapshots of its progress. His frustration grew at having the building materialize without his being there and actually seeing what was going on, as he let SMP know with a steady stream of anxious, irritated letters. Not able to be there to oversee final finishes, something he loved doing on projects he cared about, was perhaps most painful of all. The building was dedicated November 1989. He did not go.

Later Work at Portsmouth Abbey

Behind all of Belluschi's work in the 1980s was Alvar Aalto. Perhaps in response to postmodernism with which he felt so at odds, perhaps because of the renewed interest in regionalism in reaction to the universality and placelessness of modernism, perhaps as a result of a conference held at the newly completed Aalto library at Mt. Angel Abbey in 1980, the design and philosophy of the Finnish architect whom Belluschi respected more than any of the great twentieth-century masters was much in his mind.[58] It was Aalto Belluschi looked to as he resumed work on what was one of the most personally rewarding endeavors of his career: the completion of two libraries for the Portsmouth Abbey in Rhode Island.

In accordance with the master plan Belluschi had drawn up for the campus in 1959, after the church and monastery were completed in 1961 plans were announced for the construction of several new buildings and additions, to be built in two phases. The first were to be a new science building and auditorium, to be followed later by an administration building and infirmary, the whole development costing $2.3 million.

The new science building was sited on axis with the church, the two serving as complementary foci at the ends of a long grassy quadrangle, one addressing the mind, the other the spirit. The auditorium and administration building were to line the quad on one side, with classroom and library building facing them on the other.

The informality of the buildings softened the formality of the plan. They were all conceived in accordance with the general character of Belluschi's 1950s church, using simple, unadorned forms, board-and-batten stained redwood exteriors, and copper pitched roofs, and maintaining the same scale, proportions, and detailing. Unifying the complex and tying it to the region were retaining walls of local fieldstone.

*Portsmouth Abbey libraries, site plan,
October 1985.*

*Portsmouth Abbey administration and
auditorium buildings (photo: Louis
Reens).*

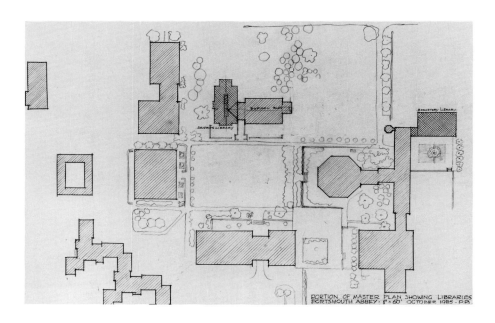

Portsmouth Abbey classroom building
(photo: Joseph Molitor).

Belluschi was the principle designer throughout. His associates changed over the years, each lending their own sensibilities to the buildings they worked on. The church and monastery were done with Anderson Beckwith & Haible; the science and auditorium buildings, done in the early 1960s, were with Robinson Green and Beretta, whom Belluschi—at this point preoccupied by various stages of work on the Pan Am Building, the Rohm & Haas Building, the Equitable Center, the Juilliard School, and St. Mary's— relied on heavily to carry out his ideas. On retiring from MIT in 1965 he asked Sasaki Associates, who had been retained for site planning and landscaping and with whom he felt he could work more closely, to associate on the architecture as well. As the pace of his other work continued to accelerate, however, he had to rely on the Sasaki team more heavily for design than he intended. Thus, though the buildings were tied together by his overall design outlook, the infirmary, administration building, dormitories, and hockey rink unmistakably bear the stamp of Ken DeMay, Sasaki's project designer.

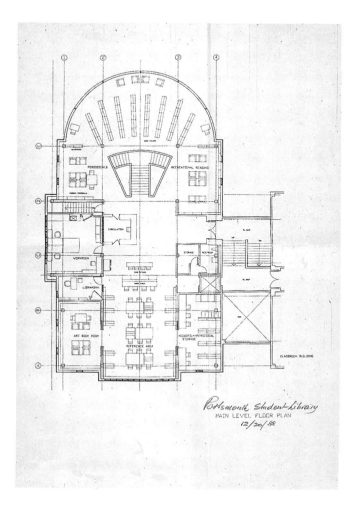

Portsmouth Abbey student library, plan, December 1988.

For the gymnasium addition and new classroom building begun in the late 1970s, Belluschi turned to Robert Brannen, who had worked with him as his assistant on the Portsmouth church in the early 1960s. Born in the Pacific Northwest and trained at the University of Washington, Brannen as a student was awed by Belluschi, whom he venerated as "one of the gods." He was also fully committed to Belluschi's regional, humanistic approach and understood it as few Easterners did. Willing to follow his design directives as faithfully as possible, Brannen proved to be one of Belluschi's most longstanding and reliable associates.

The Burden Classroom Building by Belluschi and Brannen was a simple two-story rectangular building of fireproof steel column and truss structure, with exteriors of redwood and batten sunscreens on the southern facade facing onto the central quadrangle. It bears the imprint both of Belluschi's formal language and of Brannen's technical expertise.

The last of the buildings envisioned in Belluschi's 1959 master plan were the libraries. The new student library, originally designed in 1984, then revised several times with a new circulation plan inspired by the Aalto library at Mt. Angel, formed a wing at the east end of the Burden Classroom Building; a second library for monks was added to the monastery in back of the church.[59]

The opening of the two libraries in 1991 marked the completion of the 1959 Belluschi master plan. The Portsmouth Abbey campus held special importance for him. It had been the first project he took on after moving to Cambridge, and he had followed its design and planning for some 40 years; he thus felt an emotional bond with it unlike with any other work of his later career. Drawing on an architectural idiom for which he remained best known, a language of form originating in his regional work in the Pacific Northwest characterized by simple unpretentious structures of wood, pitched roofs, straightforward use of natural materials, careful craftsmanship, and the integration of the fine arts, the Portsmouth Abbey school was one of Belluschi's most enduring statements.

PietroBelluschi

Conclusion

Awards and honors continued to pour in in the waning years of Belluschi's life. In July 1991, in a ceremony in the White House, President George Bush bestowed upon him a National Medal for the Arts. This was but one of a long list of such laurels: appointment by President Harry Truman to the National Commission of Fine Arts in 1950, election to the American Academy of Arts and Sciences in 1952, becoming a trustee of the American Federation of Arts in 1954, a Fellow of the Royal Academy of Fine Arts, Copenhagen, in 1954, and a life member of the National Institute of Arts and Letters in 1955, honorary degrees from Reed College, the University of Rhode Island, and the University of Notre Dame, and the AIA Gold Medal in 1972.

Warm, gracious, personable, and seemingly outgoing, Belluschi was in fact a very private man. Highly complex, he appeared a different person to different people: a simple, unpretentious man with no thought but to live his own life, just a decent man who loved his work, to some; an enormously ambitious, relentlessly driven, fiercely competitive, shrewdly calculating opportunist to others. Poised, self-contained, supremely self-confident to some, he seemed insecure and circumspect to others. A principled man of rare integrity to some, but described as "no saint" by one of his most loyal associates, a charismatic charlatan to still others. Seemingly simple and straightforward, he was an archdiplomat who always seemed to know what the situation called for and whose own views were never really clear. Some found his speeches and essays deeply thoughtful and intensely felt, others, including some of his best friends, considered them inflated, impressive-sounding, rhetorical fluff. He could seem forthright and openly expressive of his feelings on the one hand, reserved and guarded on the other; a man who genuinely liked other people sometimes, a reclusive, moody, introspective individual at other times; tight-fisted yet generous (if there was something in it for him; "with Belluschi there was always money in it somewhere," as one of his Portland staff members put it); modest in public, the demanding prima donna at home; compassionate social architect yet self-centered *artiste;* consummate team player yet fierce independent who liked to do things his own way; sensitive and highly refined artist yet tough businessman; candid to some, full of guile to others.

In fact, Belluschi was both a pragmatic materialist and a romantic visionary. Growing up in comfortable bourgeois circumstances he vowed to escape, Belluschi saw himself in existential terms, as the creator of his own destiny, shaping his life, as he put it, as one would a work of art. His memoirs tell the story of a rebellious wanderer exploring life in search of truth, reality, the self. The extraordinary record-keeping, with files dating back to the early 1920s of letters, newspaper clippings, and announcements, documenting every move, every mention of his name, attest his focus on self. One senses it was a need to prove himself rather than a genuine passion for architecture that drove him on.

Reserved, shy even, Belluschi was determined to make a mark. Inspired by the dream of the romantic hero, it was as if by working hard enough he could make it come true. Each new commission—Portland Art Museum, Equitable Building, St. Mary's Cathedral, Davies Symphony Hall, St. Louis synagogue—brought new promise, a flood of initial enthusiasm and messianic zeal, as if with *this* job he would prove to be the next Wright or Mies, society's savior. He remained earthbound, unable to shed those bourgeois beginnings, the materialism and middle-class ideal of money as a measure of success. Ambitious but practical, he realized that his mark was not to be made as the artistic iconoclast. Deeply intelligent and remarkably self-aware, Belluschi had a healthy sense of his own worth and the significance of his work. Yet lingering always was an air of doubt. Recipient of innumerable awards and honors, he himself questioned their legitimacy, wondering whether they were gained on the basis of his personal charm and coterie of loyal friends rather than actual merit.

At the peak of the profession in the late 1940s, Belluschi got caught in shifting values. In the aura of the *Fountainhead,* the 1950s especially saw the rise of the architect-superstar whose mark was made not on the kind of solid, economical yet quietly distinctive buildings Belluschi was known for but on their popular appeal. It launched an era of form-making, of architecture as image, that he was philosophically unprepared for and formally ill equipped to handle. He and other indigenous modernists who saw form as a consequence, rather than an end in itself, were simply eclipsed as new, media-driven trends were found visually more exciting. The profession at large was infatuated by the ideal of artistic self-expression, the Michelangelos struggling against brute philistinism, perpetuating the public image of the genius-architect working in divinely sanctioned solitude. As Philip Johnson in his break with Mies proclaimed the architect as the inspired artist, Belluschi was cast as the crass businessman, concerned only with the hard, practical realities of building ordinary buildings.

Unsympathetic to these new attitudes, Belluschi cautioned the profession against superficiality and the dangers of pure formalism, transient values, and shifting stylistic fashion. Unable to stem the tide, he yielded to peer pressure and himself got caught up in new East Coast–driven stylistic trends never really his own. As he saw his own value system challenged, he struggled to reconcile the conflicting demands of the profession, and society's need for change and novelty, with qualities that he felt would last.

Competing for success in a profession that judged buildings and determined authorship largely on the basis of form, Belluschi sized up the odds. He was not a form-giver, thus sought designers who were, guiding their work with his keen mind and discerning eye. He thrived best when working on an open, collective team where everybody contributed to the solution of a common goal; nonetheless he remained unwilling to accept the anonymity that logically accompanied the collaborative approach, unable to relinquish the glory and fame.

Especially as his reputation waned. At its brightest in the early 1950s, his star fell as tides of fashion changed and a new system of values prevailed. Students hitherto reverential turned away, finding Kahn's, Rudolph's, even Philip Johnson's work of more interest. Belluschi's subsequent work with corporate clients and large-scale developers distanced him further from progressives in the profession. How much of this was due to new taste trends rather than actual merit perhaps only time will tell.

But Belluschi's problem wasn't mere trendiness. More fundamentally it involved quality, a decline in his own artistic standards after he moved east. Losing his regional roots, he began working on foreign soil, in an unfamiliar formal language and on a larger, unfamiliar scale. More significantly, his mode of practice changed. Without his own staff trained in and sympathetic to his architectural aims, his buildings were no longer entirely, even mainly, his. Taking on more and more jobs, he stretched himself thin, overextending himself as if to make up in numbers for the loss of architectural integrity. Attaching his name to well over 1,000 projects, he purposely left no way of knowing which were really his, where he exerted real influence, where he was there in name only.

Then too he alienated academics, those who wrote articles, published books, and established reputations—for better or worse, the real driving force behind the profession. Belluschi's conciliatory manner, granting the client whatever he or she demanded, struck many as prostitution of the highest order, a flagrant disregard for the public interest and a lack of integrity for the ideals of the architectural profession at large.

He made many enemies. His power as an advisor, member of design review boards, and juror was resented, as directly or indirectly he stood in the way of scores of young architects—the Venturis, Giurgolas, Sterns, and Graveses—whose design directions differed from his own. Had Belluschi, rather than Philip Johnson, been Portland's competition advisor on the Public Services Building, Graves's building would never have been built. And while few might call it great, by all accounts it proved a watershed, opening doors to new, creative ways.

On the other hand, Belluschi's impact on twentieth-century architecture was unquestionably profound. His simple, unpretentious churches of the 1940s and 1950s served as a model for scores of churches across the country; his straightforward yet distinctive house designs were picked up by builders, contractors, and developers everywhere and absorbed into the common vernacular.

Serving as a role model for a generation of students in the postwar years, he perpetuated those architectural values later lost in the media whirl, instilling an appreciation of simple, rational, appropriate buildings. In a position of exceptional power especially in the 1960s and 1970s, he helped launch the careers of a significant number of young architects whose success they owe to him and his support. As a design critic, he contributed immeasurably to making ordinary buildings better. His skill in bringing out the best in his collaborators, catalyzing ideas and inspiring the design process so that in the end the building sang rather than just sat there, unmistakably left its mark. His ability to talk convincingly to clients heightened their awareness of and demand for high-quality de-sign. A persuasive, eloquent spokesman for architecture, he served as an invaluable liaison between the public and the profession, establishing standards and raising expec-tations for quality in the community at large. Belluschi always appealed to something higher, even though he himself was not always able to bring it about.

Belluschi's buildings remain and speak for themselves. At their best, they stand as a legacy of classic values and a testimony to his real concern for quality. The Portland Art Museum, St. Thomas More Church, Equitable Building, Burkes House, Cottage Grove church, Church of the Redeemer—all maintain their power still. Simple, honest, and direct in conception, addressing first and foremost the use for which the building was intended, his forms were never arbitrary but allowed simply to evolve naturally as the process unfolded. His efforts to understand his clients, their particular wants, needs, and values, led to forms tailored to them emotionally as well as physically. Sensitive to human aspirations in the broadest sense, his buildings were equally responsive to the region and the particularities of place.

The quality of Belluschi's buildings at their best comes through in their visual order. Marked by clean lines and crisp forms, sensitive scale, harmonious proportions, quality of materials, fine craftsmanship and detailing, they are composed with a simplicity and restraint that belies their sophistication. Most of all, they excel in their intellectual integ-rity, at once intensely personal and deeply thought.

Order and harmony, he once said, result from a sympathetic understanding of what goes on around us. Pure Belluschi.

Pietro Belluschi died 14 February 1994.

Appendix: Selected List of Buildings and Projects

Buildings and Projects, 1925–1950

The following list represents the major buildings and projects Belluschi designed or worked on between 1925, when he entered the Doyle office, and 1950, when he left his firm in Portland to become dean at MIT. It is arranged chronologically by the year the building or project was conceived, commissioned, or begun; within each year, works are arranged alphabetically. Cost figures, when included, are drawn from published sources or from Belluschi's own files.

1925   Griffith Apartment House, Portland, Oregon.
> (One of several apartment houses the Doyle firm was engaged in when Belluschi first joined it.)

Multnomah Falls Lodge, Multnomah Falls, Oregon.

Pacific Building, Portland, 1925–1926.
> (Under construction when Belluschi entered the Doyle office.)

U.S. National Bank of Portland, Portland.

1926   Cloud Cap Inn addition, Mount Hood, Oregon (project).
> (Belluschi drawing in Oregon Historical Society, dated 1927.)

Multnomah Stadium, Portland.

Public Services Building, Portland, 1926–1927.

Terminal Sales Building, Portland, 1926–1927.

1927   Department store, Boise, Idaho.

First National Bank, Boise, Idaho.
> (Belluschi served as advisor to the client, as by this time Doyle was ill. The Doyle office had been commissioned to oversee the project. Attributed to Belluschi in books on Boise architecture, though there is no evidence he had any impact on its design.)

Pacific Telephone and Telegraph Main Office Building, Portland.
> (In addition to the main office in Portland, the Doyle office was also responsible for branches in Salem, Grants Pass, Klamath Falls, Eugene, and elsewhere throughout the state.)

Portland Art Museum, Portland (alterations).

1928   Corbett Residence, Portland, 1928–1929.
> (Building was commissioned shortly after Doyle died; the design was solely Belluschi's.)

Linfield College Administration Building, McMinnville, Oregon.
> (There were close to a dozen other buildings, including the library, that the Doyle office did for Linfield College between 1928 and 1950, when Belluschi left for MIT. Although he was chief designer, in his work for Linfield College he followed closely Doyle's original schemes.)

Pacific Telephone and Telegraph Building, East Side Office, Portland.

1929   Benson Hotel, Portland (remodel).

Reed College Library, Portland, 1929–1930.
> (One of several buildings Belluschi or the office designed for Reed College. Others include the Science Building, 1945, and a dormitory, 1946. The library was expanded in the 1960s in conjunction with a new master plan by Harry Weese & Associates of Chicago, and remodeled in the 1980s by Zimmer Gunsul Frasca.)

Tommy Luke Florist, Portland.

Union Station, Portland (alterations).

1930   Commonwealth/Equitable Building, Portland (project).

1931   Commonwealth Building, Portland, 1931–1932 (remodel of existing building).

Corvallis Public Library, Corvallis, Oregon.

Equitable Savings & Loan Building, Portland, 1931–1932 (remodel of existing building).

Portland Art Museum, Portland, dedicated 1932.
> (This was the first or Ayer Wing, to which a second wing, the Hirsch Wing, was added in 1937; the school building was added in 1968, with Belluschi in association with Zimmer Gunsul Frasca.)

Richard Shore Smith House, Eugene, Oregon.

1934   Fifth Avenue Shop, Portland (alterations).

House for an artist in Town, Portland (project), 1934–1935.

Timberline Lodge, Timberline, Oregon (project).
> (A preliminary project Belluschi did with John Yeon, who was evidently primarily responsible for the design.)

1935   General Electric Supply, Portland (remodel).

McMinnville (Linfield College) Library, McMinnville, Oregon, 1935–1936.
> (Located on the Linfield College campus, this was officially commissioned by the City of McMinnville as the McMinnville Public Library to qualify for federal funds; it was later assumed by the College, becoming the Linfield College Library.)

Oregon State Capitol competition, Salem (project).

Sister's house, Quercianella, Italy, 1935–1940.
> (A house Belluschi designed on his own, with no connection to the Doyle office.)

1936   Adams House, Portland.
> (Charles F. Adams, Jr., was the president of the First National Bank and senior trustee of the Portland Art Museum. Published in *American Home,* September 1941.)

Bank of California, Portland (remodel).

(The Bank of California was an old Doyle client; Belluschi continued to do a number of additions and alterations throughout the late 1930s and 1940s.)

Belluschi House, Council Crest, Portland, 1936–1937.

(Preliminary drawings are dated July 1936; construction was begun shortly thereafter, and the Belluschis moved in May 1937. Initial cost: $3,600. The house sold in 1944 to Jed Davidson, a local lawyer, then again in 1983 to John Braestrup, who remodeled it with Belluschi's advice.)

Finley Mortuary, Portland, 1936—1937.

(Remodel of an existing colonial building and addition of a new chapel, the Morninglight Chapel.)

Watzek House, Portland, 1936–1938.

(John Yeon, designer, with working drawings done in the Belluschi office. Site was purchased 5 November 1936; Watzek moved in December 1937.)

Willamette University Library, Salem, Oregon, 1936–1938.

(One of several buildings Belluschi did for Willamette University. Others include the Science Building, 1938, Music Building (remodel), and Men's Dormitory, 1943).

1937 Portland Art Museum, Hirsch Wing, 1937–1939.

(Cost of the 15,000 sq ft addition was $220,000).

Sutor House, Portland, 1937–1938.

(Jennings Sutor was a bachelor, editor of the *Oregon Journal,* and a collector of Asian art. Initial cost: $14,000.)

1938 Umatilla County Courthouse, Pendleton, Oregon (project).

Vista Apartments, Portland.

(Originally the Vista Avenue Housing Project, subsidized by federal funds.

Willamette University Science Building, Salem, Oregon, 1938–1941.

(Initial cost: $151,081.)

1939 Lane Investment Building, 2040 SW Jefferson Street, Portland (remodel).

(This appears to have been the building Belluschi purchased and later converted into new office spaces for the Doyle firm.)

Model House, Northwest Home Show, Portland (project).

(The house was later built; Belluschi remodeled it in 1944.)

National Cash Register Store, Portland (alterations).

(Located in the old Pittock Building, this was the modernized storefront Hitchcock called to national attention in his article "An Eastern Critic Looks at Western Architecture," *California Arts & Architecture,* December 1940.)

Nelson Reed House, Klamath Falls, Oregon.

Northwest Airlines Ticket Office, Portland, 1939; 1944 (remodel).

Riverview Cemetery Chapel, Portland, 1939–1940.

St. Thomas More Catholic Church, Portland, 1939–1940.

(This was in effect Belluschi's first church. The building was enlarged and a school added in the late 1940s, then remodeled again in the 1950s, substantially changing his original concept. Cost of the original church: $12,564.)

Weiner Store, Portland (remodel). (Remodeled again in 1945).

1940 Joss House, Portland, 1940–1942. (The house was designed for Philip A. Joss and his wife, who continue to live in the house to-

day; it was built by Burt Smith, the same contractor used for both the Watzek and Sutor houses; cost was $5,303.)

Myers House, Seattle, Washington.

(Clients were Harry M. Myers and his wife.)

Platt House, Portland, 1940–1941.

(Designed for John and Jane Platt who still live in the house; budget was $8,000).

Spencer Farmhouse, Sauvies Island, Oregon.

(This was a job Belluschi liked to joke about, as evidence of the kind of work he was reduced to doing in the Depression years; according to the documents, however, the work consisted of a dairy barn and silage tank agitator added in the 1940s.)

U.S. National Bank, Ladd-Bush Branch, Salem, Oregon.

(Published in *Architectural Forum,* April 1940; built for $68,875 in 1940.)

1941 Coates House, Netarts Bay, Tillamook, Oregon, 1941–1946.

(Original client was William R. Coates; according to notes in the Belluschi files, the final cost in 1946 was $80,000. Published in *Arts + Architecture,* January 1944, *House and Garden,* March 1945, *Progressive Architecture,* May 1946, and elsewhere.)

Kerr Beach House, Gearhart, Oregon.

(Designed for Peter Kerr; cost in 1941, according to the Belluschi files, was $30,000.)

Sacred Heart Parish School, Lake Oswego, Oregon.

(Cost when completed in 1942: $18,945.)

Stearns Memorial Fountain, Portland.

(According to Belluschi, he did not design it, though it was done in his office; an article in the *Oregonian,* however, attributes it to him.)

Wherrie Tailoring Company, Portland (storefront remodel).

1942 A.F.L. Boilermakers Union Building, Portland (remodel).
(Cost of the modernization in 1942 was $224,000; published in *Architectural Forum,* May 1946.)

Bagley Downs Shopping Center, Vancouver, Washington.
(Published in *Architectural Forum,* January 1946).

Belluschi offices and apartments, Portland (remodel).
(Located at 2040 SW Jefferson Street, Portland, this was apparently the building, formally a garage or distribution center owned by the *Oregon Journal,* that Belluschi had bought in 1939. He remodeled it at this time into offices and apartments with the help of federal funds. The office moved in on 1 March 1942. Cost was $60,000.)

Housing project for the Housing Authority of Portland, Portland.
(Original project consisted of site planning, 2,000 housing units, a community building, and a shopping center; more units were added in 1943 as well as other subsidiary buildings.)

Housing project for the Housing Authority of Vancouver, Vancouver, Washington.
(Site planning and 978 units in 1942; to which 2,100 units of row housing were added in 1942, and in 1943 a theater, infirmary, and child care center.)

Japanese Relocation Center, U.S. Army Engineers, Portland.
(Other buildings for the U.S. Army Engineers in the Pacific Northwest consisted of another hospital in Walla Walla, Washington, a Reconsignment Depot in Pasco, Washington, and service clubs, training facilities, and barracks in Anchorage, Alaska.)

McLoughlin Heights Shopping Center, Vancouver, Washington.
(Shopping center published in the *Architectural Record,* and later in MoMA's *Built in USA, 1932–1944.*)

Pocatello Air Base hospital, Pocatello, Idaho.
(A 209-bed hospital done for the U.S. Army Engineers.)

1943 Cake House, Deschutes River, Oregon (project).
(For Ralph Cake, of the Equitable Savings & Loan Company.)

Dormitories and other facilities, Federal Pacific Housing Authority, Vancouver, Washington.
(Included row houses, trailer units, single-family houses, and at least one commercial building in Toledo, Ohio, as well as in Vancouver.)

Junior Chapel, First Methodist Church, Portland (alterations).
(Published in the *Architectural Record* in September 1945; a modest remodel that helped to establish Belluschi's reputation as a church designer.)

KGW-KEX radio station, Portland (remodel).

Office Building for *Architectural Forum* (project).
(Commissioned in February 1943 and published in the *Forum,* May 1943; served as prototype for the Equitable Building of 1948.)

United War Chest Offices, Portland (remodel).
(Published in *Architectural Forum,* June 1945.)

Vincent House, Palm Springs, California.
(Dean Vincent, client; original project was apparently of adobe.)

Willamette University dormitories, Salem, Oregon.

1944 Aloha Farmhouse, Aloha, Oregon (remodel).

(Site was purchased 4 April 1944; consisted of 6-acre farm with year-round creek, crayfish, fruit and nut trees, barn, and small house. Remodeled to serve as family home.)

Beauty shop, Portland.
(Sponsored by the Pittsburgh Plate Glass Company; published in *Progressive Architecture,* August 1944.)

Burkes House, Portland, 1944–1948.
(Originally commissioned in April 1944 as a one-room house, the project was revised after the war. It was completed in 1948 at a cost of $75,000. Belluschi bought the house himself in 1972 for $86,000, and lived in it, basically untouched, until he died in February 1994. His wife, Marjorie, continues to live there.)

Courtemanche Warehouse, McMinnville, Oregon.

Holy Family Parish, Portland (school building and convent).

KALE Radio Station and transmitter, Portland.

Korten Music Store, Longview, Washington.

Multnomah Hotel, Portland (remodel).
(Work consisted of modernizing the lobby, banquet room, mezzanine, and assembly room.)

Oregon Statesman Printing Plant, Salem, Oregon.

Public Services Building, Portland (addition).
(The building was one Belluschi worked on when he first joined the Doyle office in 1925; it served as one of his sources for the Equitable Building, which at this time was in the design phase.)

Smith House, Eugene, Oregon.

Sprague Vacation House, Santiam River, Oregon, 1944–1947.

(Charles A. Sprague, the client, was governor of the state at the time.)

Ungar Department Store, Portland (alterations and additions).

U.S. National Bank of Oregon, Portland.

(In addition to the main office building in Portland, there were numerous branch offices designed by the Belluschi office throughout the state, including ones in Tigard, The Dalles, Salem, Roseburg, and Medford.)

1945 Bank of California, Portland (project).

Belluschi offices (Lane Investment Building), 2040 SW Jefferson Street, Portland (remodel).

(Published in *Architectural Forum,* April 1947, and *Architectural Record,* February 1948.)

Bow Herbert Highway Restaurant and hotel chain (project).

Carl Greve Jewelry Store, Portland, 1945–1946.

(Published in *Architectural Forum,* May 1948.)

Catlin School Gymnasium, Portland, 1945–1947.

(Published in *Progressive Architecture,* February 1949.)

Central Lutheran Church, Eugene, Oregon, 1945–1955.

(Master plan was drawn up in 1945; church completed by SOM, Portland.)

Church of the People, Seattle, Washington (project).

(Published in *Progressive Architecture,* August 1947.)

Edris Morrison Photo Studio, Portland, 1945–1946.

(Cost in 1946, without architect's fees, was $68,026. Published in *Arts & Architecture,* April 1949, and *Progressive Architecture,* February 1949.)

Electrical Distribution Company warehouse, Portland.

(Published in *Progressive Architecture,* March 1948.)

Equitable Building, Portland, 1945–1948.

(Net cost in 1948, without architect's fees: $3,123,387. Widely published.)

Gallucci House, Beaverton, Oregon.

House for *Parents* magazine (project).

Jessup House, Eugene, Oregon (project).

Minimum House for *Life* magazine (project).

Oregonian Building, Portland, 1945–1948.

(Cost in 1948, without architect's fees, was $3,695,527. Published in *Progressive Architecture,* February 1949.)

Oregon State Hospital addition, Salem, Oregon, 1945–1948.

(Cost in 1948, without architect's fees, was $1,532,310. Published in *Architectural Record,* October 1950.)

Portland Federal Savings & Loan, Portland.

Reed College women's dormitory and science complex, Portland.

(The chemistry building was completed in 1949. Other buildings in the science complex, begun in the Belluschi office, were completed by SOM after Belluschi moved to MIT. The women's dormitory, by Belluschi and SOM, was published in *Architectural Forum,* January 1955.)

Seaside Apartments, Seaside, Oregon.

(Published in *Architectural Record,* May 1946.)

Solar House, Libbey-Owens-Ford Company, 1945–1946 (project).

(Published in *Your Solar House,* Marion J. Simon, ed., 1947; built later as part of the Cedar Hills housing development.)

Stuart Strong House, Sherwood, Oregon.

(Published in *Progressive Architecture,* April 1948.)

Sweeney Straub & Dim Printing Plant, Portland.

Waddles Drive-In restaurant, Portland.

(Published in *Progressive Architecture,* June 1947.)

1946 Belluschi House, Palatine Hill, Portland (remodel).

(This was the house into which Belluschi and his family moved after leaving the Aloha Farmhouse; he intended it as a temporary residence only, until he had time to design a new house of his own.)

Clinic building for Campbell, Clark, and Wolf, Salem, Oregon.

(Published in *Architectural Forum,* July 1948.)

Clinic building for doctors Miller and Smith, Portland.

Doughnut Corporation of America, factory and warehouse, Portland.

Emmanuel Lutheran Church, Longview, Washington.

(Designed, according to Belluschi, primarily by Ken Richardson.)

First National Bank of Portland, Salem Branch, Salem, Oregon, 1946–1947.

(Published in *Progressive Architecture,* February 1949, as well as elsewhere.)

Immanuel Lutheran Church, Silverton, Oregon, 1946–1947.

(Enlargement of a small Gothic revival church in a rural community. Belluschi was later asked to remodel and enlarge it again in the 1960s, and to rebuild the church entirely in 1975, when the original church was destroyed by fire.)

Indian Hill Housing Project, Tacoma, Washington (project).

Kerr House, Elk Rock, Oregon (project).

(The client, Peter Kerr, was also the owner of the Kerr Beach

House, 1941, and the father of Jane Platt of the Platt House, 1941.)

Linfield Pioneer Hall, Linfield College, McMinnville, Oregon, 1946–1947.

Menefee House, Yamhill, Oregon, 1946–1948.
(One of Belluschi's most celebrated houses of the 1940s, it won a *Progressive Architecture* award in 1948 and was widely published, both in the U.S. and abroad. Cost in 1948: $120,000.)

Moore House, Portland, 1946–1949.
(Built for Dr. Merle Moore. One of Belluschi's favorite houses, mostly because of the compact plan. Published in *Architectural Forum*, November 1951; cost in 1949 was $70,000.)

Pacific Telephone & Telegraph new headquarters building, Oak Street, Portland.

Radditz House, Portland, 1946–1947.
(Client's wife was the daughter of the owner of a plywood company; materials for the house were supplied by him. Final summary of costs, not counting materials, in 1946: $16,796.)

St. Philip Neri Catholic Church, Portland, 1946–1952.

Wilson (Charles) House, Warm Springs, Oregon, 1946–1948.

Wilson (Robert) House, Warm Springs, Oregon, 1946–1947.
(Designed as a vacation house for Charles's brother, Robert, it cost $75,000 in 1949, according to Belluschi's figures. Published in *Architectural Record*, July 1951, and in *Progressive Architecture*, August 1952.)

YWCA, Salem, Oregon, 1946–1952.

Zell Brothers Store, Portland (alterations).

1947   Blitz-Weinhard Company, Portland (remodel).

Borg-Warner Prefabricated House (project).

House for Mme Belluschi (project).
(A house Belluschi planned to build for the family in Portland before accepting the offer at MIT.)

Idaho Statesman Newspaper Plant, Boise, Idaho, 1947–1951.

Littman House, Portland (project).
(Designed for sculptor Frederic Littman, with whom Belluschi frequently collaborated.)

Malarkey Garage Building, Sun Valley, Idaho.

Waverly Country Club, Portland (alterations and additions).

Zion Lutheran Church, Portland, 1947–1950.
(One of Belluschi's most celebrated churches; built in 1950 for $187,600.)

1948   American Red Cross headquarters, Portland (alterations).

Blodgett House, Santa Barbara, California (project).

Bruno House, Tualatin Valley, Oregon.

Cedar Hills Shopping Center, Portland.
(Winner of a *Progressive Architecture* citation; published in *Progressive Architecture*, March 1957. Much of the work was done by SOM after Belluschi left for MIT.)

Central Lutheran Church, Portland, 1948–1950.

Cromwell Tailors, Portland (alterations).

Federal Reserve Bank Building, Portland, 1948–1949.

First Presbyterian Church, Cottage Grove, Oregon, 1948–1951.

Malarkey Cottage, Sun Valley, Idaho.
(Built for Huntington Malarkey; cost: $35,000.)

Olds & King Department Store, Portland (alterations).

Willamette University dormitory, Salem, Oregon.

1949   Cedar Hills Housing Development, Portland.
(Developer was Commonwealth, Inc., for whom Belluschi had designed the Commonwealth/Equitable project of 1930.

Kroeker House, Oak Grove, Oregon, 1949–1950.
(Client was J. Donald Kroeker, the engineer who worked with Belluschi on the Equitable and other buildings.)

Ressler House, Milwaukie, Oregon, 1949.
(Cost in 1949, according to Belluschi, was $20,000.)

Sacred Heart Church (Our Lady of the Lake) and Parish School, Oswego, Oregon.

Stewart House, St. Helens, Oregon, 1949–1951.

Walls House, Portland, 1949–1950.
(Built for D. H. Walls, later bought by Mr. and Mrs. William Stevens. Cost in 1950 was $60,000.)

1950   Equitable Building Penthouse, Portland.

Ester Foster Shop, Salem, Oregon.
(Published in *Architectural Forum*, July 1950.)

Griffith House, Oswego, Oregon, 1950–1951.
(Arthur G. Griffith, client.)

Johnson House, Orenco, Oregon.
(E. H. Johnson, client; published in Stubblebine, ed., *The Northwest Architecture of Pietro Belluschi*.)

Larson Landing Field, Moses Lake, Washington.
(Site plan for U.S. Army Air Corps.)

Marion County Courthouse, Salem, Oregon, 1950–1954.
(Cost of the 60,000 sq ft building when completed was $12,000,000.)

McChord Landing Field, Wisconsin. (Site plan for U.S. Army Air Corps.)

Nordstrom's Shoe Store, Portland, Oregon.
(Published in *Architectural Forum,* July 1950.)

Payless Drugstore, Portland.

Buildings and Projects, 1951–1990

The following list consists of the more significant buildings and projects Belluschi either designed or was in some capacity involved in between 1951 and 1990, typically in association with another architectural office. His role varied, from principal designer, to design consultant or advisor, to name only. The dates vary, with the initial date sometimes indicating when the project was commissioned, sometimes when Belluschi was brought in.

1951   Curator's cottage, Daughters of the American Revolution, Champoeg, Oregon.

1952   Mondawmin Shopping Center, Baltimore, Maryland, 1952–1956.
(In association with Kenneth Welch, Dan Kiley, and others; James Rouse, developer. Published in *Architectural Forum,* March 1953, and again in December 1956.)

Portsmouth Abbey (Priory School for Boys), master plan, church, and monastery, Portsmouth, Rhode Island, 1952–1960.
(Belluschi's scheme, initially drawn up in 1954, was revised in 1957. The church and monastery were completed in 1960, with Anderson Beckwith & Haible, associate architect. Cost: $824,114. It was widely published.)

Skidmore House, Winter Haven, Florida, 1952–1955.
(Belluschi's design, with working drawings by SOM, New York, for Louis B. Skidmore, client.)

YWCA Recreation Center, Pittsburgh, Pennsylvania, 1952–1960.

(In association with SOM, New York, which, according to Belluschi, took over the job; his contribution was thus minimal. Published in *Architectural Record,* March 1964.)

1953   Bathroom for the Tile Council of America, 1953–1954 (project).

Boston Back Bay Center, Boston, Massachusetts, 1953–1955 (project).
(Boston Center Architects, with Belluschi, TAC, Walter F. Bogner, Carl Koch & Associates, and Hugh Stubbins, Jr., in joint venture. Roger L. Stevens, developer. Widely published.)

Ciurlo Apartment House, Quercianella, Italy, 1953–1954.
(Belluschi provided only drawings, prepared in his Fairfield house office.)

Temple Israel, Swampscott, Massachusetts, 1953–1956.
(In association with Carl Koch & Associates. Published in *Architectural Record,* December 1954, and *Progressive Architecture,* June 1959, as well as elsewhere.)

Tucker-Mason School for the Deaf, Portland, Oregon. Completion date: 1953.
(In association with SOM, Portland, which was primarily responsible for the design.)

1954   Church of the Redeemer, Baltimore, Maryland, 1954–1958.
(Joint venture with Rogers, Taliaferro & Lamb. Cost in 1958 was $950,000. Received Award of Merit, AIA Honor Awards, 1960, and 25-year award, Baltimore Chapter of the AIA, in 1986. Widely published.)

First Lutheran Church of Boston, Boston, Massachusetts, 1954–1957.
(Belluschi, architect, with assistance of George Wallace. Cost in 1957 was $269,000. Original scheme published in *Architectural Record,* December 1954; final church included in Joseph

Hudnut, "The Church in the Modern World," *Architectural Forum,* December 1958, as well as elsewhere.)

First Presbyterian Church, Boulder, Colorado, 1954–1958.
(Hobart Wagoner, architect; Belluschi, consultant. Published in *Architectural Record,* May 1958.)

Potomac Plaza Apartments, Washington, D.C., 1954 (project).
(With Eduardo Catalano, on the site where the Watergate Apartments were later built. Project consisted of site plan and detailed report only.)

Trinity Lutheran Church, Walnut Creek, California, 1953–1956.
(Joint venture with SOM, San Francisco, which was largely responsible for its design. It was widely published.)

1955   Cedar Lane Unitarian Church, Bethesda, Maryland, 1955–1958.
(In association with Keyes, Lethbridge & Condon. Cost: $310,000. Published in *Progressive Architecture,* June 1959).

Lincoln Center, New York, New York, 1955–1962.
(Belluschi on initial planning team, with Wallace Harrison; Philip Johnson and others were brought in shortly thereafter. The project, of which the Juilliard Building was an inherent part but not built until later, was widely published.)

Rhode Island School of Design, dormitories and dining hall, Providence, Rhode Island, 1955–1959.
(Consultant to Robinson, Green & Beretta. Winner of a *PA* award, it was published in *Progressive Architecture,* January 1959, and again in September 1960.)

1956   Baltimore Civic Center, Baltimore, Maryland, 1956–1957 (project).
(Site plan and detailed report only. With Eduardo Catalano.)

Seattle Public Library, Seattle, Washington.

(Advisor to the client.)

Temple Adath Israel, Merion, Pennsylvania, 1956–1959.

(In association with Charles Frederick Wise. Cost including landscaping and furnishings: $754,790. Widely published.)

1957 Bennington College Library, Bennington, Vermont, 1957–1959.

(Joint venture with Carl Koch & Associates. Published in *Architectural Forum,* February 1960, *Progressive Architecture,* September 1960, *L'Architecture d'aujourd'hui,* June 1961, *Fortune,* May 1963, and *Architectural Record,* May 1963. Won top honors in the first Library Buildings Award Program sponsored by the AIA, American Library Association, and National Book Committee.)

Life Magazine House, San Mateo, California, 1957–1958.

(Joseph L. Eichler, builder; Quincy Jones, associate architect. Published in *Life,* 6 October 1958. See also Minimum House for *Life* magazine project, 1945.)

Lutheran Church, Richland, Washington (project).

1958 Baychester Development, Brooklyn, New York.

(Site plan and detailed report. William Zeckendorf, client; with Eduardo Catalano.)

Juilliard School of Music, Lincoln Center, New York, New York, 1958–1969.

(With Eduardo Catalano in association with Helge Westermann. Received 1970 Bard Award for Excellence in Architecture and Urban Design. Published in *Look,* 19 January 1960, *Architectural Forum,* January 1969, *New York Times,* 8 October 1969, *Architectural Record,* January 1970, as well as elsewhere.)

Pan Am Building, New York, New York, 1958–1963.

(Walter Gropius and Pietro Belluschi, design architects, in association with Emery Roth & Sons. Cost of the 2,400,000 sq ft building: $100 million. Widely published in the popular as well as professional press.)

1959 Boston Opera House, Boston, Massachusetts, 1959 (project).

(With Shepley Bulfinch Richardson & Abbott.)

Golden Gateway Housing Project, San Francisco, California, 1959–1961.

(Client: Perini Land & Development Company. Wurster Bernardi & Emmons, architect; DeMars & Reay, associate architect. Belluschi served as advisor to the client.)

Goucher College Center, Towson, Maryland, 1959–1963.

(With Rogers Taliaferro & Lamb.)

Park Avenue Congregational Church, Arlington, Massachusetts, 1959–1961.

(With Carl Koch & Associates. Cost in 1961: $191,260.)

Temple B'rith Kodesh, Rochester, New York, 1959–1963.

(With Waasdorp Northrup & Austin.)

Trinity Episcopal Church, Concord, Massachusetts, 1959–1963.

(Joint venture with Anderson Beckwith & Haible.)

West Palm Beach development, West Palm Beach, Florida (project).

(Advisor to Perini Corporation, developer. This was one of a number of projects for Perini, among them the Golden Gateway development in San Francisco and Bushell Plaza in Hartford, Connecticut, on which he served as advisor and for which he was paid an annual retaining fee plus all expenses.)

1960 Charles Center, Baltimore, Maryland, 1960–1971.

(Belluschi was member of the Architectural Review Board. See also Baltimore Civic Center project, 1956–1957.)

Trinity Church addition, Copley Square, Boston, Massachusetts (project).

(Joint venture with Shepley Bulfinch Richardson & Abbott. Cost estimate of the new chapel: $600,000. The Belluschi scheme was published in *Architectural Record,* June 1961.)

1961 Century City, Los Angeles, California, 1961–1962.

(Belluschi served as advisor only, mainly on the master plan, as consultant to the ALCOA Company.)

First Community Church, Columbus, Ohio, 1961 (project).

(Joint venture with Brubaker/ Brandt.)

565 Technology Square, Cambridge, Massachusetts, 1961–1965.

(Joint venture with Eduardo Catalano. MIT and Cabot Cabot & Forbes, clients. Published in *Architectural Forum,* January 1961.)

Hawaii State Capitol, Honolulu, Hawaii.

(Member, Advisory Committee on Design.)

May Memorial Unitarian Church, Syracuse, New York, 1961–1965.

(Joint venture with Pederson Hueber & Hares. Cost: $373,140. Published in *Architectural Record,* December 1965.)

National Center for Atmospheric Research, Boulder, Colorado, 1961–1963.

(I. M. Pei, architect; Belluschi, advisor to the client on selection of the architect.)

1962 Church of the Christian Union, Rockford, Illinois, 1962–1966.

(Joint venture with C. Edward Ware. Belluschi, principal designer.)

Equitable Center, Portland, Oregon, 1962–1965.

(Joint venture with Wolff Zimmer Gunsul Frasca. Belluschi, principal designer. Cost: $4,000,000. Published in *Architectural Record,* December 1965.)

First Methodist Church, Duluth, Minnesota, 1962–1971.

(Joint venture with Melander & Fugelso Associates.)

Northern States Power Company Building, Minneapolis, Minnesota, 1962–1965.

(With Ellerbe & Company.)

Portland Design Commission, Portland, Oregon, 1962–1973.

(Belluschi, advisor.)

Rohm & Haas Building, Philadelphia, Pennsylvania, 1962–1964.

(With George M. Ewing, Architects & Engineers. Published in *Architectural Forum,* September 1965, and *Architectural Record,* January 1966, as well as elsewhere.)

University of Rhode Island student housing, Kingston, Rhode Island, 1962–1964.

(Belluschi and Sasaki Walker & Associates, in joint venture with Kent Cruise & Aldrich. The work won a *PA* 12th Annual Design Award and was widely published.)

1963 Eutaw Place Baptist Church, Baltimore, Maryland, 1963–1969.

(Joint venture with Warren Peterson.)

J. F. Kennedy Memorial Library, Cambridge, Massachusetts, 1963–1968.

(Belluschi served as advisor to the client. The site, after a long, heated dispute, was changed to Boston; architect upon Belluschi's recommendation, was I. M. Pei.)

Monmouth Museum, Monmouth, New Jersey, 1963–1970.

(Jules Gregory, associate architect. According to Robert Brannen, who was assisting Belluschi at the time, Belluschi was consulted on but did not initiate the design concept.)

Oregon Historical Society Building, Portland, Oregon, 1963–1965.

(Advisor to the client. Architect: Wolff Zimmer Gunsul Frasca. Belluschi's input minimal.)

St. Margaret of Cortona Catholic Church, Columbus, Ohio, 1963–1970.

(Joint venture with Brubaker & Brandt.)

St. Mary's Cathedral, San Francisco, California, 1963–1970.

(Belluschi and Pier Luigi Nervi in association with McSweeney, Ryan & Lee.)

U.S. Embassy Residence, Paris, France, 1963–1972 (restoration).

(Restoration and remodeling of existing Rothschild house, rue du Faubourg St.-Honoré, Paris. Belluschi with assistance of Robert Brannen. Published briefly as a news item in the *New York Times.*)

1964 Akron Public Library, Akron, Ohio, 1964–1969.

(Consultant to Tuckman & Canute, architect.)

Bank of America Building, San Francisco, California, 1964–1969.

(Belluschi primarily responsible to the client, with Wurster Bernardi & Emmons, and SOM, architects of record. Cost of the 52-story building: $85,000,000. Received 1970 Architectural Award of Excellence, American Institute of Steel Construction. Widely published.)

Bishop W. Angie Smith Chapel, Oklahoma City University, Oklahoma City, Oklahoma, 1964–1968.

(Belluschi, designer, in association with John Reid, architect.)

Christ the King Lutheran Church, Chicago Loop, Chicago Illinois (project).

(Joint venture with Eduardo Catalano.)

National Gallery of Art, East Wing, 1968–1978.

(Belluschi advisor to client J. Carter Brown on selection of architect; discussed but did not initiate design concept. I. M. Pei, architect.)

Portland Art Museum, school wing and sculpture court, Portland, Oregon, 1964–1970.

(In association with Wolff Zimmer Gunsul Frasca; Robert Frasca largely responsible for design. Published in *Architectural Record,* April 1972.)

Portsmouth Abbey School for Boys, science building and auditorium, Portsmouth, Rhode Island, 1964–1966.

(With Robinson Green & Beretta.)

St. Joseph Catholic Church, Roseburg, Oregon, 1964–1968.

(Belluschi with Wolff Zimmer Gunsul Frasca, which was largely responsible for the design; has monumental stained glass window by Gyorgy Kepes.)

Temple B'nai Jeshurun, Short Hills, New Jersey, 1964–1968.

(In association with Kelly & Gruzen.)

University of Virginia Fine Arts & Architecture Center, Charlottesville, Virginia, 1964–1970.

(Belluschi and Kenneth DeMay, of Sasaki Dawson DeMay Associates, designers; Rawlings & Wilson, associate architect.)

1965 Calvary Temple, Hartford, Connecticut (project).

(Joint venture with Robert Brannen. Belluschi consulted on but did not initiate the design concept.)

Chatham West Housing, Brockton, Massachusetts.

(Design consultant to client, Beacon Construction Company. Joint venture with Jung/Brannen Associates; Office of Samuel Paul, associate architect. Belluschi consulted on but did not initiate the design concept.)

Columbus, Indiana, 1965–1966.
(Advisor to client on the landmark town's progressive architecture.)

Fidelity-Philadelphia Trust Company Building, Philadelphia, Pennsylvania, 1965–1966.
(Design consultant to George M. Ewing Company.)

Lutheran Chapel and Student Center, University of Pennsylvania, Philadelphia, Pennsylvania, 1965–1968.
(Principal designer, with Robert Brannen, assistant; Ewing Cole Erdman & Eubank, associate architect. According to Brannen, Belluschi advised on but did not initiate the design concept.)

MacGregor Dormitory, MIT, Cambridge, Massachusetts 1965–1970.
(Joint venture with TAC.)

Magsaysay Office Building, Manila, The Philippines, 1965–1987.
(Consultant for the Ford Foundation; joint venture with Alfredo J. Luz, Associates.)

Oak Street Housing, Brockton, Massachusetts, 1965.
(Design consultant to client, Beacon Construction Company; Samuel Paul, architect.)

Portsmouth Abbey dormitory, gymnasium, and library, Portsmouth, Rhode Island, 1965–1967.
(With Sasaki Dawson DeMay.)

SeaFirst National Bank (First National Bank of Seattle), Seattle, Washington, 1965–1969.
(With Naramore Bain Brody & Johanson, Seattle.)

Sunset Mountain Park Development, Los Angeles, California, 1965–1966.

(Won *PA* Design Award; Belluschi on Planning Advisory Committee.)

Technology Square Office Tower, Cambridge, Massachusetts, 1965–1971 (project).
(32-story office building; Cabot Cabot & Forbes, client. Belluschi with Emery Roth & Sons, associate architects.)

Temple Israel, Wynnefield, Pennsylvania, 1965 (project).
(With C. Frederick Wise.)

Tobin Elementary School, Cambridge, Massachusetts, 1965–1971.
(With Sasaki Dawson DeMay; Kenneth DeMay, principal designer.)

Washington Bridge North, Providence, Rhode Island, 1965–1966.
(Design consultant to Robert L. Pare & Charles A. Maguire & Associates, engineers.)

Wellesley Office Park, Wellesley, Massachusetts, 1965–1975.
(Robert Brannen, assistant, then joint venture with Jung/Brannen Associates. Norman Levanthal, of Beacon Construction Company, client. Complex of five speculative office buildings, to which several more were later added.)

1966 Baystate West Complex, Springfield, Massachusetts, 1966–1972.
(Joint venture with Eduardo Catalano. Complex includes a bus terminal, coliseum, central business district, hotel, private club.)

Blossom Center for the Performing Arts, Cleveland, Ohio, 1966–1968.
(Belluschi design consultant to Dalton, van Dijk, Johnson & Partners.)

Boston Company Building, Boston, Massachusetts, 1966–1969.
(Cabot Cabot & Forbes, client. Joint venture with Emery Roth & Sons; Belluschi, principal designer. Cost, according to Belluschi, was about $40,000,000.)

Center Plaza Building, Civic Center, Boston, Massachusetts, 1966–1969.
(Consultant to the client, Beacon Construction Company. Welton Becket & Associates, architect.)

Christ Church, Frederica (Sea Island Church), Saint Simons Island, Georgia, 1966–1968 (project).
(In association with Robert Brannen, Architect, later Jung/Brannen Associates. Belluschi discussed but did not initiate the design concept.)

Clark Art Institute addition, Williamstown, Massachusetts, 1966–1973.
(In association with TAC.)

Embarcadero Center, San Francisco, California, 1966–1971.
(Advisor to the San Francisco Redevelopment Authority.)

Humanities and Life Science Center, University of Louisville, Louisville, Kentucky, 1966–1969.
(Design consultant with Sasaki Dawson DeMay; Kenneth DeMay, principal designer.)

Immanuel Lutheran Church, Silverton, Oregon, 1966–1967 (alterations and enlargement).
(Belluschi, principal designer; Anthony Belluschi, assistant.)

Kerr-McGee Building, Oklahoma City, Oklahoma, 1966–1974; 1981.
(Joint venture with Frankfurt Short Emery McKinley.)

LaGuardia High School for the Performing Arts, Lincoln Center, New York, New York, 1966–1967.
(With Eduardo Catalano, who was primarily responsible for design, and Helge Westermann, associate architect.)

Motion Picture Association of America headquarters building, Washington, D.C., 1966–1967.
(Consultant to Vlastimil Koubek, architect.)

Pacific Gas & Electric Building, San Francisco, California, 1966–1972.

(Hertzka & Knowles, architects; Belluschi served as advisor to the client.)

Residence for the Dean, MIT, Cambridge, Massachusetts, 1966 (project).

University of Louisville, Humanities and Life Sciences Center, Louisville, Kentucky.
(With Sasaki Dawson DeMay. Kenneth DeMay, principal designer.)

1967 Calvary Church, West Hartford, Connecticut (project).
(In association with Jung/Brannen Associates.)

Covenant Presbyterian Church, Albany, Georgia, 1967–1972.
(In association with Robert Brannen.)

Fort Myer Post Chapel, Norfolk, Virginia, 1967–1971.
(Belluschi, designer, in association with Johnson & Johnson.)

Keystone Building, Boston, Massachusetts, 1967–1971.
(36-story building, with Emery Roth & Sons. Belluschi, principal designer.)

Oregon Graduate Center, Portland, Oregon, 1967–1970.
(With Zimmer Gunsul Frasca, which was primarily responsible for the design.)

University of Colorado Engineering Science Center, Boulder, Colorado, 1967.
(Belluschi and Sasaki, Walker & Associates, consultants. Published in *Fortune, Progressive Architecture.*)

University of Massachusetts, master plan, Boston, Massachusetts, 1967–1970.
(Belluschi and Sasaki Dawson DeMay, consultants.)

University of Notre Dame, Institute of Advanced Religious Studies, Notre Dame, Indiana, 1967–1979.
(Consultant with Sasaki and DeMay. Kenneth DeMay, principal architect.)

1968 Baltimore County Courthouse Complex, Baltimore, Maryland, 1968–1971.
(Consultant to architect, the Office of Gaudreau.)

Century 21 Complex, Philadelphia, Pennsylvania (project).
(Included Drexel Hotel, sometimes called the Kennedy Boulevard Hotel. With Jung/Brannen Associates.)

Diablo Canyon Power Plant, San Luis Obispo, California, 1968–1970.
(Consultant to the client, with Wurster Bernardi & Emmons; Pacific Gas & Electric architects largely responsible for design.)

Douglass College Arts Center, Rutgers State University, New Brunswick, New Jersey, 1968–1982.
(Joint venture with Jung/Brannen Associates. Advisor only.)

Hawaiian Electric Company office building and warehouse garage, Honolulu, Hawaii.
(Consultant to Au, Cutting, Fairweather & Smith.)

Kennedy Memorial Chapel (project).
(Sketches prepared for Senator Edward Kennedy in honor of Robert Kennedy.)

Parliament Building, Seoul, South Korea, 1968–1971.
(Advisor only.)

Portsmouth Abbey School for Boys, administration building, dormitory, and skating rink, Portsmouth, Rhode Island, 1968–1970.
(With Sasaki Dawson DeMay.)

Princeton University Faculty Club addition, Princeton, New Jersey, 1968–1970.
(In association with C. Harrison Hill, university architect, and Warren Platner, associate architect. Published in *Architectural Forum*, June 1970; Gubitosi and Izzo, p. 84.)

Sacramento Convention and Community Center, Sacramento, California, 1968–1973.

(Consultant to Sacramento Architects Collaborative. Belluschi provided the basic concept and oversaw design.)

Sixty State Street Building, Boston, Massachusetts, (project).
(Joint venture with Emery Roth & Sons. Cabot Cabot & Forbes, client. Belluschi was principal designer.)

Springfield Convention Center, Springfield, Massachusetts, 1968–1972.
(Joint venture with Eduardo Catalano.)

1969 Del Monte Office Building, San Francisco, California, 1969–1972.
(Stone Marraccini & Patterson, architect; Belluschi consultant on design.)

Dewey Square (later, One Financial Center), Boston, Massachusetts, 1969–1984.
(Rose Associates, New York, developer. Joint venture with Jung/Brannen; Emery Roth & Sons, associate architect.)

Ethel Walker School, Performing Arts Center, Simsbury, Connecticut.
(Joint venture with Jung/Brannen Associates. Belluschi advisor only.)

Federal Reserve Bank Building, Philadelphia, Pennsylvania, 1969–1976.
(Ewing Cole Erdman & Eubank, architect.)

1970 IBM Building, Baltimore, Maryland, 1970–1975.
(Joint venture with Emery Roth & Sons; Belluschi, principal designer.)

Kahneetah Lodge, Warm Springs, Oregon, 1970–1972.
(Wolff Zimmer Gunsul Frasca, architect; Belluschi, advisor only.)

Trojan Nuclear Power Plant, Columbia River, Oregon, 1970.
(Portland General Electric, client. Wolff Zimmer Gunsul Frasca, architect; Belluschi advisor only.)

1971 Beth Israel Hospital, addition, Boston, Massachusetts, 1971–1973.
>   (Advisor to the client; Perry Dean & Stewart, architect.)

Chestnut Hill Shopping Center, Newton, Massachusetts, 1971–1973.
>   (Joint venture with Jung/Brannen Associates. Sumner Schein, architect. Belluschi, advisor only.)

Oak Street Housing (Pine Grove Suburban Estates), Brockton, Massachusetts.
>   (Federally subsidized housing; Norman B. Leventhal, of the Beacon Construction Company, client. Belluschi in joint venture with Jung/Brannen Associates; Samuel Paul, associate architect.)

Oregon State University, Great Hall, Corvallis, Oregon, 1971–1976 (project).
>   (With Jung/Brannen Associates.)

State University of New York, Buffalo, New York, 1971–1975 (project).
>   (Master plan for Spine I and II. Consultant with Sasaki Dawson DeMay Associates.)

1972 Cuyahoga County Justice Center, Cleveland, Ohio, 1972–1976.
>   (Consultant to Prindle, Patrick & Partners.)

Meyerhoff Symphony Hall, Baltimore, Maryland, 1972–1982.
>   (Joint venture with Jung/Brannen Associates, Robert Hsiung, principal designer.)

Wolfson Center for Environmental Design, University of Cincinnati, Cincinnati, Ohio, 1972–1976.
>   (Design consultant to the Erwin S. Wolfson Foundation; Tweddell Wheeler Strickland & Benmer, architect.)

1973 Davies Symphony Hall, San Francisco, California, 1973–1980.
>   (Belluschi, initial architect; SOM, San Francisco, brought in as associate, then took over. Charles Bassett, designer.)

Hopkins International Airport, Cleveland, Ohio, 1973–1976.
>   (Richard L. Bowen & Associate, architect; Belluschi, design consultant.)

One Maine Savings Bank, Portland, Maine, 1973–1974.
>   (Joint venture with Jung/Brannen. Belluschi, advisor only.)

Performing Arts Center garage, San Francisco, California, 1973–1974.
>   (Design consultant.)

Phillips Academy dormitory, Andover, Massachusetts.
>   (Joint venture with Jung/Brannen Associates; Anthony Belluschi, project director. Pietro Belluschi served as advisor only.)

Pink Grove Townhouses, Brockton, Massachusetts.
>   (Federally subsidized housing; Beacon Construction Company, client. Joint venture with Jung/Brannen Associates; Samuel Paul, associate architect. Featured as one of the Apartments of the Year in *Architectural Record,* mid-May 1973.)

Savannah Bank & Trust Company Building addition, Savannah, Georgia, 1973–1975.
>   (Consultant to Thomas E. Stanley & Associates.)

1974 Brubaker House, Columbus, Ohio.
>   (In association with Belluschi/Daskalakis.)

Executive Office Building, Olympia, Washington (project).
>   (Consultant to The Richardson Associates, Seattle.)

Oregon State Capital expansion, Salem, Oregon, 1974–1977.
>   (Consultant to Wolff Zimmer Gunsul Frasca.)

University of Health Sciences, Uniformed Services, Bethesda, Maryland, 1974–1987.
>   (Consultant to Schrader & Dalton Dalton Little Newport.)

U.S. National Bank (Bancorp) headquarters building, Portland, Oregon, 1974–1983.
>   (SOM, Portland, architect; Belluschi consultant to the client.)

1975 Beckman House, Etna, California (project).
>   (With Belluschi/Daskalakis.)

Constellation Place, Baltimore, Maryland (project).
>   (Louis Kahn project; Belluschi called in as consultant to the client.)

Immanuel Lutheran Church, Silverton, Oregon, 1975–1979.
>   (With Belluschi/Daskalakis; Settecase Smith Doss, architect. Belluschi principal designer.)

Lingnan College Library and Auditorium Building, Hong Kong, 1975–1981.
>   (Joint venture with Jung/Brannen Associates, consultant to Arthur Kwok. Belluschi advisor only.)

University of Ancona engineering complex, Ancona, Italy.
>   (Joint venture with Jung/Brannen Associates. Belluschi advisor only.)

1976 Ohio State University, Agronomy, Natural Resources and Plant Pathology Building, Columbus, Ohio, 1976–1980.
>   (Consultant, with Brubaker/Brandt.)

Pentagon City Office Buildings, Arlington, Virginia, 1976–1981.
>   (Joint venture with Jung/Brannen Associates and Vlastimil Koubek. Belluschi advisor only.)

Police Headquarters, Cleveland, Ohio.
>   (Consultant with Richard L. Bowen & Associates.)

St. Francis Hospital additions, Tulsa, Oklahoma.
>   (Consultant with Hudgins Thompson Ball & Associates.)

Sarasota Detention Center, Sarasota, Florida.
> (Pringle, architect; Belluschi, design consultant.)

University of Jeddah, Saudi Arabia, 1976–1978 (project).
> (Master plan, Belluschi, consultant for Project Planning Associates, Ltd, Toronto; with Jung/Brannen Associates and Sasaki Dawson DeMay.)

U.S. Post Office, Manchester, New Hampshire.
> (Consultant; Anderson Nicols & Co., architect and engineer.)

1977   Bethesda Naval Hospital, Bethesda, Maryland.
> (Consultant; Ellerbe Co., architect.)

Campbell House, MacKenzie Bridge, Oregon, 1977–1979.
> (Belluschi designer, in collaboration with Payne Settecase Smith & Partners.)

George Fox College gymnasium, Newburg, Oregon.
> (Consultant with Daniel Mann Johnson & Mendenhall.)

Justice Center, Portland, Oregon, 1977–1983.
> (Consultant with Zimmer Gunsul Frasca; State Highway Department, client.)

Portland General Electric Office Building (Willamette Center), Portland, Oregon.
> (Consultant with Zimmer Gunsul Frasca.)

World Bank Building, Washington, D.C., 1977–1980.
> (Consultant with Vlastimil Koubek.)

1978   Blake Estates, Bedford, Massachusetts, 1978–1980.
> (Federally subsidized housing; Beacon Construction Company, client. Belluschi in joint venture with Jung/Brannen in association with Samuel Paul, architect. This was one of a number of housing developments Belluschi was involved in in the 1960s and 1970s with

the Beacon Company. Among others were the Blue Ridge Estates, Bramblewood Estates, and Dominion Place in Richmond, Virginia; Whittier Terrace, Worcester, Massachusetts; Chatham West Apartments and Pine Estates in Brockton, Massachusetts. Belluschi typically served as advisor only.)

Christ the King Catholic Church, Milwaukie, Oregon, 1978–1986.
> (Joint venture with Yost Grube Hall; Belluschi principal designer.)

Dante Alighieri Society Building, Cambridge, Massachusetts, 1978–1985.
> (Joint venture with Jung/Brannen Associates; Belluschi principal designer.)

One Post Office Square, Boston, Massachusetts, 1978–1982.
> (Consultant with Jung/Brannen Associates; Belluschi advisor only.)

Papworth House, Portland, Oregon, 1978–1980.
> (Belluschi, designer.)

Portsmouth Abbey School for Boys, classroom and student and monastery libraries, Portsmouth, Rhode Island, 1978–1991.
> (Belluschi, designer, with Jung/Brannen Associates.)

1979   Charleston Hotel and Convention Center, Charleston, South Carolina, 1979–1980 (project).
> (Consultant to the client, Theodore B. Gould, president, Charleston Center Corporation.)

Miami Center, Miami, Florida, 1979–1983.
> (Client: Theodore Gould, president of Holywell Corporation. Project only partially realized. Included a convention center, 750-room convention hotel, performing arts center, condominiums, 62-story office building, and garage. Only 40-story Ball Building and Pavillon Hotel completed. Belluschi, principal

designer, with Pietro Belluschi Architect Associates.)

University of Portland Chapel, Portland, Oregon, 1979; 1985–1986.
> (Joint venture with Yost Grube Hall; Belluschi, principal designer. Initial contact was in 1979; at the request of the client, Belluschi wholly revised the design in 1985. The chapel was completed in 1986.)

1980   Apartment house, New York, New York.
> (Consultant to the client, Rose Associates, New York.)

Condominium apartments, Singapore.
> (Consultant with Arthur Kwok.)

Hotel Meridien, Boston, Massachusetts, 1980–1982 (adaptive reuse).
> (Joint venture with Jung/Brannen Associates; Belluschi advisor only.)

Vista House Condominiums, Portland, Oregon (project).
> (Belluschi consultant; Selwyn Bingham, developer; Payne Settecase Smith Doss, architect.)

Yakima Indian Cultural Center, Yakima, Washington.
> (Belluschi consultant; A. Robert Williams and Doudna Williams, architects.)

1981   Gould House, Charlottesville, Virginia (project).
> (Theodore Gould, client.)

1982   St. Matthew's Lutheran Church, Beaverton, Oregon, 1982–1984.
> (Joint venture with Yost Grube Hall; Belluschi, principal designer.)

Washington State Convention and Trade Center, Seattle, Washington, 1982–1989.
> (Consultant with TRA and HNTB, architects; Danadjieva & Koenig Associates, associated designer. Belluschi advisor only.)

1983   One Financial Center, Boston, Massachusetts.
         (Joint venture with Jung/Brannen Associates. Originally called Dewey Square; design changed substantially with change of site. Final version, Belluschi advisor only. Client: Rose Associates, New York.)

       State Office Building, Van Nuys, California.
         (Consultant with Western Pacific Collaboration.)

       University of Louisville School of Business, Louisville, Kentucky, 1983–1984.
         (Consultant with Louis & Henry, Inc. Belluschi advisor only.)

1984   Fillmore Housing Project (Fillmore Center), San Francisco, California, 1984–1990.
         (Belluschi consultant to the client, Donald Tishman, developer. Original architect Drosilin & Kassovic, then Daniel Mann Johnson & Mendenhall. Belluschi advisor only.)

1985   Stimson Building, Seattle, Washington (project).
         (Consultant to John Graham & Company.)

1986   Packard House, Portland, Oregon, 1986–1988.
         (Belluschi, designer; John Hinchliff, architect.)

       United Hebrew Synagogue, St. Louis, Missouri, 1986–1989.
         (Belluschi, principal designer; Stone Marraccini & Patterson, architect.)

1987   Murray Hills Christian Church, Beaverton, Oregon, 1987–1989.
         (Joint venture with Yost Grube Hall; Belluschi, principal designer.)

       Provident Tower, Baltimore, Maryland (project).
         (Hadley Properties of Seattle, developer.)

       Saltzman House, Portland, Oregon, 1987–1988.

         (Jack J. Saltzman, client; with Yost Grube Hall.)

       Trinity Lutheran Church, Sheridan, Oregon, 1987–1990.
         (Joint venture with Yost Grube Hall; Belluschi, principal designer.)

1988   St. Luke's Episcopal Church, Seattle, Washington (project).
         (Consultant to Chester L. Lindsay, architect.)

1989   Church of the Resurrection (Catholic), West Linn, Oregon (project).
         (Consultant to J. David Richen, architect.)

       George Fox Bell Tower, Newberg, Oregon.
         (In 1977 Belluschi had served as consulting architect with DMJM in designing a gymnasium for George Fox College. The bell tower, designed solely by Belluschi who donated his services, was dedicated in 1990. The college awarded him an honorary Doctor of Fine Arts degree in 1991.)

       Vista House Condominiums (revised scheme), Portland, Oregon (project).
         (Selwyn Bingham, developer; consultant to Yost Grube Hall, architect.)

1990   Our Savior's Lutheran Church, Lake Oswego, Oregon.
         (Consultant to Yost Grube Hall, architect.)

Notes

1 Italian Origins

1. My account of Belluschi's childhood has been drawn principally from his unpublished memoirs kept in his personal files in Portland. Written between 1979 and 1982, they were based on a record of his travels that he kept "as far back as I can remember." According to his wife Marjorie, he reconstructed the early years from memory. She was unsure when he actually began keeping the record, though it was before they met in the 1950s.

   The memoirs are surprisingly accurate, albeit embellished, measured against documents such as passports, registration forms, and letters found in his vast files. They are also for the most part consistent with my interviews with him conducted for the Archives of American Art, Smithsonian Institution, in 1983, and some 150 hours of taped interviews with him since then. In the late 1970s he began thinking of a book devoted to his life and work, and in 1979 asked Elisabeth K. Thompson, former West Coast editor of the *Architectural Record* and a personal friend whom he had known since the late 1930s, to write it. His memoirs were evidently written with this in mind. After working on the material for several years, Thompson dropped the book project, in part because of its length and complexity, in part because of the difficult, often troubling questions it raised (taped interviews, Elisabeth K. Thompson/MLC, Berkeley, June–July 1986; June–July 1987). I would like to thank Mrs. Thompson for her generosity in passing on to me her thoughts on Belluschi and his work. Although our perspectives differ, I benefited greatly from her insights.

   Because Belluschi enjoyed writing and wanted his memoirs to provide an engaging tale, one should bear in mind his tendency toward literary flair. I have verified and in some case adjusted his account when necessary, based on interviews with his family members, colleagues, and friends, plus photographs and other documentation.

2. Father's memoirs (written in 1932, and kept in Belluschi's personal files), 4ff. Pietro himself translated them between 1958 and 1970, and evidently they served as the model for his own memoirs begun some nine years later. The differences between the two documents are telling, Belluschi's as romanticized as his father's are dry and factual.

See also Smithsonian interviews, 1–2.

3. Father's memoirs, 1.

4. Smithsonian interviews, 2.

5. Belluschi memoirs, 1.

6. Belluschi memoirs, 1–2.

7. Father's memoirs, 29–30.

8. Belluschi memoirs, 1–2.

9. Belluschi memoirs, 3; Smithsonian interviews, 2.

10. Father's memoirs, 35; Belluschi memoirs, 21.

11. Belluschi memoirs, 7–10.

12. Belluschi memoirs, 7–8; Smithsonian interviews, 3–4.

13. Taped interview, PB/MLC, Portland, 14 November 1986; Belluschi memoirs, 8; PB/MLC, 15 May 1989.

14. Smithsonian interviews, 4.

15. Belluschi memoirs, 7.

16. Belluschi memoirs, 13.

17. Belluschi memoirs, 33ff.

18. Belluschi letter to Mr. Gene Rea, of *Il Progresso Italo-Americano,* 15 January 1951 (Belluschi files). This was a response to Rea's request for biographical information for a feature article on Belluschi as a prominent American of Italian origin.

19. Taped interview, PB/MLC, 15 May 1989.

20. Taped interview, PB/MLC, 9 December 1986.

21. Belluschi letter to the Consulate of Italy, Boston, Massachusetts, 20 July 1972 (Belluschi files). Belluschi had seen an article in the *Boston Globe* of 16 July 1972 on Italian veterans of World War I, and was irate that his name was not included; his letter, requesting acknowledgment of his participation, carefully documented his war experience.

22. Belluschi memoirs, 28–30.

23. Belluschi memoirs, 30; Belluschi letter to Jo Stubblebine, 25 February 1952 (Belluschi files).

24. Belluschi to Rea, *Il Progresso Italo-Americano,* 15 January 1951. Shortly thereafter, Belluschi began referring to this degree as "Dottore-Ingegneria," which was typically translated as doctor of engineering. See for example Stubblebine, *The Northwest Architecture of Pietro Belluschi,* 1, where the degree was defined as a doctor of architectural engineering. Stubblebine was one of the four or five women who worked in the Belluschi office in the 1940s, and wrote the book under his direction, relying solely on material he provided. Belluschi was unhappy with the quality of the photographs and layout and later denied he had anything to do with the book. See for example the letter he sent to the book review department of the *Architectural Record,* Belluschi to George R. Darcy, 5 January 1953 (Belluschi files).

25. In his memoirs, Belluschi mentions (with his characteristic show of humility) his sense of inferiority "made obvious by observation of great creative people and the enormity of total human knowledge and potential that I could see at MIT of which I possessed only a minute part." Others attribute it more simply to his lack of academic training, lack of formal architectural training, or, in the opinion of some, lack of innate talent. On Belluschi's awareness of his own ill fit as dean at MIT, see Chenoweth, "Pietro Belluschi: The Architect as Prophet," 16.

26. Belluschi was often deliberately vague about his training, which has been variously described as civil engineering, architectural engineering, or architecture. See for example Stubblebine, *Northwest Architecture,* 1. Her book, the only major publication on his work prior to this one, provided much of the basic biographical material relied on by subsequent authors. See, for example, Wilson, *The AIA Gold Medal,* 214.

27. Taped interview, PB/MLC, 16 January 1988.

28. Belluschi memoirs, 37; Smithsonian interviews, 6.

29. Belluschi memoirs, 36–37; Smithsonian interviews, 6.

2 Early Years in Portland

1. Belluschi letter to Elisabeth K. Thompson, 6 October 1980 (Belluschi files).

2. Fred Asa Barnes, Director, School of Civil Engineering, Cornell University, letter re: Pietro Belluschi, 10 October 1923 (Belluschi files); Smithsonian interviews, 7; Belluschi memoirs, 36–39; taped interview, PB/MLC,

9 September 1985; Belluschi letter to Elisabeth K. Thompson, 6 October 1980; Stubblebine, *Northwest Architecture of Pietro Belluschi*, 1–3.

3. Announcement of the College of Architecture, Cornell University, 1923/24 (Belluschi files).

4. Irene di Robilant letter to Belluschi, 19 May 1924 (Belluschi files). One might wonder if Belluschi was interested in Japan because of Wright's work there on the Imperial Hotel. I find no evidence of this, however, nor did he recall knowing anything about it. Belluschi on occasion maintained that he remained in this country because of the political situation with Mussolini, but again I find no evidence of this in the documentation.

5. Taped interview, PB/MLC, 11 August 1985; Livingston Farrand, President of Cornell University, letter, To Whom it May Concern, 9 June 1924 (Belluschi files).

6. Father's memoirs, 47; 1920s correspondence (Belluschi files); Caetani telegram to Belluschi, 27 June 1924 (Belluschi files).

7. Stanley Easton, Manager, Bunker Hills and Sullivan Mining Company, letter, To Whom it May Concern, 4 April 1925 (Belluschi files).

8. Schwantes, *The Pacific Northwest, an Interpretive History*, 194.

9. Pell, "The Architecture of Albert Ernest Doyle," 20; Vaughan and Ferriday, *Space, Style and Structure*, 1: 324.

10. The Public Services Building, designed by Greene before he left and construction of which was begun in December 1927, was a 14-story steel-framed office building, with exteriors of brick and terra-cotta, and base of granite. Italianate in inspiration with an Ionic colonnaded loggia at the summit and broad arcaded base, it was the tallest building in the city at the time. Belluschi was responsible for much of the detailing, including the design of the ornate elevator doors. Outline Specs for Office Building, 6th & Salmon streets, 23 November 1928 (Belluschi Collection, Syracuse); *Oregonian Daily Newspaper* (Portland), undated clipping, circa October 1926 (Belluschi files).

11. Taped interview, PB/MLC, 26 February 1988, See also Clausen, "Belluschi and the Equitable Building in History."

12. *Oregonian*, 16 August 1926. See also Deering, "Mountain Architecture—An Alternative Design Proposal," 182–183; Vaughan and Ferriday, *Space, Style and Structure*, 468.

13. Undated newspaper clipping, Belluschi files. Cavalier toward the discipline of the historian (though not to the legacy of history), Belluschi always carefully marked the appropriate pages and underscored his own name in these collected clippings but rarely recorded titles or dates.

In a recent publication of Boise historic buildings, Belluschi alone rather than the Doyle office was credited with the First National Bank. Arthur Art of the Idaho Historical Society, letter to Belluschi, 27 November 1984 (Belluschi files).

14. Belluschi letter to MLC, 9 February 1985; Belluschi memoirs, 45; taped interview, George Kotchik/MLC, Portland, 7 April 1987. Kotchik was a member of the Doyle office in the late 1930s and early 1940s. On the name of the firm, see also chapter 4, note 56.

15. *Daily Journal of Commerce* (Portland), 24 July 1928; State Board of Examiners, letter, 27 July 1928 (Belluschi Collection, Syracuse); taped interview, PB/MLC, 11 August 1985; father's memoirs, 47.

16. Taped interview, Ken Richardson/MLC, Seattle, 30 December 1986. Richardson was a longstanding member of the Doyle firm, having joined it as an office boy in 1927. He remained with the office after Belluschi bought out the other partners in 1943 and changed the name to Pietro Belluschi Architect, then later sold it to SOM when he went to MIT in 1951. Richardson was one of Belluschi's chief designers, especially for the houses and churches.

17. Taped interview, PB/MLC, 4 February 1987.

18. Belluschi (in Rome) letter to Dave Jack, A. E. Doyle and Associates, 4 June 1929 (Belluschi files).

19. Dave Jack letter to Belluschi, 28 June 1929 (Belluschi files); taped interview, PB/MLC, 30 June 1992. A memo in Belluschi's files suggests that his primary interest in Paris was recent decorative work. His note recorded several books he bought there: *Répertoire du Goût Moderne, Nouvelles Boutiques, Façades et Intérieurs, Mobilier et Décoration*, and Le Corbusier's *Almanach d'Architecture Moderne* (Belluschi files).

20. Belluschi letter to Jeffrey G. Carter, Project Director, National Register Nomination, Reed College, 2 November 1981 (Belluschi files). See also Smithsonian Interviews, 11, and Ritz, *A History of the Reed College Campus and Its Buildings*, 38–39. Ritz was a member of the Belluschi office in the 1940s and worked closely with Belluschi in preparing the text.

21. MacColl, *Growth of a City*, 65, 187.

22. Articles, *Oregonian*, June–July 1929; *Oregon Journal*, 9 June 1929. Among the clients of the Commonwealth project who were later to retain Belluschi on other jobs were State Senator Henry Corbett, Charles Adams, president of the Portland Art Museum Association, and Aubrey Watzek, the wealthy lumberman and lawyer who was to commission the Watzek House, the first of the series of regional houses of the late 1930s and 1940s.

See also MacColl, *Growth of a City*, on the Equitable/Commonwealth consortium; and Clausen, "Belluschi and the Equitable Building."

23. *Sunday Oregonian*, 20 April 1930 (Belluschi files); taped interview, Ken Richardson/MLC, 30 December 1986.

24. Taped interview, PB/MLC, 19 August 1985; *Oregonian*, 15 November 1931; *Oregonian*, 30 November 1931; Estimate for Alterations, Equitable Savings and Loan Building, L. H. Hoffman (contractor), 28 January 1932, and other documents (Belluschi Collection, Syracuse).

25. Taped interviews, PB/MLC, 7 November 1986; 14 November 1986; 12 August 1988.

26. *Spectator* (Portland), 11 January 1930.

27. Taped interviews, PB/MLC, 26 February 1988; 4 February 1989; Kimball, "Louis Sullivan, an Old Master."

28. *Spectator*, 1 June 1929, 13. The 1930 national AIA convention in Washington, D.C., which Willcox and Ellis but not Belluschi attended, discussed the modernism debate. *Pacific Builder & Engineer*, 21 June 1930, 8.

29. Gutheim, "The Turning Point in Mr. Wright's Career" (on the Kahn lectures), 48; taped interview, George Kotchik/MLC, 7 April 1987. Belluschi owned a copy of the Kahn lectures (*Modern Architecture: Being the Kahn Lectures for 1930 by Frank Lloyd Wright*, 1931), but whether he attended

Wright's University of Oregon lecture delivered on 7 March 1931 is unclear. My thanks to Keith Richards, Archivist, University of Oregon, for verifying the date of the Wright lecture.

30. *Notable Pioneers in the History of Oregon* (Oregon Lung Association, 1983).

31. *The Oregon Artist, Journal of the Museum Art School* (Portland), fall 1955.

32. Taped interview, PB/MLC, 15 May 1989. This legacy was also passed on to Joshua C. Taylor, who studied at the Portland Art Museum before moving to Chicago to teach at the University of Chicago as professor of art history and the humanities, then to Washington, D.C. Shortly after Belluschi assumed the deanship at MIT in 1951, Taylor invited him to exhibit his work in a special exhibition held apparently at the University of Chicago (exhibition announcement, Belluschi files).

33. Taped interview, PB/MLC, 26 January 1985.

34. Taped interviews, PB/MLC, 15 May 1985; 11 August 1985; Belluschi address, Association of Collegiate Schools of Architecture, Vancouver, B.C., March 1985; taped interviews, Margaret Fritch/MLC, Seattle, 17 April 1987; John Yeon/MLC, Portland, 15 December 1986.

35. Taped interview, John Yeon/MLC, 15 December 1986. On Yeon, who died 13 March 1994, see also the obituary in the *Oregonian,* 15 March 1994.

36. *Oregon Artist,* fall 1955. On Doyle's work on the coast, see also Vaughan and Ferriday, *Space, Style and Structure,* 1: 343.

37. Interviews, John Yeon/MLC, 15 December 1986; April 1987.

38. Taped interviews, PB/MLC, 11 August 1985; 14 November 1986; Vaughan and Ferriday, *Space, Style and Structure,* 1: 345–347. In 1989, the Wentz Cottage was purchased by Pietro's elder son Peter Belluschi and subsequently remodeled under his supervision.

3 The Portland Art Museum and the Emergence of Modernism

1. MacColl, *Growth of a City,* 461.

2. Taped interview, Frank Allen/MLC, Portland, 16 November 1986.

3. Summary of Reports, Portland Art Association, January 1 to December 31, 1930 (Portland, February 1931), 18.

4. Belluschi memoirs, 49; *Annual Reports,* Portland Art Association, 1910, 1911, 1916; *Oregon Artist,* 1, no. 1 (Spring 1952).

5. Museums were increasingly seen as public institutions geared to artistic education of the populace at large, rather than monarchic palaces or ceremonial sanctuaries for the protection of art. See Stein, "The Art Museum of Tomorrow" (*Architectural Record,* 1930); Coleman, *Museum Buildings* (1950).

6. A. E. Doyle, "A New Art Museum," typed manuscript, 12 July 1926 (Belluschi Collection, Syracuse).

7. President's Report, Portland Art Museum, February 1931; *News Telegram,* 26 May 1931 (Belluschi files).

8. Taped interviews, William Givler/MLC, Portland, 19 January 1987; Margaret Fritch/MLC, Seattle, 17 April 1987; Frank Allen/MLC, Portland, 16 November 1986; Burke Morden/MLC, Portland, 5 April 1987. Givler joined the Portland Art Museum faculty as a painter in 1931 and continued teaching there until his retirement in 1974. Margaret Fritch was the first woman to become a registered architect in the state of Oregon. She worked for Jamieson Parker in 1928–1929, then again in 1933–1934.

9. Charles Adams and Pierre Hines, Portland Art Museum Building Committee, letter to A. E. Doyle & Associates, 9 March 1931 (Belluschi Collection, Syracuse).

10. "Reference for Museum," handwritten list in Belluschi's hand, undated but includes reference to an article published in the *Architect and Engineer* of January 1931 (Belluschi Collection, Syracuse). Contrary to Belluschi's frequent assertion that he designed the new museum in 1929, the documentation indicates that though preliminary discussion may have occurred earlier, actual designing did not begin for another couple of years.

11. A. E. Doyle & Associate, P. Belluschi, Memorandum for the Proposed Portland Museum of Art, 26 March 1931 (Belluschi Collection, Syracuse).

12. Belluschi letter to Anna Crocker, 28 March 1931 (Belluschi Collection, Syracuse).

13. L. Earle Rowe letter to Belluschi, 1 May 1931 (Belluschi Collection, Syracuse).

14. Taped interview, Ken Richardson/MLC, Seattle, 30 December 1986. Richardson was working in the Doyle office at the time; it was he who built the model.

15. Belluschi letter to Frank Lloyd Wright, 3 July 1931 (Belluschi files).

16. Wright letter to Belluschi, 6 July 1931 (Belluschi files). Published in Wright, *Letters to Architects* (1984), 88.

17. [Belluschi], Notes on New Portland Art Museum, undated (Belluschi Collection, Syracuse).

18. Anna B. Crocker letter to Belluschi, 19 August 1931 (Belluschi Collection, Syracuse). Her letter reveals a remarkable awareness of contemporary architectural concerns. She clearly served as one of Belluschi's key mentors, advising him, for example, how—with what course of reasoning and in what tone—to reply to the criticisms raised by Jamieson Parker, the architect to whom the job was expected to go and to whom trustees of the museum turned for advice, in response to Belluschi's preliminary plans. "Going back to his [Jamieson Parker's] first objection, it is evident that you approach the whole subject of architecture from a different angle from his. You are putting forth the plan and elevation as a solution, not of your ideal approach to the problem of an art museum, but as a plan covering the concrete needs of the interior. . . ."

19. *Bulletin, Museum of Art,* Portland, 1, no. 4 (January 1932); Jones, "Architecture Astray" (*Atlantic Monthly,* January 1931); taped interview, PB/MLC, 17 March 1985.

20. Hitchcock, "An Eastern Critic Looks at Western Architecture," 21.

21. Correspondence, A. Lawrence Kocher to William Crowell, April–May 1933 (Belluschi Collection, Syracuse).

22. Belluschi letters to Dave Jack, June–July 1933 (Belluschi files).

23. Belluschi, "Le Portland Art Museum," *Mouseion. Organ de l'Office International des Musées,* Paris, 33-34 (1936), 53-81; letter to Belluschi, Office International des Musées, 27 July 1936 (Belluschi files).

24. Belluschi, "Lecture on Modern Architecture," Portland Art Museum, 13 November 1935 (Belluschi Collection, Syracuse).

25. See "Artists and Architects: Interpreting Man's Spiritual Dreams," 1979 (reproduced in appendix of Clausen, *Spiritual Space*).

26. "Architecture: Its Relation to Civilization," undated manuscript (Belluschi Collection, Syracuse); Belluschi letters to Crocker and Wentz, November–December 1932 (Belluschi files); Belluschi, "Lecture on Modern Architecture," Portland Art Museum, 13 November 1935 (Belluschi Collection, Syracuse).

27. Marcel Breuer, "Where Do We Stand?" (Zurich, 1934), reproduced in Blake, *Marcel Breuer* (1949), 119–122. Whether Belluschi knew Breuer or his essays at the time is not known; he looked at *Bauformen* regularly, but as he did not read German, it is hard to discern how much he knew of the philosophy behind the Bauhaus forms. My sense is, not much.

28. Unidentified clipping (*Oregonian*? *Oregon Journal*?), 20 June 1935 (Belluschi files).

29. Hitchcock and Seale, *Temples of Democracy: The State Capitols of the USA* (1976), 290–291.

30. Taped interviews, PB/MLC, 15 December 1986; 12 November 1987.

31. Taped interview, PB/MLC, 21 November 1987; *Pacific Builder & Engineer* 42 (20 June 1936), 4.

32. Statement of Commissions for 1935, A. E. Doyle & Associate, 31 December 1935 (Belluschi Collection, Syracuse).

33. "Description of Corvallis Public Library Building," 19 April 1932, A. E. Doyle & Associate (Belluschi Collection, Syracuse). The building was extensively remodeled in 1990.

34. Belluschi letter to The Ball Studios, Corvallis, Oregon, 3 December 1931 (Belluschi Collection, Syracuse).

35. Doyle had prepared a master plan for Linfield College in 1919 that included a preliminary proposal for a new administration building. The building was built under Belluschi's direction in 1928, largely along Doyle's lines. In 1935, still without a library, the college turned again to the Doyle firm. In order to qualify for PWA funds available only for public works, the site for the new library was deeded to the city of McMinnville, which in turn leased it to the college for 99 years. The plan followed the basic format of the Reed College Library, with a simple cross-axial plan, entry on axis with the main circulation lobby, and large, well-lit reading rooms to either side; stacks were behind the circulation desk, with additional stacks and reading rooms in the basement. The structure was of reinforced concrete, with brick veneers and white wood trim. The Linfield library was given a Georgian rather than Tudor Gothic styling, in keeping with the rest of the campus. The building was completed in November 1936, at a cost of $62,000 (*Oregon Journal*, 29 January 1928; Holmes, *Linfield's Hundred Years*; "Linfield College Library," typed manuscript, Belluschi Collection, Syracuse).

The Willamette University Library conformed to the same basic type, but was larger and the plan more complex. It too was Georgian in keeping with the Willamette campus, with a steep hipped roof surmounted, on the insistence of the client, by a cupola. It was completed in 1938 at a cost of $84,000. On the Willamette Library, see *Pacific Builder & Engineer* 45 (20 May 1939), 4.

36. Germane here, and reflecting today's interest in typology, is Colquhoun, "The Type and its Transformations." For a recent view of regionalism, see Frampton, "Towards a Critical Regionalism"; and Frampton, "Response" [on regionalism], in DeLong, Searing, and Stern, *American Architecture: Innovation and Tradition*. Frampton curiously does not mention Belluschi, though his work and particularly his essay on regionalism in the *Architectural Record* of December 1955 (see chapter 7 below) were recognized as pivotal at the time. Belluschi was later invited to contribute to a special issue on regionalism in *Center, A Journal for Architecture in America* 3 (1987), but declined.

37. On the Finley Mortuary, see Clausen, *Spiritual Space*, 42–45.

38. Special Education Committee, AIA, letter to A. E. Doyle & Associate, 31 January 1938; *Oregonian*, 13 March 1938; *New York Times*, 20 April 1938; *Pacific Builder & Engineer*, 15 October 1938.

39. Hitchcock, "An Eastern Critic Looks at Western Architecture," 21. On regionalism, see note 36 above and chapters 4 and 7 below.

4 Regional Modernism: The Houses

1. Unidentified newspaper clipping (*Oregonian*?), 11 July 1935 (Belluschi files).

2. *Oregonian*, 6 May 1934.

3. Brown, "The New Regionalism in America," 41.

4. On Emerson and the transcendentalist tradition, see Albanese, *Nature Religion in America*, chapter 3. My special thanks to Grace Greene for bringing this work to my attention. See also Kuspit, "Regionalism Reconsidered," on regionalism in art and its revival.

5. Riley, *The International Style* (1992), 85.

6. Mock, *Built in USA: Since 1932* (1945), 124–125; see also Kuspit, "Regionalism Reconsidered," 66.

7. On the Northwest painters, see Johns, *Modern Art from the Pacific Northwest*, especially 1–2, and Kingsbury, *Northwest Traditions*.

8. *Oregonian*, 18 March 1934; *Oregonian*, 6 May 1934; Kuspit, "Regionalism Reconsidered," 65.

9. *Oregonian Sunday Journal*, 22 April 1934; *Oregonian*, 15 April 1934.

10. Drawings signed and dated by Belluschi (Belluschi Collection, Syracuse). Belluschi sold the Council Crest house in 1944 to Jed Davidson, for whom he later did some remodeling. The house has since changed owners and been substantially altered.

11. *Oregonian*, 29 May 1939.

12. The projected cost was $3,900; actual cost was $4,100. According to an article in the *Architectural Forum* (see following note), the final cost was $5,100, which may have included landscaping and furnishings. Exteriors were treated with iron chloride.

13. *Architectural Record*, February 1939, 56–58; *Oregonian*, 28 May 1939; *Architect & Engineer*, May 1939, 27; *Architectural Forum*, October 1939, 330.

14. "One Hundred One New Houses," *Architectural Forum*, October 1939, 330.

15. Preliminary sketch, Watzek House, 19 December 1936 (Belluschi Collection, Syracuse); Yeon to Belluschi, 14 October 1944 (Belluschi files); interview, Yeon/MLC, 29 May 1987.

16. Wyman Bear did the working drawings, George Kotchik, who had just joined the office, did the mechanical drawings, and Frank Allen did the detailing. Taped interview, Frank Allen/MLC, Portland, 16 November 1986.

17. Yeon letter to Belluschi, October 1944 (Belluschi files); taped interviews, Kotchik, Allen, Belluschi, Yeon/MLC, 1986–1989.

18. Yeon letter to Belluschi, October 1944 (Belluschi files); Watzek correspondence (Belluschi Collection, Syracuse).

19. "A Country House in the Oregon Hills," *Architectural Record,* December 1940, 57–61.

20. Watzek correspondence (Belluschi Collection, Syracuse).

21. John Yeon, lecture, University of Washington, May 1986; interview, Yeon/MLC, 29 May 1987. My thanks to Lucy Sloman for her generosity in passing on her notes of the lecture, which I was unable to attend.

22. Belluschi letter to Elisabeth Kendall, 16 November 1940 (Belluschi Collection, Syracuse); Yeon letter to Belluschi, October 1944; Belluschi unmailed letter to Yeon (Belluschi files); Watzek correspondence (Belluschi Collection, Syracuse).

23. Fitch, *American Building,* fig. 149. All drawings, including Yeon's preliminary sketch for the Watzek House, are in the Belluschi Collection at Syracuse.

    Yeon's fears of Belluschi's assuming credit for the Watzek design were well founded, as the correspondence from Corinne Rogers, a graduate student in the library school at Pratt who was compiling a bibliography of homes by modern architects, documents. In 1953 she wrote Belluschi asking for clarification of the designer of Council Crest house; finding that it was credited to A. E. Doyle & Associate, she wondered if in fact he was responsible for it. Belluschi's reply was unambiguous: "I was responsible for all designs of A. E. Doyle & Associate after Mr. Doyle's death, which was in 1928; the name of the firm was not changed to mine until 1943." (Corinne Rogers letter to Belluschi, 9 February 1953; Belluschi letter to Rogers, 12 February 1953, Belluschi files.)

24. The same contractor, Burt Smith, was also used in both cases. Taped interview, Frank Allen/MLC, 16 November 1986.

25. Taped interview, PB/MLC, 26 January 1985.

26. At one point, Belluschi accompanied Sutor to San Francisco to select furnishings for the house at Gumps, an exclusive store specializing in fine imported Oriental ware.

27. Drawings, Sutor House (Belluschi Collection, Syracuse).

28. On the Irimoya roof type, see Drexler, *The Architecture of Japan,* 45.

29. Most pertinent might have been Wright's 1931 *Modern Architecture,* a copy of which Belluschi possessed. He was also familiar with the *Autobiography,* although according to him he read it only selectively.

30. Jiro Harada's lectures were published as *The Lesson of Japanese Architecture* in 1936, reprinted in 1954. The book was reviewed in the *Architectural Forum* immediately after its initial publication. Belluschi had a copy of the 1936 edition in his personal library, along with numerous other publications on Japanese architecture and landscaping, long before interest in them became fashionable nationally. His interest, shared by others among his West Coast contemporaries, was in the fit of Japanese architecture within the natural landscape, as well as its economy of means; later, the focus was more on its structure, and on the analogies between timber construction and modern structures of reinforced concrete and steel. Among the books in Belluschi's collection dealing with both Japanese architecture and landscaping was Tetsuro Yoshida, *Das japanische Wohnhaus,* 1935 (reviewed in the *Forum,* January 1936), a book Bruno Taut much admired, and Samuel Newsom's *Japanese Garden Construction,* 1939. The latter served as the point of departure for much of Belluschi's work on the Sutor House, Cottage Grove Presbyterian Church, and others; see text below.

31. Harada, *Lesson of Japanese Architecture,* 10.

32. Although Belluschi later repeatedly denied the influence of barns, according to Walter Creese he had at least at one point several fine photographs of Oregon barns by the photographer Ray Atkeson tacked up in the office. My thanks to Creese for this note. See also Stubblebine, *Northwest Architecture of Pietro Belluschi,* 4–5.

33. Hitchcock, "An Eastern Critic Looks at Western Architecture," 21.

34. The Northwest Home Show, sponsored by the Federal Housing Administration, Portland Realty Board, and *Oregonian,* was aimed at spurring growth in the home building industry. Though the office was not paid for the work, Belluschi was shrewd enough to see it as an opportunity to break into the growing market for the low- or moderate-cost house.

35. Belluschi, typewritten description of projects, dated 9 May 1942 (*Progressive Architecture* file, Belluschi Collection, Syracuse).

36. Antonin Raymond, *Architectural Details* (1937), especially plates 12, 39, and 61; Belluschi letter ordering a copy, 15 March 1939 (1930s correspondence, Belluschi Collection, Syracuse).

37. "Mairea, House in Noormarkku; Workers' Houses and Pulp Mill in Sunila," *Architectural Forum,* June 1940, 401–403, 406–409; Belluschi letter requesting additional copies (Belluschi Collection, Syracuse).

38. Stubblebine, *Northwest Architecture of Pietro Belluschi,* 72–73.

39. *Architectural Forum,* May 1936, 390.

40. Typed record of costs compiled by Marjorie Belluschi (Belluschi files).

41. Yeon letter to Belluschi, October 1944 (Belluschi files).

42. *Oregonian,* 14 September 1941.

43. *Oregon Journal,* 23 February 1941; 25 February 1941.

44. *Oregon Journal,* 28 February 1941.

45. Katherine Morrison Ford, "Modern Is Regional."

46. *Sunset Magazine,* June 1941. John Yeon had made the same point in his Portland Art Museum lecture almost a decade earlier.

47. Kenneth Reid of *Pencil Points* letter to Belluschi, 4 June 1941 (*Progressive Architecture* file, Belluschi Collection, Syracuse).

48. Charles Magruder, managing editor, *Pencil Points,* letter to Belluschi, 4 August 1941 (*Progressive Architecture* file, Belluschi Collection, Syracuse). See also the letter of George Sanderson of *Architectural Record* to Belluschi, 22 August 1941, on their eagerness to publish the St. Thomas More church (*Architectural Record* file, Belluschi Collection, Syracuse).

49. Taped interview, Walter Gordon/MLC, Portland, 10 January 1987.

50. Taped interview, George Kotchik/MLC, 7 April 1987; interviews with Frank Allen, Mary Alice Hutchins, Marge Wintermute, 1986–1987.

51. Taped interview, Gordon/MLC, 10 January 1987.

52. Smithsonian interviews, Archives of American Art, 1983, 25. Some measure of this success is indicated by the documents Belluschi filed with the Navy Department, Washington, D.C., in 1943 in his application for war-related work. The figures he cited in response to the request for a financial record of the last five years are highly revealing:

1936: $126,162
1937: $365,000
1938: $1,183,572 [Finley Mortuary; Watzek House]
1939: $592,900
1940: $964,400
1941: $728,650
1942: $15,341,520 [Bagley Downs and McLoughlin Heights shopping centers; war industry workers housing for Housing Authority of Vancouver and Housing Authority of Portland; Pocatello Air Base Hospital, Pocatello, Idaho; series of hospitals, barracks, a Japanese Relocation Center, Reconsignment Depot, and so on, for U.S. Army Engineers]
1943: $1,855,000 (first six months only)

Belluschi listed 40 ongoing projects at the time of application. (Form AE-1, C&L Division, Navy Department, Bureau of Yards & Docks, Washington, D.C.; 1940s correspondence, Belluschi files.)

53. Smithsonian interviews, 108.

54. Architectural Record, November 1942, 66–67; Mock, Built in USA: Since 1932, 106–107.

55. Taped interviews, Walter Gordon/MLC, Newport, Oregon, 10 January 1987; Elisabeth K. Thompson/MLC, Berkeley, 6 July 1986; Richard Ritz/MLC, Portland, 7 January 1987.

56. The name "A. E. Doyle & Associate" was often used interchangably with "A. E. Doyle & Associates," especially after the 1935 restructuring.

57. Oregon Journal, 1 March 1942; Daily Journal of Commerce, Portland, 2 March 1942. Belluschi evidently received a substantial inheritance around this time, which helped him to buy out the firm as well as acquire the Jefferson St. building. Taped interview, George Kotchik/MLC, Portland, 7 April 1987.

58. Walter Gordon letter to MLC, 20 March 1987.

59. Oregon State Law, Sect. 68–304, amendment March 1935, Oregon Code 1930. My thanks to Portland lawyer D. Ormseth for his help in securing this information.

60. William Hennesey, architect, editor, American Home, letter to Belluschi, 20 September 1944 (American Home file, Belluschi Collection, Syracuse).

61. Douglas Haskell letter to Belluschi, 21 September 1944 (Architectural Record file, Belluschi Collection, Syracuse).

62. George Nelson letter to Belluschi, 18 May 1944 (Architectural Forum, Belluschi Collection, Syracuse).

63. Henry Wright letter to Belluschi, 18 October 1944 (Architectural Forum file, Belluschi Collection, Syracuse).

64. The McLoughlin Heights Shopping Center was credited to Belluschi, the Watzek House to A. E. Doyle, with John Yeon as designer. It was Yeon's concern that he receive credit here that led to the heated exchange of letters among Yeon, Belluschi, and MoMA in 1944 (Belluschi files; Watzek correspondence, Belluschi Collection, Syracuse).

65. Architectural Forum, May 1944.

66. Belluschi's involvement in the postwar planning and redevelopment of Portland, including his criticisms of the Moses report of 1941–1942, merits more discussion; for want of space, it is only touched on here.

67. MacColl, Growth of a City, 554, 609ff.

68. Taped interview, Frank Allen/MLC, Portland, 6 December 1986.

69. One of its fervent admirers was the photographer Roger Sturtevant, who also found it the most difficult of Belluschi houses to photograph.

70. Belluschi letter to John Entenza, editor of California Arts + Architecture, in response to Entenza's request for any new material on postwar projects "and/or any other projects you feel would be of interest," 2 January 1945 (Architectural Press file, Belluschi Collection, Syracuse).

71. Taped interviews, Frank Allen/MLC, Portland; Henry Klein/MLC, Mt. Vernon, Washington; Ken Richardson/MLC, Seattle.

72. California Arts + Architecture, January 1945; Architectural Forum, May 1951; Vitrum, March 1953; Stubblebine, Northwest Architecture of Pietro Belluschi, 92–95; Arts + Architecture, no. 4, 1985.

73. The Moore House, on a particularly restricted site in the hills above Portland, demanded a compact, efficient plan and was one Belluschi himself was particularly proud of; other houses of this time include the two Wilson houses on the Deschutes River in eastern Oregon, a hot dry desert climate very different from that he was used to in the Portland area. Again, they merit more discussion than can be given here.

74. House & Garden, March 1949, 105.

75. Saturday Evening Post, March 1949, 105ff.

76. Saturday Evening Post, March 1949, 105; draft of article for House & Garden, undated but circa 1950 (Belluschi files).

77. Typed record of costs compiled by Marjorie Belluschi (Belluschi files). The figure quoted in Time, 15 August 1949, 60, was $60,000.

78. Progressive Architecture, June 1949, 61–66; New York Times, 30 October 1949; House & Garden, March 1949, 105–109; Architectural Review, London, October 1951, 227; Interiors, August 1949, 81; Time, 15 August 1949, 60; Saturday Evening Post, March 1949, 105.

79. The Radditz House was unpublished. The client, who worked for a local plywood company, supplied the materials and much of the labor; accurate costs are thus difficult to gauge.

80. Published in Simon, Your Solar House (1947), 122–123.

81. Paxton, editor of Life, letter to Belluschi, 11 October 1945 (Belluschi Collection, Syracuse).

82. Life, 28 April 1947, 83–87; Life, 6 October 1958, 88ff. On Eichler houses, see Wright, Building the Dream, 248–251.

83. Taped interview, PB/MLC, 4 February 1987. The Seaside Apartments project, though not built, was published in Architectural Record, May 1946, 77–79.

5 Modernism versus Tradition: The Churches

1. Clausen, *Spiritual Space,* 8. Because much of the material on Belluschi's churches and philosophy of church design is discussed in that book, my treatment of it here is brief.

2. On the Riverview Chapel, a small Tudoresque brick building in keeping with the character of the cemetery setting built in 1939–1940, see Clausen, *Spiritual Space,* 46–47.

3. On the Finley Mortuary, see Clausen, *Spiritual Space,* 12, 42–45, and chapter 3, above.

4. St. Paul, Karuizawa, *Architectural Record,* January 1936, 32–36. Belluschi also acquired Raymond's book *Architectural Details* in March 1939, just as he began the design of St. Thomas More. See Clausen, *Spiritual Space,* 15, and chapter 4, above.

5. Mircea Eliade, *The Sacred and the Profane* especially the introduction and chapter 1. Eliade's book informs generally this entire chapter.

6. "Designed by Pietro Belluschi," *New Pencil Points [Progressive Architecture],* December 1942, 59–75; Christ-Janer and Foley, *Modern Church Architecture,* 37–39.

7. *New Pencil Points [Progressive Architecture],* July 1942, 59—63. The church was also published in *Western Building,* April 1942; *Liturgical Arts,* May 1949, 92–93; Stubblebine, *Northwest Architecture of Pietro Belluschi,* 92–103; Belluschi, "The Churches Go Modern," *Saturday Evening Post,* 4 October 1958; Hudnut, "The Church in a Modern World," *Architectural Forum,* December 1958; Christ-Janer and Foley, *Modern Church Architecture,* 37–39. See also Clausen, *Spiritual Space,* 14–15, 48–51. St. Thomas More was later enlarged, with a transept and choir and then a school building added: *Liturgical Arts,* February 1953, 51; *Architectural Record,* March 1960, 32–33.

8. *Progressive Architecture,* August 1947, 60–61. See also Clausen, *Spiritual Space,* 16, 53–54.

9. Reimers & Jolivette (contractors) letter to Belluschi, 24 September 1949 (St. Philip Neri file, Belluschi Collection, Syracuse).

10. Reimers & Jolivette correspondence with Belluschi, 1949–1950 (St. Philip Neri file, Belluschi Collection, Syracuse).

11. Walter Gordon letter to MLC, 15 October 1988. See, for example, the Bryggman Chapel, Finland, *Architectural Forum,* December 1949, 57–59; Madonna of the Poor, Via Osteno, Milan, in Kidder Smith, *The New Churches of Europe,* 190–193.

12. On Saarinen's Christ Church Lutheran, Minneapolis, see Christ-Janer and Foley, *Modern Church Architecture,* 146.

13. Taped interview, PB/MLC, 30 June 1992. The interior of the church has since been modified and the baldachino replaced.

14. The exteriors were of a buff brick that was not, according to the correspondence, of Belluschi's choice. The bonding pattern, too, was more obtrusive than was characteristic. Many of these design decisions were made after he moved east.

15. Taped interviews, Frank Allen/MLC, 16 November 1986; 6 December 1986; Ken Richardson/MLC. See also Clausen, *Spiritual Space,* 59–63.

16. See, for example, Raymond, *Architectural Details,* pl. 16.

17. Taped interview, Frank Allen/MLC, 11 August 1988.

18. Although Belluschi is often said to have been the first to use glulams, they had in fact been around for some time. Their use only became widespread, however, after World War II. See Stalnaker and Harris, *Structural Design in Wood,* 152. Bernard Maybeck had of course also used them in Hearst Hall on the University of California campus at the turn of the century. See Cardwell, *Bernard Maybeck, Artisan, Architect, Artist,* 46–48. On the postwar drive to be "first," see Clausen, "Belluschi and the Equitable Building," 125–126.

19. Christ-Janer and Foley, *Modern Church Architecture,* 140–141.

20. Taped interview, Frank Allen/MLC, 11 August 1988.

21. The grooved decking and glass blocks were used at the suggestion of Frank Allen, who had been trained at Portland Polytechnic, a school for the manual arts, and joined the Doyle firm as office boy in the early years of the Depression. Grooved decking subsequently became a formula in Belluschi's churches.

22. Belluschi, notes, Central Lutheran dedication brochure (Belluschi files).

23. *Architectural Forum,* December 1951, 166. These figures were typically supplied by the architect himself and are not always consistent. They should be used as a rough gauge for comparative purposes only.

24. "The Church at Cottage Grove," *Presbyterian Life* (Dayton, Ohio), 17 September 1955, 20–23.

25. Christ-Janer and Foley, *Modern Church Architecture,* 213–214.

26. Ibid., 214.

27. Taped interview, PB/MLC, 9 December 1986.

28. Taped interview, Ken Richardson/MLC, 30 December 1986.

29. On Tillich and his connection with Belluschi, see Clausen, *Spiritual Space,* 24–26.

30. Richard Neutra letter to Belluschi, 11 March 1953 (Belluschi files). This was a letter Belluschi made innumerable copies of and distributed widely. It should be noted that at the time Neutra issued this praise, he was hoping for work with the State Department on the design of foreign embassy buildings, for which Belluschi was one of the key advisors. See chapter 7, below.

31. Taped interview, Robert Frasca/MLC, 6 December 1986, and other interviews.

32. As early as June 1945, Kenneth Storwell of the *Architectural Record* wrote Belluschi soliciting any work he might have on religious architecture, then several months later *Progressive Architecture* contacted him about publishing the Junior Chapel, First Methodist Church, Portland. In November the editor of the Architectural Book Division of Reinhold Publishing Company, describing Belluschi as "the ideal man" for the job, asked him to author a book on churches. It was a book Belluschi would have liked to do, but he gave up the idea for want of time. Requests for anything he might have to contribute on church architecture continued to pour in throughout 1947–1950. A *Forum* special issue on churches in December 1949 quoted Belluschi at length on his philosophy of church design, noting that he had recently designed eight churches, four of which were Protestant, four Roman Catho-

lic. They were featured separately in a later issue (Belluschi Collection, Syracuse).

On the boom in church architecture in the postwar era, see *Architectural Forum,* July 1949, 9, and Clausen, *Spiritual Space,* 21ff.

6 The Equitable Building and the Postwar Boom

1. Hosfield, "A Study of the Architecture of Pietro Belluschi" (M. Arch. thesis, University of Oregon, 1960), 50. Hosfield's figures were based on documentation in the B/SOM office before the material was shipped to the Arents Research Library, Syracuse, and compiled with the help of Richard Ritz, one of the architects in the Belluschi office who remained with the practice after Belluschi sold it to SOM and left for MIT. The thesis was conducted under the direction of Marion Dean Ross of the University of Oregon, who was a great admirer of Belluschi's work.

2. Belluschi memoirs, 90; taped interview, PB/MLC, 28 July 1988; MacColl, *Growth of a City,* 562–563. For a fuller discussion of the Equitable Building, see Clausen, "Belluschi and the Equitable Building in History."

3. "New Buildings for 194X," *Architectural Forum,* May 1943, 69; Clausen, "Belluschi and the Equitable Building," 112–113.

4. "New Buildings for 194X," 108–111. On the Ketchum project, see "Store Block," *Architectural Forum,* October 1940, 294.

5. "Offices for Northwest Airlines," *Progressive Architecture–Pencil Points,* October 1943, 71; Clausen, "Belluschi and the Equitable Building," 115–116.

6. Belluschi letter to Cake, 7 February 1945 (Equitable file, Belluschi Collection, Syracuse).

7. Documents, Equitable file, Belluschi Collection, Syracuse.

8. Taped interview, PB/MLC, 29 July 1988; Belluschi memoirs, 91; taped interviews, Richard Ritz/MLC, 7 January 1987; Frank Allen/MLC, 16 November 1986.

9. Belluschi, "Notes on the New Equitable Building," typescript, 10 January 1946 (Belluschi files).

10. Taped interview, PB/MLC, 19 July 1985; documents, Equitable file, Belluschi Collection, Syracuse.

11. Belluschi to MLC, 24 February 1986.

12. "Products and Practice: The Heat Pump," *Architectural Forum,* November 1946, 161–164; "Office Building Initiates Prefabricated Aluminum Facing," *Architectural Forum,* April 1947, 101; "Equitable Builds a Leader," *Architectural Forum,* September 1948, 98.

13. "Equitable Builds a Leader," 105.

14. Libbey-Owens-Ford letter to Belluschi, 7 March 1947 (Equitable file, Belluschi Collection, Syracuse).

15. Correspondence, Pittsburgh Plate Glass and Belluschi, April 1946 (Equitable file, Belluschi Collection, Syracuse).

16. *Architectural Forum,* May 1949, 12.

17. Calder letter to Belluschi, 13 March 1947 (Belluschi files); Calder exhibition, MoMA, New York, 1943–1944; *Architectural Forum,* January 1944, 4; taped interview, Walter Gordon/MLC, Portland, 3 September 1988.

18. Taped interview, Walter Gordon/MLC, Portland, 3 September 1988. The lobby was subsequently remodeled and the mural destroyed. It was restored under Belluschi's supervision in the late 1980s by Soderstrom Architects of Portland, with a new Belluschi mural, and published in *Progressive Architecture,* April 1989, 90–93. Belluschi's 1989 mural is reproduced in Clausen, "Belluschi and the Equitable Building," 128.

19. Taped interviews, Ken Richardson/MLC, 30 December 1986; Richard Ritz/MLC, 12 January 1987; PB/MLC, 13 October 1990. See also Clausen, "Belluschi and the Equitable Building," 122–124; and Rowe, "Chicago Frame," which includes the Equitable Building.

20. Documents, Equitable file, Belluschi Collection, Syracuse.

21. *Progressive Architecture,* January 1950, 50; Clausen, "Belluschi and the Equitable Building," 125–126.

22. "Equitable Builds a Leader," 98; *Progressive Architecture,* January 1950, 49ff; "One Hundred Years of Significant Building: Office Buildings," *Architectural Record,* June 1956, 147ff; Clausen, "Belluschi and the Equitable Building," 127–128, which dis-

cusses also the subsequent waning of the Equitable's fame.

23. "New Oregonian Building Specially Planned," *Oregonian,* 27 April 1947; *Masco News,* Masons Supply Co., Portland, July 1948.

24. *Oregonian,* 29 September 1946; taped interview, Ken Richardson/MLC, 20 December 1986. The building, completed in 1948 at a cost of $4 million, twice the original estimate, is still fully operational today, having undergone no major modifications. It was illustrated in "The Architect and His Community," *Progressive Architecture,* February 1949, 43–47. On the role of the press in the making of history, see Clausen, "Belluschi and the Equitable Building," or more generally, Williamson, *American Architects and the Mechanics of Fame,* especially 176ff. and 207ff.

25. A sampling: [Carl Greve Jewelry Store], *Architectural Forum,* May 1948, 52; [Nordstrom Shoe Store], *Architectural Forum,* July 1950, 65; [Cedar Hills Shopping Center, commissioned in 1948], *Progressive Architecture,* March 1957 (where it won a *PA* citation). See also Louis Parnes, *Planning Stores That Pay: Organic Design and Layout* (1948), a standard text on store design in the late 1940s, which includes several Belluschi buildings.

26. "Studio for a Photographer," *Progressive Architecture,* February 1949, 50–51.

27. Documents, Edris Morrison Studio file, Belluschi Collection, Syracuse.

28. *Sunday Oregon Journal,* 26 September 1948; taped interviews, Mary Alice Hutchins/George Wallace/MLC; Frank Allen/MLC, 1987–1988.

29. "Drive-In Restaurant near Jantzen Beach, Oregon," *Progressive Architecture,* June 1947, 61–62. Waddle's is still in use today, though there has been considerable remodeling, especially of the sign.

The Bow Herbert Highway Restaurant, another Belluschi project of 1945, was equally revealing of the times. The Chicago developer Bow Herbert, of the Scientific Management Company, asked him to design a prototype for a restaurant chain to be built throughout the West Coast and eventually the nation. The job was small but potentially very lucrative. It remained a project only.

Belluschi letter to Herbert, 20 August 1945 (Belluschi Collection, Syracuse).

30. Among Belluschi's educational buildings in the Portland area are the Willamette University men's dormitory (1945–1948); Catlin School Gymnasium, Westover Terrace (1945–1947), published in *Progressive Architecture,* February 1949; and the Sacred Heart Parish School in Oswego, 1949, which was completed by SOM.

31. A. E. Doyle & Associate [Belluschi] letter to Dexter Keezer, president of Reed College, 3 September 1936 (Belluschi Collection, Syracuse).

32. *Oregonian,* 20 March 1950.

33. *Pacific Parade Magazine, Sunday Journal,* Portland, 16 September 1945.

34. Taped interviews, PB/MLC, 4 February 1987; 17 December 1986.

35. Although in interviews later Belluschi remembered little of the science building and thought SOM was wholly responsible, he evidently was involved, at least on some level, as documents at Syracuse include a bill he sent SOM for $8,694 for work on the physics wing and $4,300 on the biology wing (correspondence, Early West Coast Work file, Belluschi Collection, Syracuse).

36. [Oregon State Mental Hospital, receiving and treatment unit], *Architectural Record,* October 1950. The state commissioned the Doyle office to add the unit to the state hospital in 1941; the job was held up because of the war, after which plans changed and the capacity doubled. The building was not completed until 1948. Though it was thoroughly modern in design, the scale and choice of materials were determined by the existing buildings, which were largely Victorian. Belluschi letter to Emerson Goble, managing editor of the *Record,* 23 August 1950 (Belluschi Collection, Syracuse). Belluschi was also responsible for a number of hospitals in Oregon, Washington, and Idaho built during the war and commissioned by the U.S. Government.

37. *Capital Journal,* Salem, 22 January 1949.

38. *Capital Journal,* 25 January 1949.

39. Editorial column, *Capital Journal,* 8 September 1949. "Marbleized barns" was a reference to the several banks Belluschi had recently done in Salem.

40. Sprague House, Santiam River, Oregon, 1944–1947; Sprague's defense of Belluschi is in the *Stateman,* 20 January 1950.

41. Interview, Richard Ritz/MLC, Portland, 7 January 1987. Belluschi remained owner of the Jefferson Street building, as well as several other investment properties in Oregon, after he moved to MIT. He rented the building to SOM when they joined forces in 1951; after SOM moved to its own quarters in the early 1960s, he rented it to Joachim Grube, with whom he eventually associated for a series of late churches. On Belluschi's work with Grube, see Clausen, *Spiritual Space.*

42. Belluschi cited a figure of 40 in Paul Heyer, *Architects on Architecture* (1966, revised ed. 1978), which apparently included the office's outside consultants. *Progressive Architecture* reported a high of 22 staff members in its article on the Belluschi office (February 1949, 40–41).

43. Interview, Henry Klein/MLC, Mt. Vernon, Washington, 12 December 1986; Gordon, "The Architecture of Pietro Belluschi," 32ff.

44. Smithsonian interviews, 38. Henry Klein was one of the newcomers to the office in the late 1940s from outside the region. Born in Germany and trained at Cornell, he was drawn to the region by the mystique of the Northwest painters as well as Belluschi's fame; he came to Portland specifically to work with Belluschi. Interview, Klein/MLC, Mt. Vernon, Washington, 12 December 1986.

45. Interviews, Walter Gordon/MLC, 31 May 1987; Henry Klein/MLC, 12 December 1986; Walter Gordon/MLC, 3 September 1988. See also Pickens, "Contemporary Regional Architecture," *AIA Journal,* September 1946, 114.

46. *Progressive Architecture,* February 1949, 40. By all of the criteria suggested by Blau, *Architects and Firms: A Sociological Perspective on Architectural Practice,* 92ff.— opinion of peers, recognition in the national press, number of awards received—Belluschi was a model of success. See also Williamson, *American Architects and the Mechanics of Fame,* on the closely related issue of measuring fame.

For a series of recent discussions reflecting widespread interest in the practice of architecture in general, see Gutman, *Architectural Practice: A Critical View* (1988), and Cuff, *Architecture: The Story of Practice* (1991).

47. Taped interview, Kotchik/MLC, Portland, 7 April 1987.

48. Interview, Richard Ritz/MLC, Portland, 7 January 1987.

49. Belluschi's perspective sketch, "House for Mme Belluschi, Easter 1948" (Belluschi files).

50. *University of Washington Daily,* Seattle, 14 May 1948.

51. Taped interviews, John Storrs/MLC, 13 May 1988; Richard Ritz/MLC, 7 January 1987; Henry Klein/MLC, 12 December 1986; Robert Frasca/MLC, 6 December 1986.

52. On regional biases in the press, see Williamson, *American Architects and the Mechanics of Fame,* 209.

53. Taped interviews, Elisabeth K. Thompson/MLC, Berkeley, 1986–1987.

54. Taped interview, PB/MLC, 13 May 1988.

55. Blake obituary note on Haskell, *AIA Journal,* September 1979, 122, 124; taped interview, PB/MLC, 13 May 1988. For background on Haskell's views, especially of the early years, see "Douglas Haskell and the Criticism of International Modernism," in Wilson and Robinson, *Modern Architecture in America,* 165–183. My thanks to Walter Creese for calling this essay to my attention.

56. Taped interviews, Elisabeth K. Thompson/MLC, Berkeley, 18 June 1986; John Storrs/MLC, Portland; Henry Klein/MLC, Mt. Vernon; William Weber of SOM/MLC, San Francisco, 1986–1987. On the two branches of modernism, see (as useful background) Henry-Russell Hitchcock, *Modern Architecture* (1929), where he discusses the American current of Wright, Sullivan, and the Chicago School as distinguished from the Europeanists, and notes the bias of New York and other East Coast cities toward France and the Beaux-Arts ideal; Bruno Zevi, *Towards an Organic Architecture* (1950); and Andrea O. Dean, *Bruno Zevi on Modern Architecture* (1983). J. M. Richards, *An Introduction to Modern Architecture* (1st ed. 1940; revised 1953 and 1956), especially 103–109, sees the phenomenon from a very different perspective in time.

57. Presentation of PA National Awards, 6 June 1949 (*Progressive Architecture* file, Belluschi Collection, Syracuse).

58. Wurster, *AIA Journal*, July 1948, 30ff.

59. Mumford, "Skyline," *New Yorker*, 11 October 1947. It was in this essay that Mumford inadvertently described West Coast regionalism solely in terms of the Bay Area style, narrowing its definition and catalyzing much of the discussion about "styles" at the MoMA symposium in 1948. *MoMA Bulletin* 15, no. 3 (Spring 1948). For a reflection of the now commonplace misconception of early modernism in America, and its Eurocentric bias and identification in solely Californian terms, see Michael Glickman, review of *Arts + Architecture: The Entenza Years*, edited by Barbara Goldstein, in *Blueprint*, April 1991, 56–57.

60. Belluschi letter to Arthur McVoy, 14 April 1947 (AIA file #2, Belluschi Collection, Syracuse).

61. Susan Comfort letter to Belluschi, 18 August 1948 (AIA file, Belluschi Collection, Syracuse); taped interview, PB/MLC, 7 November 1983.

62. *AIA Journal*, August 1948, 59–60.

63. See E. Cooper, "Young Architects Revolt against Staid Conservative AIA," *New York Times*, 11 March 1949, 45.

64. *Architectural Forum*, April 1949, 17; *Architectural Record*, April 1949, 7.

65. Pickens, "Contemporary Regional Architecture," *AIA Journal*, September 1947, 114; *New York Times*, 14 October 1948.

66. On the West Coast as a leading force in regionalism, see Belluschi, Portland Art Museum talk, 1941, quoted in *Architectural Record*, April 1953. This view was also held internationally. See, for example, the Australian exhibition in which U.S. representatives were Belluschi, Wurster, and others from the West Coast. Belluschi, Wurster, Dinwiddie, and Kump were also among those Americans asked to participate in a Pan American exhibition on contemporary architecture in the United States sponsored by the Congreso Panamericano de Arquitectos at this time. This development was, of course, subsequently arrested by East Coast, European-inspired trends in the U.S.; see text below.

67. Belluschi memoirs, 64.

68. *AIA Journal*, November 1950, 22; *AIA Memo-Newsletter*, August 1953, 2.

69. Belluschi memoirs, 64.

70. Taped interview, James Killian/MLC, Boston, 18 September 1987.

71. Killian, *The Education of a College President*, 124; taped interview, Killian/MLC, Boston, 18 September 1987.

72. Belluschi's starting salary at MIT in 1951 was $15,500. According to what he told reporters in 1980, he had been making ten times that in Portland before he left. Belluschi interview, *Willamette Week*, 17 May 1980.

73. William Wurster letter to Belluschi, 10 August 1950 (Belluschi files).

74. Belluschi, in *Oregonian*, 12 September 1950.

75. *Oregon Journal*, 2 November 1950.

76. *Oregonian*, 2 November 1950.

77. The legal haranguing over finances, office responsibility, liability issues, and particularly the handling of a $65,000 loan Belluschi took out to meet the payroll the month he left turned nasty, and negotiations broke down. Belluschi subsequently abandoned the idea of continuing the office, and began looking for other solutions. Taped interviews, PB/MLC.

78. Taped interviews, Richard Ritz/MLC, Portland, 7 January 1987; PB/MLC, 4 February 1987.

79. Taped interview, David Pugh of SOM/MLC, Portland, 6 April 1987.

80. Taped interviews, PB/MLC, 16 January 1988; 29 July 1988; Ritz/MLC, 7 January 1987.

81. Belluschi, convocation speech, *Reed College Bulletin*, 1951; "Architecture and Society," *AIA Journal*, February 1951, 85–89; *Architectural Record*, February 1951.

7 MIT, Boston, and Change in Practice

1. When Belluschi moved east, most of the books in the Doyle library remained in the SOM office until they were claimed by Doyle's grandson, George McMath, who subsequently sold them to Reed College. Belluschi's own library consisted largely of Frank Lloyd Wright, books on Japanese architecture, contemporary Danish, Swiss, and Italian work (including the Estampi series), books on churches and abbeys, Le Corbusier, Breuer, Niemeyer and other new work in South America (e.g., *Brazil Builds*), plus a number of other older classics such as Hitchcock's *Painting Toward Architecture* (1948). Relatively modest at first, his collection grew to some 3,000 volumes by the time he left Boston, at which time he sold it, retaining only his favorites. After his return to Portland his collection began growing again and by the 1980s was substantial. Taped interview, PB/MLC, 15 December 1986; list of items in Belluschi library, Belluschi Collection, Syracuse.

2. Taped interviews, Peter Belluschi/MLC, Seattle, 31 July 1989; George Wallace/MLC, Stayton, Oregon, 31 May 1987.

3. Taped interviews, Elisabeth K. Thompson/MLC, Berkeley, 1987–1987; Peter Belluschi/MLC, Seattle, 31 July 1989; Tony Belluschi/MLC, Portland, 8 September 1990; Lawrence Anderson/MLC, Lincoln, Massachusetts, 2 April 1989; Gyorgy Kepes/MLC, Cambridge, 29 March 198; Eduardo Catalano/MLC, 29 March 1989.

4. Margaret Henderson Floyd, "Ralph Rapson: Modernism Implemented at MIT," in Floyd, *Architectural Education and Boston*, 92; taped interviews, Lawrence Anderson/MLC, Lincoln, Massachusetts, 1987.

5. *Boston Herald*, 20 May 1951.

6. *Architecture*, March 1987, 17.

7. Taped interview, James Killian/MLC, Cambridge, 18 September 1987. Killian was succeeded by Julius Stratton, an equally strong Belluschi supporter, in 1957. Dr. Killian and I met just several months before he died.

8. Taped interview, Killian/MLC, 18 September 1987. Belluschi was virtually unmentioned in Floyd, *Architectural Education and Boston*, again suggesting that his impact on the architecture department and its curriculum was minimal.

9. Lawrence B. Anderson, "Architectural Education MIT: The 1930s and After," in Floyd, *Architectural Education and Boston*, 87.

10. Belluschi address on architectural education, 20 November 1951, MIT. Incomplete typed manuscript (Speeches, Belluschi Collection, Syracuse).

11. Interviews, Lawrence Anderson/MLC, Lincoln, Massachusetts, 1987; Anderson, "Architectural Education MIT," 87–90. See also Gutman, *Architectural Practice*; Blau, *Archi-*

tects and Firms; and Cuff, Architecture: The Story of Practice.

12. Edward Gunts, "The Fountainhead at 50," Architecture, May 1993, 35–37; Michael Crosbie, editorial, Progressive Architecture, April 1993, 7; Berkeley, Architecture: A Place for Women, xxii, 238; Clausen, "Belluschi and the Equitable Building in History"; Williamson, American Architects and the Mechanics of Fame, 226. Still more recently, see Stephen Kliment's editorial, Architectural Record, August 1993, 9.

13. A not so subtle example of this was the envelope bearing as a return address Belluschi's portrait and the inscription "Arise and Build," a messianic message relating to his church and synagogue work at the time. See also the discussion of St. Mary's Cathedral, where this messianic view—reinforced by Irving Stone's best-selling novel The Agony and the Ecstasy, a fictionalized account of Michelangelo's heroic struggles against the pope in the building of St. Peter's published in 1961—was carried to new heights, in Clausen, Spiritual Space, 126–135.

14. Belluschi letter to Killian, 13 June 1952 (MIT. Office of the President, 1930–1959, AC4. Institute Archives and Special Collections, MIT Libraries).

15. Architectural Record, August 1955, 16ff.

16. Smithsonian interviews, 37; taped interview, PB/MLC, 17 December 1986. Belluschi, it should be noted, was still involved with SOM professionally through the Portland office of B/SOM. He was also working with the New York office on a new YWCA building in Pittsburgh, as well as designing a house for Louis Skidmore in Warm Springs, Florida. On the Pittsburgh YWCA, see Architectural Record, March 1964, 159–164; on the Skidmore House, see text below.

17. Mumford, "Skyline," excerpted in MoMA Bulletin 15, no. 3 (Spring 1948). See also Architectural Review, September 1948.

18. Belluschi remarks on modern architecture, delivered in seminar, "Principles and Techniques of Modern Architecture," held at Middle Atlantic Regional AIA Conference, June 1951, and reprinted in AIA Journal, September 1951, 99ff. See also Belluschi, typed manuscript, Boston Architectural Club address, February 1951 (Speeches, Belluschi Collection, Syracuse).

19. Zevi, Towards an Organic Architecture (1951); see also the review in Architectural Forum, January 1951, 196. For a somewhat different perspective on the controversy, see Benevolo, History of Modern Architecture, 2: 629ff.

20. Frederick Gutheim, review of Talbot Hamlin, Forms and Functions of Twentieth Century Architecture, in Architectural Forum, June 1952, 152–154.

21. Eero Saarinen, "Six Broad Currents of Modern Architecture," Architectural Forum, July 1953, 111–115. Shortly after the Forum article appeared, Saarinen wrote Belluschi, apologizing for using the word "handicraft," which Saarinen believed Forum editors seized upon and blew out of proportion. Saarinen letter to Belluschi, 20 August 1950 (Belluschi files).

22. Kennedy, "After the International Style, Then What?" Architectural Forum, September 1953, 130–133.

23. Gordon, "The Threat to the Next America," House Beautiful, April 1953, 126ff. While Belluschi accepted Gordon's arguments and indeed used them frequently (though without acknowledging their source) he typically denigrated her to his colleagues; in a letter of 4 May 1953 to John Merrill of B/SOM, for example, Belluschi warned him of her "hotheadedness." (Belluschi files).

24. Architectural Record, August 1953, 9ff.; Belluschi, "The Spirit of the New Architecture," Architectural Record, October 1953, 143–149.

25. Hitchcock, "The International Style Twenty Years After," Architectural Record, August 1951, 89–97.

26. "Next 50 Years," Architectural Forum, January 1951, 165ff. See also Peter Blake, Architectural Forum, May 1958, 131 (on Mies's dominance); Architectural Forum, July 1958, 60 (on the Seagram Building).

27. Sigfried Giedion, "The State of Contemporary Architecture—The Regional Approach," Architectural Record, January 1954, 132–137. Giedion was engaged in preparing the first Japanese edition of Space, Time and Architecture at the time. On the Japanese influence in the 1950s, see chapter 4 above; see also F. S. C. Northrop, The Meeting of East and West, 1946 (reprinted in 1979).

28. Pietro Belluschi, "The Meaning of Regionalism," Architectural Record, December 1955, 131–139.

29. Taped interview, PB/MLC, Portland, 19 August 1985.

30. Taped interviews, Alex Cvijanovic of TAC/MLC, Cambridge, 30 March 1989; Jean-Paul Carlhian/MLC, Boston, 29 March 1989. See also Wurster, "The Social Front of Modern Architecture in the 1930s."

31. See in this regard the Haskell obituary, AIA Journal 68 (September 1979), 122, 124; and Thomas Schumacher's review of Robert Stern, New Directions in American Architecture (1969), in Architectural Forum, March 1970, 58–59. For a broader perspective on the European-versus-American-modernism, or modernism-versus-regionalism, debate in the late 1940s and 1950s, see Benevolo, History of Modern Architecture, 1960 (rev. ed. 1966), 2: 671; for a more contemporary perspective, see Lefaivre and Tzonis, "Lewis Mumford's Regionalism." The recent surge of interest in regionalism, and especially Frampton's "Towards a Critical Regionalism," which calls for a regional approach, should be of particular interest in this context.

32. Belluschi, "Principles and Techniques of Modern Architecture," AIA Journal, September 1951, 99–103. See also his MIT address on architectural education, 20 November 1951 (Speeches, Belluschi Collection, Syracuse).

33. Belluschi address, Washington University, St. Louis, excerpted in St. Louis Globe Democrat, 20 November 1952.

34. "Belluschi Appraises the Gropius Challenge," Architectural Forum, May 1952, 113. See also Forum, February 1954, 156–157.

35. "On the Responsibility of the Architect," Perspecta (Yale Architectural Journal), no. 2, 1953. Belluschi's allusions to jukeboxes and the Grand Central Station seem uncanny in light of his subsequent involvement in the Pan Am Building built over the Grand Central railyard, and still later the Graves building in Portland. See text below.

36. "That Human Being Called the Client," AIA Conference, October 1953, Architectural Forum, November 1953, 58.

37. "Introduction," Form-Givers at Mid-Century (1959), 6–7.

38. Letters to the editor, *Architectural Forum,* May 1959, 114; unidentified note in Belluschi's hand (Belluschi files).

39. According to a letter he sent Elisabeth K. Thompson in preparation for the book on him she was to write, he also found the FBO one of the personally most rewarding (Belluschi letter to Thompson, 6 October 1980, Belluschi files). It seems, though, that this was an instance where Belluschi may have been thinking of his role in history, as he doesn't discuss the FBO in his memoirs nor did it come up in the Smithsonian interviews.

40. My thanks to Walter Creese for this observation, as well as his comments on this section which did much to broaden my thinking.

41. "Congressional Architecture Critics Object to the Contemporary Design of U.S. Embassies," *Architectural Forum,* March 1954, 45; *Forum,* April 1954, 172.

42. Belluschi letter to Judith Lanius, 16 December 1982, in response to her request for information about the FBO (Belluschi files); taped interviews, PB/MLC, 11 August 1985; 14 November 1986; 29 July 1988.

43. "U.S. Architecture Abroad—Modern Design at Its Best," *Architectural Forum,* March 1953, 101–115. On Bunshaft, see Krinsky, *Gordon Bunshaft of Skidmore, Owings & Merrill.*

44. *Boston Globe,* 4 January 1958.

45. *Architectural Forum,* April 1954, 172.

46. *Architectural Forum,* October 1953, 34; Belluschi letter to Lanius, 16 December 1982.

47. *Architectural Forum,* October 1953, 34.

48. Belluschi memorandum to Nelson A. Kenworthy, Foreign Buildings Operation, Department of State, Washington, D.C., 27 January 1954 (Belluschi files).

49. *AIA Journal,* February 1983, 36.

50. Belluschi letter to Kenworthy, 27 January 1953 (Belluschi files).

51. *Architectural Forum,* May 1955; *Architectural Record,* June 1956; October 1957, 237–242.

52. Taped interviews, PB/MLC.

53. *The Architecture of Diplomacy,* an exhibition of the Embassy and Consulate Buildings Commissioned by [the] Office of Foreign Buildings, Department of State, U.S. Government, 1953–1957 (Belluschi files).

54. *Architectural Forum,* March 1957, 7, 9; February 1958, 12–13, 16; *Time,* July 1960.

55. On the ambassador's residence in Paris (formerly the Rothschild mansion, Rue du Faubourg St.-Honoré), done with the assistance of Robert Brannen, see *New York Times,* 10 November 1969, 1, 22.

56. Slayton letter to Belluschi, thanking him for entertaining him in Portland, 7 September 1978; contract, Dept. of State and Belluschi, 25 June 1979 (Belluschi files).

57. *AIA Journal,* February 1983, 40; interview, Fred Bassetti/MLC, Seattle. Interest in the Foreign Buildings Operation and its role in American architectural history, a good study of which is long overdue, is beginning to stir. Among several recent inquiries are Loeffler, "The Architecture of Diplomacy: Heyday of the United States Embassy-Building Program, 1954–1960," and Robin, *Enclaves of America: The Rhetoric of American Political Architecture Abroad, 1900–1965.* See also Loeffler's review of Robin in the *Journal of the Society of Architectural Historians,* March 1994, 109–111, and the reviews by Arani Parikh, in *Design Book Review,* and Charles Goodsell, in *Journal of Architectural Education.*

58. My thanks again to Walter Creese for this observation.

59. Belluschi letter to Jo Stubblebine, 25 February 1952 (Belluschi files).

60. Smithsonian interviews, 48; Richards, *An Introduction to Modern Architecture,* 1940, 14; taped interviews, Mary Alice Hutchins/MLC, Portland, 1987–1988; Lawrence B. Anderson/MLC, Lincoln, Massachusetts, 16 September 1987.

61. *Oregonian,* 12 April 1956.

62. *Architectural Record,* December 1956, 178.

63. Blake, "Modern Architecture: Its Many Faces."

64. Hudnut, "The Church in a Modern World."

65. *Architectural Record,* July 1959, 147.

66. Taped interview, George Wallace/MLC, Stayton, Oregon, 31 May 1987. See also Clausen, *Spiritual Space,* where the Boston Lutheran as well as other Belluschi churches and synagogues of this era are discussed more fully.

67. Estimated cost of the Central Lutheran, Eugene, in 1955 was $100,000. *Architectural Record,* December 1955, 188; according to Marjorie Belluschi's records, the cost was $103,000, which may have included furnishings (Belluschi files).

68. Hudnut, "The Church in a Modern World."

69. Taped interviews, PB/MLC, Portland, 10 December 1987; 15 May 1989.

70. Portsmouth began as a priory and was advanced to the status of abbey in 1959. On the Portsmouth Abbey church, see Clausen, *Spiritual Space,* 81–85.

71. Father Hilary Martin of the Portsmouth School had studied architecture, practiced briefly in California, and returned to MIT for a master's in planning, which is where he came in contact with Belluschi. Taped interview, Father Peter Sidler, Portsmouth, 1 April 1989.

72. *Architectural Record,* December 1954, 140–142.

73. On the Temple Israel, Swampscott, see Clausen, *Spiritual Space,* 86–88.

74. More accurately, tinted glass. On Belluschi's use of modern colored glass, see Clausen, *Spiritual Space,* especially the discussion of Church of the Redeemer, 98–99.

75. On Lippold, see Carter, Burnham, and Lucie-Smith, *Richard Lippold Sculpture* (1990), which includes the Lippold baldachino in the interior of Belluschi's St. Mary's Cathedral and features it on the cover.

76. Anderson, Beckwith & Haible letter to Thomas Motley, 3 November 1960 (Trinity Church, Concord, file, Belluschi Collection, Syracuse).

77. Lawrence Anderson letter to MLC; taped interview, Father Peter Sidler/MLC, Portsmouth, 1 April 1989.

78. Bennett J. Sims, in Christ-Janer and Foley, *Modern Church Architecture,* 182.

79. Taped interview, Francis Taliaferro and Archibald Rogers of RTKL Associates/MLC, Baltimore, 7 April 1989. I'd like to extend a special thanks to Francis Taliaferro, and to Archibald Rogers who has since died, for the generosity of their time and thoughts in discussing their work with Belluschi.

80. Ibid; "The Chimes: Church of the Redeemer," 13 March 1955 (Archives, Church

23. *AIA Journal,* Mid-May 1980, 32. On Belluschi as a juror, see also "Big Name Architects," *Progressive Architecture,* December 1987, 9; Lipstadt, *The Experimental Tradition: Essays on Competitions in Architecture,* 97, 100, and elsewhere. Belluschi himself provided the material for the portions on him (correspondence, Lipstadt and Belluschi, Belluschi files). See also Collins, *Architectural Judgement,* 147, 189.

24. Taped interviews, I. M. Pei/MLC, New York City, 21 April 1989; PB/MLC, 7 November 1986; 29 March 1988.

25. Smithsonian interviews, 75. It should be noted, in light of Belluschi's tendency to self-aggrandizement, that he was not mentioned by Wiseman in his recent biography of Pei as having been of any particular importance in Pei's career. On the other hand, in my interview with Pei, while he was circumspect about Belluschi's work he very clearly felt indebted to Belluschi for his consistent support. Carter Wiseman, *I. M. Pei: A Profile in American Architecture* (1990); taped interview, Pei/MLC, 21 April 1989. On Pei, see also Arthur Herzog, "He Loves Things to Be Beautiful," *New York Times* 14 March 1965, 34, where it is noted that prior to the Kennedy Library commission (for which Belluschi was one of the architectural advisors), Pei was "relatively unknown"; Herzog also cites Pei's Earth Science Building at MIT and Everson Museum, Syracuse, for both of which Belluschi was instrumental in getting him the commission. On the general issue of professional opinion, connoisseurship, and individual taste (as opposed to objective criteria) in architectural judgment, see Collins, *Architectural Judgement,* especially 142ff.

26. Taped interview, Archibald Rogers/MLC. On Rouse and the Greater Baltimore Committee, see Hall, *Cities of Tomorrow,* 348.

27. Belluschi letter to J. Jefferson Miller, Chairman, Committee for Downtown, 15 January 1957 (Baltimore file, Belluschi Collection, Syracuse).

28. *Baltimore News Post,* 16 January 1957.

29. Philip A. Stedfast letter to Belluschi, 30 September 1957 (Baltimore file, Belluschi Collection, Syracuse).

30. *Architectural Forum,* May 1969, 48ff.

31. See files on Baltimore, particularly the Charles Center and development of the Inner Harbor, in the Belluschi Collection, Syracuse; also, discussion of Belluschi's role in the Boston Redevelopment Authority, below, and letters (especially the correspondence between Edward J. Logue and the City of Boston, Law Department, 16 September 1965, specifically addressing the issue).

32. Taped interview, Larry Reich/MLC, Baltimore, 18 April 1989 (Reich was the director of city planning, Baltimore); Martin L. Millspaugh letter to Belluschi, 11 March 1975 (Charles Center file, Belluschi Collection, Syracuse). Millspaugh was the deputy general manager of the Charles Center Management Office in the mid-sixties, and later president of the Charles Center–Inner Harbor Management Co.

33. Taped interviews, Elisabeth K. Thompson/ MLC, Berkeley, 1986–1987.

34. On St. Mary's Cathedral and the problems Belluschi encountered with the archbishop, social protestors, seismologists, etc., see Clausen, *Spiritual Space,* 33–34, 126–135.

35. Press release, Embarcadero Center Project, which was approved by the San Francisco Redevelopment Agency on the recommendation of its Architectural Advisory Committee, 14 February 1967; Belluschi's remarks, Report of the Advisory Committee to the Urban Redevelopment Authority in San Francisco, 14 February 1976; the response of the Joint Committee on Urban Design, AIA, AIP, ASCA, 13 March 1967 (San Francisco Redevelopment Agency file, Belluschi Collection, Syracuse).

36. *San Francisco Examiner/Chronicle,* 9 April 1967; Editorial, "The City's Growth to a New, Larger Scale," *San Francisco Chronicle,* 14 April 1967.

37. Other architects on the jury were William Wurster, Ralph Rapson, and Walter Netsch; Lawrence Anderson served as professional advisor. *Architectural Forum,* September 1962, 5, 7.

38. Taped interview, Edward Logue/MLC, Boston, 30 March 1989; *Architecture,* July 1985, 61 (on Logue).

39. Belluschi letter to Charles Hilgenhurst, 24 July 1965 (Boston Redevelopment Authority file, Belluschi Collection, Syracuse).

40. Robert M. Meserve, president of the Boston Bar Association and chair of the blue ribbon panel, letter to Belluschi, 24 November 1964 (Belluschi files).

41. Minutes, meeting of Design Advisory Committee, 8 July 1969 (Belluschi files).

42. Taped interview, Hideo Sasaki/MLC, Lafayette, California, 5 July 1987. On the Gropius years at Harvard and his efforts at greater collaboration among departments, see Marc Treib, ed., *Modern Landscape Architecture: A Critical Review* (1992), essays by Lance M. Neckar, especially 153–154, and Peter Walker, 252–253. My thanks to Walter Creese and David Streatfield for their suggestions in this context.

43. Taped interview, Sasaki/MLC, 5 July 1987.

44. *Architectural Forum,* October 1966, 54–62.

45. *Architectural Forum,* July 1960, 88ff.; June 1961.

46. Which is precisely what the article "Can Investors Afford Architecture?" in the *Architectural Forum,* September 1961, 94ff., recommended. See also Gutman, *Architectural Practice,* 12.

47. Taped interview, Norman Leventhal/MLC, Boston, 7 April 1989.

48. Taped interview, Robert Campbell/MLC, Boston, 28 March 1989; "Working in Suburbs a Boon, Say Tenants" (on the Wellesley Office Park), *The New England Business Journal,* 6 August 1974; Robert Campbell, "The Monster That Ate Suburbia," *Boston Globe,* 5 May 1985 (on industrial parks and their havoc); Scott Melnick, "Quality Development Pays Off in Suburbia," *Building Design and Construction,* February 1986.

49. Taped interview, Edward Logue/MLC, Boston, 30 March 1989.

50. Taped interview, Leventhal/MLC, 7 April 1989. I'd like to thank Mr. Leventhal not only for his time but also for his assistance in having this tape transcribed.

51. Taped interviews, PB/MLC, Robert Brannen/MLC, Boston, 6 April 1989; Yu Sing Jung/MLC, Boston, 11 April 1989. Belluschi became involved in the development in late 1967, when Matthew Weinstein, a major sponsor of the Temple Adath Israel synagogue that Belluschi had designed in 1956 in Merion, an affluent suburb outside Philadelphia, contacted him about designing a motor inn in downtown Philadelphia, in anticipation of the 1976 bicentennial. Spurred on by Belluschi's suggestions, the project

grew into a major urban complex, sponsored by a business consortium of which Weinstein was a partner.

52. *Philadelphia Inquirer,* 4 October 1968; Robert Brannen letter to MLC, 5 November 1993.

53. Memo, Minutes of Meeting, Kennedy Building Project (as it was also called, as it was to be located on Kennedy Boulevard), 7 February 1968 (Jung/Brannen files). The spine concept Bacon was excited about was, like the convention hotel, conceived by Portman (Portman and Barnett, *The Architect as Developer,* 47).

54. Taped interviews, PB/MLC, 7 November 1986; 15 May 1989. The Century 21 project, also called the Drexel Plaza Project, or sometimes the Kennedy Boulevard Project, was published in *Progressive Architecture,* July 1968, 130.

55. Both Jung and Brannen had worked in Eduardo Catalano's office in the mid-1960s before their association in 1968. Brannen was from the Pacific Northwest, hence particularly sympathetic to Belluschi's approach, and had left the Anderson, Beckwith & Haible office to work with him as his assistant on Portsmouth Abbey. On the Jung/Brannen firm, which grew from four people in 1968 to 189, 86 of whom were architects, in 1985, see *Architectural Record,* January 1980, 86–87; *Boston Globe,* 27 January 1987; *Progressive Architecture,* April 1987; *Architectural Record,* January 1988, 27, 29; and text below.

56. Taped interviews, Rogers/MLC, Taliaferro/MLC, 17 April 1989.

57. Belluschi letter to Dr. Otto F. Kraushaar, President, Goucher College, 25 February 1959; Kraushaar to Belluschi, 16 May 1959 (Goucher College file, Belluschi Collection, Syracuse). See also the discussion of the Juilliard commission in chapter 7. On the delicacy, or ethicality, of the situation, see Collins, *Architectural Judgement,* 152.

58. Muriel Emanuel et al., *Contemporary Architects* (1980), 679.

59. Ruttenbaum, *Mansions in the Clouds,* 206; Meredith L. Clausen, "The Pan Am Building and the Death of the Street," paper delivered at the Society of Architectural Historians annual meeting, Cincinnati, April 1991.

60. Gropius, report on trip to New York, 23 December 1958 (Pan Am file, Belluschi Collection, Syracuse).

61. Belluschi, draft of contract, 25 June 1958 (Pan Am file, Belluschi Collection, Syracuse).

62. Interview, Fred Halden (Emery Roth & Sons)/MLC, New York City, October 1986.

63. Gropius, Statement to the Press, 18 December 1958 (Pan Am files, Belluschi Collection, Syracuse). On New York as the new international postwar cultural center, see Guilbaut, *How New York Stole the Idea of Modern Art;* Clausen, "The Pan Am Building and the Death of the Street."

64. The issue of the tower's roofline and how to handle the addition of the heliport was a matter of great concern to Gropius, who wanted to maintain the effect of open mullions silhouetted against the sky. It was apparently one of the few times Roth went ahead on his own without checking with Gropius for its effect on the design as a whole. Gropius letter to Ray Colcord, Jr., vice president of the Grand Central Building Inc., 15 February 1961 (Pan Am file, Belluschi Collection, Syracuse).

65. *Boston Globe,* 1 March 1959.

66. Taped interviews, Alex Cvijanovic (TAC)/MLC, Cambridge, 30 March 1989; Norman Fletcher (TAC)/MLC, Cambridge, 28 March 1989; Richard Roth and Fred Halden (Emery Roth & Sons)/MLC, New York City, October 1989; Smithsonian interviews, 83ff.

67. *Architectural Forum,* February 1955, 116.

68. "Should One of New York's Greatest Rooms Be Sacrificed to Modern Railroad Economics?," *Architectural Forum,* November 1954, 135; Haskell editorial, *Architectural Forum,* April 1955, 172.

69. *Architectural Forum,* February 1955, 76ff.

70. Haskell editorial, *Architectural Forum,* March 1955, 178.

71. Gropius, *Scope of Total Architecture: The Ideals of the Modern Movement* (1943, 1955).

72. Walter C. Reis, associate professor of architecture, Pennsylvania State University, letter to the editor, *Architectural Forum,* January 1959, 57–58.

73. *Progressive Architecture,* May 1959, 59, 61.

74. Ada Louise Huxtable, "Marvel or Monster?," *New York Times,* 24 January 1960.

75. "Architecture—Scheme for Grand Central City," *Nation,* 30 January 1960, 104–106.

76. Ibid., 105.

77. Ibid., 106.

78. Scully, "The Death of the Street," 95.

79. Wolf Von Eckardt, "Pan Am's Glass House," *New Republic* 147 (13 August 1962), 24. See also Von Eckardt, *A Place to Live: The Crisis of the Cities* (1967), 10.

80. *New York Times,* 26 November 1960.

81. Wayne Andrews, "Something Less Than Chartres" (review of Condit, *American Building Art*), *The Reporter* 25 (6 July 1961), 49–50.

82. Emerson Goble, *Architectural Record,* May 1962, 197; Edmund Bacon, letter to the editor, *Architectural Record,* June 1963, 174. On Bacon's 1950s approach to urban design (which Belluschi basically subscribed to), see his *The Design of Cities,* 1967; on its conflict with changed values in the 1960s, see Collins, *Architectural Judgement,* 176.

83. *Architectural Record,* June 1963, 174; May 1963. See also "Pan Am Building, Center of a Storm of Controversy," *New York Times,* 7 April 1963; the article, with a photograph of the new building, was featured on the front page.

84. Interview, Allan Temko/MLC, San Francisco, 22 July 1986.

85. *Wall Street Journal,* 6 March 1963; *Time,* 15 March 1963; *Business Week,* 20 July 1963, 70.

86. *New York Times,* 29 April 1962.

87. In 1991, the long-troubled Pan American World Airways collapsed in bankruptcy, and in 1992 the aluminum and neon Pan Am sign was removed and the building renamed the MetLife for the Metropolitan Life Insurance Company, which had owned the building since 1981. *New York Times,* 4 September 1992.

I am currently pursuing a project on the Pan Am Building and its role in the reaction against modernism in the early 1960s. I would like to thank members of CASVA, the Center for Advanced Study in the Visual Arts at the National Gallery of Art, Washington, D.C., for their support of the project while I was a Senior Visiting Fellow there in spring 1994.

88. "California Bank," *Architectural Forum,* May 1958, 39.

89. *San Francisco Chronicle,* 19 March 1964.

90. Project Memorandum #9, 26 May 1964 (Bank of America file, Belluschi Collection, Syracuse).

91. *San Francisco Chronicle,* 27 July 1965; *Architectural Record,* September 1965.

92. Taped interviews, Ralph Butterfield (WB&E)/MLC, San Francisco, 15 July 1986; Donn Emmons (WB&E)/MLC, 26 June 1986; Marc Goldstein (SOM)/MLC, San Francisco, 24 June 1986.

93. Taped interview, Goldstein/MLC, 24 June 1986.

94. Charles W. Moore, "The San Francisco Skyline: Hard to Spoil, but They're Working on It," *Architectural Forum,* November 1965, 47.

95. *Architectural Record,* July 1970, 126–131; *San Francisco Chronicle,* 17 January 1971.

96. *San Francisco Chronicle,* 17 January 1971.

97. Taped interview, Ralph Butterfield/MLC, 20 June 1986.

98. Taped interview, Samuel Stewart (former President of Bank of America)/MLC, San Francisco, June 1986.

99. Associates on the 565 Technology Square, 1961–1965, were Eduardo Catalano and Paul Shimamoto; on the New Equitable Center, 1962–1964, Wolff Zimmer Gunsul Frasca; and on the Northern States Power Company Building, 1962–1965, Ellerbe & Company. The IBM Building in Baltimore, 1969–1975, with Emery Roth & Sons, drew on the same basic horizontal office building type.

100. He also recommended Plexiglas be used at the Portsmouth Abbey church, there to correct leaks in the stained glass dome (Portsmouth Abbey files, Belluschi Collection, Syracuse).

101. *Architectural Record,* January 1966, 143.

102. Minutes of meeting, Belluschi, Ewing, Gordon, and Tolane, in Belluschi's office in Cambridge, 12 June 1962 (Rohm & Haas file, Belluschi Collection, Syracuse).

103. *Architectural Record,* January 1966, 148.

104. Wolf Von Eckardt, "Design of U.S. Building in Philadelphia Stirs Protests by Officials and Citizens," *Washington Post,* 23 September 1965. On Philadelphia as a leader in city planning and redevelopment in the postwar era, from the perspective of its capital investment and focusing particularly on the key role of Edmund Bacon, see Carolyn Teich Adams, *The Politics of Capital Investment: The Case of Philadelphia* (State University of New York Press, Albany, 1988).

105. *Architectural Forum,* July–August 1968, 21.

106. The position taken by Venturi and Scott Brown evident in *Learning from Las Vegas* should be seen in this context. Belluschi was their obvious, if unspoken, target.

107. Belluschi address, Ann Arbor, published in *Monitor, Journal of the Profession* (Kalamazoo, Michigan), December 1967–1968.

108. University of Michigan talk, reported in the *Detroit News,* 4 October 1967.

109. Taped interview, Gerald W. Blakeley, Jr. (President, Cabot, Cabot & Forbes)/MLC, Boston, 16 September 1987.

110. *Boston Globe,* 15 December 1968. On Nervi and Moretti's Place Victoria Towers, see *Architectural Record,* May 1962, 189–190.

111. Taped interviews, PB/MLC, 21 November 1987; 10 December 1987; 13 May 1988; 15 May 1989.

112. Belluschi letter to Don Atran (head of public relations, Emery Roth & Sons), 20 July 1971 (Belluschi files).

113. Sibyl Moholy-Nagy, *Architectural Forum,* January 1969, 44. See also Ada Louise Huxtable's review of the new Boston Government Center, which mentions the Belluschi building, calling it a "suave, technological display," *New York Times,* 17 September 1972.

114. Taped interviews, PB/MLC, 21 November 1987; 28 February 1988; 16 January 1988. See also the article by Robert Campbell, "A Learner's Lexicon to Sixty State Street," *Boston Globe,* 24 March 1974.

115. Taped interviews, Edward Logue/MLC, Boston, 30 March 1989; PB/MLC, Portland, 7 November 1986; 21 November 1987; 10 December 1987. See also documents in Keystone Building file, Belluschi Collection, Syracuse.

116. See the appendix for a more detailed list of these buildings and of the associates who worked with Belluschi on them.

117. William Schuman letter to Belluschi, 3 January 1958; interview, Schuman/MLC, New York City, 19 April 1989.

118. Among their joint ventures was the Baystate West Urban Complex in Springfield, Massachusetts, 1966–1972, published in *Architectural Record,* April 1974, 142–143. On Catalano, see Gubitosi and Izzo, *Eduardo Catalano: Buildings and Projects* (1978), and *Structures of Warped Surfaces* (1960).

119. Taped interviews, Eduardo Catalano/MLC, Cambridge, 29 March 1989; PB/MLC, 14 November 1986; 21 November 1987; 26 February 1988; 29 March 1988; 13 May 1988; 15 May 1989.

120. Frederick Taylor fax to MLC, 30 March 1994; telephone conversation and correspondence, Robert Burns/MLC, February–March 1989.

121. Burns letter to MLC, 27 March 1989.

122. Taylor fax to MLC, 30 March 1994; taped interview, William Pedersen, New York City, 19 April 1989; Robert Brannen/MLC, Boston, 6 April 1989; telephone conversation and correspondence, Burns/MLC, March 1989. Their accounts all differ slightly.

123. Burns letter to MLC, 27 March 1989. Taylor remembers the situation somewhat differently, especially with respect to the amount of Belluschi participation.

124. Mildred Schmertz, "The Juilliard School," *Architectural Record,* January 1970, 121–130.

125. Ada Louise Huxtable, "Juilliard's New Building: Esthetic Reality," *New York Times,* 8 October 1969, 59.

126. Lincoln Center Buildings Fact Sheet, undated but circa 1970, compiled by the Lincoln Center for the Performing Arts, Inc., Public Information Department (Belluschi files); telephone interview, Philip Hart (concert manager and Schubart's deputy at Juilliard in the 1960s who retired to Sante Fe, New Mexico)/MLC, 14 June 1989.

127. Ada Louise Huxtable, "Dissimilar Buildings, Similar Awards," *New York Times,* 24 May 1970.

128. My comments here, and those that follow, are based on scores of interviews with for-

mer associates, colleagues, clients, and friends, whose identity I feel obligated to protect. See also text below.

129. See for example documents in the University of Virginia Fine Arts and Architecture Building and Clark Art Institute Addition files, Belluschi Collection, Syracuse. The letters of Talcott M. Banks, of Pilmer Dodge Gardner and Bradford, on behalf of the Clark Art Institute, to Belluschi, 1965–1966, expressive of their concern over his frequent absence and the impact it was having on the design of the building, are particularly telling.

9 The AIA Gold Medal and Belluschi's Return to Portland

1. Compare, for example, Stern's view of modernism in America to that of Lewis Mumford in *Roots of Contemporary Architecture* (1952).

2. Thomas Schumacher, review of Stern, *New Directions in American Architecture,* in *Architectural Forum,* March 1970, 58–59.

3. Venturi, *Complexity and Contradiction in Architecture* (1966); Venturi, Scott Brown, and Izenour, *Learning from Las Vegas* (1972); Venturi and Scott Brown, *A View from the Campidoglio: Selected Essays 1952–1984* (1984).

4. Robert Geddes and William LaRiche, "Theory in Practice," *Architectural Forum,* September 1972, 35.

5. See *Five Architects: Eisenman, Graves, Gwathmey, Hejduk, Meier* (1975).

6. *Architectural Forum,* July–August 1973, 77–86.

7. The material here, as was customary, was provided by Belluschi himself, and should be regarded accordingly.

8. "Pietro Belluschi: Understanding Human Motivations," *Metropolis* (Portland), January 1972, 6.

9. Ibid. See also Clausen, *Spiritual Space,* where Belluschi's philosophy of church architecture is discussed in depth.

10. "Pietro Belluschi: Understanding Human Motivations," 6.

11. Interviews, occupants of the Chatham West Housing and Pine Grove Housing developments, Brockton, Massachusetts, April

1989; taped interview, Norman Leventhal/MLC, Boston, 7 April 1989. The Pine Grove complex was recognized as among the best apartments of the year by *Architectural Record* 153 (Mid-May 1973), 104.

12. "A Morning with Pietro Belluschi," *Avenu* (Portland), April 1975, 1–2.

13. Pietro Belluschi: "Understanding Human Motivations," 6.

14. Heyer, *Architects on Architecture,* 229.

15. Ibid.

16. "A Morning with Pietro Belluschi," 1–2.

17. Belluschi speech, Portland chapter of the AIA, April 1972, typed manuscript (Belluschi files).

18. Interview with Belluschi, *Portland Profile,* November–December 1972.

19. *Architectural Forum,* July 1973, 23.

20. Belluschi, "Should You Be an Architect," pamphlet published by the New York Life Insurance Company, 1955, and his 1970 update which still addressed only men. For a response, see Ellen Perry Berkeley, introduction to *Architecture: A Place for Women* (1989), xvii; the exhibit "That Exceptional One: Women in American Architecture," at the 1988 AIA Convention; "Women in Architecture Are Influential Minority," *San Diego Union,* 3 September 1989, F-10.

Some sense of Belluschi's influence, and the impact it had on the career aspirations of women, might be gained from the following letter he received in 1957:

Dr. Mr. Belluschi,
  I sent to the NY Life Insurance Co. for the pamphlet you wrote, "Should your Child Be An Architect?" You stated that you could not "in whole conscience recommend architecture as a profession for girls." Just as you said, my parents have been trying to dissuade me. However, I sincerely want to be an architect. I am seventeen years old and have had this desire for a long time.
  I have received high marks in both mathematics and art. Please explain to me these great obstacles that make it so difficult for a girl to become a successful architect. I am determined to try, but want to convince my parents that I have the ability and therefore my attempt won't be in vain. (Margaret Drake

letter to Belluschi, 6 August 1957, Belluschi files)

Or this one in 1962:

Dear Mr. Belluschi,
  I would appreciate knowing why you think that architecture is not a recommended field for girls, as you stated in the article which you wrote in the New York Life Insurance booklet "Career Opportunities." Some girls are just as talented and intelligent as some boys. Why then can't females have the same opportunities to become architects as males do?" (Cheryl Moch letter to Belluschi, 12 November 1962, Belluschi files)

21. *Architectural Forum,* March 1973, 58–61; *AIA Journal,* June 1974, 9; "A Morning with Pietro Belluschi."

22. Text of citation, presented by Max D. Urbahn, President, and P. M. Nolton, Secretary; AIA Convention, Houston, 10 May 1972.

23. Belluschi, "The Unchanged in a Time of Change," *AIA Journal,* July 1972, 25.

24. Marion Dean Ross, "The Attainment and Restraint of Pietro Belluschi," *AIA Journal,* July 1972, 17–24; Elisabeth K. Thompson, "Pietro Belluschi: The 1972 Gold Medalist," *Architectural Record,* April 1972, 119–126.

25. Waldo B. Christensen, Director, Northwest District, AIA, Washington, D.C., letter to Holman J. Barnes, president of the Oregon Chapter AIA, Portland, Oregon, 4 January 1954; Barnes letter to Belluschi, 5 January 1954 (which enclosed a copy of Christenson's confidential letter to Barnes) (Belluschi files).

26. Taped interviews, Archibald Rogers/MLC, Baltimore, 17 April 1989; Elisabeth K. Thompson/MLC, Berkeley; documents, Belluschi AIA Gold Medal nomination file.

27. Documents, Belluschi AIA Gold Medal nomination file; taped interview, Lawrence Anderson/MLC, Lincoln, Massachusetts.

28. In the case of the Northern California chapter, this may have been a matter of official policy.

29. Taped interview, Archibald Rogers/MLC, 17 April 1989. The need for a periodical reevaluation of AIA Gold Medal criteria was

recently the focus of Stephan Kliment's editorial in *Architectural Record,* August 1993, 9.

In a highly revealing article, Huxtable addressed the role and status of African-American architects practicing in the United States in the early 1970s, pointing out the presence of many talented but yet unrecognized black architects. Ada Louise Huxtable, "The Black Man and His Architecture," *New York Times,* 3 May 1970.

30. Jane Holtz Kay, "Architect Pietro Belluschi: Broker between Budgets and Beauty," *Boston Globe,* 14 May 1972; taped interview, Kay/MLC, Boston, 29 March 1989.

31. Interviews, Mary Alice Hutchins/MLC; PB/MLC, 1987–1989. Hutchins was one of the architects who joined the Belluschi office during the war years; she remained with him as their specifications writer until he left for MIT in 1951. I want to thank her especially for her generosity in putting me up in Portland innumerable times during the course of the Belluschi interviews, and for sharing her memories of Belluschi and the ways of the office. I learned a great deal from her, and value our tie.

32. Chenoweth, "The Architect as Prophet"; transcript of taped interview, published in *Architects Talk,* Occasional Paper #4, Center for Environmental Research, University of Oregon, February 1978.

33. Belluschi was, of course, receiving a full pension from MIT, in addition to his consulting fees. He also owned a number of investment properties in Oregon.

34. Belluschi letter to John Merrill, Jr., SOM, 29 June 1959 (New Equitable Center file, Belluschi Collection, Syracuse).

35. The firm traces its origin to 1942, as Wolff & Phillips; it became Wolff & Zimmer in 1954, then Wolff Zimmer Gunsul Frasca in 1966, after a number of name changes in the 1960s. It became recognized as the Zimmer Gunsul Frasca Partnership in 1977. For more on the background of the office and its more recent makeup, see the firm profile, "Turning a Dream into Skylines," in *Oregon Business* (Portland), October 1983, 22–32.

36. Correspondence, Belluschi and Cake, 1959–1960 (New Equitable Center file, Belluschi Collection, Syracuse).

37. *Architectural Record,* December 1965, 144; Belluschi letter to Ralph Cake, 31 May 1962, 1 August 1962 (New Equitable Center file, Belluschi Collection, Syracuse).

38. The exteriors were faced with precast Mosai panels of white sand, cement, and quartz aggregate, coming in units some as large as 12 feet in size; each unit formed a completely finished wall inside and out, with window frames and air conditioning ducts cast in the panels themselves. As these were not available locally, they had to be manufactured by a company in Seattle. Taped interview, Norman Zimmer/MLC, Portland, 10 May 1989. Zimmer is the senior partner of ZGF.

39. Typed copy of Belluschi's remarks, groundbreaking day, 5 June 1963 (Belluschi files).

40. News release, 1 March 1965 (Belluschi files). The Equitable Center was granted a design award by the local AIA chapter and also given a somewhat perfunctory one-page write-up in the *Architectural Record,* December 1965.

41. Taped interviews, Zimmer/MLC; Frasca/MLC, Portland. On the importance of this kind of career connection, see Williamson, *American Architects and the Mechanics of Fame.* Belluschi, who rose on the coattails of Doyle and in turn spawned a number of what were to become nationally known firms, is a classic example of the closely controlled, powerful networking process she describes.

42. There is extensive documentation of the 1960s Portland Art Museum addition in both the Belluschi files in Portland and the Belluschi Collection at Syracuse. Most of the pre-ZGF correspondence is in Syracuse.

43. Robert Frasca began in architecture at Cincinnati, then transferred to the University of Michigan to finish his degree; he went on to get a master's in planning at MIT. Graduating in 1959, he was eager to design; drawn to the Pacific Northwest largely on the basis of what he had heard about it through Belluschi and his work, he came to Portland and worked for a year with Wolff & Zimmer. He then left on a traveling fellowship to Europe for a year, returning to the Zimmer office in early 1962, just as the New Equitable Center project was getting started. Frasca went on to become the firm's chief designer, establishing it as one of the leading architectural firms in the country. *Oregon Business,* October 1983, 23; taped interview, Frasca/MLC, 6 December 1986.

44. Interview, Thomas Vaughan/MLC, Portland, 1987.

45. Taped interviews, PB/MLC, 15 December 1986; 13 May 1988. See also Jane Van Cleve, "Conversations with Pietro Belluschi," *Willamette Week,* Portland, 17 March 1980, 11ff., and Belluschi's letter to the editor published in the following issue.

46. Belluschi's relationship with Jung/Brannen took at least five different forms: Belluschi as principal designer, as designer in association with Robert Brannen, as principal designer in association with the J/B staff, as designer in association with J/B Associates, and as design consultant, with J/B Associates as architects of record (document prepared for MLC, 6 March 1989, J/B Associates).

47. Interviews, Belluschi, Brannen, Hsiung/MLC, Boston, April 1989; Brannen/MLC, 15 September 1987. The One Maine Savings Bank was published in Thompson, *Maine Forms of American Architecture* (1976).

48. Robert Brannen letter to Audrey Michaels, Public Relations, 27 May 1982 (Belluschi files); "Joseph Meyerhoff, Patron of BSO, Dies," *Baltimore Sun,* 4 February 1985.

49. Interviews, Brannen, Hsiung/MLC, Boston, April 1989.

50. Scott Melnick, "Steel Frame Adds Flexibility" (Meyerhoff Symphony Hall), *Building Design & Construction,* June 1984.

51. *Baltimore Sun,* 17 September 1982.

52. Gubitosi and Izzo, *Pietro Belluschi, Edifici e Progetti, 1932–1973.* Both the substance of the text and the photos were provided by Belluschi himself. The catalogue included among his buildings the Pan Am Building, KahNeeTa Resort Hotel, BayState West Urban Complex, SeaFirst Bank in Seattle, Dining Room Addition to the Faculty Club, Princeton University, and the Lutheran Church, Walnut Creek, California, all of which were designed principally by his associates.

53. Memo of meeting, office of J/B Associates, Inc., Boston, with professors Alfredo Trifogli, mayor of Ancona and president of the University of Ancona, Gubitosi, and Izzo, and Dr. Ussia, of the Italian-American Foundation, Boston, 12 September 1974 (Belluschi files); interviews, Belluschi, Brannen/MLC.

54. Paolo Bruni letter to Belluschi, 4 October 1985 (Belluschi files); interviews, Belluschi, Brannen/MLC. Belluschi did not recognize photographs of the finished building that I brought him after visiting it in 1991.

55. On the rise of the Jung/Brannen firm, see *Architectural Record,* January 1980, 86; "The Growing Imprint of Jung/Brannen," *Boston Globe,* 27 January 1987; *Architectural Record,* January 1988, 27–29.

56. Interviews, PB/MLC; Kenneth DeMay (of Sasaki Associates) letter to The Rev. Dom Peter Sidler, Portsmouth Abbey, 28 January 1971 (Belluschi files).

57. Taped interview, PB/MLC, 26 February 1988.

58. Their work was undertaken under the auspices of Mr. Zellerbach, and was without a formal contract. Interview, Vernon DeMars/MLC, San Francisco, August 1987.

59. Taped interviews, Vernon DeMars/MLC, John Wells/MLC, San Francisco, 4 August 1987.

60. Taped interviews, Sam Stewart/MLC, Belford Brown/MLC, San Francisco, July–August 1987. On Belluschi's receiving the commission while serving in the capacity of advisor to the client, see also the discussion of Goucher College and the Juilliard School, above; Collins, *Architectural Judgement,* 152.

61. Belluschi had a reputation in the Bay Area, as well as elsewhere, as a master salesman, someone who could charm anyone, especially ladies, into anything. He was also known locally more for sweet talk than hard action. "He would say how he's going to design something and how everybody will love it. It sounded great, everybody loved what he said. But it was never clear he ever actually did anything." "Dangerously seductive," I was warned by another well-meaning associate. These comments are bound to ring hollow to some, sound fatally accurate to others.

62. Interviews, DeMars/MLC, Wells/MLC, July–August 1987. I want also to thank Jack Sidener, who was responsible for the perspective sketches Belluschi typically used in his publicity, for all his help here and elsewhere. Those were splendid, enriching times.

63. *San Francisco Chronicle,* 14 July 1975.

64. Belluschi had tear sheets of the Akron Concert Hall, which was published in the *Architectural Forum,* December 1973, in his San Francisco Symphony file.

65. Robert Commanday, "New Symphony Hall Plans—Intimacy of Interrelationship," *San Francisco Chronicle,* 1 June 1975. Commanday's article was illustrated with a photograph of Belluschi and a Sidener sketch of the interior of the proposed hall.

66. Belluschi, "Notes on the Design of San Francisco Symphony Hall," typed manuscript (press release), Belluschi files.

67. Ibid.; Belluschi elevation, *San Francisco Chronicle,* 14 July 1975; Commanday, "New Symphony Hall Plans."

68. Taped interviews, DeMars/MLC, San Francisco, July 1987; Sam Stewart/MLC, San Francisco, 7 August 1987; Belford Brown/MLC, Walnut Creek, California, 11 August 1987; PB/MLC, Portland, 26 August 1985; 9 September 1985; 21 July 1986; 21 November 1987; 16 January 1988; 15 May 1989.

69. Belluschi letter to Belford Brown, Coordinator, Sponsors of the San Francisco Performing Arts Center, 4 February 1976 (Belluschi files).

70. Taped interview, Belford Brown/MLC, Walnut Creek, 11 August 1987; documents, San Francisco Performing Arts Center, Belluschi files.

71. Belluschi's "Xmas sketch" and notes tabulating floor areas, December 1976 (Belluschi files); plans and other drawings, San Francisco Performing Arts Center file, Belluschi Collection, Oregon Historical Society; taped interview, Brown/MLC, 11 August 1987.

72. Belluschi's position paper, 26 January 1977 (Belluschi files, Portland).

73. Sam Stewart, President, Sponsors of the San Francisco Performing Arts Center, letter to John Merrill, Jr., SOM, 3 May 1977 (Belluschi files).

74. Bassett declined to be interviewed, and preferred that I not see SOM's files; the account here thus is incomplete. I regret not hearing their side of story, which would likely have resulted in a more balanced view of the whole. I would like to thank John Merrill, Jr., Alan Rudy, William Weber, and the archivist/librarian of SOM for giving generously of their time.

75. SOM had been involved in working on a new master plan of the Civic Center since the 1950s, hence it was not entirely unexpected that they were given the commission to do the State Office Building on a site opposite Davies Symphony Hall two years after the Davies commission. It complemented Davies in its curved facade.

76. Taped interview, Belford Brown/MLC, 11 August 1987.

77. Taped interview, Koubek/MLC, Washington, D.C., 18 August 1988. The demolished mansion was the Tuckerman House, built 1886, at 16th and I streets; see James M. Goode, *Capital Losses: A Cultural History of Washington's Destroyed Buildings* (Smithsonian Institution Press, Washington, 1979), 105–106. Belluschi later regretted having recommended its demolition. Taped interview, PB/MLC, 29 July 1988.

78. Interview, Koubek/MLC, 18 August 1988; Gould letter to Koubek, 22 February 1980 (Belluschi files).

79. Correspondence, Belluschi to his lawyers regarding insurance liability for the various Belluschi offices, October 1988 (Miami Center, Belluschi files).

80. Taped interviews, PB/MLC, 26 February 1988; 15 May 1989.

81. *Miami Herald,* 10 April 1979.

82. Ibid.

83. Beth Dunlop, *Miami Herald,* 5 July 1981.

84. Paul Goldberger, "Glitter of Miami from Afar Dulls in Close-Up," *New York Times,* 25 December 1983.

85. Paula Harper, "Power Skyline—Report from Miami," *Art in America,* September 1988, 55–65.

86. Gould, typed draft, The Miami Center brochure sent to Belluschi for his review. Other than correcting several spelling errors, Belluschi approved it with no changes (Miami Center, Belluschi files).

87. "Bank Forecloses on Miami Center," *Miami Herald,* 28 July 1984.

88. Stoel Rives Boley Fraser & Wyse, Portland (Belluschi's lawyer), letter to Belluschi, 18 August 1986, with check enclosed for $345,752 as result of the bankruptcy proceedings; taped interview, PB/MLC, 4 September 1988; documents, Miami Center, Belluschi files.

89. On the architect's obligation to society versus to the client, see Collins, *Architectural Judgement,* 205.

10 Belluschi in the 1980s: Confronting Postmodernism and the Return to Basics

1. Among the host of recent publications on postmodernism as a broad cultural phenomenon, see Berman, *All That Is Solid Melts into Air: The Experience of Modernity* (1982); Harvey, *The Condition of Post-Modernity* (1989), who argues from a political-economic perspective, and Hutcheon, *A Poetics of Postmodernism: History, Theory, Fiction* (1988), whose approach is more literary. My thanks to colleagues Jeff Olson in urban geography and anthropology and Steve Taubeneck in Germanics for their contributions to my thinking about postmodernism.

   On the role of MoMA in shaping public taste, see Smith, *Making the Modern: Industry, Art, and Design in America,* 354ff., and Williamson, *American Architects and the Mechanics of Fame,* 198ff., 226.

2. The grand master of these stylistic neologisms is of course Charles Jencks. See for example *Language of Post-Modern Architecture* (1977, enlarged edition 1981); *Late-Modern Architecture* (1980); "Death for Rebirth" and "Post-Modernism between Kitsch and Culture," in *Post-Modernism on Trial,* AD Profile no. 88, 1990.

3. *AIA Journal,* January 1978, 49ff.; mid-May 1978, 160.

4. *AIA Journal,* July 1978, 16ff.

5. Ada Louise Huxtable, "Philip Johnson and the Temper of the Times," *New York Times,* 13 May 1979.

6. "Convention Speakers Question, Needle and Berate the Profession," *AIA Journal,* July 1979, 14, 18.

7. Unpublished manuscript, Belluschi speech, AIA National Convention, Kansas City, 4 June 1979 (Belluschi files).

8. Paul Goldberger, "Architects' 'Hedonist' Bent Attacked," *New York Times,* 7 June 1979; Robert Campbell, "Architecture's Noisy Soul-Searching," *Boston Globe,* 24 June 1979.

9. Jeanne Davern letter to the editor, *Architectural Record,* February 1979, 4.

10. Ada Louise Huxtable, "The Present: The Troubled State of Modern Architecture," *Bulletin, American Academy of Arts and Sciences,* January 1980, 23–37. Belluschi was a member of the American Academy and regularly received its publications. Huxtable's essay was subsequently reproduced in the *Architectural Record,* January 1981, 72–79, as well as elsewhere.

11. Ibid.

12. James Marston Fitch, "A Funny Thing Happened . . . ," *AIA Journal,* January 1980, 66–68.

13. Kathie Durbin, "The Building of the Future, the Shape of Things to Come," *Passages* (Northwest Orient Airlines), May 1982, 34–38.

14. Among the original eleven architects invited to submit proposals were Frank Gehry from Los Angeles and Sim Van Der Rin/Calthorp of the Bay Area. Pastier, "First Monument of a Loosely Defined Style: Michael Graves' Portland Building," 235.

15. The situation with Johnson was considerably more complicated, especially politically, than described here. As Pastier points out, the decision ultimately hinged on the issue of the budget, not on Philip Johnson. But Johnson's role was obviously powerful, and the jury acknowledged leaning heavily on his advice when it came to decide. It seems clear, in fact, that Johnson's voice carried the show.

16. Pastier, "First Monument of a Loosely Defined Style," 236. My thanks to Robert Harris for passing on his observations on the competition.

17. Report of the jury to Portland City Council, 29 February 1980 (Belluschi files).

18. Belluschi testimony to Portland City Council, 12 March 1980 (Belluschi files).

19. Pastier, "First Monument of a Loosely Defined Style."

20. Earl Bradfish, Director of General Services, City of Portland, letter to Belluschi, 11 April 1980 (Belluschi files).

21. Belluschi letter to Bradfish, 15 April 1980 (Belluschi files).

22. Undated, unidentified clipping with article by Sandra Fairbanks and photograph of the building under construction by Galen Crantz, dated March 1981 (*Progressive Architecture? AIA Journal? Skyline?*) (Belluschi files).

23. Ginny Butterfield, "Inside Out: Outside, Portland Building Makes Bold Statement; Inside, It's Completely Tongue-Tied," *Oregon Magazine,* October 1982, 72–73. See also *Oregonian,* 20 May 1987 (where the building is described as "pretty much of a disaster"); *Oregonian,* 7 June 1987 ("very user unfriendly"); and *Connoisseur,* April 1989 ("form determined by architect's ability to draw rather than user's actual needs . . .").

24. Butterfield, "Inside Out."

25. Belluschi, "Architectural Milestones," *AIA Journal,* May 1973, 29–31.

26. Belluschi's comments here, voiced in an interview, are particularly difficult to paraphrase. To my note about his absorbing the philosophy, not the form, of modernism, he responded (verbatim transcription):

   This is really the core of what I believe. There are some people, and I mention all the famous architects, sometime they feel that contrived forms give you great pleasure. And I wouldn't deny that some of those forms, they are creative, and related to the pure aesthetics [which is] also satisfying. But I, from the average architect, at least from my own limited ability to create these forms, there is nothing more satisfying than seeing the logic sustaining the aesthetic. Because if—and you don't have to be completely rational, but there has to be something that sustains, and then to me, at least, the response of this wonderful solution of a problem which is a practical nature but has an aesthetic, contains an aesthetic essence, is really the thing that satisfies for a longer time and probably also for as long as you care to think in terms of the future. So this has been from the very beginning, that's when I made a comment about the back of the building being more satisfying, wasn't really quite true. Because sometimes they were so and sometimes they weren't. But the fact [is] I never lost sight of the reason why the building was to be erected. And the fact that it became an aesthetic pleasure was due to the fact that that was revealed in a very sus . . . [doesn't finish], could be very obviously or not so obviously, but that's still the essence. And in fact if you have philosophy of that, that's it! And of course you fail many times. But you never fail in believing that. (Taped interview, PB/MLC, 15 December 1986)

Because Belluschi's thinking is sometimes tangled, his comments nuanced, his manner of speaking often truncated and incomplete and his voice soft and heavily accented, tapes of interviews are very difficult to transcribe, as the transcript of the 1983 Smithsonian Institution interviews attests. Knowing this, I transcribed the Belluschi tapes, as well as all others used in this project, myself.

27. Taped interview, PB/MLC, Portland, 15 December 1986.

28. Taped interview, PB/MLC, 14 November 1986.

29. Belluschi, ACSA speech, Vancouver, March 1985; taped interview, PB/MLC (on Belluschi's advice on Kahn's Baltimore project).

30. Taped interview, PB/MLC, 29 March 1988.

31. On St. Mary's and the derivation of its form, see Clausen, *Spiritual Space,* 126–135.

32. Taped interviews, PB/MLC, 17 December 1987; 15 May 1989; 30 June 1992. As advisor to the president of the Oregon Health Sciences University, Belluschi argued on behalf of Richard Meier's proposal for a new Eye Clinic, despite the fact that it was fully consistent with Meier's own personal style and bore little relationship to its regional setting. As built, it also went way over budget. In light of Belluschi's opposition to the Michael Graves project on the grounds that it had no sense of place, this indicates Belluschi's notorious ability to rationalize convincingly whatever it was he wanted or believed was right.

It should be noted that Robert Frasca was also competing for the Eye Clinic job.

33. Taped interview, PB/MLC, 19 August 1985.

34. Taped interview, PB/MLC, 7 November 1986.

35. The Dante Alighieri Building was commissioned by the Dante Alighieri Society, a nonprofit organization aimed at furthering relations between Italy and the United States. The project went through several false starts with another architect before Belluschi, who was serving as the advisor to the client, took over. The site was a prominent, irregularly shaped corner lot near Kendall Square in Cambridge; the program called for offices, a large multipurpose room for art exhibits, films, banquets, etc., library-reading room, classroom facilities, and kitchen. In discussing the project with the client, Belluschi maintained that despite the limited budget, the potential was there for a "small masterpiece," and he envisioned it as a visible symbol of Italian culture. His solution, a two-story polygonal building of brick with travertine trim and low, hipped terracotta roof, deliberately drew on the simple Tuscan farmhouse for inspiration. Done in association with Jung/Brannen, Belluschi's concept was developed by Robert Hsiung. The building was completed in June 1985 at a cost of $2 million. Belluschi, who by this time was hungry for work, donated his services; Jung/Brannen, however, had problems getting paid. (Correspondence, Dante Alighieri Building, Belluschi files.)

36. Belluschi, *AIA Journal,* May 1983, 238–239.

37. See Breuer, "Where Do We Stand?" of 1934, reproduced in Peter Blake, *Marcel Breuer: Architect and Designer* (1949), 119.

38. Typed manuscript, ACSA conference, Vancouver (Belluschi files).

39. Belluschi, unpublished manuscript, Notre Dame speech, April 1985 (Belluschi files). Belluschi's talk delivered to the Boston Architectural Club in November 1986 bore much the same message.

40. Associates on the Seattle Convention Center were The Richardson Associates; on One Financial Center, Jung/Brannen; on the University of Kentucky Business School, Louis & Henry, Inc.; on the Fillmore Housing Development, DMJM.

41. *Willamette Week,* 17 March 1980.

42. Belluschi letter to Elisabeth K. Thompson, 30 September 1982 (Belluschi files).

43. *Willamette Week,* 17 March 1980.

44. Interviews, Phillip Jacobson (principal of TRA, architects of the Seattle Convention Center)/MLC, Seattle; Donald H. Tishman (of Tishman & Housing Associates, Sausalito, developers of the Fillmore housing project)/MLC, San Francisco. On the Fillmore Center, the largest and most controversial redevelopment project in the city's history, financed in part by minority investors, see *New York Times,* 9 December 1990; 5 February 1989.

45. "Design Unveiled for Proposed World's Tallest Office Building in Newark," *Newark Greater News,* 23 May 1987; taped interview, PB/MLC, 29 March 1988. See also "Another Belluschi Is an Architectural Light," *Oregonian,* 27 June 1988, where a perspective of the proposed Grant USA Tower is reproduced.

46. Taped interviews, PB/MLC, 11 August 1985; Tony Belluschi/MLC, 8 September 1990.

47. Interview, Robert Packard of ZGF/MLC, 9 September 1989. Final cost of the Packard House was $190,000, just slightly over budget.

48. Belluschi, "Architects and Artists—Interpreting Man's Spiritual Dreams," *Faith and Form,* 1979, reprinted in Clausen, *Spiritual Space,* 198–201.

49. See for example the Bishop Angie Smith and Fort Myer Post chapels, in Clausen, *Spiritual Space,* 148–149, 156–159. Belluschi's file on the Silverton church contained tear sheets of Saarinen's North Christian Church in Columbus, Indiana, as well as others.

50. Belluschi hand-written letter to Tony and Emmanuel [Daskalakis, of Belluschi/Daskalakis], 23 January 1977 (Belluschi files). Belluschi was very familiar with the Richardson church, as he had been commissioned to design an addition in 1960 (see Clausen, *Spiritual Space,* 112–113). My thanks to Walter Creese for noting this connection.

51. Clausen, *Spiritual Space,* 160–163. According to Belluschi, he gave Tony the job because he knew he needed work and wanted to give him the jump start he had provided others.

52. Belluschi, "Memo to files," July 1986 (Belluschi files).

53. Belluschi'a hand-written statement, undated but sometime in the fall of 1986 (St. Louis synagogue, Belluschi files).

54. A number of these drawings are among those he donated to the Octagon Museum of the American Architectural Foundation in 1990. On the exhibition of Beaux-Arts drawings, see Arthur Drexler, *The Architecture of*

the Ecole des Beaux-Arts (1977), which accompanied the show. The exhibition itself was held 29 October 1975–4 January 1976. Among the publications reflecting the resurgence of interest in architectural drawings in the later 1970s are Gebhard and Nevins, *200 Years of American Architectural Drawing* (1977), and Nevins and Stern, *The Architect's Eye: American Architectural Drawings 1799–1987* (1979).

55. Taped interview, PB/MLC, Portland, 23 June 1990. For a fuller discussion of the St. Louis synagogue, including an illustration of the 1927 synagogue in Portland, see Clausen, *Spiritual Space,* 35, 174–177.

56. Belluschi letter to Rob [Robert Barringer] of Stone Marraccini and Patterson, St. Louis, 13 March 1987 (Belluschi files).

57. Belluschi letter to Rob, 4 January 1988; taped interview, PB/MLC, 16 January 1988; Belluschi letter to Rob, 18 January 1988 (Belluschi files).

58. Symposium on Aalto and the Humanities, Mt. Angel Abbey, St. Benedict, Oregon, held 28 June 1980, in conjunction with an exhibition of Aalto's work; taped interview, PB/MLC, 13 November 1990.

59. Belluschi preliminary drawings, proposed student and monastery libraries, 1984 and 1985; site plan with libraries, October 1985 (Belluschi files).

Selected Bibliography

Belluschi's papers are housed in collections at the Arents Library, Syracuse University, and at the Oregon Historical Society, Portland; there are also some remaining files in Belluschi's own personal collection, as well as plans, drawings, and other documents in the offices with which he associated throughout the country. The University of Oregon also has a collection of Belluschi photographs.

Selected Essays by Belluschi

"An Architect's Challenge." *Architectural Forum,* December 1949, 72. (On church design.)

"Architecture and Society." *AIA Journal,* February 1951, 85–89. (Published also in *Architectural Record,* February 1951, 117–118, and in the *Reed College Bulletin,* 30, no. 3, 1951.)

"Principles and Techniques of Modern Architecture." *AIA Journal,* September 1951, 99–103.

"Shopping Center." In *Forms and Functions of Twentieth Century Architecture,* edited by Talbot Hamlin, vol. 4. Columbia University Press, New York, 1952, 114–139.

"Gropius Appraises Today's Architect as 'Master Builder,' Belluschi Appraises the Gropius Challenge." *Architectural Forum,* May 1952, 111–113.

"On the Responsibility of the Architect." *Perspecta* no. 2 (Yale Architectural Journal), 1953, 45–55.

"The Spirit of the New Architecture" *Architectural Record,* October 1953, 143–149. (Address delivered to the AIA national convention.)

"An Appraisal of Our Contemporary Architecture." *Bulletin of the American Academy of Arts & Sciences,* December 1953, 4–7. (From his address to the AIA convention, Seattle, June 1953.)

"Who Should Study Architecture?" *Architectural Record,* August 1954, 194ff.

"How Should Architecture Be Taught?" *Architectural Record,* September 1954, 182ff.

"Should Your Child Be an Architect?" Booklet published by the New York Life Insurance Company, 1955, reprinted continuously until well into the 1970s; excerpted in *Saturday Evening Post* and *Ladies Home Journal,* as well as elsewhere.

"The Challenge of St. John's Cathedral." *Architectural Forum,* May 1955, 162–163. (Reprint of his AIA, New York chapter, address.)

"The Meaning of Regionalism." *Architectural Record,* December 1955, 131–139.

[Introduction], *Form-Givers at Mid-Century.* Time Magazine and the American Federation of Arts, New York, 1956, 6–8.

"A New Century of Architecture." *AIA Journal,* June 1957, 180–186. (Reprint of his address to the AIA Centennial in Washington, D.C.; also published in *Pacific Architect & Builder,* August 1957, 14, 40–42; and excerpted in *Architectural Forum,* July 1957, 191ff.)

[Architectural Education]. *The Student Publication of the School of Design,* North Carolina State College, Raleigh, North Carolina, vol. 8, no. 1, spring 1958.

"Why Hire an Architect?" *House & Garden,* June 1958, 66ff.

"The Churches Go Modern." *Saturday Evening Post,* 4 October 1958. Reprinted in Clausen, *Spiritual Space,* 192–194.

"The Aesthetics of the City." *Proceedings of the American Academy of Arts & Letters,* National Institute of Arts & Letters, 1962.

"Eloquent Simplicity in Architecture." *Architectural Record,* July 1963, 131–135. Reprinted in Clausen, *Spiritual Space,* 195–198.

"Architecture as an Art of Our Time." In *The People's Architects,* edited by Harry S. Ransom. University of Chicago Press for Rice University, Chicago, 1964, 96–110.

[Comments]. In *Architects on Architecture,* edited by Paul Heyer. Walker and Company, New York, 1966, 1978, 225–233.

"The Unchanged in a Time of Change." *AIA Journal,* July 1972, 25. (On receiving the AIA Gold Medal.)

"Architectural Milestones." *AIA Journal,* May 1973, 29–31. (On competitions, juries, design guidelines.)

"New Architecture." *Arts + Architecture,* August 1973.

"Architects and Artists—Interpreting Man's Spiritual Dreams." *Faith and Form,* Journal of the Interfaith Forum on Religion, Art and Architecture, Spring–Summer 1979, 8–9. Reprinted in Clausen, *Spiritual Space,* 198–201.

[On postmodernism]. Address to the Society of Architectural Historians, Northwest Chapter, November 1984. Unpublished manuscript, Belluschi files.

Principal Works Used or Cited

Albanese, Catherine L. *Nature Religion in America.* University of Chicago Press, Chicago, 1990.

Anderson, Lawrence B. "Architectural Education MIT: The 1930s and After." In *Architectural Education and Boston,* edited by Margaret Henderson Floyd. Boston Architectural Center, Boston, 1989, 87–90.

Anderson, Martin. *The Federal Bulldozer: A Critical Analysis of Urban Renewal, 1949–1962.* MIT Press, Cambridge, Mass., 1964.

Andrews, Wayne. "Something Less Than Chartres" (review of Condit, *American Building Art*). *The Reporter,* 6 July 1961, 49–50.

"The Architect and His Community." *Progressive Architecture,* February 1949, 43–47.

The Architecture of Diplomacy. Exhibition of the Embassy and Consulate Buildings Commissioned by [the] Office of Foreign Buildings, Department of State, U.S. Government, 1953–1957.

The Architecture of Skidmore, Owings & Merrill, 1950–1962. Verlag Gerd Hatje, Stuttgart, 1962; Praeger, New York, 1963.

"Architecture of the Northwest." *Architectural Record,* April 1953, 133–178.

Bacon, Edmund N. *The Design of Cities.* Penguin Books, New York, 1967, revised ed., 1974.

Banham, Reyner. *The New Brutalism.* Reinhold Publishing, New York, 1966.

Bannister, Turpin C., ed. *The Architect at Mid-Century: Evolution and Achievement.* Reinhold Publishing, New York, 1954.

[Belluschi] Interview transcript. Taped interview with Pietro Belluschi in Portland, Oregon, August 22–23, September 4, 1983. Meredith L. Clausen, interviewer. Northwest Oral History Project, no. 12. Archives of American Art, Smithsonian Institution, Washington, D.C., 1983.

"Belluschi Named to Receive AIA's Highest Honor." *AIA Journal,* February 1972, 6ff.

"Belluschi to Receive AIA Gold Medal." *Progressive Architecture,* February 1972.

Benevolo, Leonardo. *History of Modern Architecture.* MIT Press, Cambridge, 1971, 2 vols.

Berkeley, Ellen Perry. *Architecture: A Place for Women.* Smithsonian Institution, Washington, D.C., 1989.

Berman, Marshall. *All That Is Solid Melts into Air: The Experience of Modernity.* Simon and Schuster, New York, 1982.

Blake, Peter. [Douglas Haskell obituary]. *AIA Journal,* September 1979, 122, 124.

Blake, Peter. *Marcel Breuer: Architect and Designer.* MoMA, New York, 1949.

Blake, Peter. "Modern Architecture: Its Many Faces." *Architectural Forum,* March 1958, 77–81.

Blau, Judith R. *Architects and Firms: A Sociological Perspective on Architectural Practice.* MIT Press, Cambridge and London, 1984.

Boyd, Robin. *The Puzzle of Architecture.* Melbourne University Press, London and New York, 1965.

Breuer, Marcel. "Where Do We Stand?" In Peter Blake, *Marcel Breuer: Architect and Designer.* MoMA, New York, 1949, 119.

Brown, Richard Maxwell. "The New Regionalism in America." In William G. Robbins et al., *Regionalism and the Pacific Northwest.* Oregon State University, Corvallis, 1983.

Built in U.S.A. A Survey of Contemporary American Architecture. MoMA, New York, 1945.

Built in U.S.A.: Post-War Architecture. MoMA, New York, 1952.

Burchard, John E., and Albert Bush-Brown. "Where Does Architecture Go From Here?" *Harpers Magazine,* May 1957, 36–40.

Campbell, Robert. "Architecture's Noisy Soul-Searching." *Boston Globe,* 24 June 1979.

Campbell, Robert. "A Learner's Lexicon to Sixty State Street." *Boston Globe,* 24 March 1974.

Campbell, Robert. "The Monster That Ate Suburbia." *Boston Globe,* 5 May 1985.

Cardwell, Kenneth H. *Bernard Maybeck, Artisan, Architect, Artist.* Peregrine Smith, Inc., Santa Barbara and Salt Lake City, 1977.

Carter, Curtis L., Jack W. Burnham, and Edward Lucie-Smith. *Richard Lippold Sculpture.* Morgan Press Inc., New York, 1990.

Catalano, Eduardo F. *Structures of Warped Surfaces.* School of Design, Raleigh, N.C., vol. 10, no. 1, 1960.

Chenoweth, Art. "The Architect as Prophet." *Northwest Magazine,* Portland, 5 December 1976.

Christ-Janer, Albert, and Mary Mix Foley. *Modern Church Architecture.* McGraw-Hill, New York, 1962.

Clausen, Meredith L. "Belluschi and the Equitable Building in History." *Journal of the Society of Architectural Historians,* June 1991, 109–127.

Clausen, Meredith L. "Northgate Shopping Center: Paradigm from the Provinces." *Journal of the Society of Architectural Historians,* May 1984, 144–161.

Clausen, Meredith L. "The Pan Am Building and the Death of the Street." Paper delivered at the Society of Architectural Historians annual meeting, Cincinnati, April 1991.

Clausen, Meredith L. *Spiritual Space: The Religious Architecture of Pietro Belluschi.* University of Washington Press, Seattle, 1992.

Coleman, Laurence Vail. *Museum Buildings.* American Association of Museums, Washington, D.C., 1950.

Collins, Peter. *Architectural Judgement.* McGill-Queens University Press, Montreal, 1971.

Colquhoun, Alan. "The Type and Its Transformations." In *Essays in Architectural Criticism.* MIT Press, Cambridge and London, 1981.

Creese, Walter. "The Equitable Revisited." *Architectural Forum,* June 1968, 40–45.

Creighton, Thomas. "The New Sensualism." *Progressive Architecture,* September 1959, 141ff.

Cuff, Dana. *Architecture: The Story of Practice.* MIT Press, Cambridge and London, 1991.

Dean, Andrea O. *Bruno Zevi on Modern Architecture.* Rizzoli, New York, 1983.

Deering, Thomas P., Jr. "Mountain Architecture—An Alternative Design Proposal." M. Arch. thesis, University of Washington, Seattle, 1986.

Drexler, Arthur. *The Architecture of Japan.* MoMA, New York, 1955.

Drexler, Arthur. *The Architecture of the Ecole des Beaux-Arts.* MoMA, New York, 1977.

Eliade, Mircea. *The Sacred and the Profane: The Nature of Religion.* Harcourt Brace Jovanovich, New York, 1957.

"Equitable Builds a Leader." *Architectural Forum,* September 1948, 97–106.

Fitch, James Marston. *American Building: The Forces That Shape It.* Houghton Mifflin Co., Boston, 1947 and 1948.

Fitch, James Marston. "A Funny Thing Happened. . . ." *AIA Journal,* January 1980, 66–68.

Five Architects: Eisenman, Graves, Gwathmey, Hejduk, Meier. Oxford University Press, New York, 1975.

Floyd, Margaret Henderson, ed. *Architectural Education and Boston.* Centennial Publication of the Boston Architectural Center, 1889–1989. Boston Architectural Center, Boston, 1989.

Ford, Katherine Morrison. "Modern Is Regional." *House & Garden,* March 1941, 35–37.

Form-Givers at Mid-Century. Time Magazine and The American Federation of Arts, New York, 1959.

Frampton, Kenneth. "Response" [on regionalism]. In David DeLong, Helen Searing, and Robert Stern, eds., *American Architecture: Innovation and Tradition.* Rizzoli, New York, 1986.

Frampton, Kenneth. "Towards a Critical Regionalism." In *The Anti-Aesthetic: Essays on Postmodern Culture,* ed. Hal Foster. Bay Press, Port Townsend, Washington, 1983.

Gebhard, David, and Deborah Nevins. *200 Years of American Architectural Drawing.* Watson-Guptill Publications, New York, 1977.

Geddes, Robert, and William LaRiche. "Theory in Practice." *Architectural Forum,* September 1972, 35.

Giedion, Sigfried. "The State of Contemporary Architecture—The Regional Approach." *Architectural Record,* January 1954, 132–137.

Gitlin, Todd. *The Sixties: Years of Hope, Days of Rage.* Bantam Book, Toronto and New York, 1987.

Goldberger, Paul. "Architects' 'Hedonist' Bent Attacked." *New York Times,* 7 June 1979.

Goldberger, Paul. "Glitter of Miami from Afar Dulls in Close-Up." *New York Times,* 25 December 1983.

"The Gold Medalists: A Brief Look at Five (Kenzo Tange, Marcel Breuer, Pietro Belluschi, R. Buckminster Fuller, and Wallace Harrison)." *AIA Journal,* June 1979, 41–77.

Goodsell, Charles. Review of Robin, *Enclaves of America. Journal of Architectural Education,* February 1994, 178–179.

Gordon, Elizabeth. "The Threat to the Next America." *House Beautiful,* April 1953, 126ff.

Gordon, Walter. "The Architecture of Pietro Belluschi." *Northwest Review,* University of Oregon, Eugene, Oregon, Fall–Winter, 1954.

Gordon, Walter. "Designed by Pietro Belluschi." *Pencil Points,* July 1942, 70–73.

Gropius, Walter. *Scope of Total Architecture: The Ideals of the Modern Movement in Architecture, City Planning, and Design.* Collier Books, New York, 1943, 1954.

Gubitosi, Camillo, and Alberto Izzo. *Eduardo Catalano: Buildings and Projects.* Officina Edizioni, Rome, 1978.

Gubitosi, Camillo, and Alberto Izzo. *Pietro Belluschi. Edifici e progetti, 1932–1973.* Officina Edizioni, Rome, 1974.

Guilbaut, Serge. *How New York Stole the Idea of Modern Art: Abstract Expressionism, Freedom, and the Cold War.* University of Chicago Press, Chicago and London, 1983.

Gunts, Edward. "The Fountainhead at 50." *Architecture,* May 1993, 35–37.

Gutheim, Frederick. Review of Hamlin, *Forms and Functions of Twentieth Century Architecture.* In *Architectural Forum,* June 1952, 152–154.

Gutheim, Frederick. "The Turning Point in Mr. Wright's Career." *AIA Journal,* June 1980, 48.

Gutman, Robert. *Architectural Practice: A Critical View.* Princeton Architectural Press, Princeton, 1988.

Hall, Peter. *Cities of Tomorrow.* Blackwell Books, Oxford, 1988.

Hamlin, Talbot, ed. *Forms and Functions of Twentieth Century Architecture.* Columbia University Press, New York, 1952, 4 vols.

Harada, Jiro. *The Lesson of Japanese Architecture.* The Studio Ltd, London, 1936; reprinted Dover Publications, New York, 1985.

Harper, Paula. "Power Skyline—Report from Miami." *Art in America,* September 1988, 55–65.

Harvey, David. *The Condition of Post-Modernity.* Basil Blackwell, Oxford, 1989.

Heyer, Paul. *Architects on Architecture.* Walther & Company, New York, 1966; revised edition, 1978.

Hitchcock, [Henry-] Russell. "An Eastern Critic Looks at Western Architecture." *California Arts + Architecture,* December 1940, 21–23, 40–41.

Hitchcock, Henry-Russell. "The International Style Twenty Years After." *Architectural Record,* August 1951, 89–97.

Hitchcock, Henry-Russell. *Modern Architecture: Romanticism and Reintegration.* Payson and Clarke, Ltd, London, 1929.

Hitchcock, Henry-Russell, and Philip Johnson. *The International Style: Architecture since 1922.* W. W. Norton, New York, 1932.

Hitchcock, Henry-Russell, Philip Johnson, and Lewis Mumford. *Modern Architecture—International Exhibition.* MoMA, New York, 1932.

Hitchcock, Henry-Russell, and William Seale. *Temples of Democracy: The State Capitols of the USA.* Harcourt Brace Jovanovich, New York and London, 1976.

Holmes, Kenneth L., ed. *Linfield's Hundred Years, a Centennial History of Linfield College.* McMinnville, Oregon.

Hosfield, John. "A Study of the Architecture of Pietro Belluschi." M.A. thesis, University of Oregon, Eugene, 1960.

Hudnut, Joseph. "The Church in a Modern World." *Architectural Forum,* December 1958, 89–93.

Hutcheon, Linda. *A Poetics of Postmodernism: History, Theory, Fiction.* Routledge, New York and London, 1988.

Huxtable, Ada Louise. "Architecture: Towers, Bunkers, Bombsites." *Oregonian,* Friday, circa June 18, 1970.

Huxtable, Ada Louise. "Dissimilar Buildings, Similar Award." *New York Times,* 24 May 1970, section 8, 1, 7.

Huxtable, Ada Louise. "In Portland, Ore., Urban Decay Is Masked by Natural Splendor." *New York Times,* 19 June 1970.

Huxtable, Ada Louise. "Juilliard's New Building: Esthetic Reality." *New York Times,* 8 October 1969, 59.

Huxtable, Ada Louise. "Marvel or Monster?" *New York Times,* 24 January 1960.

Huxtable, Ada Louise. "Philip Johnson and the Temper of These Times." *New York Times,* 13 May 1979, section 2, 27–28.

Huxtable, Ada Louise. "The Present: The Troubled State of Modern Architecture." *Bulletin, American Academy of Arts and Sciences,* January 1980, 23–37. Reproduced in *Architectural Record,* January 1981, 72–79.

Jacobs, Jane. *The Death and Life of Great American Cities.* Random House, New York, 1961.

Jencks, Charles. "Death for Rebirth" and "Post-Modernism between Kitsch and Culture." In *Post-Modernism on Trial,* Architectural Design Profile No. 88. Academy Group Ltd, London, 1990.

Jencks, Charles. *The Language of Post-Modern Architecture.* Rizzoli, New York, 1977.

Jencks, Charles. *Late-Modern Architecture.* Rizzoli, New York, 1980.

Johns, Barbara. *Modern Art from the Pacific Northwest.* Seattle Art Museum, Seattle, 1990.

Johnson, Philip. Review of Boyd, *The Puzzle of Architecture.* In *Architectural Forum,* June 1966, 72–73, 93.

Jones, Chester Henry. "Architecture Astray." *Atlantic Monthly,* January 1931, 64–74.

Kallmann, G. M. "Action Architecture." *Architectural Forum,* October 1959, 132ff.

Kay, Jane Holtz. "Architect Pietro Belluschi: Broker between Budgets and Beauty." *Boston Globe,* 14 May 1972, 25ff.

Kennedy, Robert Woods. "After the International Style, Then What?" *Architectural Forum,* September 1953, 130–133.

Kepes, Gyorgy. *The MIT Years 1945–1977.* MIT Press, Cambridge and London, 1978.

Kidder Smith, G. E. *The New Churches of Europe.* Holt, Rinehart and Winston, New York, 1964.

Killian, James R. *The Education of a College President.* MIT Press, Cambridge and London, 1985.

Kimball, Fiske. "Louis Sullivan, an Old Master." *Architectural Record,* April 1925, 289–304.

Kingsbury, Martha. *Northwest Traditions.* Seattle Art Museum, Seattle, 1978.

Krinsky, Carol H. *Gordon Bunshaft of Skidmore, Owings & Merrill.* Architectural History Foundation and MIT Press, Cambridge, 1988.

Krinsky, Carol H. *Rockefeller Center.* Oxford University Press, New York, 1978.

Kuspit, Donald B. "Regionalism Reconsidered." *Art in America,* July/August, 1976, 64–69.

Lefaivre, Liane, and Alexander Tzonis. "Lewis Mumford's Regionalism." *Design Book Review,* no. 19, Winter 1990, 20–25.

Lipstadt, Hélène, ed. *The Experimental Tradition: Essays on Competitions in Architecture.* Architectural League of New York and Princeton University Press, New York, 1989.

Loeffler, Jane C. "The Architecture of Diplomacy: Heyday of the United States Embassy-Building Program, 1954–1960." *Journal of the Society of Architectural Historians,* September 1990, 251–278.

MacColl, E. Kimbark. *The Growth of a City: Power and Politics in Portland, Oregon, 1915–1950.* Georgian Press, Portland, 1979.

"MAS [Modern Architecture Symposium] 1964: The Decade 1929–1939." *Journal of the Society of Architectural Historians,* March 1965, 3–107.

Mock, Elizabeth, ed. *Built in USA: Since 1932.* MoMA, New York, 1945.

Moore, Charles W. "The San Francisco Skyline: Hard to Spoil, but They're Working on It." *Architectural Forum,* November 1965, 47.

Mumford, Lewis. *Roots of Contemporary American Architecture.* Dover Publications, New York, 1952.

Mumford, Lewis. "Skyline." *The New Yorker,* 11 October 1947.

Nevins, Deborah, and Robert Stern. *The Architect's Eye: American Architectural Drawings 1799–1978.* Pantheon Books, New York, 1979.

"New Buildings for 194X." *Architectural Forum,* May 1943, 108–111.

Newhouse, Victoria. *Wallace K. Harrison, Architect.* Rizzoli, New York, 1989.

"New Regionalism." *Center, a Journal for Architecture in America,* vol. 3. School of Architecture, University of Texas at Austin, and Rizzoli Press, New York, 1987.

Newsom, Samuel. *Japanese Garden Construction.* Domoto, Kumagawa and Perkins, Tokyo, 1939.

Northrop, F. S. C. *The Meeting of East and West.* Ox Bow Press, Woodbridge, Conn., 1946, 1979 reprint.

Notable Pioneers in the History of Oregon. Oregon Lung Association, Portland, Oregon, 1983.

"On the Responsibility of the Architect." *Perspecta,* Yale Architectural Journal, no. 2, 1953, 45–57.

Parikh, Arani. Review of Robin, *Enclaves of America. Design Book Review,* no. 29–30, Summer–Fall 1993, 77–79.

Parnes, Louis. *Planning Stores That Pay: Organic Design and Layout.* Dodge Corporation, New York, 1948.

Pastier, John. "First Monument of a Loosely Defined Style: Michael Graves' Portland Building." *AIA Journal,* May 1983, 235–236.

Pell, Paul T. "The Architecture of Albert Ernest Doyle." M.A. thesis, Reed College, Portland, 1976.

Pickens, Buford. "Contemporary Regional Architecture." *AIA Journal,* September 1947, 114.

Plunz, Richard. *A History of Housing in New York City.* Columbia University Press, New York, 1990.

Portman, John, and Jonathan Barnett. *The Architect as Developer.* McGraw-Hill, New York, 1976.

Rand, Ayn. *The Fountainhead.* Bobbs-Merrill, New York, 1943.

Randall, Kathleen. "Lincoln Center for the Performing Arts: Cultural Visibility and Postwar Urbanism." M.S. thesis in Historic Preservation, Columbia University, New York, 1992.

Ransom, Harry S., ed. *The People's Architects.* University of Chicago Press for Rice University, Chicago, 1964.

Raymond, Antonin. *Architectural Details.* Architectural Book Publishing, New York, 1937, 1947.

Richards, J. M. *An Introduction to Modern Architecture.* Penguin Books, Middlesex, 1940, 1953, 1956.

Riley, Terrence. *The International Style: Exhibition 15 and the Museum of Modern Art.* Rizzoli, New York, 1992.

Ritz, Richard. *A History of the Reed College Campus and Its Buildings.* Reed College, Portland, 1990.

Robbins, William G., et al. *Regionalism and the Pacific Northwest.* Oregon University Press, Corvallis, 1983.

Robin, Ron. *Enclaves of America: The Rhetoric of American Political Architecture Abroad, 1900–1965.* Princeton University Press, Princeton, 1992.

Ross, Marion Dean. "The Attainment and Restraint of Pietro Belluschi." *AIA Journal,* July 1972, 17–24.

Rowe, Colin. "Chicago Frame." In *The Mathematics of the Ideal Villa and Other Essays.* MIT Press, Cambridge, 1976.

Ruttenbaum, Steven. *Mansions in the Clouds: The Skyscraper Palazzi of Emery Roth.* Balsam Press, New York, 1986.

Saarinen, Eero. "Six Broad Currents of Modern Architecture." *Architectural Forum,* July 1953, 111–115.

Schmertz, Mildred. "The Juilliard School." *Architectural Record,* January 1970, 121–130.

Schumacher, Thomas. Review of Stern, *New Directions in American Architecture.* In *Architectural Forum,* March 1970, 58–59.

Schwantes, Carlos A. *The Pacific Northwest, an Interpretive History.* University of Nebraska Press, Lincoln and London, 1989.

Scully, Vincent. "The Death of the Street." *Perspecta,* Yale Architectural Journal, no. 8, 1963, 91–102.

Simon, Maron J. *Your Solar House.* Simon and Schuster, New York, 1947.

Smith, Terry. *Making the Modern: Industry, Art, and Design in America.* University of Chicago Press, Chicago, 1993.

Spreiregen, Paul D. *Design Competitions.* McGraw-Hill, New York, 1979.

Stalnaker, Judith J., and Ernest C. Harris. *Structural Design in Wood.* Van Nostrand Reinhold, New York, 1989.

Stein, Clarence. "The Art Museum of Tomorrow." *Architectural Record,* January 1930, 5–12.

Stern, Robert. *New Dirctions in American Architecture.* George Braziller, New York, 1969.

Stone, Irving. *The Agony and the Ecstasy: A Novel of Michelangelo.* Doubleday and Company, Garden City, New York, 1961.

Stubblebine, Jo, ed. *The Northwest Architecture of Pietro Belluschi.* F. W. Dodge Corporation, New York, 1953.

Thompson, Deborah, ed. *Maine Forms of American Architecture.* 1976.

"U.S. Architecture Abroad—Modern Design at Its Best." *Architectural Forum,* March 1953, 101–115.

Van Cleve, Jane. "Conversations with Pietro Belluschi." *Willamette Week,* 17 March 1980, 11ff.

Vaughan, Thomas, and Virginia G. Ferriday. *Space, Style and Structure: Building in Northwest America.* Oregon Historical Society, Portland, 1974, vols. 1 and 2.

Venturi, Robert. *Complexity and Contradiction in Architecture.* MoMA, New York, 1966.

Venturi, Robert, and Denise Scott Brown. *A View from the Campidoglio: Selected Essays 1953–1984.* Harper & Row, New York, 1984.

Venturi, Robert, Denise Scott Brown, and Steven Izenour. *Learning from Las Vegas.* MIT Press, Cambridge and London, 1972.

Von Eckardt, Wolf. *A Place to Live: The Crisis of the Cities.* Delta Books, New York, 1967.

Williamson, Roxanne. *American Architects and the Mechanics of Fame.* University of Texas Press, Austin, 1991.

Wilson, James. *Urban Renewal: The Record and the Controversy.* Joint Center for Urban Studies of MIT and Harvard University, MIT Press, Cambridge and London, 1966.

Wilson, Richard Guy. *The AIA Gold Medal.* McGraw-Hill, New York, 1984.

Wilson, Richard Guy, and Sidney Robinson, eds. *Modern Architecture in America: Visions and Revisions.* Iowa State University, Ames, 1991.

Wiseman, Carter. *I. M. Pei: A Profile in American Architecture.* Harry N. Abrams, New York, 1990.

Wright, Frank Lloyd. *An Autobiography.* Horizon Press, New York, 1932, 1943, 1977.

Wright, Frank Lloyd. *Letters to Architects.* California State University, Fresco, 1984.

Wright, Frank Lloyd. *Modern Architecture: Being the Kahn Lectures for 1930 by Frank Lloyd Wright.* Princeton University Press, Princeton, 1931.

Wright, Gwendolyn. *Building the Dream: A Social History of Housing in America.* New York: Pantheon, 1981.

Wurster, Catherine B. "The Social Front of Modern Architecture in the 1930s." *Journal of the Society of Architectural Historians,* March 1965, 48–52.

Yoshida, Tetsuro. *Das japanische Wohnhaus.* Verlag Ernst Wasmuth, Berlin, 1935.

Young, Edgar B. *Lincoln Center: The Building of an Institution.* New York University Press, New York and London, 1980.

Zaitzevsky, Cynthia. "Education and Landscape Architecture." In *Architectural Education and Boston,* edited by Margaret Henderson Floyd. Boston, 1989, 20–34.

Zevi, Bruno. *Towards an Organic Architecture.* Faber & Faber Limited, London, 1950.

Acknowledgments

The research on this project involved considerable travel. I am grateful for travel grants from the American Council of Learned Societies and National Endowment for the Humanities, as well as support from the Graduate School Research Fund, University of Washington. Without their help, my work could not have been done.

I would like to acknowledge individually the many people who have assisted in one way or another with the project. As it extends over a number of years and overlapped several other projects, it involved a number of people whose names I may have inadvertently overlooked. I would like to extend my thanks to them all.

For their generosity in both time and insights, I am grateful for interviews with: Carl Abbott, professor of urban studies, and professor Stefano Zegretti, Portland State University, Portland; Frank Allen, Lew Crutcher, Walter Gordon, Henry Klein, George Kotchik, Mary Alice Hutchins, Ken Richardson, Richard Ritz, Marge Wintermute, and George Wallace of the Belluschi office in Portland; Lawrence B. Anderson, former head of the Department of Architecture and Dean of the School of Architecture and Planning at MIT; Anthony Belluschi and Peter Belluschi; Sol Bianchi, director of facilities, and Philip Hart, concert manager, of the Juilliard School; Gerald W. Blakeley, Jr., partner, Cabot, Cabot & Forbes, Boston; Belford Brown of the Davies Symphony Hall, San Francisco; Leland Brubaker, of Brubaker and Brandt, Columbus, Ohio; Robert Burns, Associate Dean, School of Design, North Carolina State University, Raleigh; Robert Campbell, architectural critic, *Boston Globe;* Nick Cardell, Jr., Laurence Kinney, David C. Ashley, A. Douglas Aird, and Robert Coye of the May Memorial Unitarian Church, Syracuse; Jean-Paul Carlhian of Shepley, Bulfinch, Richardson & Abbott, Boston; Eduardo Catalano; Stanley M. Cole and Alexander Ewing of Ewing Cole Cherry Parsky, Philadelphia; Crawley Cooper, Robert Hsiung, YuSing Jung, Austin Rasco, and Elizabeth Redmond of Jung/Brannen Associates; Alex Cvijanovic, formerly of TAC, Cambridge; Frederic Day of Carl Koch and Associates; Alan G. Deale, former minister of the Church of the Christian Union, Rockford, Illinois; Kenneth DeMay of Sasaki Associates, Watertown, Massachusetts; Vernon DeMars and John Wells of DeMars & Wells, San Francisco; Robert Durham, former AIA president, Seattle; Donn Emmons and Ralph Butterfield of Wurster/Bernardi & Emmons; Norman Fletcher of TAC, Cambridge; Richard Foster, Marc Goldstein, John O. Merrill, Alan Rudy, and Bill Weber of SOM, San Francisco; Margaret Fritch; William H. Givler of the Portland Art Museum; Victor Gorlach, Fred Halden, and Richard Roth, Sr., of Emery Roth & Sons, New York; Mark Grabowski, manager of operations, Meyerhoff Symphony Hall, Baltimore; Joachim Grube of Yost Grube Hall, Portland; Lawrence Halprin, landscape architect, San Francisco; George L. Hanna of Hertzka & Knowles, San Francisco; Frances E. Hares of Hueber Hares Glavin, Syracuse; Mr. and Mrs. Philip Joss, Portland; Jane Holtz Kay, architectural critic, *Boston Globe;* John B. Kenward, former Executive Director, Portland Development Commission; Gyorgy Kepes, Cambridge; James R. Killian, former President, MIT; Paul Kirk, Seattle; Carl Koch of Carl Koch & Associates; Vlastimil Koubek, Washington, D.C.; Eric Ladd, Neahkanie, Oregon; Norman B. Leventhal of the Beacon Companies, Boston; Merlin Lickhalter of Stone Marraccini Patterson, St. Louis; Edward Logue, former head of the Boston Redevelopment Authority; George McMath; Jeffrey Alan Merkel, pastor of the Lutheran Church and Student Center, University of Pennsylvania; Henry Millon, Director, Center for Advanced Study in the Visual Arts, National Gallery of Art, Washington, D.C.; Burke Morden, Portland; Thomas Mulvey of the Rohm & Haas Company, Philadelphia; Ittsei Nakagawa of the Pacific Gas & Electric Company, San Francisco; Claude Oakland, San Francisco (Life Magazine House); Robert Packard and Norman Zimmer of Zimmer Gunsul Frasca, Portland; William Pedersen of Kohn Pedersen Fox, New York; I. M. Pei of I. M. Pei & Partners, New York; Reverend D. Hugh Peniston of the Cottage Grove Presbyterian Church, Cottage Grove, Oregon; Mr. and Mrs. John Platt, Portland; David Pugh of SOM, Portland; Carroll S. Rankin, San Francisco (Life Magazine House); Archibald Rogers and Francis T. Taliaferro of RTKL, Baltimore; Dan Rose of Rose Associates, New York; Hideo Sasaki of Sasaki Associates; William Schubart, Director of Lincoln Center; William Schuppel, of McSweeney, Ryan & Lee, San Francisco; Theodore Schultz, of Bolt Beranek & Newman, Boston; Father Peter Sidler of the Portsmouth Abbey; Reverend Bennett Sims of the Church of the Redeemer, Baltimore; William L. Slayton, formerly Director of the Foreign Buildings Operation, State Department, Washington, D.C.; Paul Spreiregen, Washington, D.C.; Samuel B. Stewart of the Bank of America, San Francisco; John Storrs, Portland; Julius Stratton, former President, MIT; Hugh Stubbins, Boston; Frederick Taylor of the Eduardo Catalano office; Donald Tishman of Tishman Developers, San Francisco; Allan Temko, architectural critic of the *San Francisco Chronicle;* Thomas Vaughan, former director, Oregon Historical Society, Portland; Ralph Vitello of the Sacramento Architects Collaborative; Tony P. Wrenn, archivist, AIA, Washington, D.C.; and John Yeon, Portland.

For their wise and generous counsel, I want to acknowledge Walter Creese and William Jordy for their comments on the text, and my colleagues at the University of Washington historians David Pinkney and William Rorabaugh, landscape architect David Streatfield, and architect Phillip Jacobson; for the many years of companionship, his sharp eye and extraordinary range of talents, Jack Sidener; for their assistance in library work, Susan Seyl and MC of the Oregon Historical Society, Carolyn Davis and Kathleen Manwaring of the Arents Research Library, Syracuse, and Betty L. Wagner, Diane Senders, Mary Ellen Anderson, and Jo Nilsson of the University of Washington. My thanks, too, to Pamela Perrin Zytnicki, Marjorie Burston, Laura Burns Carroll, Russ Craig, and Elizabeth Guffie for their research assistance.

For her assistance, warmth, and generous spirit, a special thanks to Elisabeth K. Thompson. I would also like to acknowledge Jean Jack, whose support on every level sustained me throughout, and of course, Marjorie Bruckner Belluschi, Pietro's loyal companion without whom he could never have accomplished what he did, and without whose unflagging assistance throughout the years my study would have remained sorely incomplete. I cherish her and hope we remain lifelong friends. And finally, my thanks to family members and friends for their forbearance.

Index

Page numbers in italics indicate illustrations.